Odious Debt

THE HISTORY AND THEORY OF INTERNATIONAL LAW

In the past few decades the understanding of the relationship between nations has undergone a radical transformation. The role of the traditional nation state is diminishing, along with many of the traditional vocabularies which were once used to describe what has been called, ever since Jeremy Bentham coined the phrase in 1780, 'international law'. The older boundaries between states are growing ever more fluid, new conceptions and new languages have emerged which are slowly coming to replace the image of a world of sovereign independent nation states which has dominated the study of international relations since the early nineteenth century. This redefinition of the international arena demands a new understanding of classical and contemporary questions in international and legal theory. It is the editors' conviction that the best way to achieve this is by bridging the traditional divide between international legal theory, intellectual history, and legal and political history. The aim of the series, therefore, is to provide a forum for historical studies, from classical antiquity to the twenty-first century, that are theoretically informed and for philosophical work that is historically conscious, in the hope that a new vision of the rapidly evolving international world, its past and its possible future, may emerge.

PREVIOUSLY PUBLISHED IN THIS SERIES

A Century of Anarchy?
War, Normativity, and the Birth of Modern International Order
Hendrik Simon

The Individual in International Law
Anne Peters, Tom Sparks

Pufendorf's International Political and Legal Thought
Peter Schröder

Victims
Perceptions of Harm in Modern European War and Violence
Svenja Goltermann

Sovereignty, International Law, and the Princely States of Colonial South Asia
Priyasha Saksena

Sepúlveda on the Spanish Invasion of the Americas
Defending Empire, Debating Las Casas
Luke Glanville, David Lupher, Maya Feile Tomes

Odious Debt

Bankruptcy, International Law, and the Making of Latin America

EDWARD JONES CORREDERA

Senior Research Fellow, Max Planck Institute for Comparative Public Law and International Law, Germany
Assistant Lecturer, Universidad Nacional de Educación a Distancia, Spain

OXFORD
UNIVERSITY PRESS

OXFORD
UNIVERSITY PRESS

Great Clarendon Street, Oxford, OX2 6DP,
United Kingdom

Oxford University Press is a department of the University of Oxford.
It furthers the University's objective of excellence in research, scholarship,
and education by publishing worldwide. Oxford is a registered trade mark of
Oxford University Press in the UK and in certain other countries

Published in the United States of America by Oxford University Press
198 Madison Avenue, New York, NY 10016, United States of America

British Library Cataloguing in Publication Data

Data available

Library of Congress Control Number: 2024943016

ISBN 9780192888280

DOI: 10.1093/9780191982200.001.0001

Printed and bound by
CPI Group (UK) Ltd, Croydon, CR0 4YY

MIX
Paper | Supporting
responsible forestry
FSC® C013604

Series Editor's Preface

'Waves of debt surged and swelled before breaking on Spanish shores.' In this masterful book, Edward Jones Corredera writes the story of how debt becomes a vessel of transnational meaning—one that is instrumental to the making of Latin America.

'What do postcolonial states owe to empires they once toppled?', Jones Corredera asks. If an 'odious debt' is one 'incurred by or for tyrannical means,' is it morally and legally acceptable not to repay it?

One can also ask: aren't *all* debts odious? Not if the moral universe in which debts are incurred considers them as synonymous with sins. Debts, much like sins, break against the shores of time. If the Original Sin 'entered the world' as a fracture in the atemporal chain of innocence, postcolonial states break the impassive flow of '*Ewigkeit*'—the ill-fated assumption that empires and states last forever, as recently observed by Natasha Wheatley in her *The Life and Death of States*.

What happens after the death of an empire is not only a question of moral and legal solvency. It is a question of soteriology. One of the many merits of this book is that it offers, with impressive and evocative storytelling, an international legal history of debt and its moral economy. International law has been, as a discipline, long lost on its quest for secularisation—a professional habitus in which, the author denounces, 'ideas are decontextualized, telescoped, foreshortened, and sublimated for modern use,' and the so-called 'founding fathers of international law' like Hugo Grotius and Alberico Gentili are portrayed as unrealistic precursors of *laicité*. Instead, questions of grace and salvation were at the very core of debates on the Protestant Reformation, debates in which Hugo Grotius himself was actively involved, and that informed the very language of early modern international law, empire, and revolt. Jones Corredera shows how, unsurprisingly, Latin American lawyers turned to Grotius to compare their situation with the Dutch Revolt. Historical analogy allowed these lawyers to write 'a history of their own making,' because 'the Protestant law of nations was an unreliable narrator of Spanish imperial history.'

Furthermore, the analogy between sins and debts is a textual pillar of Catholicism. Jones Corredera, relying on the historian Peter Brown, notes that 'in the Latin original version of the Lord's Prayer, the term for sins was *debita*, or debts; one asked God to forgive one's sins, or *dimitte nobis debita nostra*'. While 'prayer and almsgiving could cancel one's debts to God through the remission of sins,' conversely, 'the non-payment of one's debts was a type of perjury, a breach of contract, and could lead to excommunication.'

Latin American lawyers used an intricate and highly creative vocabulary of debt to craft both their constitutional thinking and international aspirations. While the very term 'odious debt' suggests that it was right not to compensate an oppressive regime, at the same time, newly established liberal states in Latin America cared about their reputation: a new state which does not value property rights, defending instead the breaching of contracts, appears vulnerable and weak. This might have potentially discouraged new investments, and thus the regular flow of debts crashing against Atlantic shores.

This story has largely been forgotten. Jones Corredera warns us that its international dimension has escaped us, too. In one of the book's most powerful and radical claims, Jones Corredera recentres the history of Latin America *via* its contribution to international law by looking closely at the histories of Mexico, Colombia, Argentina and their legal protagonists. As the author argues, 'the settlement of debts inherited from the Spanish monarchy, and the negotiation of loans owed to the rest of the world, were central to the formation of modern international law across the region. Latin American jurists did not seek to generate a creole legal consciousness or meet a standard of civilisation: they sought to settle their debts with the wider world, create constitutional states, and straighten the crooked timber of international law.'

From this perspective, debt acts as a prism to investigate the nature of obligation, and its two-pronged domestic and international dimension. Jones Corredera asks: 'what type of obligations and responsibilities ought to be at the core of global relations?' This book reminds us that this question, whatever its answer, is at the very core of international law, should it ever need saving.

Francesca Iurlaro

Acknowledgements

The core themes in this book were informed by a number of academic events funded by the DAAD-Cambridge Hub, co-organised with Joshua Smeltzer during our doctoral studies, on the global legacies of Reinhart Koselleck at the University of Cambridge. These ideas gradually acquired a greater degree of coherence during the lockdown phase of the Covid-19 pandemic in the United Kingdom and in Germany. My thoughts were informed by daily exchanges with Joshua, Mark Somos, Francesca Iurlaro, Emma Curran, and George Gallwey. As we ambled through the deserted streets of Cambridge once a week, conversations with Yonatan Glazer-Eytan about long-standing themes in Spanish history helped me reconsider the early modern confessional politics. As the world slowly opened up, a number of presentations and discussions informed the outline of the book. One of them, at the Bilbao seminar convened by Javier Fernández Sebastián, stands out because of the extraordinary scope of the discussion. Fernández Sebastián encouraged me to bring together my research on time and credit and my work on the Spanish Enlightenment. Marcos Reguera and Matthew Cleary, in turn, helped me work through the complexities of this exercise in reconciliation. This book is, in part, an effort to respond to this challenge in a way that would be of interest to scholars of international law. In addressing this task over a number of years, I accrued the greatest intellectual debt to Mark, a patient mentor.

I am grateful to Anne Peters and Armin von Bogdandy for hosting discussions about the book at the Max Planck Institute for Comparative Public Law and International Law, and for their feedback on the earlier drafts of the manuscript. I am equally indebted to my colleagues at the Institute, above all Florian Kriener, Áine Fellenz, Lea Berger, and Erin Pobjie, and the team members of the Grotius Census Project. A number of other academics had a significant influence on the direction of this book. José María Iñurritegui Rodríguez provided me with a range of brilliant insights as he listened to some of these ideas as the manuscript reached a more mature stage, and facilitated their further growth. The writing of this book overlapped with discussions with José María and Melissa Calaresu regarding the translation of my first book into Spanish; having grown up in Spain, this process of transliteration from one cultural context to another generated new ideas about the 'homogenization' or 'homologation', to use José María's terms, of concepts. Over a number of exchanges about the translatability of my first book, Pablo Fernández Albaladejo synthesised and contextualised my earlier work better than I ever could. He also drew my attention to the broader significance of fiscalism and Augustinianism in Spanish history; this book connects early modern nightmares of Habsburg bankruptcies, the rise of dreams of revolutionary credit, and the return of the monsters produced by the sleep of reason. José María Portillo, in turn, took an exemplary avuncular disposition towards me and fostered my desire to reconsider the role of religion in Spanish political economic thought.

At the Seminar of the Cambridge Centre for Political Thought, Jeremy Adelman provided me with sweeping and wide-ranging feedback on a number of themes, including the relationship between revolutionary credit and modern debates about default and failure. David Armitage nudged me to consider the contemporary resonance of discussions about debt and war and their relationship to processes of civil fragmentation. José Luis Egío García encouraged me to think anew about the relationship between Spanish legal history and Mexico's present. Matilde Cazzola prompted me to think about philanthropy and charity and expanded my understanding of the anglophone debates on these topics. Morgan Golf-French helped in innumerable ways. Xabier Lamikiz and Alejandra Irigoin were kind itinerant mentors: they always helped me navigate the economics of the Spanish Empire and modern academia. However, they bear no responsibility for my analysis of the political economic visions studied in this book. David Jiménez Torres and Jonathan Nathan drew my attention to some of the cultural dimensions of credit and debt in nineteenth-century Europe and Spain and were always ready with helpful advice. Broader conversations with Stefan Vogenauer, Thomas Duve, Sabarish Suresh, and other members of the sister institute in Frankfurt, the Max Planck Institute for Legal History and Legal Theory, allowed me to reconsider some of the links between the early modern world and contemporary Latin America that I had developed in my first book. My work on the reception of Grotius in the Spanish-speaking world was informed by the publication of my article on the topic in the *English Historical Review*; I am grateful to the editors and the two anonymous readers for their insightful comments on the manuscript.

A number of presentations in Cambridge, Manchester, Madrid, Bilbao, Brussels, Paris, Heidelberg, and Frankfurt, and a range of conversations over the years, allowed me to develop some of the original ideas of the book. I am grateful to Tania Ixchel Atilano, Paulette Baeriswyl, Arnulf Becker Lorca, Nicolas Bell-Romero, Hans Blom, Nina Boy, Hugo Bromley, Chris Brooke, Raphaël Cahen, Anthony Carty, Clorinda Donato, Frederik Dhondt, Hugo Drochon, Sean Fleming, Marta García Garralón, Fernanda Gallo, Matthias Goldmann, Tom Hopkins, María Luz González Mezquita, Shiru Lim, Andreas Kulick, Charlotte Johann, Francisco Miguel Martín Blázquez, David Martín Marcos, Mariano Martin Schlez, Darina Martykánová, Peter Morgan, Stephen Neff, Isaac Nakhimovksy, Liliana Obregón, William O'Reilly, Niklas Olsen, Dorinda Outram, Sam Pallis, Florencia Peyrou, Luna Sabastian, Juan Pablo Scarfi, Juan Luis Simal, Glenda Sluga, Tom Sparks, José Javier Rodríguez Solís, Christopher Rossi, Alexia Yates, Inge van Hulle, and Felix Waldmann for our exchanges, and for many of their comments and feedback on my work at various stages of the research. I am grateful to Ana Maria Otero

Cleves, Luis Galán-Guerrero, and Juan Neves Sarriegui for their assistance with my research in Colombia.

This book is built on research carried out at the Biblioteca Nacional de España, the Biblioteca del Palacio Real, the Biblioteca Tomás Navarro Tomás, the libraries of the Max Planck Institute for Comparative Public Law and International Law and Max Planck Institute for Legal History and Legal Theory, the Cambridge University Library, the Churchill Archives Centre in Cambridge, the Squire Law Library, the British Library, the LSE Library, also known as the fourth circle of hell, the Bibliothèque nationale de France, the Daniel Cosío Villegas Library at the Colegio de México, the Archivo General de la Nación de Colombia, the Biblioteca Luis Ángel Arango, the library of the Instituto Caro y Cuervo, and the Biblioteca Nacional Mariano Moreno.

The research for this book was supported by funding from the German Research Foundation and the Grotius Census Project at the Max Planck Institute for Comparative Public Law and International Law, an Affiliated Postdoctoral Membership at Clare Hall, a postdoctoral scholarship at the Universidad de Educación a Distancia in Madrid, and Portillo's project on 'Desimperialización y procesos de construcción nacional en el Atlántico Hispano', funded by the Spanish Ministry of Science and Innovation. Robert Cavooris at Oxford University Press was extraordinarily helpful in helping me turn the book proposal into a manuscript and Lisa Butts, the project editor, was always thoughtful and accommodating. Finally, I owe a great debt of gratitude to Jenny Arthur for her conscientious reading of the text.

Contents

We are accustomed from our earliest youth to see in the history of the Roman people public acts of injustice, so atrocious in themselves, always coloured with specious names, always accompanied by a proud eulogy on Roman virtues. The abolition of debts plays a great part from the earliest times of the republic. A withdrawal of the people to Mount Aventine, when the enemy was at the gates of Rome, forced the Senate to pass a sponge over the rights of creditors. The historian excites all our interest in favour of the fraudulent debtors who paid their debts by a bankruptcy, and does not fail to render odious those who were despoiled by an act of violence. And what was gained by this injustice? Usury, which had served as a pretext for the robbery, could not but be augmented the very next day after the catastrophe; for the exorbitant rate of interest was only the price of the risk caused by the uncertainty of engagements. The foundation of the Roman colonies has been celebrated as a work of profound policy. It always consisted in despoiling part of the lawful proprietors of a conquered country to create establishments in the way of favour or reward.

Jeremy Bentham, *Principles of the Civil Code*

Introduction

There is no such thing as a dead letter in Latin America: all past laws, covenants, and obligations retain a degree of historical authority. And yet this is a story about how, in the construction of Latin American nations and empires, forbearance and forgiveness were consigned to oblivion. In the Spanish Empire, debts to God, the community, and the Crown were commutative, relational, and confessional obligations grounded on principles of justice. A law of nations, designed by Hugo Grotius and other Protestant authors who cast the Spanish Crown as their foil, questioned whether it was licit to default on debts and renege on contracts signed with a tyrannical Iberian monarch. Latin American officials, many of whom had risked their lives in the fight for the survival of the Crown of Spain, saw this tyrant as an agent of redemption, an arbiter of piety, and the guarantor of law and order. To create sovereign states according to the law of nations, they had to overhaul their histories of their colonial past to establish what they owed this empire. It was crucial to establish whether money had been used for the sake of imperial expansion, for the profit of the Iberian Peninsula, for the benefit of the American subjects, with or without the people's consent, or in a way that bound the descendants of the conquerors and the conquered. Debts with which the Spanish government had encumbered the Spanish Americans after their revolution were, in the words of Carlos María de Bustamante, 'violent oblations': sacrilegious raids on Catholic values of charity and community. The settlement of the debts owed to Spain, the handmaiden of Catholicism, and to Britain, the empire that financed the Latin American struggle for freedom, required a turn to history to locate Latin America's place in the world.

Yet the Protestant law of nations was an unreliable narrator of Spanish imperial history. It replaced Spanish imperial principles like reputation, mercy, clemency, and grace with terms like interest, amnesty, and revolution; it drew the attention of rulers and rebels to the question of consent. It exchanged commutative ideas of debt for contractual forms of association. As Latin American officials assiduously studied the doctrines of the law of nations to reconfigure their bonds with neighbouring states and meet their commutative obligations to the world, war from within and without prevented the repayment of debts and catalysed the negotiations of further speculative loans. Latin Americans sought to find communion, forgiveness, and peace through international law while the United States pursued,

Odious Debt. Edward Jones Corredera, Oxford University Press. © Edward Jones Corredera 2024.
DOI: 10.1093/9780191982200.003.0001

in the words of John Adams, a 'reformation' of the American world through arbitration, unilateral rule-making, and intervention.[1]

Latin American officials were forced to correct the norms of international law. In their refusal to surrender to their manifest destiny, their disillusionment with the catechisms of the moral code of the law of nations fuelled the growth of a clear-eyed vision of international affairs: Latin American officials developed a critique of the impact of their colonial, foreign, and public debts on their relations with the wider world. Debt remained a means to fulfil those social and political expectations that wars foreclosed. War undermined a nation's capacity to repay its debts and foster its 'national peace'.[2] Default could not be exploited to deprive a state of the administration of territories that, through careful governance, could generate the necessary wealth to pay back its debts.[3] War, not insolvency, was the gravest sin. The sanctity of contracts was used to legitimate conflict but the use of violence undermined the sacred purpose of debt: to fulfil the state's obligations to the community. Impunity, as Juan Bautista Alberdi noted, did not confer absolution.[4] Mexican, Argentinian, and Colombian statesmen declared that invasions, conquests, and war should not be used to enforce the payment of state debts since public debt, according to Luis María Drago, ought to be used to redeem commutative ends.

Latin American officials sought to fulfil the Enlightenment's promise to create a global system of irenic capitalism. Bankruptcy, they hoped, would outlaw war over finance. Bankruptcy laws and proceedings protected merchants—could they not protect nations? Default had wrought endless misery and strife—it was at the root of countless interventions in Latin America. Universal bankruptcy rules, grounded in the law of nations, ought to provide an equitable set of global norms that determined what one owed another when all other political and economic bonds and pacts failed.

Just as modern international law forgot Latin America, this tradition of legal thought was largely forgotten. Hard-nosed Latin American statesmen turned to new discourses like Marxism to decry the law of nations as an immoral economy. Yet the most important radical author of the period, José Martí, drew on one term more than any other to defend his programme of socialist reform, emancipation, and regional solidarity: redemption. Officials in the United States in turn recovered the original principle of tyranny embedded in Grotius' law of nations to reject the payment of Cuban loans after its rebels shook off the shackles of Spanish

[1] Jay Sexton, *The Monroe Doctrine: Empire and Nation in Nineteenth Century America* (New York: Hill and Wang, 2011), p. 29.

[2] Manuel Payno, *México y sus cuestiones financieras con la Inglaterra, la España y la Francia* (Mexico City: Cumplido, 1862), p. 312.

[3] As argued by Manuel Crescencio Rejón. Rejón was the founder of the Mexican Writ of Amparo. The Writ of Amparo gives individuals the right to contest administrative actions on the basis of their unconstitutionality. Josefina Zoraida Vázquez, *Manuel Crescencio Rejón* (Mexico City: Senado de la República, 1987), p. 127.

[4] Juan Bautista Alberdi, *El crimen de la guerra* (Buenos Aires: Cadal, 2020), p. 333.

rule. Since Cuba's debt had not been drawn with its consent or for its benefit, they reasoned, it ought to go unpaid. This logic was encapsulated in a term that continues to elicit intense discussion to this day. That term is odious debt.

Alexander Sack's odious debts

In modern international law, the principle of odious debt states that those debts incurred by tyrannical means, or for despotic ends, should be considered illegitimate. These loans therefore ought not to burden peoples that have freed themselves from such a system of rule. It is generally seen as a modern phenomenon with some cursory older precedents.[5] Since the theory has never been implemented, it remains a debate and a source of contention among economists and lawyers. It is, at its core, a dilemma regarding the relationship between consent, one of the core principles of international law, and default, one of the gravest sins in political economy.

The history of odious debt, as it is traditionally told, begins in Paris with the writings of the Russian lawyer, Alexander Nahum Sack. In 1927, Alexander Nahum Sack published his *Les effets des transformations des états sur leurs dettes publiques et autres obligations financières*.[6] In this text he coined the term odious debt. He noted how he had begun to study the connections between loans and state succession 10 years earlier, as a result of Vladimir Lenin's repudiation of the Tsarist debt.[7] His work contributed to a global surge in interest in credit, blame, and solidarity that followed the end of World War I, from the Indian revolutionary Lala Lajpat Rai's *England's Debt to India*, Marcel Mauss' commentaries on forgiveness and German reparations, and his seminal *Essai sur le don* (The Gift), to the Mexican diplomatic efforts to counter the political influence of the United States by developing new ideas of credit.[8]

[5] On its uses in the United Nations see Jeff King, *The Doctrine of Odious Debt in International Law: A Restatement* (Cambridge: Cambridge University Press, 2016), pp. 30–61. Lee Buchheit and others have sought to find solutions to the problem of odious debt by shifting the terms of the debate to the terrain of domestic law. Mitu Gulati, Lee Buchheit, and Robert B. Thompson, 'The Dilemma of Odious Debts', *Duke Law Journal* 56 (2007), pp. 1201–1262.

[6] Alexander Nahum Sack, *Les effets des transformations des états sur leurs dettes publiques et autres obligations financières. Traité juridique et financier, etc.* (Paris: Sirey, 1927).

[7] On the legal logic behind this repudiation see Odette Lineau, *Rethinking Sovereign Debt: Politics, Repudiation, and Legitimacy in Modern Finance* (Cambridge: Harvard University Press, 2014), pp. 57–99.

[8] Lenin's library featured a copy of Rai's work. Ilasai Manian and V. Rajesh, *The Russian Revolution and India* (London: Routledge, 2020), p. 62. Grégoire Mallard, *Gift Exchange: The Transnational History of a Political Idea* (Cambridge: Cambridge University Press, 2019); Christy Thornton, *Revolution in Development Mexico and the Governance of the Global Economy* (Berkeley: University of California Press, 2021); on Russia and the Soviet cancellation of the Tsarist debts to Persia and China see King, *The Doctrine*, pp. 82–84. On the counterintuitive forecasts of foreign lenders anticipating the economic effects of the revolution see Kim Oosterlinck, *Hope Springs Eternal: French Bondholders and the Repudiation of Russian Sovereign Debt* (Oxford: Oxford University Press, 2016).

Principles and doctrines in international law are associated with Sack, as they are with other authors studied in this book, such as Luis María Drago and Carlos Calvo. But in the case of these three men, their biographies, and their own reflections on the context of their works, are generally overlooked by scholars. Recently, Sarah Ludington and Mitu Gulati have produced a brief and much-needed biography of Sack: born in Moscow in 1890, Sack studied economics and law and, during World War I, went on to fight for the Russian army. He left Russia soon after, perhaps as a result of the limits imposed on his life by his Jewish origins, and worked as a lecturer in Paris, The Hague, and New York. Later in life, he was critical of the Bolsheviks in his writings and even sued the *New York Times* when the newspaper accused him of supporting the Communist cause. New York University, his last employer, fired him during a round of cuts, and he spent his final years in a retirement home.[9] Over the course of the twentieth century, his vision of odious debt was popularised by international legal scholars, while Sack's desultory life was largely forgotten.

In Sack's own preface to the work, he noted that two historical events that took place in the same year encouraged him to write the book: the Russian Revolution and the proclamation of independence of Poland.[10] This was not a study fostered by dry readings of debt repudiation but one that shed light on a range of contemporary dilemmas: the spoils of war, the mindset of diplomats as they assimilated imperial defeat and, crucially, the pursuit of self-determination and independence. In the chapter where Sack defined the term odious debt, his first historical reference was found in a footnote, via the writings of the humanitarian lawyer Gaston Jèze, to the Mexican default on the debts incurred by Emperor Maximilian I.[11] The French establishment of a Habsburg sovereign as Emperor of Mexico, premised on the need to enforce the restitution of foreign claims, was the most grotesque demonstration of the century of the excesses of European imperialism in Latin America—so much so that it overshadowed, in the national Mexican memory, the experience of the Mexican-American War and the United States' acquisition of half of Mexico's land.[12] It was an experiment that quickly unravelled because Maximilian was in principle too despotic for Mexican liberals and in practice too liberal for the officious Catholic Church. He was also burdened by debts he could never pay. Sack noted that debts incurred for and by Maximilian's administration had not been contracted to meet the needs or the interests of the Mexican people. The successor state thus had no need to repay them.[13] Sack further observed that odious debts were those that were not contracted to satisfy the needs or the interests of the state,

[9] Sarah Ludington and Mitu Gulati, 'A Convenient Untruth: Fact and Fantasy in the Doctrine of Odious Debts', *Virginia Journal of International Law* 48:3 (2008), pp. 595–639, pp. 607–615.
[10] Sack, *Les effets*, p. vii.
[11] Sack, *Les effets*, pp. 157–158.
[12] Peter Guardino, *The Dead March: A History of the Mexican-American War* (Cambridge: Harvard University Press, 2018), p. 4.
[13] Sack, *Les effets*, pp. 157–158.

but to strengthen a despotic state. To illustrate his view that debts incurred to colonise a territory ought not to be paid by the people, he cited a second American example: the 1898 United States' default on Cuba's debts to Spain. As a result of the Spanish–American War, North American representatives had claimed that Spain had imposed debts on Cubans against their interests and without their consent.[14]

On the basis of these case studies and a number of other historical examples, most of which were drawn from modern European history, Sack gradually developed a formula of odious debts. Sack explained that, for a debt to be considered odious a government would have to prove, and an international tribunal would have to recognise, the following facts: first, that the purposes behind the negotiation of the debt by a past government had been odious and clearly against the interest of the population of part of or the entirety of the territory. Secondly, it would have to demonstrate that debtors had been aware of the projected odious uses of the debts. Once these criteria had been met, it remained incumbent on the lenders to show that the profits produced from these debts had not been used for odious ends that could harm part of or the totality of the population of the state.[15]

Sack was not the first lawyer to consider the legitimacy of debt in these terms; indeed, Sack caught the tail end of a story about the Hispanic world that had been written over four centuries, and which had gained salience in nineteenth-century Latin America. Latin American officials had debated the legitimacy of debt as they sought to resolve the following dilemma: what do postcolonial states owe to empires they once toppled?

Latin American lawyers turned to international law and found, as one Colombian congressman wrote, that after recovering their freedom, Portugal and the Netherlands had never even considered paying the debts they owed to Spain. The United States had also failed to deliver on its promise to repay Britain following the War of Independence.[16] And yet Latin American states debated whether or not to honour their debts to Spain as they drafted their constitutions. Why did Latin American officials consider repaying, and in some cases repay, the tyrannical

[14] Sack, *Les effets*, p. 159.

[15] Sack, *Les effets*, p. 163.

[16] Jerónimo Torres, *Opinión del Senador que suscribe sobre la obligación que tiene la República de reconocer los capitales recibidos a censo en este país por el Gobierno antiguo* (Bogotá: Imprenta de Salazar, 1826), p. 9. In 1824, Brazilian diplomats made the exact same argument when addressing their counterparts in Portugal, as noted by Mohammed Bedjaoui in one of his most famous interventions on the matter of state debts; see Mohammed Bedjaoui, *Ninth Report on Succession of States in respect of matters other than treaties*. United Nations Doc. A/CN.4/301. Volume 2. Part 1 (New York: Yearbook of the International Law Commission, 1977), p. 93. On the important differences between the independence revolts of the 1820s and the mid-twentieth-century movement for decolonisation see Frederick Cooper, 'Decolonizations, Colonizations, and More Decolonizations: The End of Empire in Time and Space', *Journal of World History* 33:3 (2022), pp. 491–526. On decolonisation and the origins of interest in colonial debts and colonialism in international law see Grégoire Mallard, 'We Owe You Nothing: Decolonization and Sovereign Debt Obligations in International Public Law', in Pierre Penet and Juan Flores Zendejas eds., *Sovereign Debt Diplomacies: Rethinking Sovereign Debt from Colonial Empires to Hegemony* (Oxford: Oxford University Press, 2021), pp. 189–212.

Spanish Crown? Was the confessional communion that connected the flourishing Latin American states to the rump Spanish Empire grounded on a type of obligation that defied the lessons of the history of international law? As officials debated these questions, jurists formulated new concepts and classifications to analyse the legitimacy and illegitimacy of debt. The nineteenth-century Latin American solutions to the dilemmas posed by the odiousness of tyrannical debts played played a structuring role in the region's wars of independence, the drafting of its constitutions, its waning federal ambitions, and the configuration of its relations with the rest of the world.

A new history of odious debt

Today, we are witnessing a fundamental transformation in the study of global history. The transition from the early modern age to the modern era is no longer seen, as the historians Friedemann Pestel and Jan Jansen have recently remarked, as an 'age of revolutions' but as an 'age of compensations'.[17] With the rise of new states across the Atlantic world, the pursuit of a moral economy collided with the codification of international law. Nowhere was this clash of values clearer than in the international application of ideas, laws, and doctrines on debt and bankruptcy.[18] This book is a study of Latin American visions of the morality of debt, default, and bankruptcy. Each of the case studies in this book, on Mexico, Colombia, and Argentina, contextualises how Latin American constitutional debates discussed the themes embedded in these modern definitions of odious debt.

Three viewpoints emerged from the Latin American analysis of the odiousness of debt: in one reading, colonial bills were debts owed to an oppressive regime that had continued to wage a costly and unjust war on the new states. It was therefore right to avoid compensating the enemy. This revolutionary fervour was, however, mollified by the desire to establish a liberal state based on the right to property, whereby contracts made in good faith by private creditors had to be respected: liberal officials argued that if a state were to renege on the debts based on Spanish colonial laws, prospective investors would take their money elsewhere and all norms and institutions based on these rules would be open to debate. This would leave the nation in a state of anarchy and likely foster popular support for the return of the Spanish Crown. A third viewpoint was shaped by the demands of expediency and

[17] As noted by Friedemann Pestel and Jan Jansen in the call for papers for the 'Compensations and Reparative Politics: A View from the Nineteenth Century' conference at the University of Heidelberg in November 2024.

[18] For the changes brought about by the 1848 revolutions in Europe see Christopher Clark, *Revolutionary Spring: Fighting for a New World* (London: Penguin, 2023), pp. 93–168. On how these debates emerged from earlier discussions about the tension between property and equality see Michael Sonenscher, *Capitalism: The Story behind the Word* (Princeton: Princeton University Press, 2022).

raison d'état: to recognise this debt would only make the internal debt swell, undermine the state's capacity for reform, and dent its defence spending in a way that would render the state more vulnerable to a Spanish invasion. As Colombian and Argentinian congressmen explained to their peers ahead of the drafting of their constitutions, the establishment of public credit would constitute a form of bankruptcy. What was the moral solution to the inevitable? The answers to this question provided the building blocks for the construction of Latin American fiscal policies, constitutionalism, and international law.

This book focuses on three historical narratives. This is, above all, a new history of the moral economy of the Hispanic world from the 1520s to the 1920s. This study of the making of Latin America raises questions about whether cultural ideas of fairness and obligations that constitute the moral economy are compatible with the epistemological approach to matters of war, peace, and justice that shape international law.[19] For Latin American views on what one owed another differed from those that emerged in the Protestant world. From the sixteenth century to the final decades of the nineteenth century, Spanish and Latin American officials propagated commutative and confessional ideas of debt and obligation while a revolution in the logic of economic obligation transformed the politics of the Protestant world.[20] Contractual responsibilities replaced commutative duties in political economic thought and international law.[21] In the Spanish-speaking world, by contrast, debt remained a way to deliver on one's responsibilities to the community.[22] *Deber* was a moral act. In the word *deber* – both a noun, duty, and a verb, meaning to owe and to be obliged to do something – the Spanish language retained the multiple connotations of the Latin *debeo*, or *debere* – to owe, and to be bound by, something – and confessionalised the term. Debt was duty: to owe another was to be duty-bound to pay them. The entry on *deber* in the most influential early modern Spanish dictionary emphasised the moral dimension of the term, for it signalled that one was 'obliged to pay, satisfy, or honour a debt, an obligation, a contract: and

[19] See also the valuable Marxist critique of international law, one which excluded Latin America, in Ntina Tzouvala, *Capitalism as Civilization: A History of International Law* (Cambridge: Cambridge University Press, 2020). See also E. P. Thompson, 'The Moral Economy of the English Crowd in the Eighteenth Century', *Past & Present* 50 (1971), pp. 76–136; John Stevenson, 'The "Moral Economy" of the English Crowd: Myth and Reality', in Anthony J. Fletcher and John Stevenson eds., *Order and Disorder in Early Modern England* (Cambridge: Cambridge University Press, 1985), pp. 218–238.

[20] Craig Muldrew, *The Economy of Obligation: The Culture of Credit and Social Relations in Early Modern England* (London: Palgrave Macmillan, 1998); Paul Slack, *From Reformation to Improvement: Public Welfare in Early Modern England* (Oxford: Oxford University Press, 1998).

[21] This shift was central to the formation of ideas of the private and the public legal spheres, which had a contingent historical trajectory and cannot be projected back in history in a context like that of the Spanish Empire. For a history built on this problematic divide see Martti Koskenniemi, *To the Uttermost Parts of the Earth: Legal Imagination and International Power 1300–1870* (Cambridge: Cambridge University Press, 2021). For a defence of this work as a 'legal history of capitalism' see David Kennedy and Martti Koskenniemi, *Of Law and the World: Critical Conversations on Power, History, and Political Economy* (Cambridge: Harvard University Press, 2023), pp. 210–262.

[22] Bartolomé Clavero, *Antidora. Antropología católica de la economía moderna* (Milan: Giuffrè, 1991), pp. 93–100.

to not say or do that which is not just or honest'.[23] In early Latin American congressional debates, with the assimilation of international law into the organisation of these new states, it became imperative, and ever more challenging, to establish who made up the community and what one owed another—and the other.[24] Justice was, after all, not a matter of law—it was the domain of theology and history.[25]

By drawing attention to these understudied congressional debates, this book provides a new intellectual history of the rise of international law in Latin America. The settlement of debts inherited from the Spanish monarchy, and the negotiation of loans owed to the rest of the world, were central to the formation of modern international law across the region. Latin American jurists did not seek to generate a creole legal consciousness or meet a standard of civilisation: they sought to settle their debts with the wider world, create constitutional states, and straighten the crooked timber of international law.[26] The definitions of legitimate and illegitimate debt that surfaced from these deliberations fostered the consolidation of states and constitutions in Latin America, and a number of canonical figures in the field of constitutional and international law, including Andrés Bello, Simón Bolívar, Lorenzo de Zavala, Manuel Payno, Juan Bautista Alberdi, Ezequiel Rojas, Carlos Calvo, and Luis María Drago, devoted years of their lives to the resolution of Latin American foreign debts. In the shared ambitions of Latin American lawyers, from the basin of Mexico City through the mountainous fastnesses of the Andes to the shores of Buenos Aires, we find the origins of a form of regional international law that held the moral economy of obligation up as a mirror to the law of nations.

The focus on a number of congresses and the codifying efforts of international lawyers has overshadowed the foundational, structural, and polyvalent functions

[23] The French *devoir* and the Italian *dovere* also retain this layered meaning. Real Academia Española ed., *Diccionario de Autoridades*. Volume 3 (Madrid: Viuda de Francisco del Hierro, 1732), p. 30. The entry on 'To Owe' in Samuel Johnson's contemporary *Dictionary* featured references to obligation but not justice; the bleaker entry on 'debt' noted that this term referred to that which 'one man owes to another' and that 'which any one is obliged to do or suffer'. See the corresponding entries in Samuel Johnson, *A Dictionary of the English Language*. 1755, 1773. Edited by Beth Rapp Young, Jack Lynch, William Dorner, Amy Larner Giroux, Carmen Faye Mathes, and Abigail Moreshead. 2021 (Online).

[24] These ideas were blended with indigenous notions of obligation that are beyond the scope of this book. For a recent overview on these themes see Brian P. Owensby, *New World of Gain: Europeans, Guaraní, and the Global Origins of Modern Economy* (Redwood: Stanford University Press, 2021).

[25] On theology and justice in the Spanish Americas see Tamar Herzog, *Defining Nations: Immigrants and Citizens in Early Modern Spain and Spanish America* (New Haven: Yale University Press, 2003), p. 169.

[26] On how scholars of empire have challenged epiphenomenal readings of law in the Spanish Empire see Tamar Herzog, 'Is Spain Exceptional? Reflections on Thirty Years of Research and Writing', in Edward Jones Corredera ed., *Supplicant Empires: Searching for the Iberian World in Global History* (Turnhout: Brepols) (Forthcoming). Liliana Obregón, 'Between Civilisation and Barbarism: Creole Interventions in International Law', *Third World Quarterly* 27:5 (2006), pp. 815–832 and Liliana Obregón, 'Completing Civilization: Creole Consciousness and International Law in Nineteenth-Century Latin America', in Anne Orford ed., *International Law and Its Others* (Cambridge: Cambridge University Press, 2006), pp. 247–264; Liliana Obregón, 'The Forgotten 19th Century: A New History of a "Latin American" International Law', *Annuaire de La Haye de Droit International* 13 (2000), pp. 27–32; Martti Koskenniemi, *The Gentle Civilizer of Nations: The Rise and Fall of International Law 1870–1960* (Cambridge: Cambridge University Press, 2001), pp. 127–137.

of international law in national debates—and in the very definition of the idea of Latin America.[27] Carlos Calvo, for example, known as a defender of the Monroe Doctrine and the founding father of non-interventionism in Latin America, originally argued in favour of the establishment of a French sphere of influence over the 'Latin race'—and it was on the basis of this racialised world view that French authors coined the term 'Latin America'.[28] The seeds of Calvo's clause and his doctrine emerged from diplomatic negotiations with Britain over the Canstatt affair and, more specifically, from the letter of a secretary to the British Prime Minister Henry John Temple, Lord Palmerston. Reluctant to resuscitate the debates of the Don Pacifico affair, and busy with the resolution of disputes in Mexico, Italy, and the United States, the Prime Minister refused to meet Calvo. Palmerston's secretary responded to Calvo by curtly denying him the possibility of a meeting and informing him that these differences had to be resolved '*in Paraguay*, in a way that was to the absolute satisfaction of Her Majesty's Government'.[29] In these dismissive words of Palmerston's secretary, Calvo saw the 'deciphering of the enigma' of international law.[30] The resolution of the matter had to take place in Paraguay: it had to be settled, as the Calvo Clause would later dictate, according to local norms. This, then, is a book about the formation of international law by agents in motion who negotiated these loans while self-fashioning as agents of redemption and looking at history 'out of their corner of their eye'.[31]

Finally, this book offers a new intellectual history of the role of confessional ideas in the formation of ideas of debt, government or sovereign debt and default—and bankruptcy.[32] The presentist terms "sovereign debt" or "sovereign default" assume that modern ideas of statehood, reputation, and welfare are organic when they in fact require global histories of their own. The Latin American side of this

[27] Juan Pablo Scarfi, *The Hidden History of International Law in the Americas: Empire and Legal Networks* (Oxford: Oxford University Press, 2017), p. 6; Obregón, 'Completing Civilization', pp. 247–264; Aimer Granados García, 'Congresos e intelectuales en los inicios de un proyecto y de una conciencia continental latinoamericana, 1826–1860', in Aimer Granados García and Carlos Marichal eds., *Construcción de las identidades latinoamericanas: ensayos de historia intelectual (Siglos XIX y XX)* (México: Colegio de México, 2004), pp. 39–69; José Briceño Ruiz, 'Los congresos hispanoamericanos en el siglo XIX: identidad, amenazas externas e intereses en la construcción del regionalismo', *Ciclos en la historia, la economía y la sociedad* 26:45 (2015), pp. 88–117; Arnulf Becker Lorca, *Mestizo International Law: A Global Intellectual History 1842–1933* (Cambridge: Cambridge University Press, 2015), pp. 104–107. On the late nineteenth-century origins of the standard of civilisation see, most recently, Tzouvala, *Capitalism as Civilization*, pp. 1–43.

[28] Raymond Jonas, *Habsburgs on the Rio Grande: The Rise and Fall of the Second Mexican Empire* (Cambridge, MA: Harvard University Press, 2024), pp. 11–25.

[29] Carlos Calvo, *Una página de derecho internacional: o La América del Sur ante la ciencia del derecho de gentes moderno* (Paris: Durand, 1864), p. 274. This text will be discussed in a separate article: see Edward Jones Corredera, 'The Laws of Debt: The Paraguayan War (1864–1870) and the Drago Doctrine', in Raphaël Cahen, León Castellanos- Jankiewicz, and Hendrik Simon eds., *The Monroe Doctrine: History, Interpretations, Legacy* (Under review).

[30] Calvo, *Una página*, p. 273.

[31] Germán Colmenares, *Las Convenciones contra la Cultura* (Bogotá: Tercer Mundo, 1987), p. 67.

[32] Recent research on these topics includes Simon Hinrichsen, *When Nations Can't Default* (Cambridge: Cambridge University Press, 2023); Didac Queralt, *Pawned States: State Building in the Era of International Finance* (Princeton: Princeton University Press, 2022).

story reveals the need for a careful study of the composite parts of these terms, for the early nineteenth century was a time when courts, crowns, clerics, and knaves overhauled the definition of ideas of sovereignty, debt, and default, an age that saw the birth of inchoate and conflicting ideas of creditworthiness. In Latin America, a nation's sovereignty was contested and its debt was not its own: strands of foreign debt and public debt were knotted together so strongly that officials spent decades trying to untangle them.[33]

Bankruptcy, however, was a legal recourse with a long and chequered history, and it was a legal mechanism which Latin American officials sought to scale up from civil to international law.[34] Bankruptcy law emerged in medieval Europe to prevent an absconding debtor from running away from those creditors had brought claims against them—indeed, before the word bankruptcy was coined in its original Italian term, the *bancarotta*, the term *fugitivi* was used to settle cases of insolvency because most insolvent debtors would flee their jurisdiction.[35] Others took shelter in churches, which caused tensions between civil and ecclesiastical authorities, and continued to exasperate Spanish officials in the eighteenth century.[36] But bankruptcy law also grew to protect debtors from the punishment or enslavement by creditors.[37] The rise of debtors' prisons generated secular spaces in religious societies that coerced, sheltered, and punished insolvent merchants. The promise of credit inspired Benjamin Constant, Pierre-Joseph Proudhon, and István Széchenyi—but the perils of these gaols, and the risk of insolvency, became the source of myth and mire in the lives and novels of Charles Dickens; Charlotte Brontë; Gustav Freytag, the author one of the most popular German nineteenth-century novels, *Soll und Haben* (Debit and Credit); George Gordon Byron, Lord Byron; Honoré de Balzac; and Fyodor Dostoevsky.[38] Until the nineteenth century,

[33] On the rise of ideas of creditworthiness during this period see Beatrice de Graaf, *Fighting Terror after Napoleon: How Europe Became Secure after 1815* (Cambridge: Cambridge University Press, 2020), pp. 302–356.

[34] Some of these ideas anticipate the main themes of my next book, a work in progress, preliminarily titled: *Bankruptcy: How Hopes & Fears of Default Took Over the World.*

[35] A point repeatedly noted by Israel Treiman; see Israel Treiman, 'Acts of Bankruptcy: A Medieval Concept in Modern Bankruptcy Law' *Harvard Law Review* 52:2 (1938), pp. 189–215, p. 192; Israel Treiman, 'Escaping the Creditor in the Middle Ages', *Law Quarterly Review* 43 (1927), pp. 230–231; Marta Lupi, '*Ius Mercatorum* and Statutes of Florence during the 14th and 15th centuries: The Case of Bankruptcy', *GLOSSAE. European Journal of Legal History* 16 (2019), pp. 204–227, p. 214.

[36] *Ordenanzas de la Ilustre Universidad y Casa de Contratación de la M.N. y M.L. villa de Bilbao: insertos sus reales privilegios* (Bilbao: en la oficina de la viuda de Antonio de Zafra y Rueda, 1738), p. 132.

[37] F. J. J. Cadwallader, *In Pursuit of the Merchant Debtor and Bankrupt: 1066–1732.* Two volumes. Volume 1 (Unpublished PhD Thesis) (University of London, 1965), pp. 10–11; Francisco Tomás y Valiente, 'La prisión por deudas en los Derechos castellano y aragonés', *Anuario de Historia del Derecho Español* 30 (1960), pp. 249–490, pp. 393–394.

[38] V. Markham Lester, *Victorian Insolvency: Bankruptcy, Imprisonment for Debt, and Company Winding-Up in Nineteenth-Century England* (New York: Oxford University Press, 1995); Tawny Paul, *The Poverty of Disaster: Debt and Insecurity in Eighteenth-Century Britain* (Cambridge: Cambridge University Press, 2019), pp. 31–66; Margot Finn, *The Character of Credit. Personal Debt in English Culture, 1740–1914* (Cambridge: Cambridge University Press, 2003); Joanna Innes, *Inferior Politics:*

however, the characteristics of bankruptcy law in Europe and the Americas remained intensely local—with one exception: all of these norms held that only merchants could go bankrupt.[39] Insolvent nations and impecunious empires did not go bankrupt—they signed new loans at a premium and went to war.

This study of Latin American debates on debt and default generates new ideas about bankruptcy and demonstrates that the Hispanic world sought to enlighten capitalism: since bankruptcy was still described as a foreign term in the main early modern Spanish dictionary that retained the definition of debt as 'sin, guilt, or offence', Latin American officials would come to understand the meaning of bankruptcy on their own terms.[40] In the eyes of Latin American officials, bankruptcy revealed who had the power to forgive and forget. Even after Latin American officials accepted that foreign credit was not a demiurgic force that could create states out of smoke and speculation, debt retained its capacity to unite communities and nations around a shared salvific purpose: a government's policy towards insolvency therefore determined what one owed another when all other social and economic bonds and pacts failed. Those who shaped bankruptcy rules therefore establish a hierarchy of contracts and promises. Bankruptcy and debt had little to do with money: these were mechanisms that exposed, often with brutal clarity, who had the power to make or break a contract. How insolvency was then resolved on a global scale exposed what contracts and agreements were foregrounded by international actors when written promises and pledges were voided as a result of one's failure to pay.[41] In Mexico, bankruptcy served to force empires and foreign creditors to respect the nation's sovereignty; in Colombia, bankruptcy promised to redistribute risk and reward; in Argentina, bankruptcy was seen as a shared sacrifice, the final payment of the struggle for independence, and the cost of Buenos Aires' supremacy. The moral economy of bankruptcy, in light of these reforms, challenged the political economy of the law of nations.

Social Problems and Social Policies in Eighteenth-Century Britain (Oxford: Oxford University Press, 2009), pp. 227–278; Erika Vause, *In the Red and in the Black: Debt, Dishonor, and the Law in France between the Revolutions* (Charlottesville: University of Virginia Press, 2018); Julie Claustre, *Dans les geôles du roi. L'emprisonnement pour dette à Paris à la fin du Moyen Âge* (Paris: Éditions de la Sorbonne, 2007). On Széchenyi see Clark, *Revolutionary Spring*, p. 231.

[39] Naturally obtaining a clear definition of a merchant and clarifying who had jurisdiction over the settlement of these matters was a challenge. See Clavero, *Antidora*, pp. 174–180.

[40] Real Academia Española ed., *Diccionario de Autoridades*. Volume 3, p. 247; Real Academia Española ed., *Diccionario de Autoridades*. Volume 1 (Madrid: Real Academia Española, 1726), p. 542. Clavero, *Antidora*, p. 180.

[41] Katharina Pistor has recently referred to bankruptcy as 'the acid test for the rights and privileges the parties negotiated or that state law granted them long before default loomed on the horizon. If these rights cannot be enforced in bankruptcy, they are not worth much'. Katharina Pistor, *Code of Capital: How the Law Creates Wealth and Inequality* (Princeton: Princeton University Press, 2019), p. 137. The late Nigel Dodd once noted that German and French theorists saw debt as a contract while Americans saw debt as a form of money; see his *The Social Life of Money* (Princeton: Princeton University Press, 2014), p. 94.

Moral bankruptcy: how Latin America corrected international law's historical fictions

We are frequently told that one of the defining characteristics of the history of Hispanic empires and states, from the sixteenth to the twentieth centuries, is the persistence of government declarations of bankruptcy.[42] But, throughout this period, only merchants could file for bankruptcy.[43] Moreover, historians continue to argue that patrimonial structures in the Hispanic world stalled the rise of capitalist principles and institutions across its territories. What explains this contradiction in terms? This is the first book to study the seeds of this contradiction, from the famous defaults of the Habsburg Spanish emperors and the catastrophic crashes of Latin American states, from Philip II's bankruptcy to the Baring Crisis and the Carranza Doctrine. It is worth noting that in most of these cases, including the two most famous instances, Philip's non-payment of 1575 and Benito Juaréz's moratorium of 1861, these governments merely suspended or deferred payments.[44] How did the moral shame associated with bankruptcy mark these reforms?

This book shows that the association of the political and economic history of the Spanish Empire with bankruptcy was first made by the founder of international law—and it quickly became entrenched in the law of nations. In one of his many brilliant rhetorical moves, Hugo Grotius bound a king to the moral code of a merchant. Grotius argued that Philip II's suspension of payments to his lenders and his soldiers fuelled the sack of Antwerp, a bloody episode in history that bolstered the growth of the Black Legend of Spanish barbarity and backwardness.[45] Grotius, and the leaders of the Dutch Revolt, used this narrative to connect the economy of salvation to the economy of contract: the King, they argued, had breached the sacred covenant.[46] The law of nations of Grotius and Vattel turned Philip's non-payment into a morality tale that suggested that the King was forced to repay his debts to Dutch lenders to improve his creditworthiness and retain his empire, that the economy of contract could make a king yield, and that the Dutch Republic, through its respect for contract rights, had dealt a death blow to the Spanish Empire.

[42] Carmen Reinhart and Kenneth Rogoff, *This Time Is Different: Eight Centuries of Financial Folly* (Princeton: Princeton University Press, 2009), p. xxx, pp. 70–86.

[43] Jay Cohen, 'The History of Imprisonment for Debt and Its Relation to the Development of Discharge in Bankruptcy', *The Journal of Legal History* 3:2 (1982), pp. 153–171, pp. 159–160.

[44] For the sake of ease of reading, I nonetheless refer to these resolutions as a type of bankruptcy.

[45] Jan Waszink has argued that this was an important theme in the text; see his introduction in Hugo Grotius, *Annals of the War in the Low Countries*. Editing, Translation, and Introduction by Jan Waszink (Leuven: Leuven University Press, 2023), p. 217.

[46] Martin van Gelderen, *The Political Thought of the Dutch Revolt 1555–1590* (Cambridge: Cambridge University Press, 1992), pp. 110–165.

It was a compelling piece of propaganda.[47] As the founding fathers of Latin American states noted time and time again, as a historical recollection of events it was quite wrong. Twelve years after this affair, Philip was able to raise enough loans to send the armada on its fateful mission to invade England.[48] Some of the debts owed to Dutch subjects were only settled by Philip's son and grandson at the Twelve Years' Truce and the Treaty of Munster.[49] Above all, Latin American creole officials identified with the culture that grew during and after Philip II's death, in the seventeenth and eighteenth centuries, and profited from the overall rise in the silver trade—this was an age of Enlightenment in the Spanish Empire.[50] By the early nineteenth century, many Latin American officials did not regard the King of Spain as a tyrant—even, as we will see, when his representatives refused to pay the debts the Crown owed to the Spanish Americas.

Latin American prelates, politicians, and philosophers therefore had to correct the history of international law. They methodically compared and contrasted their own colonial and revolutionary histories with the chronicles of the law of nations. They introduced terms like liquidation, consolidation, and bankruptcy into their national debates through translations and comparative histories. By the late nineteenth century, lawyers and priests had generated new ideas about the moral economy of debt. They sought to realise Grotius' honourable ambitions: to bind emperors and kings to the local laws of the nation where debts had been negotiated. Latin American officials harnessed international law to universalise bankruptcy

[47] The study of propaganda and communication strategies during and after the Dutch Revolt has recently produced some fascinating research: see Judith Pollmann, *Catholic Identity and the Revolt of the Netherlands, 1520–1635* (Oxford: Oxford University Press, 2011); Geert H. Janssen, *The Dutch Revolt and Catholic Exile in Reformation Europe* (Cambridge: Cambridge University Press, 2014); Monica Stensland, *Habsburg Communication in the Dutch Revolt* (Amsterdam: Amsterdam University Press, 2012); Hugh Dunthorne, *Britain and the Dutch Revolt, 1560–1700* (Cambridge: Cambridge University Press, 2013).

[48] He also had to introduce the *millones* tax, which has been the subject of a great deal of research. Mauricio Drelichman and Hans-Joachim Voth, 'The Sustainable Debts of Philip II: A Reconstruction of Castile's Fiscal Position, 1566–1596', *The Journal of Economic History* 70:4 (2010), pp. 813–842, p. 819; James Conklin, 'The Theory of Sovereign Debt and Spain under Philip II', *Journal of Political Economy* 106:3 (1998), pp. 483–513.

[49] Randall C. H. Lesaffer and Erik-Jan Broers, 'Private Property in the Dutch-Spanish Peace Treaty of Münster (30 January 1648)', *Tilburg University Legal Studies Working Papers* 2 (2007), pp. 2–44. On the Dutch Republic's management of its own debts see W. Fritschy, 'A "Financial Revolution" Reconsidered: Public Finance in Holland during the Dutch Revolt, 1568–1648', *Economic History Review* 56:1 (2003), pp. 57–89.

[50] Jorge Cañizares-Esguerra, *How to Write the History of the New World: Histories, Epistemologies, and Identities in the Eighteenth-Century Atlantic World* (Stanford: Stanford University Press, 2001); Carlos Eire, *Reformations: The Early Modern World, 1450–1650* (New Haven: Yale University Press, 2016), pp. 466–497; Edward Jones Corredera, *The Diplomatic Enlightenment: Spain, Europe, and the Age of Speculation* (Leiden: Brill, 2021); Lisa Voigt, *Spectacular Wealth: The Festival of Colonial South American Mining Towns* (Austin: University of Texas Press, 2016); Maria Soledad Barbón, *Colonial Loyalties: Celebrating the Spanish Monarchy in Eighteenth-Century Lima* (Notre Dame, IN: University of Notre Dame Press, 2019); David Brading, *The First America: The Spanish Monarchy, Creole Patriots, and the Liberal State, 1492–1867* (Cambridge: Cambridge University Press, 1991).

proceedings; bankruptcy law, after all, gave merchant debtors the chance to gather funds and make their case before a court. It measured culpability on the basis of one's intentions. Latin American states were deprived of rights that were afforded to merchants. Their leaders, argued Alberdi, were treated like criminals who were shunted into debtors' prisons—at a time when European states were abolishing these institutions on the basis of humanitarianism.[51] All nineteenth-century European states, as Payno noted, were overly indebted and staved off default through imperial expansion—but there was no point in waging war against one another and further increasing one's debts. The world deserved better. Latin American statesmen, in the face of US and European opposition, sought nothing less than to create a global system of moral debt relations that did not punish a nation's financial failure with outright war. Paradoxically, it was only in the nineteenth century, as US legislators eased bankruptcy laws at home and European governments relaxed punishments for personal insolvency, that US and European leaders pursued an increasingly predatory attitude towards the non-payment of Latin American states.[52]

Why should lawyers study Latin American history?

In international law, Latin American debates on debt and default have been entirely forgotten. Indeed, international lawyers frequently forget periods, global regions, and the weight of economics in global affairs. Modern international law has a problem with time and space: the study of the origins of doctrines encourages the pursuit of historical solutions to a problem, rather than the study of the origins of the problem that once led to its proposed solution.[53] The roots of said problems are always wrenched from their local soil. Ideas are decontextualised, telescoped,

[51] Vause, *In the Red and the Black*, p. 249. Though scholars have noted that these legal norms did not exactly end, rather the social composition of those jailed over debt changed. See Finn, *The Character of Credit*, pp. 186–187.

[52] Peter J. Coleman, *Debtors and Creditors in America: Insolvency, Imprisonment for Debt, and Bankruptcy, 1607–1900* (Madison: The State Historical Society of Wisconsin, 1974), p. 27; David A. Skeel Jr., *Debt's Dominion: A History of Bankruptcy Law in America* (Princeton: Princeton University Press, 2003), pp. 23–70. On the challenges of cross-border insolvency legislation today see Irit Mevorach, *The Future of Cross-Border Insolvency: Overcoming Biases and Closing Gaps* (Oxford: Oxford University Press, 2018).

[53] For a valuable reflection on the complexities of resolving this distinction see François Furet, 'De l'histoire-récit à l'histoire-problème', *Diogène* 89 (1975), pp. 113–130 and more broadly his *L'Atelier de l'histoire* (Paris: Flammarion, 1982). See also Quentin Skinner's study of the mythology of doctrines of a different kind in Quentin Skinner, 'Meaning and Understanding in the History of Ideas', *History & Theory* 8:1 (1969), pp. 3–53, p. 7. In the context of international law, David Kennedy drew attention to this issue decades ago: David Kennedy, 'International Law and the Nineteenth Century: History of an Illusion', *Nordic Journal of International Law* 65 (1996), pp. 385–420, pp. 388–397. The study of problems instead of solutions was also at the core of many of the writings of Reinhart Koselleck which have informed this author.

foreshortened, and sublimated for modern use.[54] Cultural readings of economics, religion, and the memorialisation of successful and failed constitutional experiences are all frequently neglected.[55] Many of the problems and prognoses that are seen as new today are revealed, through the study of Latin American history, to be long-standing problems associated with early modern debates on revolution, sovereignty, and consent. As we will see, the shift from the odiousness of the debt to the odiousness of the regime, which scholars have depicted as a contemporary one, had a formative role in the pursuit of Latin American independence and in the formation of statehood.[56] Whether consent or the control of a territory ought to be at the core of definitions of sovereignty, in turn, was a crucial debate in the region's mid-nineteenth-century constitutional debates.[57] Elements that are seen as constituent parts of a process of recognition in international law today—revolution, independence, self-determination, statehood, and the establishment of a constitution—had entirely different origins and, at times, conflicting ends.[58] While the late James Crawford, the leading scholar on state succession, argued that 'nothing in early international law precluded the solution of the legal problems raised by the creation and existence' of states, Latin American states found that the acceptance of colonial and foreign debt undermined both the nominal recognition

[54] For the latest summary of the debate see Samuel Moyn, 'International Law and the Politics of History. By Anne Orford. Cambridge, UK: Cambridge University Press, 2021. Pp. xii, 382. Index', *American Journal of International Law* 116:4 (2022), pp. 895–900. For my views on the flaws with the epistemological foundations of the field see Edward Jones Corredera, 'Why International Lawyers Measure Time with a Telescope: Grotian Moments & Richard Falk's Histories of the Future', *Grotiana* 42:2 (2021), pp. 212–228.

[55] Thanks to the work of Juan Pablo Scarfi, Liliana Obregón, and Arnulf Becker Lorca, cited throughout this book, this has started to change. Note, in particular, Scarfi's observation on the need to study 'the cultural and intellectual impact of international law in the Americas'. See Scarfi, *Hidden History*, p. xxxii.

[56] Joseph Stiglitz, 'Odious Rulers, Odious Debts', *The Atlantic*, November 2003; Patrick Bolton and David Skeel. 'Odious Debts or Odious Regimes?', *Law and Contemporary Problems* 70:4 (2007), pp. 83–107. Gulati et al., 'The Dilemma', p. 1203. As scholars have pointed out, Sack understood that the American position was not the established one, and that the Spanish argument had been considered 'flawless' at the time. Gaurang Mitu Gulati, Sarah Ludington, and Arthur Mark Weisburd, 'A Convenient Untruth: Fact and Fantasy in the Doctrine of Odious Debts (with Response: Reflections on 'A Convenient Untruth')', *Virginia Journal of International Law* 48:3. Duke Law School Legal Studies Paper No. 174, pp. 1–47, p. 37; Bolton and Skeel, 'Odious Debts or Odious Regimes?', pp. 83–107, pp. 94–197; James V. Feinerman, 'Odious Debt, Old and New: The Legal Intellectual History of an Idea', *Law and Contemporary Problems* 70:4 (2007), pp. 193–220, p. 195, n. 9; Odette Lienau, 'Who is the "Sovereign" in Sovereign Debt?: Reinterpreting a Rule-of-Law Framework from the Early Twentieth Century', *Yale Journal of International Law* 33:1 (2008), pp. 63–111. On the argument that the odiousness of the regime may be disregarded in assessments of odious debts see Kim Oosterlinck, Ugo Panizza, Mark Weidemaier, and Mitu Gulati, 'The Odious Haitian Independence Debt', *Journal of Global Development* 13:2 (2022), pp. 339–378, p. 371.

[57] A distinction at the core of the important book by Odette Lineau, *Rethinking Sovereign Debt*.

[58] On the difficulties of theorising recent efforts at achieving self-determination see Matthew Craven, *The Decolonization of International Law: State Succession and the Law of Treaties* (Oxford: Oxford University Press, 2007), pp. 88–92.

of their independence and their capacity to exercise their sovereignty in an international stage.[59]

Latin American thinkers provided sophisticated answers to questions that continue to shape current discussions on odious and sovereign debts: scholars have noted how, over the past 30 years, 'debts that might be regarded as "odious" in international law' have been 'subject to enforcement (or at any rate litigation) in national courts applying domestic private law'.[60] This lack of definition continues to affect Latin America's international relations: since the issuing of Venezuela's current public debt bonds took place under New York law, debt negotiations could only be pursued by a Venezuelan president that is recognised by the United States government. Since the current leader of Venezuela is on the United States' list of sanctions the stalemate seemed, at the time of writing this book, impossible to resolve.[61] The norms governing the 'international law on sovereign debt' are undeveloped and know 'no settled definition of sovereign debt'.[62]

Does it matter that Latin America's history has been forgotten? It matters because the recovery of these ideas sheds new light on the development of modern debates of international law—and its neglect, and its mistaken understanding, of Latin American history. The most important modern study of odious debt was conducted by the Algerian diplomat Mohammed Bedjaoui, Special Rapporteur of the International Law Commission with respect to Succession of States in relation to matters other than treaties, and a Judge of the International Court of Justice.[63] When Bedjaoui studied the matter of debt and state succession in the Latin American context, he noted that 'in most of the cases involving Spain and her former colonies, the debts assumed by the successor States were assumed by means of internal legislation, even before the conclusion of treaties with Spain, which often merely took note of the provisions of those internal laws'. Bedjaoui judged the size and character of this iceberg from the parts above the waterline: by neglecting to consider the role of international law in the formation of the internal legislation or national political debates, he diverted his view towards the matter of Latin America's treaties with European powers, and argued that 'none of the treaties, however, speak of rules or principles of international law governing succession to State debts. Indeed, many of the treaty provisions indicate that what was

[59] James Crawford, *The Creation of States in International Law* (Oxford: Oxford University Press, 2007), p. 12.

[60] See King, *The Doctrine*, p. 127; See also Jarrod Hepbur, *Domestic Law in International Investment Arbitration* (Oxford: Oxford University Press, 2017).

[61] Mayela Armas, 'Venezuela's Maduro Seeks to Revive Stalled Debt Talks, Bondholders Unimpressed', *Reuters*, 30 September 2019.

[62] Michael Waibel, *Sovereign Defaults before International Courts and Tribunals* (Cambridge: Cambridge University Press, 2011), p. 12.

[63] On Bedjaoui's influence on international legal views on debt see Mallard, 'We Owe You Nothing', pp. 189–212.

involved was a "voluntary and spontaneous" decision on the part of the newly independent State'.[64]

There was nothing spontaneous about the Latin American approach to the negotiation of foreign debt: the language of treaties failed to convey the international legal thought and the complexity of the political processes that yielded these accords, along with the rejection with which these words were met in some corners of the region. Whether the payment of colonial debts was 'voluntary' or not was a source of contention for most of the century in Mexico, Colombia, and Argentina. Bedjaoui never cited the origins of these terms: the first treaty that featured these words, and which Spain used as the basis for other accords with its former colonies, was the one signed between Spain and Mexico in 1836.[65] The terms declared that Mexico recognised 'voluntarily and spontaneously' as its own the debt contracted by the metropolitan Spanish government.[66] As this book shows, these well-meaning terms caused endless problems for Mexico and the new republics.[67] By the middle of the century, Spain, according to Mexico's agent in charge of resolving these debts, continued to consider Mexico 'a rebel state'.[68] Indeed, it was Mexico's postponement of the repayment of a number of foreign debts, including Spanish claims, that encouraged Spain to join France and Britain in the blockade that culminated in the rise of Maximilian I.

International law, in this way, forgot about Latin America and its history. Today, debates on odious debt rarely acknowledge the salience or the long history of debates on foreign debt in Latin American politics. The question of foreign debt remains an open wound in Latin America, and its history has served as a rhetorical device to be deployed for political ends.[69] In the 1980s in Argentina the promise

[64] The phrase is taken from Gallagher and Robinson's famous article on informal empire: John Gallagher and Ronald Robinson, 'The Imperialism of Free Trade', *The Economic History Review* 6:1 (1953), pp. 1–15, p. 1. Bedjaoui, *Ninth Report*, p. 94. Bedjaoui mostly paraphrased Feilchenfeld's views on the topic. See Ernst H. Feilchenfeld, *Public Debts and State Succession* (New York, Macmillan, 1931), pp. 254–255.

[65] The terms of Spain's earliest treaties of recognition with its former provinces, Chile, Ecuador, and El Salvador, all followed these terms. Other nations, including Peru, Venezuela, and Argentina, were reluctant to accept these terms and delayed negotiations over the matter of debt: in the case of Mexico, Colombia, and Argentina, these terms would be frequently revised and debated in Latin American congressional and diplomatic gatherings. For a valuable edited collection of these treaties see Carlos Daniel Malamud ed., *Ruptura y reconciliación España y el reconocimiento de las independencias latinoamericanas* (Madrid: Fundación Mapfre, 2012).

[66] See the careful analysis of Antonia Pi-Suñer Llorens, *El General Prim y la "Cuestión de Mexico"* (Published PhD Thesis) (Mexico City: Universidad Nacional Autónoma de México, 1991). See the treaty in Agustín Sánchez Andrés, 'México', in Malamud ed., *Ruptura y reconciliación*, pp. 37–52, pp. 50–52.

[67] Pi-Suñer Llorens, *El General Prim*, pp. 67–80. For a summary of the response of the other republics to the Spanish use of these terms see William Spence Robertson, 'The Recognition of the Spanish Colonies by the Motherland', *The Hispanic American Historical Review* 1:1 (1918), pp. 70–91.

[68] Manuel Payno, *México y el Sr. embajador Don Joaquín Francisco Pacheco* (Mexico City: J. Abadiano, 1862), p. 18.

[69] Best captured in Eduardo Galeano, *Las venas abiertas de América Latina* (Mexico City: Siglo XXI, 1971) and Miguel Ángel Centeno, *Sangre y deuda: Ciudades, Estado y construcción de nación en América Latina* (Bogotá: Universidad Nacional de Colombia, 2014). See also Alejandro Olmos Gaona,

of the repudiation of foreign debt, and the commitment to focus instead on the well-being of the people, was a central political message of the regime.[70] In Cuba, Fidel Castro dedicated several books and a number of lengthy interviews to historical digressions on the need for Latin America to denounce the illegitimacy of its foreign lenders.[71] Castro portrayed the default on foreign loans as the natural and long-awaited conclusion of the independence process started in the 1820s by Latin American revolutionaries.[72] In a speech praising the 'recovery of the banners of Simón Bolívar', Hugo Chávez spoke against the 'neo-liberal model' of the International Monetary Fund (IMF) and described the nation's obligations to the international body as 'a never-ending debt!'.[73] Chávez sought to create an alternative socialist Latin American lending mechanism backed by a boost in profits derived from oil exports.[74] The influential Venezuelan academic and former minister Ricardo Hausmann has advocated that his country should simply deny the legitimacy of foreign loans.[75] As I was finishing this book, the Argentinian President Javier Milei was threatening to default on the nation's constitutional obligations by drawing on the logic once espoused by Bernardino Rivadavia. The principles of odious debt remain a source of hope and fear for Latin American officials.

Memory, forgetting, and forgiving in Latin American history

Today, the rise of climate, slavery, and war reparations has triggered the growth of debates about the historical responsibility of states, sovereigns, and empires for the predicaments of modern nations—a complex exercise in retroactive law, revisionist historiography, and *ars memoria* which has come to shape current political discussions.[76] The study of historical accountability and economics of blame and restitution are already generating new readings of history—and clashing with

La deuda odiosa: el valor de una doctrina jurídica como instrumento de solución política (Buenos Aires: Ediciones Continente, 2005).

[70] Winthrop Wright, *British-Owned Railways in Argentina: Their Effect on the Growth of Economic Nationalism, 1854–1948* (Austin: University of Texas Press, 1974), pp. 262–269. On this debate in the context of the 1980s see Lee C. Buchheit and G. Mitu Gulati, 'Odious Debts and Nation-Building: When the Incubus Departs', *Maine Law Review* 60:2 (2008), pp. 478–485, p. 483.

[71] Alfonso Rosa, *Fidel Castro y la deuda externa* (Havana: Editora Política, 1989).

[72] Rosa, *Castro y la deuda externa*, pp. 7–9, pp. 82–85.

[73] 'Speech by President Hugo Chávez at the opening of XII G-15 Summit', *Venezuela Analysis*, 1 May 2004.

[74] Saul Hudson, 'Venezuela to Quit IMF, World Bank', *Reuters*, 1 May 2007.

[75] Ricardo Hausmann, Alejandro Grisanti, and José Ignacio Hernández, 'How to Address Venezuela's Crushing Debt Burden', *Project Syndicate*, 10 July 2019.

[76] Ana Lucia Araujo, *Reparations for Slavery and the Slave Trade: A Transnational and Comparative History* (New York: Bloomsbury Academic, 2017); Katrina Forrester, 'Reparations, History and the Origins of Global Justice', in Duncan Bell ed., *Empire, Race and Global Justice* (Cambridge: Cambridge University Press, 2019), pp. 22–51.

existing national priorities and moral discourses. My hope is that this book about an earlier era of imperial reparations, the economics of retroactivity, and the social life of debt will encourage a historical understanding of how ideas of retaliation, reprisal, forgiveness, and absolution continue to shape discussions about what we owe to one another across borders when most economic bonds fail. At the heart of the logic of reparations, there is a crucial and entirely understudied historical principle that the study of the age of compensations can shed light on.

In the nineteenth century, Manuel Payno and other novelists around the world drew on the figure of the devil to shed light on the darker side of fate and the tyranny of choice.[77] Payno's slim silver-tongued devil was, in the words of a scholar, 'a forgetful demon'; he displayed a disarming ambiguity towards moral dilemmas—through sleights of hand and poignant promises, he reached into the hidden depths of human hearts and intervened in mankind's affairs, past and present, to change the course of history in an instant.[78] When it came to debt and diplomacy, the devil was in the details. And it had a name: retroactivity. As revolutionaries debated when the Spanish Empire ended and the nation began, when and how, in short, they could retroactively project their visions of justice on the affairs of their forebears, retroactivity turned into the most influential historical device in the writing of Latin American history and the drafting of its laws. Constitutions, debt settlements, and treaty negotiations often had conflicting retroactive effects—this devil conjured up new histories, sat back, and watched diplomats and statesmen fight to establish a favourable hierarchy of obligations.[79] The retrospective application of debt settlements legally reassigned the weight of the legal burden of history across time and space—it determined, by law, and in spite of whatever contemporaries may have thought at the time, when a regime rose and fell, whether debts signed decades earlier were just or unjust, or whether the conquistadors who reached the Americas centuries earlier usurped an empire or built a civilisation. This devil, through this desacralisation of the last judgement, could foreshorten blame and guilt across countless generations; as he bent history to his will, he could lay the responsibility for their actions on the shoulders of the present—or free the future from the tyranny of the past. But debt was based on political economy, constitutions were based on consent, and international law was based on custom—what happened when the retroactive application of international law

[77] Antonio Castro Leal, 'Estudio preliminar', in Manuel Payno, *El fistol del diablo. Novelas de costumbres mexicanas.* Texto establecido y estudio preliminar de Antonio Castro Leal (Mexico City: Porrua, 1981), pp. ix–xxv, pp. xv–xvi; Jeffrey Burton Russell, *Mephistopheles: The Devil in the Modern World* (Ithaca, NY: Cornell University Press, 1990), pp. 168–173; Sarah Bartels, *The Devil and the Victorians: Supernatural Evil in Nineteenth-Century English Culture* (London: Routledge, 2021).

[78] Leal, 'Estudio preliminar', p. xvi.

[79] In Payno's *El fistol*, the devil grants a gift, in the form of a precious stone, a *fistol*, to his unsuspecting victims. The *fistol* represents the allure and the weight of free choice—when the main character in the novel describes this gift as a debt he can pay back to lift the weight of his obligation, the devil explains that it can be bought and sold but not permanently owned. See Payno, *El fistol del diablo*, pp. 439–453.

and debt repayment assigned blame in conflicting ways? Johann Wolfgang von Goethe's Mephistopheles would have grinned like a Cheshire cat: in the age of compensations, ethical uncertainty was the cost of progress—this was a debt that had to be paid.[80]

As foreign powers cited the sacred principles of international law to demand unfair compensation, Latin American authors like Payno turned the retroactive study of debt—of numbers, intentions, political principles, and economic hopes—into a form of historical accountability. Latin American authors, erstwhile students of the ancient fictions of Spain's civil law, used these histories of debts to challenge the historical foundations of the law of nations—and question its moral authority.[81] Constitutional reforms, the time frames of electoral politics, or a government's disavowal of the laws and contracts of a vanquished tyrannical regime, Latin American diplomats reasoned time and time again, had to be respected even when they clashed with the imperatives created by foreign accounts of past obligations.[82] Once foreign credit stopped shaping the expectation of the future the study of debt served to rewrite the past. Slowly, the analysis of debt became an exercise in historiography, and the history of Latin American foreign debt turned into a chronicle of its relations with the wider world. The study of the art of retroactivity in reparations has a long history; my hope is that this book about imperial reparations and interventions will foster its study.

In Payno's historical novel, in the aftermath of the American victory in the Mexican–American War, at the side of the US general making his victorious entrance into Mexico City was the true architect of the invasion: the devil.[83] By the middle of the nineteenth century, the Latin American memory of foreign debt was transformed by the shared experience of intervention. The doctrine of Carlos Calvo, which stated that local norms ought to settle indemnities and debt disputes of foreigners and locals equally, and the doctrine of Luis María Drago, which stated that the use of force by a foreign power could not be deployed to resolve

[80] On the ancient view that the devil was the evil debt collector and God was the redeemer see Gary A. Anderson, *Sin: A History* (New Haven: Yale University Press, 2009), pp. 193–195 and Devin Singh, *Divine Currency: The Theological Power of Money in the West* (Stanford: Stanford University Press, 2018), pp. 174–192.

[81] It was the counterpoint to the Protestant common law's obsession with what Jeremy Bentham described as a 'cobweb' of hidden and ancient sources of authority. Jeremy Bentham, 'To the Citizens of the several American United States', in Philip Schofield and Jonathan Harris eds., *'Legislator of the Worid': Writings on Codification, Law, and Education* (Oxford: Oxford University Press, 1998), pp. 113–172, p. 132. Though, as Benton and Walker have shown, Spanish civil authorities also drew on selective readings of past sources; see Lauren Benton and Kathyrn Walker, 'Law for the Empire: The Common Law in Colonial America and the Problem of Legal Diversity', *Chicago-Kent Law Review* 89 (2014), pp. 937–956, p. 950. On parallels between civil and common law see Herzog, 'Is Spain Exceptional?'. On the fictions of the law of nations see Francesca Iurarlo, *The Invention of Custom: Natural Law and the Law of Nations, ca. 1550–1750* (Oxford: Oxford University Press, 2021).

[82] On the rise of democracy in Latin America see Eduardo Posada-Carbó, Joanna Innes, and Mark Philp eds., *Re-imagining Democracy in Latin America and the Caribbean, 1780–1870* (New York: Oxford University Press, 2023).

[83] Payno, *El fistol del diablo*, p. 880.

matters concerning the public debt of a nation, can only be understood through a comparative history of the three countries considered in this book: the rise of Maximilian I as Emperor of Mexico reshaped Latin American attitudes towards Europe and foreign debt. The fragmentation of Gran Colombia and the chronic indebtedness of its former constituent parts led to the Venezuela Crisis of 1902, the subject of the letter written by Drago to the Argentinian ambassador in the United States that gave birth to his doctrine.[84] Drago's views, in turn, can only be understood by foregrounding the writings of the philosopher and diplomat Juan Bautista Alberdi and the historical experience of nineteenth-century Argentina. Finally, the study of the ambitions of Elihu Root, the United States Secretary who received a Nobel Prize for the establishment of a permanent court of justice, and his reaction to Drago's writings, must account for the North American lawyer's role in generating the legal framework used by the diplomats of the United States in the aftermath of the Spanish–American War. This logic which would later inform Sack's definition of odious debt.[85]

There are countless histories of war and debt in modern Latin America—one scholar has gone as far as to say that the 'history of independent Mexico is no more than the history of the external debt'.[86] This study is by no means a comprehensive account of the economics of Latin American debt.[87] This book studies instead the confessional, legal, and political economic debates that gave rise to lasting international disputes over debt. It frames debt—colonial, public, and foreign debt—in the context of the broader intellectual history of the rise of capitalism in the Hispanic world.[88] I have tried to contextualise nineteenth-century Latin American readings of credit, amplify and streamline many of these historiographical accounts, and provide new perspectives on the legal and political discourses that prompted the signing of these loans and facilitated the pursuit of their resolution.[89]

[84] On the differences in the definitions and uses of the Calvo Doctrine and the Calvo Clause see Waibel, *Sovereign Defaults*, pp. 263–272.

[85] On Root's broader ambitions see Anthony Anghie, *Imperialism, Sovereignty and the Making of International Law* (Cambridge: Cambridge University Press, 2012), pp. 281–291.

[86] Araceli Ibarra Bellón, *El comercio y el poder en México, 1821–1864: la lucha por las fuentes financieras entre el Estado central y las regiones* (Mexico City: Fondo de Cultura Económica, 1998), p. 47. Cited by Richard J. Salvucci, *Politics, Markets, and Mexico's 'London Debt,' 1823–1887* (New York: Cambridge University Press, 2009), p. 5.

[87] The best work on this front remains Carlos Marichal, *A Century of Debt Crises in Latin America. From Independence to the Great Depression, 1820–1930* (Princeton: Princeton University Press, 1989), recently updated in *Historia mínima de la deuda externa de Latinoamérica* (Mexico City: El Colegio de México, 2014). See, for a comparative reading on sovereign debt and state formation, Queralt, *Pawned States*.

[88] For an excellent summary of the rise of capitalism in the Spanish Empire see John Tutino, 'The Americas in the Rise of Capitalism', in John Tutino ed., *New Countries: Capitalism, Revolutions, and Nations in the Americas, 1750–1870* (Durham, NC: Duke University Press, 2017), pp. 25–70.

[89] Contributing to the literature in economic history on the topic see Kim Oosterlinck, 'The Historical Context of Sovereign Debt', in Ilias Bantekas and Cephas Lumina eds., *Sovereign Debt and Human Rights* (Oxford: Oxford University Press, 2018), pp. 13–27 and Marc Flandreau and Juan H. Flores, 'Bonds and Brands: Foundations of Sovereign Debt Markets, 1820–1830', *The Journal of*

I have avoided the use of jargon and the sums of the loans, since other scholars, frequently cited throughout this work, have carried out this work better than I ever could. I hope that by drawing attention to the soteriology of debt, certain trends that continue to shape the study of Spanish and Spanish American political thought, such as the insistence on overstating the impact of Scholastic thinkers, instead of studying theology and Spanish politics, and assuming the existence of an intellectual path dependence based on their ideas, or the division of the world into Protestant powers who erased the legacies of Catholic Hispanic cultures, will be revisited and reconsidered.[90]

The reader will find that, as we move through the three case studies and the travels of Mexican officials take us from the Cádiz Cortes to the salons of Paris and eventually to the shores of Veracruz, the focus of the lens grows sharper in order to study the specific constitutional and legal reforms that shaped Colombian and, in particular, Argentine constitutional debates, since it would be Argentinian jurists who, drawing on their national history, proposed outlawing war over finance. This book tracks how the discussions on foreign debt took on a structuring role in elite national debates that, in due course, framed regional ideas of international law, and thus generated an intellectual strand of thought that predated Marxist solidarity and its own vision of communitarianism.[91] This study provides a reconfiguration of the study of the problem of the ethics of foreign debt that, I hope, will generate further comparative research across the fields of economic and legal history.[92] In particular, I hope this study will stimulate further research on the relationship between the law of nations and the day-to-day social experience of debt—from the

Economic History 69:3 (2009), pp. 646–684. See also a deft summary of the economic history of the period in Juan Flores Zendejas and Felipe Ford Cole, 'Sovereignty and Debt in Nineteenth-Century Latin America', in Penet and Flores Zendejas eds., *Sovereign Debt Diplomacies*, pp. 49–72. For a good overview of the debates in economic history on this period of Latin American history see Juan Flores Zendejas, 'Explaining Latin America's Persistent Defaults: An Analysis of the Debtor–Creditor Relations in London, 1822–1914', *Financial History Review* 27:3 (2020), pp. 319–339.

[90] See the recent critique of the ties between Scholastic thought and human rights in Francisco Castilla Urbano, 'La Escuela de Salamanca y los derechos humanos: una difícil conciliación', *Araucaria* 25:54 (2023), pp. 534–566. There is no evidence that Latin American thinkers drew on Scholastic principles, as Manuel Chust has repeatedly argued. See Manuel Chust, 'El Rey para el pueblo, la constitución para la nación', in Víctor Mínguez and Manuel Chust eds., *El imperio sublevado: monarquía y naciones en España e Hispanoamérica* (Madrid: CSIC, 2014), pp. 225–254 and Manuel Chust and Ivana Frasquet, 'La génesis de las independencias. La complejidad de un proceso histórico de dimensiones universales', in Manuel Chust and Ivana Frasquet eds., *La patria no se hizo sola: las revoluciones de las independencias iberoamericanas* (Madrid: Silex, 2012), pp. 17–66, p. 51. See also O. Carlos Stoetzer, *The Scholastic Roots of the Spanish American Revolution* (New York: Fordham University Press, 1979); Jorge Cañizares-Esguerra, 'How the "Reformation" Invented Separate Catholic and Protestant Atlantics', *Archive for Reformation History* 108:1 (2017), pp. 245–254.

[91] Frank Dawson's work remains a valuable summary of the topic; see Frank Griffith Dawson, *The First Latin American Debt Crisis, The City of London and the 1822–25 Loan Bubble* (New Haven: Yale University Press, 1990).

[92] On the need for greater comparative history in the study of Iberian empires see the contributions by Tamar Herzog and Pedro Cardim in Jones Corredera ed., *Supplicant Empires* (Forthcoming).

crucial role of nuns as creditors in the Spanish Empire to the rise of *agiotistas* in modern Latin America.[93]

Writing this history was like chasing after a rabbit and falling down countless burrows trying to figure out how and why these debts were repudiated, then reconsidered and reappraised, and sometimes repaid. In this way, this book follows the halting, intermittent, and inconsistent nature of the efforts to track down, rearrange, and resolve symbolic and financial debts. The salience of debt in national debates ebbed and flowed; at times, overshadowed by war, discussions about past debts faded from view for years. When fragile peace settlements were reached, or when nations grew stronger and able to resume their claims against other or earlier administrations, claims resurfaced. By then, some of those states had broken up or assumed new forms of government. In the meantime, faced with inaction, the interest on debts grew and grew. The scope and time frame of the settlement of these transactions are striking: Venezuela only finished refinancing some of the loans signed in 1824 in 1931.[94] This is a history about the meaning of historiography—about what counts as history to whom.

Our story, then, is one of forgetting without forgiving.[95] It is worth noting that the last efforts of reconciliation between Spain and the Spanish Americas were premised on oblivion. Drawing on a practice that once shaped the Habsburg response to the Southern Netherlands in the aftermath of the Dutch Revolt, between 1810 and 1823 Spain tried to harness amnesty, forgetfulness, and forgiveness as a way to both compel and reward support for the Crown: the tradition of pardons based on the grace and mercy of the King was transformed into the practice of issuing '*olvidos del pasado*', 'acts of forgetfulness of the past', and these were issued to people who had shown a questionable commitment to the Crown to allow them to repay their debt to society.[96] These pardons only caused confusion about who

[93] The best works on these topics are Julio César Guillamondegui, 'La quiebra en el derecho indiano rioplatense', *Historia* 8:1 (1969), pp. 123–139; Martín Wasserman, *Las obligaciones fundamentales. Crédito y consolidación económica durante el surgimiento de Buenos Aires* (Buenos Aires: Prometeo, 2017), and Alfonso W. Quiroz, *Deudas olvidadas: Instrumentos de crédito en la economía colonial peruana 1750–1820* (San Miguel: Pontificia Universidad Católica del Perú, 1993). See also the studies of María del Pilar Martínez López-Cano, 'La Iglesia y el crédito en Nueva España: entre viejos presupuestos y nuevos retos de investigación' in María de Pilar Martínez López-Cano ed., *La Iglesia en Nueva España. Problemas y perspectivas de investigación* (Mexico City: UNAM, 2010), pp. 303–352; Carlos Mayo and Jaime Peire, 'Iglesia y crédito colonial: La política crediticia de los conventos de Buenos Aires (1767–1810)' *Revista de Historia de América* 112 (1991), pp. 147–157.

[94] Reinhard Liehr, 'La deuda exterior de la Gran Colombia frente a Gran Bretaña, 1820–1860', in Reinhard Liehr ed., *América Latina en la época de Simón Bolívar* (Berlin: Colloquium Verlag, 1989), pp. 465–488, p. 487.

[95] On the role of forgetting in the construction of the nation see Ernest Renan, 'What is a Nation?' in Ernest Renan and Matteo Giglioli, *What Is a Nation? And Other Political Writings* (New York: Columbia University Press, 2018), pp. 247–263 and Elia Palti's reflections on the topic in 'La nación argentina entre el ser y el acontecimiento. La controvertida plasmación de una visión genealógica del pasado nacional', in Guillermo Palacios ed., *La nación y su historia, independencias, relato historiográfico y debates sobre la nación* (Mexico City: Colegio de México, 2009), pp. 17–38, pp. 26–27.

[96] Pollmann, *Catholic Identity*, pp. 170–175. As Pollmann has shown, the use of oblivion was not unique to Spain. The idea of 'forgetting', in turn, played an important role in Ferdinand's propaganda;

had the authority to forgive and who ought to be forgiven. In the hope of fostering a reconciliation with their American counterparts, the liberal Spanish Cortes also discussed Vattel's writings on amnesty as a mechanism that could foster harmony.[97] But it was too late: in the Americas, the Buenos Aires government established a Law of Forgiveness; '*forgiveness* in Spanish, *amnesty* in the voice of literature, and *forgetting* in the voice of reason' had, as the revolutionary leader Bernardino Rivadavia suggested, such a long history that its origins were unclear. But its uses were manifestly clear: forgiveness would draw a line in the sand, 'end the revolution, and erase the testimony of our international differences' in the minds of those in foreign lands. It would show the world that the 'empire of the law' had won the day.[98]

Yet the memory of the revolution would be used against Rivadavia in an unsuccessful effort to prevent his rise to power. His rivals shed light on his earlier scheme to establish a Bourbon prince at the helm of Buenos Aires and published his proposals to remind readers that 'many pages of our revolution would have to be torn out to make us forget' about the ways that 'our former oppressors' and 'those we have entrusted with our salvation' had undermined its cause.[99] Oblivion remained a political tool: many of the treaties signed by Spain and the new Latin American states explicitly stated the shared desire to forget and forgive past disputes.[100] With the consolidation of electoral politics, the contested politics of amnesty would shape Latin American politics for centuries.[101]

see Ferdinand VII, *El Rey a los habitantes de ultramar* (Madrid, n.s.) and the analysis provided in Jeremy Adelman, *Sovereignty and Revolution in the Iberian Atlantic* (Princeton: Princeton University Press, 2006), pp. 304–305, and Timothy Anna, *Spain and the Loss of America* (London: University of Nebraska Press, 1983), p. 235; Ferdinand VII's invocation to treat the actions of the Cortes 'as if they had never happened' in Fabio Wasserman, 'Presentación', in Fabio Wasserman ed., *Tiempos Críticos: Historia, revolución y temporalidad en el mundo iberoamericano (siglos XVIII y XIX)* (Buenos Aires: Prometeo, 2010), pp. 11–32, p. 27. For a recent treatment on the role of pardons in the Ancien Régime see Stuart Carroll, *Enmity and Violence in Early Modern Europe* (Cambridge: Cambridge University Press, 2023), pp. 23–65.

[97] *Diario de las actas y discusiones de las cortes: Legislatura de los años de 1820 y 1821.* Volume 6, p. 139. See also how Mejía hoped to include a recognition of independence in the decree regarding the 'olvido' in Marie Laure Rieu-Millan, *Los diputados americanos en las Cortes de Cádiz (Igualdad o independencia)* (Madrid: CSIC, 1990), pp. 335–338.

[98] *Diario de sesiones de la Junta de Representantes de la Provincia de Buenos Aires* (1 May–23 December 1822) (Buenos Aires: Imprenta de la Independencia, 1823), p. 16.

[99] *Reverente Súplica al ex-rey Carlos Cuarto pidiéndole a su hijo adoptivo el infante don Francisco de Paula para coronarle en las provincias del Río de la Plata. Por los vasallos del mismo d. Manuel Velgrano y Bernardino Rivadavia* (Buenos Aires: Librería Argentina, 1825), p. 1; Juan Carlos Cardinali, *Semblanzas y conjeturas en la historia argentina* (Buenos Aires: Biblos, 2004), pp. 97–99.

[100] See also Simal's study of amnesty in Spain in the 1830s in Juan Luis Simal, *Emigrados. España y el exilio internacional, 1814–1834* (Madrid: CEPC, 2012), pp. 286–291.

[101] For a summary of the past 50 years see Lisa J. Laplante, 'Outlawing Amnesty: The Return of Criminal Justice in Transitional Justice Schemes', *Virginia Journal of International Law* 49:4 (2019), pp. 915–984. As noted by Joshua M. Rosenthal, scholars of Colombian history like Eduardo Posada Carbó have pointed to the importance of amnesty and pardons in the nineteenth century. See Joshua M. Rosenthal, 'The Indultados of Tescua: Criminal Rebellion and Judicial Reckoning during the War

Over the past two hundred years, Latin American leaders have turned to credit to accelerate their headlong flight towards statehood. The weight of obligations to their past slowed down and frequently halted their flight. Under the Spanish Empire, the Crown had the capacity to forgive criminals and fraudulent merchants; once the empire fell, praetorian ambitions often ensured that non-partisan national systems of justice failed to take hold in the three countries under study.[102] The law of nations, with its promise of secular absolution from the crimes of war and the systematic resolution of the problem of transnational debts, replaced royal grace and favour.[103] In an effort to reconcile Catholic ideas of obligation with the doctrines of international law, debt became a way to establish when the empire ended, when a nation began, and who belonged to a state; foreign loans became a bond shared with other states in Latin America and beyond, a way to understand the role of these new nations on the world's stage, a means to improve its reputation, a providential force to develop arts and industries. As defaults became more frequent, these debts pitted the obligations of these states to the world against those they owed to the people. Spanish, Mexican, Colombian, and Argentinian statesmen all believed that if the interest on the payment of debt could be postponed for a year or two, a modern system of government could be established in that time.

Yet, in Latin America, foreign credit was nothing more than a raid on the future of these young nations. Among a people that Simón Bolívar described, in his *Carta de Jamaica*, as an amalgamation of two communities, 'the proprietors of this land and the usurpers of the Spaniards', assigning blame and responsibility remained challenging.[104] The question of debt was, explained the Mexican author and political economist Manuel Payno, one that 'concerned past and future

of the Supremes', *Anuario Colombiano de Historia Social y de la Cultura* 39:2 (2012), pp. 131–156, pp. 131–132. The best work on the matter is Carlos Camacho Arango, Margarita Garrido Otoya, and Daniel Gutiérrez Ardila eds., *Paz en la República. Colombia, siglo XIX* (Bogotá: Universidad Externado de Colombia, 2018).

[102] On the association with pardons and Spanish governance in nineteenth-century Colombia see Joshua M. Rosenthal's recent work, including 'Conditional Clemency after the Golpe de Melo of 1854: Constitutionalism and Tradition in Early Republican Colombia', *Historía Crítica* 63 (2017), pp. 75–96.

[103] A summary and historiographical overview can be found in this excellent doctoral thesis: Gibran Irving Israel Bautista y Lugo, *Castigar o perdonar: El gobierno de Felipe IV ante la rebelión de 1624 en México* (Unpublished PhD thesis) (México City: UNAM, 2014), pp. 14–46. See also António M. Hespanha, *La gracia del derecho: Economía de la cultura en la Edad Moderna*. Edited by Bartolomé Clavero (Madrid: CEPC, 1993).

[104] Simón Bolívar, *Carta de Jamaica* (Madrid: Verbum, 2020), p. 17. For an alternative translation see David Bushnell ed., *El Libertador: Writings of Simón Bolívar*. Translated by Frederick H. Fornoff (Oxford: Oxford University Press, 2013), p. 18. I owe this view of credit to Peter de Bolla, who made this remark during the DAAD-Cambridge Hub conference on 'Imperial Futures' at Cambridge in 2019. On the racialised aspects of Bolívar's vision see Joshua Simon, *The Ideology of Creole Revolution Imperialism and Independence in American and Latin American Political Thought* (Cambridge: Cambridge University Press, 2017), pp. 89–127.

generations'. History, in his words, showed that 'we are still repaying that which the pirates of Jamaica stole in the past century from the Spanish galleons'.[105] As Payno showed, the vertiginous incongruity of the Spanish heritage and the Protestant law of nations could only be resolved through the rise of historical accountability. Yet history revealed that, time after time, ambition's debt was paid, but the ambition, the debt, and the payment were forgotten.[106] Peace proved to be a poor substitute for forgiveness. British statesmen wrestled with the question of expiation and, eventually, established a political economy of atonement by indemnifying slaveowners, creating a national bankruptcy law, and establishing limited liability; speculation was 'the supreme sin' and charity 'the supreme virtue'.[107] In the United States, banking and corporate laws were introduced to establish a consistent mechanism for both debtors and creditors to redress the sin of insolvency.[108]

In Latin America, international and domestic laws did not deliver absolution. To the degree that the moral code of international law replaced the Spanish philosophical foundations of justice, its model of redemption would eventually deliver tentative peace deals, but it did not carry with it the remission of past debts. As the United States enforced its own model of continental redemption, international legal aspirations such as the Monroe Doctrine at times overlapped with religious ambitions that flew in the face of Latin American interests.[109] Soon, as Payno noted, it became clear that many of the putative 'redeemers' of Mexico had failed to improve the people's well-being. Payno argued that only by tending to its needs and rejecting foreign debts imposed by predatory powers who had betrayed Mexico could the nation thrive.[110] Only by writing its own history, claimed Alberdi, could Latin America make peace with its past: the 'Latin and Roman legacy' in the Americas, he explained, included welcome attributes such as 'its legislation, its language, and its race'. But its 'inheritance should not be accepted without taking an

[105] Quoted in Barbara A. Tenenbaum and Sergio Negrete, 'Manuel Payno y los bandidos del erario mexicano, 1848–1873', *Historia Mexicana* 44:1 (1994), pp. 73–106, p. 77.

[106] William Shakespeare, *Julius Caesar*. Edited by Arthur Raleigh Humphreys (Oxford: Oxford University Press, 1998), p. 163.

[107] Catherine Hall, Nicholas Draper, and Keith McClelland, 'Introduction', in Catherine Hall, Nicholas Draper, and Keith McClelland eds., *Emancipation and the Remaking of the British Imperial World* (Manchester: Manchester University Press, 2014), pp. 1–19; Marc Flandreau, 'Pari Passu Lost and Found: The Origins of Sovereign Bankruptcy 1798–1873', *Institute for New Economic Thinking Working Paper Series* 186 (2022), pp. 1–67, p. 36; Boyd Hilton, *The Age of Atonement: The Influence of Evangelicalism on Social and Economic Thought, 1795–1865* (Oxford: Oxford University Press, 1988), p. 136, pp. 255–297.

[108] Bruce H. Mann, *Republic of Debtors: Bankruptcy in the Age of American Independence* (Cambridge: Harvard University Press, 2009), pp. 221–253.

[109] On religious, racial, and gendered elements behind the doctrine see Daniel J. Burge, *A Failed Vision of Empire: The Collapse of Manifest Destiny, 1845–1872* (Lincoln: University of Nebraska Press, 2022), pp. 9–12.

[110] Manuel Payno, *Cuentas, gastos, acreedores y otros asuntos del tiempo de la intervención francesa y del imperio. De 1861 a 1867* (Mexico City: Imprenta de Ignacio Cumplido, 1868), p. 931.

inventory of its contents, for we may otherwise be burdened with horrible debts to the Christian civilisation'.[111]

For over a century, foreign observers have claimed that the Latin American debt problem was an outcome of the failure of governments to establish a liberal economy, the result of an inability to enforce contracts or protect property through the creation of modern economic institutions.[112] Instead, further research is needed on the lack of a clear cultural, legal, and political strategy regarding penance, compensation, and punishment over past debts; the absence, in sum, of a coherent legal view on forgiveness and atonement. This book focuses on the international dimensions of these issues. But calls to never forget, from the *Nunca más* mantra in Argentina, debates about historical memory in Chile, and the pursuit of forgiveness of the erstwhile commanders of the Colombian Revolutionary Armed Forces (FARC), continue to shape the region's politics. Countless studies have emerged in Latin America to study the pervasiveness of violence in the region in what has become known as the study of 'violentology'.[113] The study of debt is part of this story. In the absence of forgiveness, one option remained: war and the prioritisation of certain debts or, in other words, default.

This book is a history of the uses of international law and political economy in the making of three states in one of the most war-torn and economically vulnerable regions in the world. It is a story about why ideas that aimed to preserve the world united failed to bind states together. It is a story that shows that international law, like every nation, is built on forgetting.[114]

Outline

Chapter 1 establishes how, when, and why debt became odious. The power of the Spanish Empire was based on confessional constancy, the promise of silver, and the threat of default. When soldiers and officials went unpaid and committed atrocities as a result of the King's mismanagement of the empire's debt, authors like Emanuel van Meteren and Grotius took note. In their analyses of the Spanish Crown, Hugo Grotius, Jean Barbeyrac, and Emer de Vattel connected the Black

[111] Juan Bautista Alberdi, 'Notas para el juicio crítico del "Derecho internacional" de C. Calvo', in *Escritos póstumos. Política exterior de la república argentina. Bibliografía.* Volume 3: (Buenos Aires: Imprenta Europa, Moreno, y Defensa, 1896), pp. 137-280, p. 257.

[112] Lars Schoultz, *Beneath the United States: A History of U.S. Policy Towards Latin America* (Cambridge: Harvard University Press, 2003), p. 376.

[113] Stephen Ferry, *Violentology: A Manual of the Colombian Conflict* (New York: Umbrage, 2012). Calls to never forget—the *Nunca más* mantra in Argentina or debates about 'historical memory' in Chile—and the pursuit of forgiveness by former commanders of the Colombian Revolutionary Armed Forces, better known as the FARC, continue to shape the region's politics. See also the study that pioneered research on this topic in Colombia: Orlando Fals Borda, German Guzman, and Eduardo Umaña Luna, *La violencia en Colombia* (Bogotá: Ediciones Tercer Mundo, 1962).

[114] Renan, *What is a Nation*, p. 96.

Legend of Spanish barbarity and backwardness to the odious nature of imperial debt. Debt was odious because it was incurred for the imperial gain of the tyrannical Spanish King rather than the good of the people.

Chapter 2 shows how writers and officials who generated the Spanish Enlightenment and spearheaded nineteenth-century Hispanic constitutional debates sought to reconcile imperial histories with Grotius' law of nations. Dissatisfied with the negotiations at the Cádiz Cortes, Latin American officials concluded that the chronic indebtedness of the Spanish Crown had eroded the bonds that once united the various provinces of the Empire. One author went as far as to argue that through *translatio imperii* the Americas were now the centre of Spanish imperial power. But most American representatives made clear that Spain owed a number of debts to the Americas. This chapter explores why the King of Spain and the Cortes failed to listen to the demands of their American brethren. In response, Latin American revolutionaries began to criticise the Crown's bankruptcy: Spanish ancestry conferred commercial benefits to creoles in the Americas, but the Spanish Crown no longer conferred much of anything—not security, not unity, not faith.[115] It merely burdened the empire with its debts. It paid to remain a member of this caste and class in the Americas—but these states, as rebels outlined in countless pamphlets, no longer had to finance the Crown's wars with their silver. This chapter then studies how Catholic ideas of debt were squared with the international legal writings of Protestant authors in debates about the right to revolution, the right to private property, and slave labour. The rise of disputes over debt accompanied cultural changes such as the growth of historiography, which encouraged a reconsideration of the terms of engagement between Latin American states and Spain, Britain, and the United States.

Chapter 3 focuses on nineteenth-century Mexican debates on colonial, foreign, and public debt and succession. Mexican officials were reluctant to break with the Spanish Empire: in 1810, following the invasion of Napoleon of the Spanish peninsula, the editors of a periodical claimed their province's role as *primus inter pares* and vindicated that '[w]e are now the true Spaniards'.[116] Following the rise of the first deliberative assemblies and the separation from the monarchy, Mexican officials drew on international law to establish the nation's debt to the Spanish Crown and to Britain. Mexicans sought to be more Catholic and more Spanish than their peninsular counterparts. Ideas about the right to revolution clashed with the liberal belief in protecting contracts, private property, and citizenship rights. This chapter then focuses on the life and writings of Manuel Payno, who was tasked with the negotiations of Mexico's foreign debt. As Mexico was faced with foreign

[115] On the commercial benefits of "Spanishness" in the Americas see Herzog, *Defining Nations*, pp. 64–118.

[116] Jaime E. Rodríguez O., *'We Are Now the True Spaniards': Sovereignty, Revolution, Independence, and the Emergence of the Federal Republic of Mexico, 1808–1824* (Stanford: Stanford University Press, 2012).

interventions over unpaid claims, Payno sought to harness international law and political economy to demand a fairer approach to the resolution of these debts. These diplomatic dilemmas compounded issues caused by a mercurial national political scene that, between 1821 and 1856, saw the rise and fall of 53 governments.[117] Following the fall of Maximilian, Payno noted that European states had defaulted on the norms of the law of nations: it was thus licit for Mexico to renege on its foreign debts, along with those loans incurred under Maximilian's government. He believed that the future of Mexico required fostering relations with Spain, for the 'Castilian race' was the most compatible with the fabric of Hispanic American interests, but was increasingly dismayed by the foreign policy of Old Spain. This disenchantment with international law and the contested heritage of the colonial past shaped Mexican political debates towards the repayment of foreign debts. In 1884, an effort to deliver a swift resolution to the settlement of British debts sparked violent protests against the government and prompted a lengthy parliamentary debate on what was owed to Spain, Britain, France, and the United States: empires that had been instrumental in fostering economic growth of Mexico but had also spearheaded interventions in the country's affairs in the recent past.

Chapter 4 considers why Gran Colombia's management of its foreign debts, drawn to finance the wars of liberation against Spain and to bolster Bolívar's ambitions, led Jeremy Bentham to advise the *Libertador* to default on the nation's loans. After creating an assembly of sovereign states in Gran Colombia, Bolívar never established what war debts from each of its composite parts were to be recognised.[118] Panama, for example, had recognised some of the Spanish colonial authorities, something which Bolívar's administration had flatly rejected.[119] As conflicts ravaged the region, military expenditure accounted for three-quarters of the revenue of the state.[120] Gripped by Bentham's teachings, Colombian officials connected past debts to a number of debates about the future of the country through the language of international law: the importance of preserving existing property rights from the colonial period, including the right to own slaves, and the idea of establishing a confederation with a clear set of rules to administer past and future debts. Following the collapse of Gran Colombia, officials from each of the parts of the rump state, New Granada, Venezuela, and Ecuador, had to establish how to divide the costs of independence. This chapter studies how officials drew on the law of nations to make sense of this endless Russian doll of debts and establish, through international law and the writings of Thomas Malthus, a fair way to distribute their payment. Two

[117] Barbara A. Tenenbaum, *The Politics of Penury: Debts and Taxes in Mexico, 1821–1856* (Alburquerque: University of New Mexico Press, 1986), p. xi.

[118] John Lynch, *Simón Bolívar: A Life* (New Haven: Yale University Press, 2006), p. 159.

[119] David Bushnell, *The Santander Regime in Gran Colombia* (Newark: University of Delaware Press, 1954), pp. 103–104.

[120] Lynch, *Simón Bolívar*, p. 159.

figures under study, Ezequiel Rojas and Manuel Murillo Toro, sought to settle the relationship between the resolution of state debts and the establishment of private property through Colombian constitutional reforms. By the end of the century, the payment of Gran Colombia's debts was framed as a symbol of regional commutative solidarity that was not extended to its age-old redeemer, Britain. James Brown Scott, however, folded Bolívar's ambitions into a system of Pan-Americanism that bolstered the interests of the United States in the region.

Chapter 5 studies the role of international law, and the settlement of war debts, in the configuration of Argentina. Buenos Aires' desire to nationalise the region's wealth collided with the provinces' defence of consent and their states' sovereignty; indeed, revolutionary officials in the port city did not even consider paying their debts to Spain. The concentration of political power in this port city overhauled the colonial geography of power established by the religious and civic authorities and which prioritised the highlands.[121] Buenos Aires rushed to sign loans with British lenders, mortgaged the public land, and set up a national bank that was dominated by British investors. As Buenos Aires and the provinces sought to find unity, the responsibility for the management of these debts became a dividing line that would shape the region's politics. Within a few years, tensions between Buenos Aires and the provinces led to the rise of the *caudillo* Juan Manuel Rosas and intensified debates about how to distribute outstanding debts. Exiled authors drew on Grotius and Vattel to justify a foreign intervention that would topple the *caudillo*. One of the authors who defended the deployment of a foreign navy to end the tyrant's rule was Juan Bautista Alberdi. In his writings, Alberdi established a constitutional blueprint for Argentina by foregrounding private interests as a means to foreclose the possibility of war. He was then asked to negotiate Argentina's foreign loans as divisions between Buenos Aires and the provinces, then known as the Argentine Confederation, intensified. Alberdi resolved questions of debt and citizenship as he negotiated a treaty of recognition with Spain. As Buenos Aires gained greater control over the administration of Argentina, the new government disavowed Alberdi's negotiations. After he lost the support and the backing of his state and faced the hardest years of his life, he received a letter from another Argentinian jurist, Carlos Calvo. This chapter concludes by introducing Alberdi's response to Calvo's ideas, the nature of their disagreement, and the profound implications it had for Alberdi's reading of international law. Calvo originally defended Napoleon III and his visions of a French-led Latin America before he shifted his views in favour of the Monroe Doctrine. The definition of the term 'Latin America' would be shaped by the regional responses to this clash between Latin and Anglo-Saxon identities and rival commercial interests. Napoleon III, and his pamphlet on the

[121] See Miron Burgin, *Aspectos económicos del federalismo argentino* (Buenos Aires, Hachette, 1960), p. 163; Alan Knight, *Bandits and Liberals, Rebels and Saints: Latin America since Independence* (Lincoln: University of Nebraska, 2022), p. 8; Adelman, *Sovereignty and Revolution*, pp. 48–49.

construction of a Canal of Nicaragua, clashed with the North American proposals for the creation of a Panama Canal and international efforts to create an Anglo-American Christian civilising mission in Central America.[122]

Chapter 6 explores in greater depth the Calvo–Alberdi debate and their conflicting visions of Latin America's experience of foreign intervention. Alberdi's reading of Calvo's *Derecho internacional* shed a critical light on the work of his rival and threw into relief important questions regarding the international lawyer's interpretation of the history of Latin America, his silences on Maximilian I and the Paraguayan War, and, above all, his views on Rosas. Alberdi emphasised how his constitutionalism could be scaled up to establish a system of international relations that would deliver peace to Latin America. Calvo and Alberdi both had a profound influence on the most important Argentinian international lawyer of his age, Luis María Drago. The legacy of the original split between Buenos Aires and the United Provinces was at the heart of the Drago Doctrine: in the lead up to the Baring Crisis, the Argentinian jurist argued before the courts that Buenos Aires could not be sued before the national courts on the basis of unpaid debts.[123] As Foreign Minister, however, Drago had to reconcile his view of debt with an increasingly interventionist North American government. This chapter concludes by examining Drago's arguments against the use of force to demand the repayment of debt and the response by United State officials. The views of the most important North American official, the Secretary of State Elihu Root, were informed by his experience in the Spanish–American War.

The Conclusion studies the relationship between nineteenth-century Latin American debates about debt and the logic behind the North American repudiation of Cuba's outstanding payments to Spain. During the Spanish–American War, the United States mobilised ideas of Spanish backwardness and barbarity to portray its involvement in Cuban affairs as a humanitarian intervention. Spain's unforgiving extractive policies towards Cuban rents were replaced by North American complaints about the island's refusal to acknowledge its debt of gratitude to its redeemers. This chapter concludes by exploring the connections between these visions of debt and modern debates on forgiveness, reparations, and consent. As a whole, this book generates a question for other scholars and practitioners of international law: is international law compatible with the global pursuit of a moral economy?

[122] Schoultz, *Beneath*, p. 153; Sexton, *Monroe*, p. 117. The United States originally sought to build their canal in Nicaragua; see Michel Gobat, *Empire by Invitation: William Walker and Manifest Destiny in Central America* (Cambridge: Harvard University Press, 2018), p. 1. On the broader French geopolitical strategy for the region see David Todd, *A Velvet Empire: French Informal Imperialism in the Nineteenth Century* (Princeton: Princeton University Press, 2021), pp. 175–226.

[123] Laura Julieta Casas, 'Alberdi y el derecho internacional. La actualidad de su pensamiento', in Carmen Fontán ed., *Juan Bautista Alberdi. Apología y crítica de su pensamiento* (San Miguel de Tucuman, Argentina: Constitución para Todos, 2011), pp. 357–370, p. 360; Daniel Guerra Iñiguez, 'Palabras preliminares', in Alfredo N. Vivot and Alberto A. Conil Paz, *Homenaje al doctor Luis M. Drago* (Caracas: Oficina Central de Información, 1976), pp. 9–33, p. 12.

1
The Origins of Odious Debt

The end of the Mediterranean World

Waves of debt surged and swelled before breaking on Spanish shores. The rhythm of European trade was shaped by the prospects of exorbitant gains generated by the ebb and flow of credit lines, bills of exchange, and diffuse debts that were negotiated in a series of seasonal commercial fairs organised throughout the Old World and the Americas. Knowledge of the tide was priceless: spurred on and sustained by the interests of the Spanish Empire, financiers at the fairs of Medina del Campo, Antwerp, Lyon, Genoa, Portobello, and Jalapa speculated on the unpredictable time frames and irregular shipments of Spanish vessels. These ships carried goods from Manila, Mexico City, and Lima. They docked in and shipped from Seville with silver, silk, and European cloth.[1] Habsburg monarchs relied on a mercurial combination of promises and expectations surrounding these shipments to pay back their debts.

In May, at the fairs, farmers, shepherds, and merchants would request loans in order to finance the sowing of seeds and the shearing of sheep. The October fairs followed the pace of the harvest and the sale of the crops. This facilitated the repayment of loans.[2] Investors awaited the fairs with anticipation. The Crown's reliance on loans emitted at these fairs, and the provision of gold and silver from the Americas, guaranteed a high supply of capital at the hands of local and foreign bankers. The function of the bill of exchange, the dominant medium of commercial transaction, was to avoid the accusation of usury. These bills would be sent to Flanders, Lyon, and Besançon. A lender would grant a loan to a borrower who would, in turn, provide the lender with a promissory note anticipating that repayment would come from a third party in a foreign city. Upon arrival in said location, the third party would be expected to pay the borrower's representative. Crucially, since these bills had to engage in an international exchange, different coins had to be used during the transaction. Since each nation had different exchange rates, financiers speculated on these loans and avoided the accusation of usury.[3]

[1] See Fernand Braudel, *La Méditerranée et le monde méditerranéen à l'époque de Philippe II*. Two volumes (Paris: Colin, 1949).

[2] Ramón Carande, *Carlos V y sus banqueros*. Volume 1 (Barcelona: Crítica, 1987), pp. 331–332.

[3] Falah Hassan Abed Al-Hussein, 'Los cambios y el mercado del dinero medinense', in Eufemio Lorenzo Sanz eds., *Historia de Medina del Campo y su tierra*. Volume 2 (Valladolid: Caja de Ahorros Provincial de Valladolid, 1986), pp. 67–92, pp. 69–70; Marjorie Grice Hutchinson, *The School of Salamánca: Readings in Monetary Theory 1544–1605* (Oxford: Clarendon Press, 1952), pp. 10–12.

Odious Debt. Edward Jones Corredera, Oxford University Press. © Edward Jones Corredera 2024.
DOI: 10.1093/9780191982200.003.0002

Conquest, colonisation, and *translatio imperii* made this world possible.[4] Across the Atlantic Ocean, Emperor Moctezuma the Elder ruled the Aztec dynasty of the Mexica Empire, a territory that stretched from today's Mexico City to Honduras, where the main tongue was Nahuatl.[5] It was organised around the idea of the *altepetl*, a city state structure that featured a market and was governed by a dynastic potentate and a patron deity.[6] Time began when the gods committed sacrifice and set the sun in motion: blood sacrifice was seen as a running debt necessary to perpetuate its movements.[7] The calendar featured 18,980 days, and the cycle was renewed through a ritual ceremony.[8] Tributes and textiles connected faith, politics, and exchange.[9] By the time Moctezuma I died, he had expanded the reach of the Mexica Empire, established a zoo near his palace in Tenochtitlan, the centre of today's Mexico City, and settled the matter of the succession to his throne.[10] Moctezuma II consolidated this bureaucratic network and ensured the smooth synchronisation of the collection of local tributes through planned public ceremonies.[11]

In 1519, Moctezuma came face to face with a representative of the King of Spain, Hernán Cortés, in an encounter between a legitimate ruler and an official who had overstretched his authority.[12] According to the Spaniard's recollection of events, Cortés eventually imprisoned Moctezuma and the Aztec emperor dutifully

See also Jeremy Adelman, *Republic of Capital: Buenos Aires and the Legal Transformation of the Atlantic World* (Stanford: Stanford University Press, 1999), pp. 152–153 and Martti Koskenniemi, 'Colonization of the "Indies". The origin of International Law?', in Yolanda Gamarra Chopo ed., *La idea de América en el pensamiento ius internacionalista del siglo XXI: Estudios a propósito de la conmemoración de los bicentenarios de las independencias de las repúblicas latinoamericanas* (Zaragoza: Institución Fernando el católico, 2010), pp. 43–63, pp. 56–60. On the complex 'triple contract' built on these ideas by the Jesuit philosopher Leonardus Lessius see Wim Decock, 'The Catholic Spirit of Capitalism?', in Wim Decock, Jordan J. Ballor, Michael Germann, and Laurent Waelkens eds., *Law and Religion: The Legal Teachings of the Protestant and Catholic Reformations* (Göttingen: Vandenhoeck & Ruprecht, 2014), pp. 22–44, pp. 25–36.

[4] The best summary of the political thought of the period is Anthony Pagden, 'Conquest and the Just War: The "School of Salamanca" and the "Affair of the Indies"' in Sankar Muthu ed., *Empire and Modern Political Thought* (Cambridge: Cambridge University Press, 2012), pp. 30–60.

[5] On the survival of historical narratives in this tongue during the colonial period see Camilla Townsend, *Annals of Native America: How the Nahuas of Colonial Mexico Kept Their History Alive* (Oxford: Oxford University Press, 2017).

[6] Lane F. Fargher, Richard E. Blanton, and Verenice Heredia Espinoza, 'Aztec State-Making, Politics, and Empires: The Triple Alliance', in Deborah L. Nichols, and Enrique Rodríguez-Alegría eds., *The Oxford Handbook of the Aztecs* (Oxford: Oxford University Press, 2017), pp. 143–160, p. 145.

[7] Anthony F. Aveni, 'The Measure, Meaning, and Transformation of Aztec Time and Calendars', in Nichols and Rodríguez-Alegría, *The Oxford Handbook of the Aztecs*, pp. 107–116, p. 110.

[8] Aveni, 'The Measure', p. 108.

[9] Stefan Rinke, *Conquistadors and Aztecs: A History of the Fall of Tenochtitlan* (Oxford: Oxford University Press, 2023), pp. 62–65.

[10] Camilla Townsend, *Fifth Sun: A New History of the Aztecs* (Oxford: Oxford University Press, 2019), pp. 60–67.

[11] Townsend, *Fifth Sun*, p. 72.

[12] John Elliott, 'Introduction', in *Hernán Cortés. Letters from Mexico*. Translated and edited by Anthony Pagden. With an introduction by John Elliott. (New Haven: Yale University Press, 1986), pp. xii–xiii.

followed the terms of *translatio imperii*: he surrendered and transferred the empire to Charles V as set out in the terms of the act of donation.[13] For the Americas, some jurists contended, were a donation, a gift, from God to the Crown of Spain.[14] In practice, it was only after two years of war that Cortés claimed victory and turned the *altepetl* into *encomiendas*, a system whereby the protection of a conquistador was granted to the people in exchange for their labour and tribute.[15] Gradually, the arrival of members of the Jesuit Order fostered the expansion of the Catholic Church in the region.[16] Centuries later, locals would try to demonstrate their ancestors' early adoption of Christianity in order to claim their right to territories lost during the conquest.[17] On the basis of medieval traditions, the contractual nature of female obligations in marriage was defined as a 'conjugal debt'.[18]

The discovery and exploitation of gold and silver mines encouraged the Crown to regulate the migration from the Iberian Peninsula to the Americas.[19] Crossing the Atlantic was costly, and travellers funded their voyages through credit. This indebtedness could lead to desperation and foster rapacity.[20] The enslavement of African peoples was not just financed on debt, but those slaves who reached American shores were often sold in order to settle outstanding debts.[21] Slavery, silver, and debt were closely connected. The Crown claimed a fifth of each bar of silver in order to fund the interest on the loans signed in Central Europe.[22] The profits to be made from the slave trade, along with the allure of gold and silver,

[13] John Elliott, *Empires of the Atlantic World: Britain and Spain in America 1492–1830* (New Haven: Yale University Press, 2006), p. 5; Elliott, 'Introduction', in *Hernán Cortés*, p. xliii. See also Martti Koskenniemi, *To the Uttermost Parts of the Earth Legal Imagination and International Power 1300–1870* (Cambridge: Cambridge University Press, 2021), pp. 177–211.

[14] A logic that was the subject of intense debate: see Anthony Pagden, 'The School of Salamanca, the Requerimiento, and the Papal Donation of Alexander VI', *Republics of Letters* 5 (2018), pp. 1–10; Carlos Eire, *Reformations: The Early Modern World, 1450–1650* (New Haven: Yale University Press, 2016), pp. 474–475. Anthony Pagden, *The Burdens of Empire: 1539 to the Present* (Cambridge: Cambridge University Press, 2015), pp. 52–53.

[15] Rinke, *Conquistadors*, pp. 217–233. On the legal status of the *encomienda* see Anthony Pagden, *Spanish Imperialism and the Political Imagination: Studies in European and Spanish-American Social and Political Theory 1513–1830* (New Haven: Yale University Press, 1990), pp. 92–93.

[16] Townsend, *Fifth Sun*, p. 134.

[17] Louise M. Burkhart, 'The Aztecs and the Catholic Church', in Nichols and Rodríguez-Alegría, *The Oxford Handbook of the Aztecs*, pp. 675–688, p. 688.

[18] See for example Jesús M. Usunáriz, 'El padre ante el parto en la España de los siglos XVI y XVII', *Hipogrifo. Revista de literatura y cultura del Siglo de Oro* 6:1 (2018), pp. 1–20. This term was still used in the nineteenth century.

[19] Elliott, *Empires*, pp. 49–51.

[20] An argument made by Mark Safford; see Frank Safford, *Historia de Colombia: País fragmentado, sociedad dividida.* Translated by Marco Palacios and Ángela García (Bogotá: Ediciones Uniandes, 2011), p. 43.

[21] Herbert S. Klein and Ben Vinson III, *Historia mínima de la esclavitud en América Latina y en el Caribe* (Mexico City: Colegio de México, 2013), pp. 52–103. On the economic changes brought about by the Spanish colonisation of the Americas see the two-volume work by Enriqe Semo, *La conquista, catástrofe de los pueblos originarios* (Mexico City: Siglo XXI, 2019).

[22] Kris Lane, *Potosi: The Silver City That Changed the World* (Berkeley: University of California Press, 2019), p. 41.

enticed German lenders to accept the Crown's gift of Venezuela to improve the terms of future loans.[23]

Mining required patience and extensive funds: as scholars have recently noted, in the absence of explosives, the perforation of a rock in search of ore was a slow and unforgiving process.[24] Returns were far from certain and far from immediate. Urban communities grew to satisfy the needs of the labour market in towns like Lima and Potosí.[25] Yet conquest and its rewards were more profitable and immediate than the process of urbanisation: in pursuit of the *adelantamiento*, a title that granted a conquistador the authority to conquer, colonise, and administer an area, Cortés reminded the King that he had used his own money to ensure the 'pacification' of those dominions. As a result, he was heavily in debt.[26] In an audacious tone that characterised a number of other passages in his correspondence with the King, Cortés noted that he ought to be compensated for some of these costs, for

> if this is not returned to me I shall be unable to repay my creditors and will find myself in great need. I cannot think that Your Catholic Majesty will permit this, but, rather, in addition to paying me, will grant me many great favours; for besides the fact that Your Highness is so Catholic and so Christian a Prince, my services, for their part, are not undeserving of it, as their fruits will bear witness.[27]

When he died, Cortés left many of his debts unpaid.[28] The need to establish clear parameters regarding the Crown's *dominium*, its right to property and sovereignty, along with the rights of the conquistadors, the heads of the *encomiendas*, and indigenous peoples, precipitated the establishment of a code of imperial laws.[29] The code, which was informed by the debates of the School of Salamanca, promised but failed to end the *encomienda* and the abuse of forced labour in the Americas.[30]

[23] Barbara Stein and Stanley Stein, *Silver, Trade, and War: Spain and America in the Making of Early Modern Europe* (Baltimore: Johns Hopkins University Press, 2000), pp. 40–57, pp. 43–53.

[24] Lane, *Potosi*, pp. 35–36.

[25] Lane, *Potosi*, pp. 92–116. See also Rossana Barragán and Paula C. Zagalsky eds., *Potosí in the Global Silver Age (16th–19th Centuries)* (Leiden: Brill, 2023).

[26] A year later he would be granted his wish; see Bernard Grunberg, 'Hernán Cortés: un hombre de su tiempo', in María del Carmen Martínez Martínez and Alicia Mayer eds., *Miradas sobre Hernán Cortés* (Frankfurt: Vervuert Verlagsgesellschaft, 2016), pp. 49–66, p. 56.

[27] See his fourth letter in Pagden ed., *Hernán Cortés. Letters from Mexico*, p. 329. See, most recently, a fascinating study of the role debt played in the ambitions of the conquistadors: Enrique Rodríguez-Alegría, *How to Make a New Spain: The Material Worlds of Colonial Mexico City* (Oxford: Oxford University Press, 2023), pp. 24–53.

[28] María del Carmen Martínez Martínez, 'Hernán Cortés en España (1540–1547): Negocios, pleitos y familia', in Martín Federico Ríos Saloma ed., *El mundo de los conquistadores* (Mexico City: UNAM, 2015), pp. 577–598.

[29] The best summary of this process is Anthony Pagden, 'Conquest and the Just War', pp. 30–60. On Vitoria and *dominium* see Anthony Pagden, *The Fall of Natural Man: The American Indian and the Origins of Comparative Ethnology* (Cambridge: Cambridge University Press, 1982), pp. 67–108.

[30] David Lantigua, *Infidels and Empires in a New World Order: Early Modern Spanish Contributions to International Legal Thought* (Cambridge: Cambridge University Press, 2020), pp. 141–186.

A complex caste system that built on Iberian debates on conversion and the purity of one's Christian blood was established across the Americas to classify a subject's colour, lineage, and faith.[31]

In the Andes, the Inca Empire was a dynastic union of provinces ruled by its leader, the *sapa inka*, a descendant of the son of the sun.[32] From its capital in Cuzco, the construction of huge highways across vast terrains enabled the expansion of its economic and political interests.[33] Strings known as *quipu* were knotted and used for accounting purposes and, according to a Jesuit writer, as 'memory aids'; in some regions, decimal groupings were used to administer the empire.[34] Llamas and alpacas were used for clothing, military purposes, and sacrificial rituals.[35] Quarrels over succession characterised a heavily hierarchical society.[36] In 1527, the reigning Tupa Inca Yupanqui and his heir died after they contracted smallpox, a disease spread by the Spanish colonists. Their deaths provoked a crisis of succession that saw Inca Yupanqui's son Atahualpa defeat his half-brother, Huascar, in a civil war.[37] Led by Francisco Pizarro, Spanish troops arrived in Cajamarca and were met with a divided enemy. They capitalised on this situation by capturing and executing Atahualpa.[38] Spanish authors crafted stories about how the dynastic sovereign, prior to his death, had transferred his Crown through *translatio imperii* to the King of Spain.[39] Yet Spanish forces struggled to enforce their rule as violence continued for decades. Spanish officials gradually established the *encomienda* and sought to profit from the discovery of the mines in Potosí. Administrators faced divisions among the conquistadors and intense local resistance.[40] More elusive governing tasks included the need to synchronise local calendars, measurements of age, and visions of history that closely aligned the Inca dynasty with Spain's confessional

[31] Stuart Schwartz, *Blood and Boundaries: The Limits of Religious and Racial Exclusion in Early Modern Latin America* (Waltham: Brandeis University Press, 2020), pp. 72–110.

[32] Kenneth J. Andrien, *Andean Worlds: Indigenous History, Culture, and Consciousness under Spanish Rule, 1532–1825* (Albuquerque: University of New Mexico Press, 2001), p. 27.

[33] Terence N. d'Altroy, 'Inca Political Organization, Economic Institutions, and Infrastructure', in Sonia Alconini and Alan Covey eds., *The Oxford Handbook of the Incas* (Oxford: Oxford University Press, 2018), pp. 205–226, p. 206.

[34] Kathryn Burns, *Into the Archive: Writing and Power in Colonial Peru* (Durham: Duke University Press, 2010), p. 8; Andrien, *Andean Worlds*, p. 4.

[35] D'Altroy, 'Inca Political Organization', pp. 214–215.

[36] D'Altroy, 'Inca Political Organization', pp. 208–209. On marriage norms see Jane E. Mangan, *Transatlantic Obligations: Creating the Bonds of Family in Conquest-era Peru and Spain* (Oxford: Oxford University Press, 2016), pp. 18–46. On the problems of projecting European readings of history on matters of succession on the Incan tradition see Catherine Julien, *Reading Inca History* (Iowa City: University of Iowa Press, 2000), pp. 23–48.

[37] Andrien, *Andean Worlds*, p. 36.

[38] Andrien, *Andean Worlds*, p. 38.

[39] David Brading, *The First America: The Spanish Monarchy, Creole Patriots, and the Liberal State, 1492–1867* (Cambridge: Cambridge University Press, 1991), p. 153; Alejandra B. Osorio, *Inventing Lima: Baroque Modernity in Peru's South Sea Metropolis* (London: Springer, 2008), p. 93.

[40] Sarah Elizabeth Penry, *The People Are King: The Making of an Indigenous Andean Politics* (New York: Oxford, 2019), pp. 43–78.

and monarchical time frames.[41] The use of *probanzas*, evidence of merit or ancestry, at times allowed women or mestizo subjects who could demonstrate their Incan noble heritage to improve their legal standing.[42] Gradually, cracks in the administration allowed for further contestation, as people harnessed legal norms around age and labour for their own ends. The Crown in turn sought to connect popular culture to royal rule. Officials ensured that colonial artworks laced depictions of local dynastic rulers with those of the Habsburg and Bourbon crowns.[43]

Viceroyalties were established to govern the provinces. Viceroys were meant to reflect and reproduce the King's economy of grace. Instead, they fostered public displays of largesse that bolstered the economy of favour.[44] *Consulados*, chartered corporations, were created to settle commercial affairs, including bankruptcies. Beyond large urban spaces, threads of credit were woven into the fabric of colonial authority: members of the *consulados* and mint officials speculated with the profits generated by the mines; the *alcalde mayor*, a provincial magistrate, provided indigenous peoples with supplies or specie on credit, and debt peonage grew in spite of official efforts to regulate and reduce its use.[45] Convents managed by nuns, pawn shops known as *montes de piedad*, and public granaries known as *pósitos*, all extended loans to the lay population.[46] These debts that served social ends greased the wheels of an American imperial administration that was built on the practices of the Reconquista and a strong degree of improvisation. Ming China's increasing reliance, following the collapse in value of its paper money, on Spanish American

[41] Kerstin Nowack, 'Measuring the Passage of Time in Inca and Early Spanish Peru', *Indiana* 30 (2013), pp. 77–98; Alfredo Luis Escudero, 'The New Age of Andeans: Chronological Age, Indigenous Labor, and the Making of Spanish Colonial Rule', *Hispanic American Historical Review* 103:1 (2023), pp. 1–30.

[42] Sara Vicuña Guengerich, 'Inca Women under Spanish Rule: Probanzas and Informaciones of the Colonial Andean Elite', in Mónica Díaz and Rocío Quispe-Agnoli eds., *Women's Negotiations and Textual Agency in Latin America, 1500–1799* (London: Routledge, 2016), pp. 118–141; Felipe E. Ruan, 'The Probanza and Shaping a Contesting Mestizo Record in Early Colonial Peru', *Bulletin of Spanish Studies* 94:5 (2017), pp. 843–869. Mestizos nonetheless faced ostracism from indigenous peoples and Spaniards since they were seen as illegitimate children. See Enrique Krauze, *Mexico: Biography of Power. A History of Modern Mexico, 1810–1996*. Translated by Hanz Heifetz (New York: Harper Collins, 1997), pp. 51–54.

[43] Jorge Cañizares-Esguerra, *How to Write the History of the New World* (Stanford: Stanford University Press, 2001) and Bianca Premo, 'Meticulous Imprecision: Calculating Age in Colonial Spanish American Law', *The American Historical Review* 125:2 (2020), pp. 396–406.

[44] Antonio M. Hespanha, *La gracia del derecho: economía de la cultura en la edad moderna*. Edited by Bartolomé Clavero and translated by Ana Cañellas Haurie (Madrid: Centro de Estudios Constitucionales, 1993), pp. 151–176; Alejandro Cañeque, *The King's Living Image: The Culture and Politics of Viceregal Power in Colonial Mexico* (New York: Routledge, 2004), pp. 157–184.

[45] Jeremy Baskes, *Indians, Merchants, and Markets A Reinterpretation of the Repartimiento and Spanish-Indian Economic Relations in Colonial Oaxaca, 1750–1821* (Stanford: Stanford University Press, 2000), pp. 93–108; Richard J. Salvucci, *Textiles and Capitalism in Mexico: An Economic History of the Obrajes, 1539–1840* (Princeton: Princeton University Press, 1988), pp. 112–120.

[46] Kathryn Burns, 'Nuns, *Kurakas*, and Credit: The Spiritual Economy of Seventeenth-Century Cuzco', *Colonial Latin American Review* 6:2 (1997), pp. 185–203; Donald. L. Gibbs, 'The Economic Activities of Nuns, Friars, and Their Conventos in Mid-Colonial Cuzco', *The Americas* 45:3 (1989), pp. 343–362.

silver for the payment of taxes and foreign trade bolstered Spanish finances.[47] Yet no amount of money could resolve the fundamental problem that slowly undermined Spain's public credit throughout this period: Spanish sovereigns perpetually raided the future in order to meet their imperial ambitions.[48]

Unredeemable debts

As the historian Peter Brown has noted, in the Latin original version of the Lord's Prayer, the term for 'sins' was '*debita*', or debts; one asked God to forgive one's sins, or '*dimitte nobis debita nostra*'. The term redemption, or *redimir*, derived from the Latin *redimo*, to pay back or deliver on a promise: prayer and almsgiving could cancel one's debts to God through the remission of sins.[49] In the Catholic tradition, charity foreshortened the promise of salvation and provided an accessible way to emulate and honour God's grace towards his children.[50] The non-payment of one's debts was a type of perjury, a breach of contract, and could lead to excommunication.[51] The Spanish Crown harnessed this economy of salvation to build an emphyteutic monarchy which ruled over its imperial lands on behalf of God and in exchange for the conservation of confessional interests.[52] In an imperial administration modelled on an Iberian Peninsula that was shaped by the interests of landowners, early modern Spanish theologians harnessed the Roman law principles of *dominium utile*, *utilitas publica*, and *praescriptio* to refine ideas of commutative justice and to legislate, on the basis of public utility, on matters of property and possession.[53] Under the *encomienda* or the *arrendamiento*, land was transferred to the

[47] Lane, *Potosi*, pp. 20–45; Dennis O. Flynn and Arturo Giráldez, 'Cycles of Silver: Global Economic Unity through the Mid-Eighteenth Century', *Journal of World History* 13:2 (2002), pp. 391–427.

[48] A. W. Lovett, 'The Castilian Bankruptcy of 1575', *The Historical Journal* 23:4 (1980), pp. 899–911, p. 911.

[49] Craig Muldrew, The Economy of Obligation: *The Culture of Credit and Social Relations in Early Modern England* (London: Palgrave Macmillan, 1998), p. 131; Peter Brown, *The Ransom of the Soul: Afterlife and Wealth in Early Western Christianity* (Cambridge: Harvard University Press, 2015), pp. 99–100. On the evolution of this Augustinian tradition in Spain, and the Congregatio de Auxiliis see Stuart Schwartz, *All Can Be Saved: Religious Tolerance and Salvation in the Iberian Atlantic World* (New Haven: Yale University Press, 2008), pp. 39–41.

[50] Brown, *The Ransom of the Soul*, pp. 97–99. Anderson's genealogy of this connotation in his *Sin: A History*.

[51] Robert B. Ekelund, Robert D. Tollison, Gary M. Anderson, Robert F. Hebert, and Audrey B. Davidson, *Sacred Trust: Sacred Trust: The Medieval Church as an Economic Firm* (Oxford: Oxford University Press, 1996), pp. 65–67, p. 120.

[52] Tamar Herzog, 'Independence(s): What Is a Revolutionary Law?' in Thomas Duve and Tamar Herzog eds., *The Cambridge History of Latin American Law in Global Perspective* (Cambridge: Cambridge University Press, 2024), pp. 250–282.

[53] On concepts of property rights at the core of the Spanish colonisation of the Americas see Anthony Pagden, *Spanish Imperialism and the Political Imagination: Studies in European and Spanish-American Social and Political Theory 1513–1830* (New Haven: Yale University Press, 1990), pp. 13–36; Bartolomé Clavero, *Mayorazgo: Propiedad feudal en Castilla 1369–1836* (Madrid: Siglo XXI, 1989), pp. 181–210; Annabel Brett, *Liberty, Right and Nature Individual Rights in Later Scholastic Thought* (Cambridge: Cambridge University Press, 1997), pp. 20–24; Paolo Grossi, 'La proprietà nel Sistema

landholder as a loan and labourers worked off a perpetual debt to this proprietor. Spanish philosophers mobilised ideas of charity, poverty, and salvation to defend the colonisation of the Americas; the Jesuit and Franciscan orders, along with the Inquisition, would administer this economy of grace.[54] The first Nahuatl-Spanish dictionary, written in 1555, featured multiple Nahuatl words for debt, including *inama*, a term that reflected the local commutative association of debt, shame, and restitution: 'to demand a loan from the creditor, to enquire and question those who have spoken ill of me [. . .] in order to clear my name and show my innocence'.[55] However, in Peru, *hucha*, the Quechua word for 'reciprocal obligation' and 'debt', was translated into 'sin'.[56] Indigenous tributes were confessionalised into ex-votos: a popular means to honour one's debt of gratitude towards a patron saint after an act of grace or a miracle.[57]

The economy of salvation transcended the economy of contract. In a culture where God's forgiveness did not alleviate one's responsibility to exhibit further contrition, writers registered bitter complaints about how the extravagant interests of foreign bankers who funded the Crown trumped the needs of the people.[58] Bankruptcy reflected the breach of a licit contract—although it only applied to merchants, not to kings—and defaulting on contracts with foreign bankers did not shake the foundations of the Crown's contract with the people.[59] The bond that united the King to his subjects was stronger than gold and silver. The Abrahamic image of the King as *pater familias* and the shepherd of his flock inspired what Pablo Fernández Albaladejo has described as pastoral sovereignty.[60] The King of Spain's confessional status and his relationship to God, certified by the Church, meant that the advancement of the Crown's interests carried greater importance than the fulfilment of a pecuniary contract.[61] But the logic of indulgences

privatistico della Seconda Scolastica', in Paolo Grossi ed., *La seconda scolastica nella formazione del diritto private moderno* (Milan: Giuffrè, 1973), pp. 117–223.

[54] Julia McClure, 'Poverty and Empire' in Julia McClure and David Hitchcock eds., *The Routledge History of Poverty, c. 1450–1800* (Abingdon: Routledge, 2020), pp. 39–59; Elliott, *Empires*, pp. 23–24. See also Brett, *Liberty*, p. 12.

[55] Alonso de Molina, *Vocabulario en lengua castellana y mexicana y mexicana y castellana* (Mexico City: Casa de Espinosa, 1571), p. 38

[56] Gregory Haimovich, 'Linguistic Consequences of Evangelization in Colonial Peru: Analyzing the Quechua Corpus of the Doctrina Christiana y Catecismo', *Journal of Language Contact* 10:2 (2017), pp. 193–218, pp. 204–205.

[57] Lucia García Noriega, Lgia Ochoa Leyzaola, Manuel Arbolí, and Cristina Pantoja eds., *Dones y promesas: 500 años de arte ofrenda (exvotos mexicanos)* (Mexico City: Fundación Cultural Televisa, 1996).

[58] Claudio César Rizzuto, 'The Crusading Indulgence and the Revolt of the Comunidades of Castile (1520–21): Ecclesiastical Reform and Local Religious Life', *The Catholic Historical Review* 107:4 (2021), pp. 503–527, p. 507.

[59] The best cultural history of ideas of money in the Spanish World during this period is Elvira Vilches, *New World Gold: Cultural Anxiety and Monetary Disorder in Early Modern Spain* (Chicago: University of Chicago Press, 2010).

[60] Fernández Albaladejo, *La crisis de la monarquía* (Barcelona: Crítica, 2009), pp. 367–393.

[61] For a deft summary of how Luther's critique struck at the heart of this model see Lyndal Roper, *Luther: Renegade and Prophet* (London: Vintage, 2017), pp. 4–6.

connected the spiritual and the practical demands of the Church. Martin Luther's rousing criticism of indulgences threatened to expose the unseemly relationship between a sacred covenant and pecuniary contracts. For indulgences were a form of payment for the remission of one's time in purgatory, and one which the Church had exploited in a complex scheme to repay the Fugger banking family. It was all the more important for the Holy Roman Emperor to vindicate the supremacy of the moral economy of salvation.[62] Holy needs trumped the needs of creditors: as Charles noted in his testament to his son, however 'indebted' Philip might be, he had an obligation to check the rise of French ambitions in Italy and thus 'prevent the return of war'.[63]

Debt was part and parcel of the process of Spanish monarchical succession. In 1519, the then Charles of Habsburg struggled to acquire the necessary loans to finance his travel to Frankfurt in order to attend the Imperial Diet Election. He thereby inaugurated an inauspicious dynastic tradition. Spanish sovereigns were often so short of money that they struggled to gather the sums required to finance their travels to be crowned emperor, to cement a diplomatic alliance, or to find solace in solitude after abdicating the throne. At the Imperial Diet Election, Charles also inherited a problem which he helped to perpetuate: he found out that his recently deceased grandfather, the Holy Roman Emperor Maximilian I, had left behind a heavy burden of debts which his successor would have to resolve.[64] Many of these contracts had been issued by the Fuggers' firm, whose officials liked to remind Charles, following his election as emperor, that their credit had played a crucial factor in securing the necessary votes behind his victory.[65] Decades later, as an older man, Charles wrote a letter to his son, Philip, then regent of Spain, to ask him to take responsibility for defaulting on the Habsburg Crown's debts and to spare his father the shame that would come from this announcement. At that time, however, Philip was himself struggling to gather the funds to finance his trip to the Low Countries, where he planned to request more capital to finance his wars in Italy.[66] Following his abdication, Charles would have to delay his travels to Spain because he lacked the cash needed to cover his local debts.[67]

[62] Roper, *Luther*, pp. 5–6. Peter Marshall, *1517: Martin Luther and the Invention of the Reformation* (Oxford: Oxford University Press, 2017), pp. 27–70. On the rise of Catholic criticisms of a bloated Church administration see Eire, *Reformations*, pp. 114–129. On indulgences see Rizzuto, 'The Crusading Indulgence', p. 507; Patrick J. O'Banion, 'Only the King Can Do It: Adaptation and Flexibility in Crusade Ideology in Sixteenth-Century Spain', *Church History* 81:3 (2012), pp. 552–574; Mary C. Moorman, *Indulgences: Luther, Catholicism, and the Imputation of Merit* (Ohio: Emmaus Academic, 2017).

[63] 'Instrucciones de Carlos V a Felipe II sobre política exterior', in Manuel Fernández Álvarez ed., *Corpus de Carlos V*. Volume 2 (Salamanca: Universidad de Salamanca, 1975), pp. 569–592.

[64] Carande, *Carlos V*. Volume 1, pp. 28–33.

[65] Carande, *Carlos V*. Volume 1, p. 33.

[66] María José Rodríguez Salgado, *Un imperio en transición: Carlos V, Felipe II y su mundo, 1551–1559* (Barcelona: Crítica, 1992), p. 115.

[67] Salgado, *Un imperio en transición*, p. 204.

Debt also played a structuring role in intra-imperial Habsburg political negotiations. Based on the report of a commission set up in the Low Countries, Philip II hoped to create a corporation made up of factors who would coordinate, centralise, and oversee the debts of the Habsburg Crown through a common accounting system.[68] This council would exploit its privileged access to information to speculate with currency manipulation. Its officials would use their authority to stimulate the sale of bonds. Philip's plan was met with strong opposition from the various regions of the empire who wanted to decrease, not rationalise and combine, the debts of its composite parts.[69] The King pursued a number of other measures. One possible solution was to hold all of the Spanish fairs in one location, since the Low Countries had successfully consolidated their own in Antwerp, but this proposal generated local resistance.[70] Philip tried to undermine speculation within the Iberian Peninsula: he sought to ban bills of exchange. This led to a rush to sign bills of exchange which only increased the prices of goods.[71] Philip then tried to emit *juros*, or public debt, at an unprecedented scale in order to consolidate the floating debt.[72] However, members of the Cortes purchased and speculated with the *juros*. On 5 May 1596, the King was informed that the bulk of the revenues which the *juros* depended on for the next two years had been mortgaged and thus could not be paid out.[73] Philip was left with only one option: he was forced to declare bankruptcy.[74]

Philip II sought to show that he could postpone and renegotiate earthly contracts—and avoid a default on his promise to advance the Christian faith. The conversion of new kingdoms through conquest would, after all, save countless souls.[75] The practical elements of this logic were soon put to the test: Philip found that a royal declaration of the suspension of payment allowed the Spanish Crown to regain a degree of leverage over foreign bankers, renegotiate the terms of its loans, and continue to fund the Church that preached the economy of salvation.[76] Yet there were a small number of lenders who could afford to supply the Spanish Empire with the scale of funds the Crown required. Spanish rulers played investors against one another: Genoese lenders replaced Central European bankers only to

[68] For the broader dynamics of the reform see Francisco Comín Comín, *Las crisis de la deuda soberana en España (1500–2015)* (Madrid: Catarata, 2016), pp. 44–47.

[69] Salgado, *Un imperio en transición*, pp. 350–351.

[70] Carlos Javier de Carlos Morales, *Felipe II. El imperio en bancarrota la Hacienda Real de Castilla y los negocios financieros del Rey Prudente* (Madrid: Dilema, 2009), p. 44, p. 112. On Spain's spending in the Netherlands under Philip II see A. W. Lovett, *Philip II and Mateo Vázquez de Leca: the Government of Spain (1572–1592)* (Geneva: Droz, 1977), pp. 39–59.

[71] Morales, *Felipe II*, pp. 35–36.

[72] Salgado, *Un imperio en transición*, p. 48.

[73] Morales, *Felipe II*, p. 275.

[74] Salgado, *Un imperio en transición*, pp. 350–352.

[75] Geoffrey Parker, *Imprudent King: A New Life of Philip II* (New Haven: Yale University Press, 2014), p. 236.

[76] Salgado, *Un imperio en transición*, pp. 18–19.

lose their influence to Portuguese financiers.[77] Creditors were granted increasingly favourable terms: *asientos*, contracts for short-term loans during times of financial difficulty, carried the promise that these creditors would be paid before anyone else, including the Treasury or the Court.[78]

Succession, as ever, was accompanied by a debt crisis. In 1598, a few days before Philip II's death, the Cortes informed his heir, the future Philip III, that he was about to inherit a range of debts and obligations that he did not have the means to satisfy.[79] One official lamented the indignity of the King's need to beg for money.[80] Philip III's solution was to experiment with the revaluation of the different currencies used in the Spanish Empire. The Cortes, in turn, complained that the fluctuation and abundance of the *vellón*, the currency used to trade and pay taxes within Spain, slowed down the repayment of the rents which backed the *juros*. This in turn undermined the value of the *juros* they owned.[81] In the midst of this crisis, the costly struggle against the insurgents in the Low Countries forced Philip III to declare bankruptcy. Under Philip IV, financiers learned they could buy *vellón* in Spain and sell it abroad in exchange for silver.[82] This had the effect, in the words of the wordsmith Francisco de Quevedo, of 'turning the *vellón* from a Treasury to a source of daily shocks'.[83] Lawsuits piled up on the desks of European officials over the changing value of currencies between the time the loans were negotiated and the time the goods arrived at the fairs. Philosophers like Juan de Mariana warned the Spanish Crown that it was not 'licit to devalue currencies when financing debts that were agreed when their value was higher'.[84] Monetary devaluation, argued Mariana, was a form of taxation—and an unjust one.[85] The political writer Baltasar Álamos de Barrientos noted that the accumulation of bills meant that the King did not 'own' the Crown's revenues since they were all mortgaged to pay for outstanding debts.[86] It was impossible for the government to keep up with the pace of

[77] Carlos Álvarez Nogal, 'Los banqueros de Felipe IV y los metales preciosos americanos (1621–1665)', *Banco de España: Servicio de Estudios de Historia Económica* 36 (1997), pp. 1–115, pp. 21–50.

[78] Comín, *Las crisis*, pp. 26–27.

[79] Juan E. Gelabert, *La bolsa del Rey. Rey, reino y fisco en Castilla (1598–1648)* (Barcelona: Crítica, 1997), p. 13.

[80] Gelabert, *La bolsa del Rey*, p. 13.

[81] Elena María García Guerra, *Moneda y arbitrios. Consideraciones del siglo XVII* (Madrid: Consejo Superior de Investigaciones Científicas, 2003), pp. 175–177.

[82] Carmen Sanz Ayán, *Los banqueros y la crisis de la monarquía hispánica de 1640* (Madrid: Marcial Pons, 2013), p. 19, p. 112. On the broader relationship between specie and debt see Álvarez Nogal, 'Los banqueros de Felipe IV', pp. 26–50.

[83] 'Susto de cada día'; Quoted in Sanz Ayán, *Los banqueros*, p. 62.

[84] García Guerra, *Moneda y arbitrios*, p. 39.

[85] García Guerra, *Moneda y arbitrios*, pp. 30–43; Wim Decock, 'Spanish Scholastics on Money and Credit', in David Fox and Wolfgang Ernst eds., *Money in the Western Legal Tradition Middle Ages to Bretton Woods* (Oxford: Oxford University Press, 2016), pp. 267–283, pp. 272–277.

[86] Quoted in Alberto Marcos Martín, 'Medina del Campo en la Época Moderna: del florecimiento a la decadencia. Estructura ocupacional y estructura de la demanda en los siglos XVI, XVII y XVIII: un intento de estimación de la riqueza y su distribución por categorías sociales', in Eufemio Lorenzo ed., *Historia de Medina del Campo y su tierra*. Volume 1 (Medina Del Campo: Ayuntamiento de Medina del Campo, 1986), pp. 523–634, pp. 600–601.

its public credit market: a state council informed the Crown that 'the time frames of matters regarding the treasury, *asientos*, debts, recollection, and repayment are so tight that reforms and improvements no longer suffice to forestall the harms that could arise'.[87]

The confessional constancy of the Crown, however, guaranteed the survival of the empire. So too did its army. In an effort to retain its control of "the Spanish Road", a path that stretched from Brussels to Milan, Spain spent the bulk of its imperial revenues fighting to retain control of the Low Countries.[88] When the Crown was unable to pay its soldiers, Philip II asked Fernando Álvarez de Toledo, the duke of Alba and Governor of the Low Countries, to raise loans in the region.[89] Financial support was not forthcoming. Unpaid soldiers, in order to force the King's hand, mutinied and sacked the town of Antwerp. Early modern political writers concluded that the indebtedness of the Spanish Crown had caused the cruelty perpetrated by its soldiers in Antwerp: an act of violence that fostered the growth of the Black Legend.[90] In the Act of Abjuration, the Dutch provinces would fault Philip for failing to adhere to his obligations and claim their natural right to rule on behalf of the people.[91] Failure to repay one's debts, according to this reading of events, had not just led to a breach of an earthly contract: it was an infringement of a covenant established with God. One of the authors who convinced the rest of Europe of its merits was Hugo Grotius.

Grotius changed Europe's perception of Spain. The Enlightenment marshalled his ideas and sought to replace the political and commercial arbitrariness that, in the eyes of the *philosophes*, characterised Philip II's Mediterranean World with the growth of new norms of succession, the codification of the law of nations, and the establishment of national banks in the Netherlands, Britain, and France.[92] Charles Louis de Secondat, Baron de La Brède et de Montesquieu, in his unpublished *Réflexions sur la monarchie universelle en Europe* and in his *Esprit des Lois*, noted that European 'public credit took the place of mines and diminished the profit

[87] Quoted in Gelabert, *La bolsa del Rey*, p. 78.

[88] Geoffrey Parker, *The Army of Flanders and the Spanish Road 1567–1659: The Logistics of Spanish Victory and Defeat in the Low Countries' Wars* (Cambridge: Cambridge University Press, 2004).

[89] Lovett, 'Castilian Bankruptcy', p. 899.

[90] Pagden, *Spanish Imperialism*, p. 4.

[91] Helmut Koenigsberger observed that the language of the Act of Abjuration of 1581 was rather like Philip's own language, citing a letter from the King to the Viceroy of Naples. But the main difference was that the Act made 'the fulfilment of the ruler's political obligations to his subjects the condition of the subjects' political obligation to the ruler'. Helmut Koenigsberger, *The Government of Sicily under Philip II of Spain* (London: Staples Press, 1951), p. 172, n. 2. Martin van Gelderen, *The Political Thought of the Dutch Revolt 1555–1590* (Cambridge: Cambridge University Press, 2002); Nehal Bhuta, 'The State Theory of Grotius', *Current Legal Problems* 73:1 (2020), pp. 127–176, pp. 143–148. For an economist's reading of this argument see Mauricio Drelichman and Hans-Joachim Voth, *Lending to the Borrower from Hell: Debt, Taxes, and Default in the Age of Philip II* (Princeton: Princeton University Press, 2014), pp. 271–280.

[92] Antoin E. Murphy, *John Law: Economic Theorist and Policy-maker* (Oxford: Oxford University Press, 1997), pp. 45–66.

which the Spaniards drew from theirs.'[93] In his view, Philip II's bankruptcy, and his inability to pay his troops, had fostered the Spanish Fury at Antwerp that was the final spark that ignited the fire of the Dutch Revolt and the start of Spain's 'continual state of decline': 'Philip II, who succeeded Charles V, was obliged to declare the famous bankruptcy everyone knows about; and there has scarcely ever been a prince who has suffered more than he did from the grumbling, the insolence, and the revolt of his always poorly paid troops.'[94] European affairs were no longer shaped by Spain's dynastic norms and its fairs: according to Montesquieu, 'the law of nations' was the law of the land.[95] It was no surprise that the Founding Fathers of the United States, obsessed with the memory of the Dutch Revolt, resolved to pay their army and establish a sound system of public credit to reap the fruits of their revolution.[96]

When is it moral to default on the debts of a tyrant?

Montesquieu believed that everyone knew about Spain's famous bankruptcy because most contemporary European thinkers had read Grotius' works. Born in Delft, Grotius was a polymath and a diplomat, a pedant who made the *faux pas* of advising a widowed queen to have children to resolve her political dilemmas, and a celebrity who was asked to sign copies of his works by his fans.[97] His successes are frequently studied and his failures are largely forgotten. One of his greatest errors was his intervention in the Socinian controversy, named after Lelio Sozzini and Fausto Sozzini, regarding the nature of atonement. In the minds of the leaders of the Dutch Revolt, God had delivered the Dutch from Spain: the possibility of forsaking God's benevolence provoked fear and unease.[98] The Socinians argued that Christ's death had not satisfied humanity's debt for its sins; God could simply forgive humanity with his grace. This undermined Christ's sacrifice and appeared to discourage piety and humility.[99]

[93] Charles de Montesquieu, *The Spirit of the Laws*. Edited by Anne M. Cohler, Basia Carolyn Miller, and Harold Samuel Stone (Cambridge: Cambridge University Press, 1989), p. 395.

[94] Montesquieu, *The Spirit of the Laws*, p. 393; David W. Carrithers and Philip Stewart eds., 'Statecraft', in *Montesquieu: Discourses, Dissertations, and Dialogues on Politics, Science, and Religion* (Cambridge: Cambridge University Press, 2020), pp. 155–205, p. 180.

[95] Carrithers and Stewart eds., 'Statecraft', p. 171.

[96] Kieran J. O'Keefe, 'The Dutch Revolt and Historical Memory in the American Revolution', *The International History Review* 43:3 (2021), pp. 567–578, p. 570.

[97] On pedantry see Henk Nellen, *Hugo Grotius A Lifelong Struggle for Peace in Church and State, 1583–1645* (Leiden: Brill, 2015), p. 157, p. 249; on his mishaps see p. 673; on the anecdote surrounding his autograph see p. 722.

[98] Hans Blom, 'Grotius and Socinianism', in Martin Mulsow and Jan Rohls eds., *Socinianism and Arminianism. Antitrinitarians, Calvinists, and Cultural Exchange in Seventeenth-Century Europe* (Leiden: Brill, 2005), pp. 121–147, p. 121.

[99] Nellen, *Grotius*, p. 236.

In *De satisfactione*, Grotius sought to counter this position: he suggested that this debt to God was not to be considered an economic debt, but an offence that was to be resolved through criminal law.[100] The punishment of this crime would discourage future criminality and bring those who accepted it closer to salvation.[101] Yet Dutch contemporaries saw the text as a defence of Socinian principles.[102] Grotius' view of atonement was too broad and too lax, all too similar to the universalism of Catholic Spain; it likely invoked memories of Philip's use of the idea of clemency and the use of pardons during the Dutch Revolt. The Dutch would strive to show that they were the chosen few who would continue to pay their debt to God.[103] The Act of Abjuration, after all, was based on the idea that Spain had broken a contract established by the Christian norms of natural law: the Dutch, by contrast, respected their sacred covenant.[104]

Fears that Grotius would embrace Catholicism as a result of his diplomatic service for France were entirely unwarranted and yet followed him all his life; in Spain, this stance was so common that the most influential eighteenth-century philosopher simply assumed that the conversion had taken place.[105] Grotius was nonetheless one of the most fervent and convincing critics of the norms that had fostered the growth of the Iberian empires, including the act of donation that, in Cortés' view, had legitimated *translatio imperii*.[106] Building on the works of Scholastic theologians, he shifted claims to sovereignty and possession away from *dominium* and towards *imperium*, common property, and the rights of corporations.[107] Better

[100] Jeremy Seth Geddert, 'Too Subtle to Satisfy Many: Was Grotius's Teleology of Punishment Predestined to Fail?', *Grotiana* 38 (2017), pp. 46–69, pp. 50–56.

[101] Geddert, 'Too Subtle to Satisfy Many', p. 55.

[102] Geddert, 'Too Subtle to Satisfy Many', p. 61.

[103] Spain deployed the concept of clemency in its propaganda to quell the Dutch Revolt. See Judith Pollmann, *Catholic Identity and the Revolt of the Netherlands, 1520–1635* (Oxford: Oxford University Press, 2011), p. 90 and much of Violet Soen's work, in particular, 'The Clementia Lipsiana: Political Analysis, Autobiography and Panegyric', in Erik de Bom et al., *(Un)masking the Realities of Power Justus Lipsius and the Dynamics of Political Writing in Early Modern Europe* (Leiden: Brill, 2011), pp. 207–231. On Grotius' debt to, and parallels with, the Jesuits and the Spanish Scholastics on the question of debt see Wim Decock, *Theologians and Contract Law: The Moral Transformation of the Ius Commune (ca. 1500–1650)* (Leiden: Brill, 2012), pp. 84–87, pp. 102–104, pp. 198–200.

[104] The critique had a colonial dimension, as he reasoned that 'Iberian bad faith' offended 'God, because it severs the only bond that provides security among those who meet for the first time'; see Mark Somos, 'Virtue', in Randall Lesaffer and Janne E. Nijman eds., *The Cambridge Companion to Hugo Grotius* (Cambridge: Cambridge University Press, 2021), pp. 91–117, p. 93, p. 105.

[105] Edward Jones Corredera, 'The End of Composite Monarchies: Hugo Grotius' *De iure belli ac pacis* and the Making of Mid-Century Iberian Diplomacy', *English Historical Review* (Forthcoming).

[106] Benjamin Straumann, *Roman Law in the State of Nature: The Classical Foundations of Hugo Grotius' Natural Law* (Cambridge: Cambridge University Press, 2015), p. 155, n. 112; Alfred Dufour, 'Les "Magni hispani" dans l'oeuvre de Grotius', in Frank Grunert and Kurt Seelmann eds., *Die Ordnung der Praxis. Neue Studies zur Spanischen Spätscholastik* (Tübingen: Niemeyer 2001), pp. 351–380; Annabel Brett, 'Natural Right and Civil Community: The Civil Philosophy of Hugo Grotius', *The Historical Journal* 45:1 (2002), pp. 31–51; Martine van Ittersum, *Profit and Principle Hugo Grotius, Natural Rights Theories and the Rise of Dutch Power in the East Indies, 1595–1615* (Leiden: Brill, 2006), pp. 53–80; Anthony Anghie, *Imperialism, Sovereignty and the Making of International Law* (Cambridge: Cambridge University Press, 2012), pp. 13–31.

[107] Annabel Brett, 'The Space of Politics and the Space of War in Hugo Grotius's *De iure belli ac pacis*', *Global Intellectual History* 1:1 (2016), pp. 33–60, pp. 38–40; Straumann, *Roman Law*, p. 151.

known for the way he marshalled these ideas in defence of the rights of the Dutch East India Company in *Mare liberum*, in his *Annales*, the first official history of the Dutch Revolt, Grotius framed Spain's fiscal mismanagement as a series of instances of theft and a breach of contract.[108] He criticised Philip II's bankruptcy and argued that the conflict with the Netherlands had 'eroded the Spanish financial reserves, however strong they were, to an astonishing degree; the King had incurred so many debts that with the help of a debt redemption he had robbed his creditors of their possessions'.[109] It was easy to establish Spain's reckless fiscal management as a cause for revolution. It was more challenging to clarify what ought to happen to these debts in the case of succession.

For the relationship between succession and promises, oaths, and debts was a difficult circle to square. In book two of his major work, *De iure belli ac pacis*, Grotius argued that debts contracted by a 'free people' under monarchical rule remained binding.[110] But he also noted that contracts that were deemed unjust at the time of their signing could be defaulted on. 'Some Laws are manifestly absurd and unreasonable, so also the Contracts of Princes do not oblige their Subjects, unless they carry any warrantable Reason, which in doubtful Matters ought to be presumed, in Respect to the Authority of Governors'.[111] Grotius laid out the criteria for odious contracts. To judge the 'Contracts of Princes' the crux of the question had to shift from 'the Success of the Contracts' to 'the Reasons whereon they were grounded'.[112] Citing examples found in the works of Mariana, Grotius argued that a contract that was against the interest of the people and lacked the consent of the polity's legal institutions could be reneged on. If 'at the Time when the Contract was so made', the terms 'had been judged unlawful and unjust; then may that Contract be not so much revoked as declared no longer obliging, as if it were made conditionally of being void in that Case, without which Condition it could not have been justly made'.[113]

Which laws were to be used to retroactively determine the unfairness of a contract? In the Spanish Empire, the plurality of laws contained within its multiple provinces meant these criteria were dependent on the norms of each province.

[108] Hugo Grotius, *Annals of the War in the Low Countries*. Edition, Translation, and Introduction by Jan Waszink (Leuven: Leuven University Press, 2023).

[109] Grotius, *Annals of the War in the Low Countries*, p. 217. See also Jan Waszink, 'Hugo Grotius on the Agglomerate Polity of Philip II', *History of European Ideas* 46:3 (2020), pp. 276–291. On Grotius' debt to the Scholastics' views on obligation and contract law see Decock, *Theologians and Contract Law*, pp. 209–211, pp. 598–600.

[110] Hugo Grotius, *The Rights of War and Peace*. Volume 2. Edited and with an Introduction by Richard Tuck. From the edition by Jean Barbeyrac (Indianapolis: Liberty Fund, 2005), p. 673. For a good summary on Grotius' views on the matter see Ernst H. Feilchenfeld, *Public Debts and State Succession* (New York: Macmillan, 1931), pp. 27–29. See also Richard Tuck, *The Sleeping Sovereign: The Invention of Modern Democracy* (Cambridge: Cambridge University Press, 2016), pp. 79–80.

[111] Grotius, *The Rights of War and Peace*. Volume 2, p. 813.

[112] Grotius, *The Rights of War and Peace*. Volume 2, p. 813.

[113] Grotius, *The Rights of War and Peace*. Volume 2, pp. 815–816. Note the consistency of his views in Grotius, *The Rights of War and Peace*. Volume 3, pp. 1231–1233. See also his criticism of Scholastic views on false debts in Grotius, *The Rights of War and Peace*. Volume 2, pp. 806–807.

The Spanish Crown ruled the various parts of its empire through a process of strategic ambiguity: it was reluctant to establish consistent norms of succession across the Habsburg territories; Castile was *primus inter pares*, first among equals, and officials in Portugal, Naples, Aragon, and the Americas emulated each other's policies as they engaged in a competition for ascendancy within the hierarchy established by the Crown. The Spanish Crown would often draw on writings on succession in inconsistent and mutually exclusive ways in each of these territories; it regulated and resolved succession crises by granting privileges, deploying brute force, and disseminating confessional propaganda. In effect, in times of crisis it showed its true nature: this was a patrimonial monarchy. Yet Grotius held the Crown to its promise to rule as a composite monarchy: local norms, he noted, served to hold the monarch accountable, for the 'private Acts of a King', he continued, were to be seen 'not as the Acts of the Community, but as of one of its Members', and therefore based on 'the common Rule of the Laws', even those 'Laws which make void some Acts either simply, or if the injured Person desires, shall also take place here, as if it had been agreed on upon this Condition. Thus we see some Kings have taken their Advantage of the Laws against Extortion'.[114]

It followed that the King could not breach the laws of the Low Countries to improve Spain's fiscal status, and the legality of contracts signed by the King of Spain was to be judged according to Dutch law. This was the reading of the passage rendered by Jean Barbeyrac, the eighteenth-century French philosopher and translator who reinterpreted Grotius' writings.[115] In a footnote, he observed that Grotius must have been thinking, when drafting this passage, about Spain and Philip II: 'It is imagined our Author here had his Eye on Philip II. King of Spain, who, in 1596, abolished all the Debts contracted in his Name, and seized on all the Assignments, which had been given to his Creditors'. As Barbeyrac explained, citing Emanuel de Meteren's *L'histoire des Pays-Bas*, 'the same Prince, two Years after, recalled his Ordinance, and restored his Creditors to their full Right'. Barbeyrac noted how '[b]y the new Agreement made with them he declared and openly confessed that the aforesaid Merchants and Traders had dealt fairly and honestly with him, and laid the whole Fault on himself and his own extreme Necessity'.[116]

[114] Grotius, *The Rights of War and Peace*. Volume 2, p. 804. Grotius further muddled his argument by signalling Bodin's writings on the matter for clarity on just and unjust debts of succession. Grotius, *The Rights of War and Peace*. Volume 2, p. 816.

[115] Barbeyrac focused extensively on Grotius' and Samuel von Pufendorf's writings on debt. He was the first early modern author to observe, in one of his analyses of Pufendorf's writings, that Aristotle had originally noted that some believed that the illegitimate debts of a tyrannical regime could, following its demise, be reneged on. See Samuel von Pufendorf, Le droit de la nature et des gens ou système général des principes les plus importan*t*s de la morale, de la jurisprudence et de la politique. Translated by Jean Barbeyrac (Amsterdam: Chez Kuyper, 1706), p. 468, n. 1.

[116] Grotius, *The Rights of War and Peace*. Volume 2, p. 804, n. 2. See the original in Jean Barbeyrac, *Le droit de la guerre, et de la paix. Par Hugues Grotius. Nouvelle traduction, par Jean Barbeyrac*. Volume 1 (Amsterdam: Pierre de Coup, 1724), p. 464, n. 2.

Philip II, in this analysis, had been forced by the laws of the Low Countries to repay his debts. Yet it was not clear how, within this patrimonial kingdom masked as a composite monarchy, a province with a different system of law could enforce this norm, or indeed whether it was Dutch law that had compelled the King of Spain to show greater respect for his contracts with private merchants. A second unresolved matter was whether contracts, even if they were deemed odious according to the laws of the time, could be repudiated once succession had taken place; indeed, Grotius, as Barbeyrac noted, struggled to determine which acts and properties of a sovereign were classified private and which public in the process of succession.[117]

The Swiss jurist Emer de Vattel sought to address these questions. Vattel was critical of Frederick II's assault on the European balance of power and his default on a British loan as a form of reprisal, and yet it was Philip II's attitude towards the Netherlands which was still used to exemplify a tyrannical government.[118] In his *Droit des Gens*, Vattel described patrimonial succession as 'a chimera'. To show it was nothing more than a farce, he cited Grotius' views on Philip II's grant of succession of the Netherlands to his daughter Isabella as a 'a dangerous precedent' whereby 'free citizens' were bartered like 'domestic slaves', and a breach of the authority that could only be granted by the Dutch parliamentary powers.[119] In his chapter on 'Conventions of Sovereigns with private Persons', Vattel argued that '[w]hen a lawful power' contracted a debt 'in the name of the state' it created an 'obligation' on 'all future leaders of society'. Debts between states and private parties had to be repaid because the right and property of the creditor had to be respected. 'The conductor of the nation may have dealings of his own, and private debts' but 'loans contracted for the service of the state, debts incurred in the administration of public affairs, are contracts in all the strictness of law, and obligatory on the state and the whole nation, which is indispensably bound to discharge those debts'.[120] Vattel concluded that the debt had to be repaid: 'Whether the money borrowed has been turned to the advantage of the state, or squandered in foolish expenses, is no concern of the person who has lent it'.[121]

[117] As observed by Brett in 'The Space of Politics and the Space of War, pp. 33–60, p. 40.
[118] Koen Stapelbroek, 'Vattel and the Seven Years' War' in Peter Schröder ed., *Concepts and Contexts of Vattel's Political and Legal Thought* (Cambridge: Cambridge University Press, 2021), pp. 101–120; Emer de Vattel, *The Law of Nations, Or, Principles of the Law of Nature, Applied to the Conduct and Affairs of Nations and Sovereigns, with Three Early Essays on the Origin and Nature of Natural Law and on Luxury*. Edited and with an Introduction by Béla Kapossy and Richard Whatmore (Indianapolis: Liberty Fund, 2008), p. 104. As noted by Portillo; see José María Portillo, *Una historia atlántica de los orígenes de la nación y el Estado* (Madrid: Alianza, 2022), p. 43.
[119] Vattel, *The Law of Nations*, p. 115, n.*.
[120] Shavana Musa, 'The Silesian Loan Affair and the Seven Years War', in *Victim Reparation under the Ius Post Bellum: An Historical and Normative Perspective* (Cambridge: Cambridge University Press, 2019), pp. 74–104. Vattel, *The Law of Nations*, p. 384.
[121] Vattel, *The Law of Nations*, p. 384.

It was precisely in the context of this debate that Vattel, in a footnote, drew on Grotius' *Annales* to illustrate his argument by noting how in 1596 Philip II had declared himself 'a bankrupt'—or, in the original, '*a fit banqueroute à ses créanciers*'—in order to defraud his investors 'under pretence that an unfair advantage had been taken of his necessities', only to find that he was unable to find any financiers who would willingly fund his Crown. Unable to find anyone who would 'lend him money', he was obliged to both restore the affairs to their former state and 'to heal the wound which he had given to the public faith'.[122]

This reading of Philip II's character once again reaffirmed the sense that even the great Spanish tyrant had been forced to repay his creditors and yet, in this case, Vattel interpreted Philip's resolution of the matter as a matter of political expediency. Indeed, Vattel went on to qualify his views on legitimate and illegitimate debts. While the sovereign could not hold the nation 'liable for the debts he contracts, unless they be incurred with a view to the national advantage, and in order to enable him to provide for all occurrences', if the ruler was an absolute monarch it belonged to 'him alone to decide, in all doubtful cases, what the welfare and safety of the state require'.[123] Yet in the absence of absolute necessity, if the absolute monarch were to 'contract debts of immense magnitude and capable of ruining the nation for ever, there could not then exist any doubt in the case: the sovereign has evidently acted without authority; and those who have lent him their money, have imprudently risked it'.[124] The burden of responsibility and justice thus fell on the absolute monarch and his creditors. In the case of succession, if the sovereign had granted 'any of the property of the state' to a creditor for reasons other 'than the public welfare' or 'as a reward for services rendered to the state' it followed that '[h]is successor, or the state, may at any time revoke such a grant' since it had been made without the consent of the state and with property that did not belong to the sovereign.[125] Default, argued Vattel, was, under these circumstances, a licit measure.

The Spanish Empire remained an easy foil and a complex riddle for those who sought to follow the law of nations designed by Grotius and Vattel.[126] For Philip,

[122] Vattel, *The Law of Nations*, p. 384, n. *. See also the original second edition of the book, which featured more notes than the first. Emer de Vattel, *Le droit des gens ou principes de la loi naturelle, appliqués à la conduite et aux affaires des nations et des souverains*. Volume 1 (Neuchâtel: Société Typographique, 1773), p. 381, n. *.

[123] Vattel, *The Law of Nations*, p. 385.

[124] Vattel, *The Law of Nations*, p. 385.

[125] Vattel, *The Law of Nations*, p. 385.

[126] Further research on Grotius' rhetorical move may shed light on the historical origins of the fiscal tensions embedded in the idea of a 'sovereign state' identified by Frederic William Maitland, and more recently discussed by Quentin Skinner and Sean Fleming. See Quentin Skinner, 'The sovereign state: a genealogy', in Hent Kalmo and Quentin Skinner eds., *Sovereignty in Fragments: The Past, Present, and Future of a Contested Concept* (Cambridge: Cambridge University Press, 2010), pp. 26-46, p. 46; Sean Fleming, *Leviathan on a Leash: A Theory of State Responsibility* (Princeton: Princeton University Press, 2020), p. 4. Note also that Maitland developed his ideas on debt and moral personality by drawing on the same Venezuelan debt crisis that would inspire Drago to write his famous note. See F. W. Maitland, *State, Trust and Corporation*. Edited by David Runciman and Magnus Ryan (Cambridge: Cambridge University Press, 2003), pp. 70-71.

as Vattel's assessment made clear, had not been moved by the wisdom of Dutch laws to repay his debts. Barbeyrac and Vattel focused on the bankruptcy of 1596, but Grotius appeared to have been concerned with the impact of the crisis of 1575. Nor had Philip or his heirs ceased to see the threat of bankruptcy, or the Crown's patrimonial dynastic norms of succession, as mechanisms through which to wield power in Europe or deliver acts of grace. Grotius and Vattel overplayed the significance of Philip's bankruptcy and failed to establish how to handle debts of succession. Latin American officials would have to establish what public welfare and consent meant to a confessional revolutionary nation. Above all, Latin American jurists had to correct the views of Grotius and Vattel on the political consequences of default.

The parallels between the Dutch Revolt and the Latin American pursuit of independence were commonly emphasised by countless revolutionaries, including Francisco de Miranda, Francisco Antonio Zea, and Fray Servando Teresa de Mier.[127] In the 1820s, one anonymous letter published in a Colombian newspaper, the *Correo del Orinoco*, argued that 'what the Spanish describe as peace is not what jurists understand by the term'.[128] Rather the Spanish definition of peace was based on the *Leyes de Indias*, and it meant nothing more than 'pacification', the 're-establishment of order', and 'submission'.[129] The 'patrimonial right to a territory, in the words of jurists', the author continued, 'could not deny the right of a people like Colombia to gain its own emancipation through negotiations and the protection of its natural rights'. The Crown could not claim these territories as its own and instead had to treat them as part of 'individuals in the great society of nations ruled by international law'.[130] It was the same argument made by the founder of international law: following the violent clashes in the

[127] Servando Teresa de Mier, *Historia de la Revolución de Nueva España* (Mexico City: CEMC, 1990), p. 492; David Brading, *Mito y profecia en la historia de México. Translated by Tomás Segura* (Mexico City: FDCE, 2004), p. 90; Francisco de Miranda, 'Proclamación a los pueblos del continente colombiano', *Cuadernos de Cultura Latinoamericana* 23 (1978), pp. 5–20, p. 15. Francisco Antonio Zea, 'Mediación entre España y América', in Pedro Pablo Diaz, José Luis Ramos, and Domingo Navas Spinola eds., *Varios discursos del ciudadano Francisco Antonio Zea* (Caracas: Spinola, 1825), pp. 1–80, p. 56.

[128] 'Cartas de un patriota: Carta 6'. *Correo del Orinoco*. Number 96, 17 February 1821. The author was correct; on the activities of the *juntas de pacificación* see Timothy Anna, *Spain and the Loss of America* (London: University of Nebraska Press, 1983), pp. 166–169.

[129] 'Cartas de un patriota: Carta 6'. Argüelles would try to suggest there was a parallel between pacification and the modern approach to the balance of power; see José Canga Argüelles, *Breve respuesta á la representación de los Comerciantes de Londres* (London: Caldero, 1829), p. 42. See also Jeremy Adelman, *Sovereignty and Revolution in the Iberian Atlantic* (Princeton: Princeton University Press, 2006), pp. 272–276. Pablo Murillo, the Spanish general who had sought to quell the revolts, had described the goal of his expedition as 'pacification'. Note the curious blend of the sacred right of the pardon and the Crown's conduct being dictated by the norms of humanity in *Manifiesto que hace a la nación española el teniente general don Pablo Morillo* (Madrid: Imprenta de la Calle de Greda, 1821), p. 36.

[130] 'Cartas de un patriota: Carta 6'. On broader global conceptual changes to the meaning of the idea of peace see Thomas Hippler and Miloš Vec eds., *Paradoxes of Peace in Nineteenth Century Europe* (Oxford: Oxford University Press, 2015).

Netherlands, Philip II had replaced the word 'conquest' in his ordinances with the word 'pacification'.[131]

But Bolívar also declared that 'there is no benefit to looking like Jacobins, and much less criticise monarchs, and only with respect and justice when they offend us'.[132] Latin American revolutionary scripts thus had to encode seventeenth-century revolts in an eighteenth-century framework: Colombian envoys to London were told to convey to their counterparts that '[t]he Americas have no desire to attack the Spanish government nor decapitate the King of Spain; their pretension is the same as that of the Low Countries and Portugal against the three Philips of Castile'.[133] The earliest textbook on international law published in Buenos Aires in turn drew on Grotius' commentary on Philip II in *De iure belli ac pacis* to bolster its argument that the government required the consent of the Argentine provinces in order to negotiate loans, a debate that would shape Argentina's politics throughout the century.[134] In negotiations with Britain, Mexican officials hoped to strengthen their case for independence by drawing on the history of Spanish and Dutch relations.[135] By negotiating the 1609 Twelve Years' Truce between the warring factions,

[131] John Elliott, *National and Comparative History: An Inaugural Lecture Delivered Before the University of Oxford on 10 May 1991* (Oxford: Clarendon Press, 1991), p. 19. There was thus a struggle behind the process of 'internationalisation' in Spanish-speaking political discourses; see on this internationalisation Javier Fernández Sebastián, *Historia conceptual en el Atlántico ibérico: Lenguajes, tiempos, revoluciones* (Madrid: FCEE, 2021), pp. 179–181. The principle of revolution and restoration united the Hispanic World: Latin American and Spanish thinkers celebrated the success of 'Castile' in liberating the empire from the hands of the tyrant. Yet this only made it possible for Latin American thinkers to boast about having financially contributed to the liberation of the home nation, and to criticise the hypocrisy of Spanish officials in preventing the inchoate states from achieving their desired independence. See José María Portillo, 'Los rumbos imprevistos de Cádiz', in Roberto Breña ed., *Cádiz a debate: Actualidad, contexto y legado* (Mexico City: Colegio de México, 2014), pp. 27–48, pp. 36–39. On how some of these values were granted greater prominence in Latin American debates thanks to the discussions at Cádiz see Sebastián, *Historia conceptual*, p. 265, p. 278.

[132] Juan Francisco Padín, 'Los albores del derecho internacional en la Universidad de Buenos Aires: la enseñanza de la materia según Antonio Sáenz', *Academia: Revista sobre enseñanza del derecho de Buenos Aires* 27 (2016), pp. 79–99, p. 91; Vicente Lecuna, *Relaciones diplomáticas de Bolívar con Chile y Buenos Aires: copiadas de los originales existentes en las secciones del Archivo del libertador denominadas de O'Leary y Juan de Francisco Martín.* Volume 2 (Caracas: Imprenta Nacional, 1954), p. 185. Compare with René Provost, *Rebel Courts: The Administration of Justice by Armed Insurgents* (Oxford: Oxford University Press, 2021). Roberto Breña has further suggested that the first wave of peninsular Spanish liberal thought grounded its ambitions on historicist readings of tradition. See Roberto Breña, *El primer liberalismo español y los procesos de emancipación de América 1808–1824. Una revisión historiográfica del liberalismo hispánico* (México: El Colegio de México, 2006), p. 54.

[133] In this regard, Portillo does not go far enough in indicating the distinctiveness of the historiographical challenge posed by the revolutions in Latin America; see José María Portillo, 'Constitutions', in Duve and Herzog eds., *Cambridge History of Latin American Law*, pp. 283–321; Daniel Ardila, *El reconocimiento de Colombia: diplomacia y propaganda en la coyuntura de las restauraciones, 1819–1831* (Bogotá: Universidad Externado de Colombia, 2012), p. 271. Mexican officials also sought to avoid accusations of Jacobinism in 1821; see David Brading, *Los orígenes del nacionalismo mexicano.* Translated by Soledad Loaeza Grave (Mexico City: Secretaría de Educación Pública, 1973), p. 79.

[134] Antonio Sáenz, *Instituciones elementales sobre el derecho natural de gentes.* Noticia preliminar de Ricardo Levene (Buenos Aires: Instituto de Historia del Derecho Argentino, 1939), pp. 310–311.

[135] Lucas Alamán, *El reconocimiento de nuestra independencia por España y la unión de los países hispano-americanos.* With an introduction by Antonio de la Peña y Reyes (Mexico City: Publicaciones de la Secretaría de Relaciones Exteriores, 1924), pp. 65–76.

they argued, Spain had tacitly recognised the independence of the Dutch provinces.[136] Since Spain had negotiated a truce with Mexico, it followed that this could be seen as a recognition of independence. Mexican officials were likely aware of the contemporary echoes of Adam Smith's reading of the truce: had Spain accepted Dutch independence, and established an alliance with its former enemy, the Crown's power would have grown stronger in Europe.[137]

As officials debated whether or not to pay the nation's debts to Spain, one congressman cited Vattel's analysis of Philip II's bankruptcy to argue that, since Spain had ruled by virtue of force and conquest, it followed that Mexico could default on these debts. The Mexican statesman Lorenzo de Zavala countered that Spain, while ruled by an absolute ruler, had never tried to actually waste the empire's wealth. Zavala accepted that Mexico had been under a state of occupation at the time of the conquest, yet 'the nation that exists today is for the most part based on the mix between the conquerors and the conquered, and with some derived from the African peoples that the former brought over'. Many of the debts, then, belonged to 'children of the nation' who would be able to abandon their lives of misery if these bills were acknowledged and repaid.[138] Zavala also defended the rights of the creditors: it would be unfair to deprive financiers of their funds or their profits when they may well have sought to improve the nation, and investors could not always know whether or not rulers were causing harm to their people. Latin American authors had a better understanding of the history of the Spanish Empire than Grotius or Vattel—it was, after all, a history of their own making.

[136] Alamán, *El reconocimiento*, pp. 65–76. It was only during the negotiations of the truce that Dutch envoys to British and French courts were granted the title of ambassador, and terms of the accord allowed the Dutch to trade with the rest of the world. van Ittersum, *Profit and Principle*, p. 54; Nellen, *Hugo Grotius*, p. 104.

[137] As noted by Anthony Pagden, *Lords of all the World: Ideologies of Empire in Spain, Britain, and France c. 1500–1800* (New Haven: Yale University Press, 1995), p. 193.

[138] Juan Antonio Mateos, *Historia Parlamentaria De Los Congresos Mexicanos De 1821 A 1857.* Appendix to Volume 2 (Mexico City: J.V. Villada, 1882), p. 318. The revolutionary rhetoric of a familial relationship was a colonial legacy and served to mollify the more extreme tendencies; see Anna, *Spain and the Loss of America*, pp. 3–5. José María Portillo, *Crisis Atlántica: Autonomía e independencia en la crisis de la monarquía hispana* (Madrid: Marcial Pons, 2016), pp. 194–195, p. 208; François-Xavier Guerra, *Modernidad e independencias: ensayos sobre las revoluciones hispánicas* (México: FCE, 2010), pp. 150–151.

2

Sancho Panza's Promised Land

Spain's Default on its American Debts

The end of Caritas

The unresolved tension in Grotius' thought between debt and salvation was part of a broader fractious intellectual dispute in the Protestant world over the meaning of the Protestant Reformation. The Catholic Reformation advanced the expansion of religious orders and strengthened the influence of royal grace.[1] The proliferation of indulgences accompanied the rise of printing and offered predictable returns to printers.[2] In the Americas, this movement bolstered the expansion of the Quito School of Art which merged indigenous techniques with European trends. The artworks produced in the Andes and above all in Peru, a region that may have produced 60 per cent of the global silver supply, were widely acclaimed across Europe.[3] New Spain's economy in turn improved steadily, in part thanks to China's ever-growing demand for silver.[4]

In Europe, the Crown's interests were under assault. Spain had to adapt its diplomacy to the new rules of the game, and the norms of political economy and the law of nations were increasingly built on the works of Protestant authors. As the size of credit networks expanded in England and the Netherlands, commutative

[1] Carlos Eire, *Reformations: The Early Modern World, 1450–1650* (New Haven: Yale University Press, 2016), pp. 369–413; Simon Ditchfield, 'Catholic Reformation and Renewal', in Peter Marshall ed., *The Oxford Illustrated History of the Reformation* (Oxford: Oxford University Press, 2015), pp. 152–185; Leszek Kolakowski, *God Owes Us Nothing: A Brief Remark on Pascal's Religion and on the Spirit of Jansenism* (Chicago: University of Chicago Press, 1995). The Southern Netherlands, in response to the Dutch Revolt, generated a vision of atonement that fostered unity through the Catholic Reformation; see Judith Pollmann, *Catholic Identity and the Revolt of the Netherlands, 1520–1635* (Oxford: Oxford University Press, 2011), pp. 125–158.

[2] Paul Dover, *The Information Revolution in Early Modern Europe* (Cambridge: Cambridge University Press, 2021), p. 156.

[3] Carmen Fernández-Salvador, 'Uses of Tridentine Artistic Theory in Spanish America: Imaging the Christian Painter in Colonial Hagiography', *Hispanic Research Journal* 21:5 (2020), pp. 495–510; Harry E. Cross, 'South American Bullion Production and Export, 1550–1750,' in J. F. Richards ed., *Precious Metals in the Later Medieval and Early Modern Worlds* (Durham: North Carolina University Press, 1983), pp. 397–424, pp. 402–403; Dennis O. Flynn and Arturo Giráldez, 'Born with a "Silver Spoon": The Origin of World Trade in 1571', *Journal of World History* 6: 2 (1995), pp. 201–221, p. 209, n. 11.

[4] Herbert S. Klein, 'The Great Shift: the Rise of Mexico and the Decline of Peru in the Spanish American Colonial Empire, 1680–1809', *Revista De Historia Economica—Journal of Iberian and Latin American Economic History* 13:1 (1995), pp. 35–61; Dennis O. Flynn and Arturo Giráldez. 'Cycles of Silver: Global Economic Unity through the Mid-Eighteenth Century', *Journal of World History* 13:2 (2002), pp. 391–427.

Odious Debt. Edward Jones Corredera, Oxford University Press. © Edward Jones Corredera 2024.
DOI: 10.1093/9780191982200.003.0003

Protestant ideas of debt were replaced by abstract accounting, contractual principles, and the political economy of state banks. In Spain, by contrast, commutative Catholic ideas of debt remained the law of the land and the Crown increased its sales of titles, which ballooned in the late seventeenth century, in order to lower the public debt.[5] As European diplomats based their designs on the presumption that a Spanish king could be compelled by the law of nations or economic expediency to fulfil commercial contracts, these changes generated more questions than answers for Iberian administrators.

Iberian officials nonetheless understood the uses of Grotius' ideas decades before Samuel von Pufendorf was granted a Chair at the University of Heidelberg to preach them. In the 1640s, Catalan and Portuguese rebels drew on *De iure belli ac pacis* to establish a consistent logic to succession, secession, and *aeque principaliter* across the various parts of the Spanish Crown. As new discourses and practices of diplomacy became more dominant on a European stage and influenced the relationship between these states, Iberian rebels and rulers seized on Grotius' law of nations, at times opportunistically, at times judiciously, in an effort to bind this patrimonial kingdom to the rules of a composite monarchy.[6] But the Crown also took steps to reaffirm its patrimonial norms, its confessional core, and its commutative vision of debt: following the signing of the Peace of Westphalia, Philip IV sold the Cortes on the merits of the peace with the Netherlands: for the sake of the empire's 'relief', the Crown could now 'forgive' a number of debts.[7]

The uncertainty provoked by the War of Spanish Succession, however, ensured that foreign credit dried up. As more and more of the empire's credit depended on Castilian merchants, it became harder to mask the relationship between the quotidian monetary means needed to achieve sacred ends.[8] It was no longer possible to insulate the divine covenant from the profane demands of earthly contracts. The war further demonstrated that international law had eroded and replaced Spanish dynastic norms in Europe. During the war, imperial ties were eroded: the Spanish American *consulados* protected their commercial interests and frequently ignored the Crown's orders. Creole officials fostered smuggling with Dutch, French, and British traders, all while harnessing existing colonial structures to the benefit of the local mercantile interests. Powerful companies of freed black people in Caracas would soon trade freely with their peers in Curaçao and the official in charge of collecting the *alcabala* in Potosí would serve as an official of the South

[5] Craig Muldrew, *The Economy of Obligation: The Culture of Credit and Social Relations in Early Modern England* (London: Palgrave Macmillan, 1998), p. 65, pp. 320–328; Jan Vries, *The Industrious Revolution: Consumer Behavior and the Household Economy, 1650 to the Present* (Cambridge: Cambridge University Press, 2008), pp. 40–72.

[6] See Corredera, 'The End of Composite Monarchies'.

[7] Juen E. Gelabert, *La bolsa del Rey. Rey, reino y fisco en Castilla (1598–1648)* (Barcelona: Crítica, 1997), p. 126.

[8] Anne Dubet, 'José Patiño y el crédito de Felipe V ¿Un proyecto global?', *Obradoiro de Historia Moderna* 29 (2020), pp. 17–50.

Sea Company.[9] The war ended with the victory of Philip of Anjou, later Philip V. Philip was an absolute monarch who pursued an erratic foreign policy, abdicated the throne once, and threatened to abdicate again four years later. Political economists from Lima to Caracas demonstrated that corporations and the law of nations could protect the people from his tyranny.[10] In response to the publication of the 1737 Bilbao *Ordenanzas*, a merchant code that enacted sweeping reforms of Spanish commercial law, foreign merchants demanded a meeting with the Bilbao Consulado, where they explained that, in the age of reason, the norms of trade were settled through diplomacy, not unilateral legal reform.[11] The *Ordenanzas* nonetheless provided an illustrative overview of the main types of bankruptcies that emerged in the Spanish Empire. The code divided insolvent debtors into three categories: those who had simply failed to pay on time but had the means to settle their affairs in good faith, those who had suffered misfortunes at sea and could renegotiate their loans, and those who had recklessly speculated with the money of others.[12]

Spanish officials gradually learned to harness the rules of diplomacy to limit the King's authority and establish new alliances in Europe. As Philip was forced to declare bankruptcy in the middle of two wars, with Austria and Britain, Spanish diplomats designed mechanisms to prevent the King from impetuously speculating with the money that aimed to satisfy the needs of the people.[13] José Carvajal y Lancaster, member of the Council of the Indies and erstwhile diplomat, sketched a plan to create an alliance with Britain, Portugal, and Austria against France. Inspired by the abbé de Saint-Pierre's writings, he hoped to exploit Spain's administration of the Mexican *peso*, the main currency used in Sino-European trade, in order to establish a union of European powers through a corporate coalition of princes.

There was not much point in studying the debate between Grotius and Selden, reasoned Carvajal, since 'peace treaties' and commercial interests now shaped the law of nations.[14] Royal Anglo-Spanish investment in a trading company would check the King's worst impulses, foreclose the possibility of war, and ensure that the wealth of the empire was used for the development of arts and industry. Britain, he noted, was republican enough to limit costly monarchical ventures and monarchical enough to preserve stability. This alliance would turn Spain's patrimonial kingdom into a composite monarchy. The burden of empire would be shared. The problem of the spiralling debt that resulted from inter-imperial competition,

[9] Edward Jones Corredera, *The Diplomatic Enlightenment: Spain, Europe, and the Age of Speculation* (Leiden: Brill, 2021), p. 87, p. 109.
[10] Corredera, *The Diplomatic Enlightenment*, pp. 109–124, p. 129.
[11] Corredera, *The Diplomatic Enlightenment*, pp. 119–123.
[12] *Ordenanzas*, pp. 132–134.
[13] Corredera, *The Diplomatic Enlightenment*, pp. 89–90.
[14] Corredera, *The Diplomatic Enlightenment*, p. 131.

which so worried other thinkers like David Hume, would be neutralised.[15] Control of the most important currency in world trade, managed by the two crowns, would lead to solvency and peace. Perhaps debt could retain its salvific force after all. Together, Spain and Britain would be 'lords of the seas'.[16]

Following Philip's death, the coronation of his son Ferdinand VI encouraged new hopes of reform throughout the empire. Some rebels called for revolutionary measures. In Peru, Fray Calixto de San José Túpac Inca penned an incendiary narrative where he suggested that the self-rule of indigenous communities would remedy the effects of imperial mismanagement.[17] The rebel Juan Santos Atahualpa Apu-Inca Huayna Capac in turn believed that British naval cooperation would allow him to lead indigenous peoples and reconquer Peru for the 'Incan Crown' that 'Pizarro' and the Spaniards had once usurped.[18] When Spain tried to shore up its control of the cocoa trade in Caracas through the expansion of the Caracas Company, hundreds of *mulatos*, *zambos*, and Indians marched into Caracas and gathered around the governor's house to protest against this corporation. The earliest reports submitted to the Council of the Indies suggested that the rebels would 'follow a different King' unless the company was abolished. Spanish officials had seen this play before: as one member of the Council of the Indies noted, the rebels were following the same steps as 'the Prince of Orange' in the Dutch Revolt.[19] Rumours suggested that one of the leaders of the insurrection had sailed for Cuba to foster a slave insurrection in the island.[20] Was this the beginning of the end of the Spanish Empire?

Once Carvajal y Lancaster was made Ferdinand VI's universal minister, he carried out a number of enlightened reforms to improve relations between the Crown, its territories, and the rest of the world. Carvajal y Lancaster, along with the Prime Minister Zenón de Somodevilla y Bengoechea, the marquess of Ensenada, increased the Crown's returns on the silver trade; pacified protests; fostered a debate on free trade at the Council of the Indies; created an imperial bank; promoted the expansion of academies; improved the state of the navy; created a network of industrial spies across Europe; and negotiated favourable treaties with Britain, Austria, and Portugal.[21] As these reforms were underway, Spanish authors produced a number of works on Grotius and the law of nations that aimed

[15] See Richard Whatmore, *The End of Enlightenment: Empire, Commerce, Crisis* (London: Allen Lane, 2023), pp. 19–49.

[16] Corredera, 'The End of Composite Monarchies'; Pablo Fernández Albaladejo, *La crisis de la monarquía* (Barcelona: Crítica, 2009), pp. 303–358.

[17] Alcira Dueñas, *Indians and Mestizos in the "Lettered City": Reshaping Justice, Social Hierarchy, and Political Culture in Colonial Peru* (Boulder: University of Colorado, 2010), pp. 65–71.

[18] Francisco A. Loayza, *Juan Santos: el invencible: manuscritos del año de 1742 al año de 1755* (Lima: Editorial Domingo Miranda, 1942), pp. 10–11; Corredera, *The Diplomatic Enlightenment*, p. 152.

[19] Corredera, *The Diplomatic Enlightenment*, pp. 153–154.

[20] Corredera, *The Diplomatic Enlightenment*, p. 155.

[21] Corredera, *The Diplomatic Enlightenment*, p. 140–174. On the inevitable tensions that were to surface between a universal minister and a prime minister see pp. 137–139.

to reconsider Spain's role in the world and trace a roadmap towards peace.[22] By 1753, on the basis of Spain's growing collaboration with Britain, Austria, and Portugal, Carvajal y Lancaster believed he had 'fulfilled' Saint-Pierre's dream of 'perpetual peace' in Europe.[23] World peace, he hoped, would be established by consolidating the debts of the two empires and investing in a durable balance of power.

As part of his programme of Enlightenment reform, Carvajal oversaw a commission established to consider whether the debts that were 'owed since the time of Charles V' belonged 'to the King or the Kingdom'.[24] The commission's report reflected the enduring influence of commutative visions of debt, and the idea of *deber*, on the Spanish Court and noted that 'the Kingdom has provided such great contributions in the past years', and that 'so many resources from the Americas' had arrived, that it appeared 'morally impossible' to avoid repaying the Crown's debts.[25] Yet the principle of 'charity' appeared to favour the improvement of the lives of the people over the repayment of foreign debts.[26] The 'right of the people', who suffered 'from notorious poverty' to enjoy the 'relief from taxation' suggested these sums ought to be used for the improvement of their welfare. However, the Crown also had to consider 'the right of creditors'.[27] The question of 'utility' clashed with concerns of justice: on the one hand, justice seemed to dictate that, to compensate for the delay of almost two hundred years, the heirs of the creditors should be paid first.[28] On the other hand, the more politically expedient measure was to pay the lenders who had most recently contributed to the improvement of the imperial finances. This would incentivise them to invest in the Crown again, which would allow the Crown to address poverty. Yet creating a fund to repay the debts of past and future successors to the Crown could lead to criticisms that the empire's wealth was being monopolised by the royal family and was 'of no use to the people'.[29]

The report concluded that there was a way to square the circle: the settlement of these loans, reasoned the authors of the text, would ultimately benefit the people because it would foster further investment in the Crown. Indeed, the improvement

[22] José María Iñurritegui Rodríguez, 'Traducción y geografías del interés en la temprana Ilustración hispana', *Studia Historica. Historia Moderna* 43:2 (2021) pp. 283–304; Corredera, *The Diplomatic Enlightenment*, pp. 160–174.

[23] Corredera, *The Diplomatic Enlightenment*, p. 138, pp. 175–202.

[24] 'Reflexiones sobre las deudas del Rey; si estas son del Rei [sic] o del Reino', in *Papeles referentes a las deudas de la Real Hacienda en tiempos de Fernando VI y de Carlos III* (c. 1756–1768). Biblioteca Nacional de España, MSS/13814. pp. 1–157. As noted by Lucas Alamán, *Disertaciones sobre la historia de la república Megicana, desde la época de la conquista que los españoles hicieron hasta la independencia.* Volume 3 (Mexico City: Lara, 1849), pp. 272–273.

[25] 'Reflexiones sobre las deudas del Rey', p. 3.

[26] 'Reflexiones sobre las deudas del Rey', p. 30.

[27] 'Reflexiones sobre las deudas del Rey', p. 6.

[28] 'Reflexiones sobre las deudas del Rey', p. 19.

[29] 'Reflexiones sobre las deudas del Rey', p. 32. Something that Bentham would later argue in his writings against the Spanish Crown.

of people's lives would help generate financial support for the Crown's foreign affairs, just as Britain, by safeguarding the wealth of its people, had been able to raise funds in the recent War of the Austrian Succession.[30] The report noted that Spain was an 'absolute monarchy' and thus the debts were inherited by the people and the King, who were one and the same.[31] The Crown had to find a way to liquidate the debts from past sovereigns to meet the obligations that the Habsburg dynasty had failed to fulfil—a task Ferdinand VI started but which would remain unresolved at the Cádiz Cortes.[32] Paradoxically, conservative Latin American officials would later use this debate to draw attention to the constancy of Ferdinand's fiscal reforms. Described by Lucas Alamán as 'the bankruptcy of Ferdinand VI', he noted that while this 'arbitrary procedure' of debt reorganisation was wrong, the government's creditworthiness improved because its promise to settle these payments was, he claimed, eventually fulfilled.[33]

The death of Carvajal and the emergence of the Seven Years' War put an end to mid-century Spanish efforts to find peace through the consolidation of federations.[34] Spanish officials began to use a new term—the nation—and the Crown was forced to find new sources of revenue and accept a closer union with a predatory France. The implementation of a decree on free trade prevented France from gaining complete control of Spain's imperial commerce.[35] In the Spanish Americas, the revolutionary turmoil in French and British colonies fostered violent popular revolts and encouraged the colonial elites to cooperate with the Spanish Court—and to accept its tax hikes.[36] In the face of popular riots and protests in Peru and New Granada, Joaquín de Finestrad, a Capuchin priest based in Bogotá, warned the insurrectionists against emulating foreign aspirations based on the rights of

[30] 'Reflexiones sobre las deudas del Rey', pp. 30–31.

[31] 'Reflexiones sobre las deudas del Rey', pp. 58–59.

[32] On efforts made by Philip V, Ferdinand VI, and Charles III to remedy this issue see Francisco Comín Comín, *Las crisis de la deuda soberana en España (1500–2015)* (Madrid: Catarata, 2016), pp. 103–111. On the political uses of charity in the early modern Spanish Empire see the contributions by Julia McClure and Regina Grafe in Julia McClure ed., 'Editors' Forum: Empires of Charity', *New Global Studies* 2:12 (2018). On late eighteenth-century Spanish debates on how Catholic ideas of charity could be reconciled with the rise of capitalist passions see Julián Viejo Yharrassarry, *Amor propio y sociedad comercial en el siglo XVIII hispano* (Bilbao: Universidad del País Vasco, 2018), pp. 57–72.

[33] Alamán, *Disertaciones*, p. 272.

[34] Corredera, 'The End of Composite Monarchies'.

[35] Edward Jones Corredera, 'Free Trade & the Ghost Story of the Bourbon Alliance: Spain, Free Ports, and the Mediterranean Sea, c. 1648–1765', in Giulia Delogu, Koen Stapelbroek, Antonio Trampus eds., *Free Trade and Free Ports in the Mediterranean* (London: Routledge, 2024), pp. 198-213.

[36] Gabriel Paquette, 'State-Civil Society Cooperation and Conflict in the Spanish Empire: The Intellectual and Political Activities of the Ultramarine Consulados and Economic Societies, c. 1780–1810', *Journal of Latin American Studies* 39:2 (2007), pp. 263–298; Jeremy Baskes, *Staying Afloat: Risk and Uncertainty in Spanish Atlantic World Trade, 1760–1820* (Redwood: Stanford University Press, 2013), pp. 110–145; Brian R. Hamnett, *The End of Iberian Rule on the American Continent, 1770–1830* (Cambridge: Cambridge University Press, 2017), pp. 31–52; Carlos Marichal, *Bankruptcy of Empire: Mexican Silver and the Wars Between Spain, Britain and France, 1760–1810* (Cambridge: Cambridge University Press, 2009); José María Portillo, *Una historia atlántica de los orígenes de la nación y el Estado* (Madrid: Alianza, 2022), pp. 63–64.

man: 'since you did not want to live in seas of clemency you will perish in the abysses of justice'.[37]

As revolutions spread across the Atlantic, new historical readings of the Spanish Crown emerged: one of the most astute readers of Adam Smith and Montesquieu at the service of the Crown of Spain, Alessandro Malaspina, concluded that Spain had never benefited from the silver mines. These mines had generated the illusion that Spain could rely on their production of silver as a type of eternal 'debit' that would never have to be paid, a delusion which had fostered the rise of the *ferias* and hindered the establishment of industry in the Iberian Peninsula.[38] Spain had been nothing more than a broker between creoles and European merchants and now had to establish a favourable balance of industrial production across the Iberian Peninsula and in the Americas.[39] Instead, when the wars with Britain and France intensified, Spain experimented with the establishment of its first national bank, the Banco de San Carlos, and the emission of paper money and government bonds, or *vales reales*.[40] In order to protect Spain from a French invasion, Charles IV signed a treaty of neutrality with Napoleon whereby he agreed to pay six million francs per month to France. It soon became clear that the only way to fund this monthly payment was to consolidate the *vales*. The Crown seized control of the administration of the debts, the capital, and the properties of the Church.[41] New Spain provided more than 70 per cent of the American contributions to the consolidation of this public debt.[42]

As the elites of New Spain watched their wealth disappear at pace, officials like the enlightened Bishop of Michoacán Manuel Abad y Queipo complained that New Spain had always generously sacrificed its wealth and willingly 'donated' its riches to support the Crown. This was a question of charity and *deber*: it had never asked for anything in return. New Spain had never even requested metropolitan support for the preservation of its defence. The Crown was rewarding New Spain's good faith by creating a number of onerous 'obligations' that could never be binding on a Catholic monarchy and conducting a 'universal seizure of

[37] Quoted in Jairo Antonio Melo Flórez, 'Clemencia y obediencia. El vínculo amoroso entre el rey y los vasallos del Nuevo Reino de Granada entre 1780 y 1800', *Historia Crítica* 78 (2020), pp. 25–43, p. 43. On the rise of the "*juntas de damas*" as agents of the administration of charity see Catherine M. Jaffe and Elisa Martín-Valdepeñas Yagüe eds., *Society Women and Enlightened Charity in Spain The Junta de Damas de Honor y Mérito, 1787–1823* (Baton Rouge: Louisiana State University Press, 2022).

[38] A point made by Montesquieu; see Carrithers and Stewart, 'Statecraft', pp. 180–182. Alejandro Malaspina, 'Axiomas Políticos sobre América', in Manuel Lucena Giraldo and Juan Pimentel eds., *Los 'Axiomas políticos sobre la América' de Alejandro Malaspina* (Aranjuez: Sociedad Estatal Quinto Centenario, 1991), pp. 145–200, p. 171.

[39] Malaspina, 'Axiomas, pp. 171–173, pp. 175–195.

[40] Comín, *Las crisis*, pp. 111–121; Gisela von Wobeser, *Dominación colonial. La consolidación de Vales Reales en Nueva España, 1804–1812* (Mexico City: UNAM, 2003), pp. 19–24.

[41] von Wobeser, *Dominación colonial*, pp. 27–28; Gisela von Wobeser, 'La consolidación de vales reales como factor determinante de la lucha de independencia en México, 1804–1808', *Historia Mexicana* 56:2 (2006), pp. 373–425, p. 376.

[42] Wobeser, 'La consolidación', p. 370.

all the properties of the kingdom'.[43] It was nothing less than a 'notorious offence against commutative justice'.[44] Threatened by the prospect of personal bankruptcy, Abad y Quiepo's friend, Fray Miguel Hidalgo y Costilla, began to plot against the viceregal government.[45] Across the Americas, clerics and viceroys remonstrated with the Crown and petitioned the King to end the seizure of Church goods in their lands. The Crown eventually suspended the consolidation of the *vales* but the flame of Hidalgo's revolution had already been kindled. In the midst of the revolt, thousands of people turned to confession and requested individual royal pardons to demonstrate their confessional loyalty to the Crown. Blanket pardons were administered to entire communities for the remission of sin.[46] In defence of the insurgency, Hidalgo argued that New Spain's 'dependence on the Peninsula over 300 years' had led to the Crown's 'abuse of the Mexican's wealth' which, Hidalgo predicted, 'will one day lead to their absolution'.[47]

The Holy Roman Spanish Empire

In 1810, as Hidalgo spearheaded the rebellion in New Spain and Napoleonic troops continued to march across the Iberian Peninsula, the Junta Central, the last peninsular council to rule on behalf of the Spanish Crown, was dissolved. Spanish American and Spanish representatives met at the Cádiz Cortes to sketch a new constitutional framework to protect and preserve the territorial integrity of the Spanish Empire.[48] Cádiz was a cosmopolitan town in the middle of a war zone: half of the population in the city was made up of foreigners and the port, protected by the British navy, remained open for business. Merchants and officials had to be alert to the threat of yellow fever.[49] Most of the representatives at the Cortes were religious, military, or legal officials.[50] At the first meeting of the Cortes, those present were asked to swear to 'support the Holy, Catholic, Apostolic, Roman

[43] Reprinted in José Luis María Mora's *Revista Política*: see *Obras sueltas de José María Luis Mora, ciudadano mexicano* (Mexico City: Editorial Porrúa, 1963), pp. 214–221.

[44] Masae Sugawara ed., *La deuda pública de España y la economía novohispana, 1804–1809* (Mexico City: INAH, 1976), p. 64.

[45] Hidalgo was already heavily indebted before the establishment of the *vales reales*. See Carlos Herrejón Peredo, 'El endeudamiento de Hidalgo', *Relaciones. Estudios de historia y sociedad*, 34:133 (2013), pp. 199–223; Enrique Krauze, *Mexico: Biography of Power. A History of Modern Mexico, 1810–1996*. Translated by Hanz Heifetz (New York: Harper Collins, 1997), pp. 84–96.

[46] van Young, *The Other Rebellion*, pp. 118–126.

[47] Miguel Ángel Fernández Delgado ed., *Los Sentimientos de la Nación de José María Morelos. Antología documental*. Prólogo de Patricia Galeana (Mexico City: INEH, 2013), p. 40.

[48] On the military situation and the response of the Junta Central see François-Xavier Guerra, *Modernidad e independencias: ensayos sobre las revoluciones hispánicas* (México: FCE, 2010), p. 132.

[49] Marie-Laure Rieu-Millan, 'Presencia Americana en Cádiz y en las Cortes. Encuentros y desencuentros', in Scarlett O'Phelan Godoy y Georges Lomné, eds. *Voces americanas en las Cortes de Cádiz*, pp. 21–38, pp. 23–24.

[50] Quinti Casals Bergés, 'Proceso electoral y prosopografía de los diputados de las Cortes Extraordinarias de Cádiz (1810–1813), *Historia Constitucional* 13 (2012), pp. 194–231, p. 231.

religion without admitting any other in these realms'. A Te Deum was read and only then could the representatives voice the rallying cry 'long live the nation and long live the Cortes'.[51] These congressional debates resulted in the establishment of the Cádiz Constitution, a charter which represented Spaniards from 'both sides of the Atlantic' and established that sovereignty resided with the nation. This code enshrined into law the freedom of the press, abolished the Indian tribute and the Inquisition, and curtailed the influence of clerical authorities.[52] The Constitution reaffirmed the empire's Catholic heritage: the end of the Inquisition was instead portrayed as a way to ensure the survival of the faith.[53]

Private property and definitions of liberty were subject to the administrative needs of the state and the precepts set by the Catholic faith.[54] Colonial duties were reconfigured as a civilising enterprise and were connected with broader ideas of citizenship.[55] As the late Bartolomé Clavero showed, Spanish and Spanish American officials at Cádiz endorsed the ideas of Jeremy Bentham and not those of John Locke; there was, as Bentham noted, no natural law that secured private rights. There was only a civil code.[56] While article two of the Constitution noted

[51] On the uses of the Te Deum in these debates throughout the empire see Pablo Marcos Ortemberg, 'El tedeum en el ritual político: usos y sentidos de un dispositivo de pactos en la América española y en la revolución de Mayo', *Anuario del Instituto de Historia Argentina* 10:12 (2010), pp. 199–226; Jaime Olveda, 'El repudio a la Constitución de Cádiz', in Breña, *Cádiz a debate*, pp. 321-338, pp. 325–327; José María Portillo, *Crisis Atlántica: Autonomía e independencia en la crisis de la monarquía hispana* (Madrid: Marcial Pons, 2016), p. 71.

[52] Timothy Anna, *Spain and the Loss of America* (London: University of Nebraska Press, 1983), pp. 74–75. On the tax reforms implemented during this period see Hamnett, *The End of Iberian Rule*, pp. 202–205.

[53] José María Portillo, 'De la Monarquía Católica a la Nación de los Católicos', *Historia y Política* 17 (2007), pp. 17–35, pp. 33–35.

[54] See how constitutions in the Banda Oriental addressed the question of property rights in Botana, *Repúblicas y monarquías. La encrucijada de la independencia* (Buenos Aires: Edhasa, 2016), pp. 172–174; on the way Mexican thought approached this matter see David Brading, *Los orígenes del nacionalismo mexicano.* Translated by Soledad Loaeza Grave (México: Secretaría de Educación Pública, 1973), pp. 102–105 and Charles Hale, *El liberalismo mexicano en la época de Mora.* Translated by Serio Fernández Bravo and Francisco González Aramburu (Mexico City: Siglo XXI, 2012), pp. 67–70. See also Portillo, *Crisis Atlántica*, p. 232–235; José María Portillo, 'La libertad entre evangelio y constitución: Notas para el concepto de libertad política en la cultura española de 1812', in José María Portillo and José María Iñurritegui eds., *Constitución en España. Orígenes y destinos* (Madrid: CEPC, 1998), pp. 139–178; Guerra, *Modernidad e independencias*, pp. 321–322.

[55] Portillo, *Crisis Atlántica*, p. 231; Josep Fradera, 'Reescribir las reglas del juego colonial: discurso, representación, y lobbying', in Scarlett O'Phelan Godoy y Georges Lomné eds., *Voces americanas en las Cortes de Cádiz: 1810–1814* (Lima: Institut Français d'Études Andines, 2014), pp. 141–156.

[56] Bartolomé Clavero, *Razón de estado, razón de individuo, razón de historia* (Madrid: Centro de Constitucionales, 1991), pp. 192–231. Guerra, *Modernidad e independencias*, pp. 358–359. See Portillo, *Crisis Atlántica*, pp. 179–180; José María Portillo, *Revolución de nación. Orígenes de la cultura constitucional en España, 1780–1812* (Madrid: Centro de Estudios Políticos y Constitucionales, 2000), pp. 152–153, pp. 384–397; Ignacio Fernández Sarasola, 'La proyección de los derechos individuales', in Encarna García Monerris and Carmen García Monerris eds., *Guerra, Revolución, Constitución (1808 y 2008)* (Valencia: Universidad de Valencia, 2012), pp. 239–268. On unsuccessful efforts to entrench ideas of natural law in the Constitution see Joaquín Varela Suanzes-Carpegna, *La teoría del Estado en las Cortes de Cádiz* (Madrid: Centro de Estudios Políticos y Constitucionales, 2012) and José Antonio Aguilar Rivera, 'Memoria del cogido imposible: Cádiz y el experimento constitucional atlántico', in Roberto Breña ed., *Cádiz a debate: Actualidad, contexto y legado* (Mexico City: Colegio de México, 2014), pp. 107-130, pp. 121–123.

that the nation was not and could never be the 'patrimony of a family or a person', the patrimonial principles behind existing property rights and socio-economic inequality were perpetuated by this new charter.[57] European discussions about the Cádiz debates ensured that the word 'liberalism' gained prominence in the Old World and this constitution had a profound influence on the politics of the Mediterranean World.[58] While the text was foundational in shaping Mexican constitutionalism, elsewhere in Latin America it remained a constitutional sketch that offered one of many definitions of a nation and a state.[59]

The Constitution, after all, reflected the lack of attention displayed towards the Spanish Americas at the Cortes.[60] Spanish American representatives, however, contributed to these debates with some of the most far-reaching insights about the institutional inequalities of the Spanish Empire.[61] The Peruvian José Mejía Lequerica, a Latin and philosophy professor, was a member of the committee tasked with the study of the reform of Spain's public credit.[62] When the Cortes debated whether to disavow any acts or accords that the King of Spain might sign abroad without its consent, Mejía Lequerica stood up and delivered a rousing speech on *translatio imperii*, the law of nations, and the rights of man.[63]

[57] Note the use of the Mexican *cabildo* of the idea of the empire as the King's 'mayorazgo' in Guerra, *Modernidad e independencias*, pp. 323–324. Post-independence approaches to native people and their land remained, as Portillo has noted, profoundly influenced by Spanish traditions; see Portillo, *Crisis Atlántica*, p. 225–227 and Antonio Annino, 'La Historiografía', in Rafael Rojas, Antonio Annino, and Francisco A. Eissa-Barroso, *La independencia: los libros de la patria* (México: CIDE, 2008), pp. 84–95. As Vejo has noted, the 'Political Constitution of the Spanish Monarchy', with its title, claimed to represent 'the Spanish Monarchy', and not 'the Spanish Nation', see Tomás Pérez Vejo, *3 de Julio de 1898: El significado de una fecha* (Madrid: Taurus, 2020), p. 190.

[58] Ignacio Fernández Sarasola, *La Constitución de Cádiz: Orígen, contenido y proyección internacional* (Madrid: CEPC, 2011); Maurizio Isabella, *Southern Europe in the Age of Revolutions* (Princeton: Princeton University Press, 2023), pp. 18–27; Duncan Bell, 'What is Liberalism?', *Political Theory* 42:6 (2014), pp. 682–715, p. 693.

[59] A point made by a number of scholars, including Enrique Gandía, *Rivadavia y su tiempo* (Buenos Aires: Claridad, 1990), p. 68 and p. 74; Fabio Wasserman, 'El concepto de nación y las transformaciones del orden político en Iberoamérica, 1750–1850', *Jahrbuch für Geschichte Lateinamerikas* 45 (2008), pp. 197–220', p. 207. See also Manuel Chust, 'La Constitución de 1812: una revolución constitutional bihemisférica', in Antonio Annino y Marcela Ternavasio eds. *El Laboratório constitucional iberoamericano: 1807/1808–1830* (Madrid: Iberoamericana, 2012), pp. 93–114. For the argument that the text influenced indigenous views of politics see Javier Fernández Sebastián, *Historia conceptual en el Atlántico ibérico: Lenguajes, tiempos, revoluciones* (Madrid: FCEE, 2021), p. 191 and Bartolomé Clavero, 'Cádiz entre indígenas: Lecturas y lecciones sobre la Constitución y su cultura en tierra de los mayas', *Anuario de Historia del Derecho Español* 65 (1995), pp. 931–992.

[60] Anna, *Spain and the Loss of America*, p. 113; Rieu-Millan, 'Presencia Americana', pp. 28–29 and Marie Laure Rieu-Millan, *Los diputados americanos en las Cortes de Cádiz (Igualdad o independencia)* (Madrid: CSIC, 1990), pp. 69–74.

[61] On the question of representation and race see Rieu-Millan, *Los diputados*, pp. 10–20.

[62] For a summary of his other contributions to debates see Ana Luz Borrego Vega, 'José Mejía Lequerica y José Joaquín de Olmedo', in Godoy y Lomné eds., *Voces Americanas*, pp. 207–216; Anna, *Spain and the Loss of America*, p. 68; Rieu-Millan, *Los diputados*, pp. 55–56, p. 149.

[63] Alfredo Flores y Caamaño, *Don José Mejía Lequerica en las Cortes de Cádiz de 1810 a 1813: (o sea el principal defensor de los intereses de la América española en la más grande asamblea de la península)* (Barcelona: Casa Editorial Maucci, 1913), pp. 202–213. On the origins of this view of America as its own sovereign nation see Wasserman, 'El concepto de nación y las transformaciones del orden político', pp. 210–211. Bello would draw on the idea of *translatio imperii* in his assessment of Spain's colonial

The Spanish people should square up to Napoleon, a 'Crowned Machiavelli': they had been endowed with an authority that had once only belonged to kings. Instead, he argued, the congressmen in Cádiz, the majority of which were peninsular Spaniards, were shying away from their historic responsibility.[64] Spanish Americans, by contrast, would never renege on this duty, nor would they ever be within reach of the enemy. Mejía Lequerica depicted the Spanish Empire as the bulwark of global peace against Napoleon.[65] He did not defend 'the cause of Spain' for its own sake, rather because 'the interests and rights of all mankind rest on its cause'.[66] The 'fate of humankind' depended on Europe, and Europe's own future rested on Spain and its Cortes. If the 'ship of state' capsized, the last plank standing would be America, responsible for saving 'the Cortes, the *patria*, and humanity'. Mejía Lequerica's words made clear that the Spanish Americas were now *primus inter pares*—first among equals—in the Spanish Crown.

By shifting the debate from an imperial to a universal outlook, Mejía Lequerica could defend an otherwise controversial view: the inevitability of *translatio imperii* from Spain to the Spanish Americas: 'it is important to remember that the sceptres are passed from one people to another once inequality occupies the seat of justice'. Drawing on the examples of the Egyptian, Babylonian, Persian, Syrian, and Roman empires, Mejía Lequerica explained that 'all that is born dies' and only 'truth remains'. Truth, he explained, was derived from 'the rights of man, the obligations of monarchs, and the responsibility of those judges who sit and decide the destinies of one and the other'. In this context, carrying out this obligation with 'impartiality and decorum' was 'the first principle of universal justice'. America would embrace this responsibility: if the King of Spain chose to enslave the empire to 'the French' without the consent of the Cortes, the 'honourable Castilians' could count on 'the Americans', who would act with 'fraternal love' and 'unlimited hospitality'.[67]

The time to 'say goodbye to Troy' had not yet come, continued Mejía Lequerica, offering some hope to his Spanish counterparts.[68] How then could the Spanish Empire be sustained until the monarchical question was resolved? Mejía

past; see Andrés Bello, 'Investigaciones sobre la influencia de la Conquista y del sistema colonial de los españoles en Chile', in *Obras completas de Andrés Bello*. Volume 23: *Temas de historia y geografía* (Caracas: Ministerio de Educación, 1957), pp. 153–173, pp. 165–166.

[64] Caamaño, *Don José Mejía*, p. 203. Mejía had also advocated for the introduction of the Cortes to be referred to as 'majesty', thereby appropriating the King's title, and was acutely aware of the tensions involved in the process of independence. See Jaime E. Rodríguez O., *'We Are Now the true Spaniards' Sovereignty, Revolution, Independence, and the Emergence of the Federal Republic of Mexico, 1808–1824* (Stanford: Stanford University Press, 2012), p. 152 and Portillo, *Crisis Atlántica*, p. 152–154.

[65] As Isaac Nakhimovsky has shown, US representatives would draw on similar evocative terms to describe the heroic role of Russia, the *ami des hommes*, which, following Napoleon's retreat, had helped humanity by forestalling the rise of universal despotism. See Isaac Nakhimovsky, *The Holy Alliance: Liberalism and the Politics of Federation* (Princeton: Princeton University Press, 2024), p. 90.

[66] Caamaño, *Don José Mejía*, pp. 211–212.

[67] Caamaño, *Don José Mejía*, pp. 211–213.

[68] Caamaño, *Don José Mejía*, pp. 211–213.

Lequerica drew on a powerful historical analogy: The Holy Roman Empire.[69] While it was a 'despotic monarchy', since the time of the Peace of Westphalia, the formation and ratification of treaties was organised by the 'reunion of princes' who were, like rebellious regions of the Spanish Empire, 'frequently enemies of one another, and even of the empire'. There was, in Mejía Lequerica's view, no difference between the Cortes, which 'represented a single state, with a single and uniform constitution, and reunited all its members', all of which were animated by the 'spirit of common and indivisible interest'.[70] There was therefore no reason for any other European power which had negotiated with the Imperial Diet to refuse to confer with the Cortes.[71] The treaty-based law of nations that, according to some, emerged from the negotiations of the Holy Roman Empire, a true composite monarchy, could set the example for the political administration of the Spanish Empire while the Spanish world retained its culturally and institutionally religious core.[72] In this speech, Mejía Lequerica's warning of *translatio imperii* united the logic of God's donation of the Americas to Spain and the law of nations—the Spanish Americas would now inherit the burden of empire. This was a compromise that offered the possibility of reconciliation.[73] Hispanic approaches to the law of nations would emerge in the aftermath of the failure to develop a Holy Roman Spanish Empire.

In a discussion over the creation of a Treasury Board for the whole empire, Mejía Lequerica noted that the codes that governed trade in the Peninsula and the Americas, the *Partidas* and the *Leyes de Indias*, differed greatly.[74] More broadly, the history of Spain's administration of its debt was a model of mismanagement.

[69] On how the dilemmas of reconciling 'national' law and international law were manifested in the Holy Roman Empire see Martti Koskenniemi, *To the Uttermost Parts Parts of the Earth: Legal Imagination and International Power 1300–1870* (Cambridge: Cambridge University Press, 2021), pp. 808–809.

[70] On the problem of representation during the congressional sessions see Jeremy Adelman, *Sovereignty and Revolution in the Iberian Atlantic* (Princeton: Princeton University Press, 2006), p. 195.

[71] Caamaño, *Don José Mejía*, pp. 341–342. Scholars have compared these federative schemes to the British Commonwealth, but the Holy Roman Empire is the more natural example. On the Commonwealth example see Rodríguez, '*We Are Now the true Spaniards*', p. 2: Portillo, *Crisis Atlántica*, p. 172; and on the Swiss model see Portillo, *Revolución de nación*, p. 162.

[72] Mejía's speech could be seen as a break with the earlier tradition of a uniquely Hispanic federation studied in Portillo, *Crisis Atlántica*, pp. 70–103. See also Antonio Annino et al eds., *El momento gaditano: La Constitución en el orbe hispánico (1808–1826)* (Madrid: Congreso de los Diputados, 2011), pp. 210–228. For a critique of the myth of Westphalia see Randall Lesaffer, 'Peace Treaties from Lodi to Westphalia', in Randall Lesaffer ed., *Peace Treaties and International Law in European History: From the Late Middle Ages to World War One* (Cambridge: Cambridge University Press, 2004), pp. 9–44.

[73] It was in this context that some of the invocations to the sixteenth century must be understood; *contra* Fernández Sebastián, *Historia conceptual*, pp. 292–299 and Javier Fernández Sebastián, 'A Distorting Mirror: The Sixteenth Century in the Historical Imagination of the First Hispanic Liberals', *History of European Ideas* 41:2 (2015), pp. 166–175, and on the view that this was an emancipation from the imperial, but not from its religion, see José María Portillo, *Una historia atlántica de los orígenes de la nación y el Estado: España y las Españas en el siglo XIX* (Madrid: Alianza, 2022).

[74] Caamaño, *Don José Mejía*, pp. 351–352. More recently noted in Adelman, *Republic of Capital*, p. 145.

Spanish sovereigns had failed to inspire trust in spite of their 'good will': the burden of the empire ensured that the money allocated towards debt repayment was assigned to pressing enterprises instead.[75] Before his early death, Mejía Lequerica defended the commission's plan to find a way to deploy a number of resources, including the goods of the Inquisition, to stabilise the public debt, a measure which would eventually be approved.[76]

It was not clear whether the differences between Spanish lands on both sides of the Atlantic had gone too far, or whether the Cortes' reforms were enough to galvanise the people to invest their trust in the new regime. One of the wisest measures implemented by the Cortes compelled priests to preach the virtues of the Constitution to their congregations to foster popular support for the new charter.[77] In the event, the 1812 Cádiz Constitution served as a source of Hispanic communion and as a reference for some Latin American states, most notably Mexico. But unresolved economic questions revealed and deepened the fractures between the composite parts of the empire.

Property and sovereignty in a bankrupt empire

The improvement of Spain's commercial system was one way to finance Spain's public debt and shore up colonial sympathy for the Cortes.[78] Based on his brief time in London, the Spanish official Álvaro Flórez Estrada offered a solution in his *Examen* that he hoped would please Spaniards on both sides of the Atlantic: the establishment of a system of free trade that would favour the Spanish Americas.[79] The pursuit of an economic compromise echoed the memory of the *vales* and a number of Latin American demands that were ignored by the Cádiz Cortes. The emphasis on the balance of trade at the expense of greater representation granted Latin American authors a powerful rhetorical ploy to reject the financial benefits of remaining attached to the Spanish Empire—and to deny that its survival

[75] Caamaño, *Don José Mejía*, p. 512; Hamnett, *The End of Iberian Rule*, p. 213.

[76] Caamaño, *Don José Mejía*, p. 523.

[77] Mark Lawrence, 'Constitutional Catechism and the Crowd', *La Révolution française* (Online) and Scott Eastman, *Preaching Spanish Nationalism across the Hispanic Atlantic, 1759–1823* (Baton Rouge: Louisiana State University Press, 2012); Tomás Pérez Vejo, *España en el debate público mexicano, 1836–1867: aportaciones para una historia de la nación* (Mexico City: El Colegio de México, 2008), p. 35; Brading, *Los orígenes del nacionalismo mexicano*, p. 52; Adelman, *Sovereignty and Revolution*, p. 211; Portillo, *Crisis Atlántica*, pp. 142.

[78] The Constitution's abolition of the Inquisition led to the deployment of its estate towards the repayment of debt. Ferdinand would, however, restore the Inquisition, which would continue to work effectively in certain regions, such as Mexico. Hamnett, *The End of Iberian Rule*, p. 213.

[79] Alvaro Flórez Estrada, *Examen imparcial de las disensiones de la América con la España: de los medios de su recíproco interés y de la utilidad de los aliados de la España* (Londres: Juigné, 1811). On the influence of his constitutional ideas in Latin America see Natalio Botana, *Repúblicas y monarquías. La encrucijada de la independencia* (Buenos Aires: Edhasa, 2016), p 137.

was guaranteed.[80] In 1813, the return of Ferdinand to the throne, and the rise of reactionary policies, intensified calls for a fairer political arrangement for the empire.[81]

The idea that the Spanish Crown had always been overwhelmed by its debts was a powerful rhetorical device for Spanish American revolutionaries. The Crown, argued Spanish American rebels, no longer saw debt as a means to serve the common good. Drawing on the statistics provided by Flórez Estrada and the Spanish Minister of Finance, José Canga Argüelles, the aristocrat and future President of Peru, José de la Riva-Agüero drafted his incendiary *Manifestación histórica y política*.[82] Agüero not only showed that Spanish officials had a poor understanding of the population numbers and economic conditions of Spanish Americans but, as a result of the interests on its debts, Spain could not afford to preserve its empire: 'how will Spain maintain itself with the product of its rents and deal with such a high accumulation of interests?'[83] One now had to add the 'debt of the Crown (for in Spain nothing is national, but royal)' to the imperial debt.[84] America, explained Agüero, 'detests the usurious and monopolistic spirit of Spain', and, citing Vattel, argued that since Spain had ignored international law, and the considerations of 'humanity', as it deprived America of liberty and reason, rebels were pursuing a just war.[85] Flórez Estrada, continued Agüero, had argued that 'if all men formed a single political family' the Spanish Americas 'would be more independent, because they would be free from external enemies'.[86] Flórez Estrada had used this argument not to emphasise the merits of the law of nations, but rather to emphasise the patrimonial bonds that once bound the Americas to Spain. Why then, countered Agüero, did Spain not accept Napoleon's Code and his shackles, and yield to its status as a 'slave' to France?[87]

Others built on similar tropes. The Mexican priest, Fray Servando Teresa Mier, in the midst of a *guerre de plume* between Latin American separatists and Spanish liberals in London, declared that Spain was so bankrupt it lacked the strength to

[80] Internal reports also painted a grim picture and further demands for colonial resources aggravated tensions; see Adelman, *Sovereignty and Revolution*, pp. 291–296. On Estrada's text see Portillo, *Crisis Atlántica*, pp. 163–165. On the denial of free trade as a catalyst for independence see Anna, *Spain and the Loss of America*, p. 253. On the demands for liberalisation of Latin American officials see Rieu-Millan, *Los diputados*, pp. 176–194.

[81] Hamnett, *The End of Iberian Rule*, pp. 221–231.

[82] José de la Riva-Agüero, *Manifestación histórica y política de la revolución de la América y más especialmente de la parte que corresponde al Perú, y Río de la Plata* (Buenos Aires: Expositos, 1818).

[83] Riva-Agüero, *Manifestación histórica*, pp. 175–176.

[84] Riva-Agüero, *Manifestación histórica*, p. 177. By 1818, Flórez Estrada revised his own assessment of the situation and suggested that the union with the Americas required their explicit and voluntary consent. See María Teresa Berruezo León, *La lucha de Hispanoamérica por su independencia en Inglaterra 1800–1830* (Madrid: Ediciones de Cultura Hispánica, 1989), p. 296.

[85] Riva-Agüero, *Manifestación histórica*, pp. 28–29, p. 101, p. 183, p. 88. For his criticism of Spain's monopoly see Portillo, *Crisis Atlántica*, pp. 168–170.

[86] Flórez Estrada, *Examen*, p. 340.

[87] Riva-Agüero, *Manifestación histórica*, p. 147, n. *.

defend itself and its case was beyond repair: it would never receive enough foreign aid to subjugate the Americas once again.[88] The Argentinian thinker and financier, Mariano Moreno, penned the foundational text of Argentine independence, the *Representación de los Hacendados*.[89] Addressed to Gaspar Melchor de Jovellanos, then president of the governing board in Cádiz, the *Representación* concluded with one of the most scathing critiques of the Spanish attitude towards the commercial ambitions of the colonies, one that poured salt on an open wound and drew attention to the relationship between foreign finance and Spain's own independence. Britain, argued Moreno, was the guarantor of Spanish independence: 'Today, nothing is more useful to Spain than reaffirming through all possible means the union and alliance with Britain'.[90] Under the Napoleonic invasion, Britain, 'this generous nation', had provided Spain the means to fight the enemy; 'there were no other examples of' such liberality in the history of 'friendships among nations'.[91] Higher revenues through free trade would allow the Crown and the local authorities to avoid its chronic reliance on 'begging' and 'lending', while Britain would continue to serve as the most robust 'creditor' in ensuring that 'our speculations are never too far removed from the wellbeing of their subjects'.[92] Buenos Aires' pursuit of a closer commercial alliance with Britain made the rebels nothing other than 'good Spaniards'.[93]

In 1820, a revolution in Spain forced Ferdinand into exile and the Cortes were reconstituted. Ferdinand had ignored conciliatory proposals but the Cortes hoped to capitalise on any lingering good will in the Americas.[94] A last-ditch effort to save the empire by drawing on liberal principles and the terms of the Cádiz Constitution was arranged and Spanish American representatives participated in the discussions. The Cortes were forced to address the 'illusory perspective' the Cádiz Cortes had displayed towards the war debts when they had been signed.[95] Since large parts of the territories had been occupied at the time, the 'repayment of war' had been 'deferred' to a 'happier epoch', generating an illusion about Spain's future political conditions. This delusion continued to influence the discussions at the Cortes, as representatives debated the need to settle all outstanding debts—except for those that had emerged in the Spanish Americas. Deputies lamented the tragic patterns in the empire's debt mismanagement since the age of

[88] Berruezo León, *La lucha*, p. 105.

[89] Mariano Moreno, *Representación de los Hacendados* (1809). Reprinted (Madrid: Biblioteca Virtual Universal, 2003).

[90] Moreno, *Representación*, p. 50.

[91] Moreno, *Representación*, pp. 50–51.

[92] Moreno, *Representación*, p. 50.

[93] Moreno, *Representación*, p. 51. For a succinct summary of Mariano Moreno's views and ambitions see Adelman, *Republic of Capital*, pp. 80–81.

[94] On these proposals see Anna, *Spain and the Loss of America*, pp. 166–188.

[95] *Diario de las actas y discusiones de las Cortes*. Legislatura. 1820/21 (1820). Volume 1 (Madrid: Imprenta especial de las Cortes, 1820), p. 263.

Charles V—and debated the merits of paying these historical debts to enhance Spain's credit abroad.[96]

There were broader conceptual problems regarding Spain's dues: the Cortes had to establish the difference between the debt of the nation and the debt of the Crown. The new liberal government had a chance to improve its credit abroad by paying back the Dutch debt incurred in the construction of the Canal of Aragon under the reign of Charles III.[97] The Netherlands had, however, been ruled by Spain's enemy for a number of years. Did this mean that Spain could reject the interests that accrued during said years? A commission tasked with producing a report on the topic rejected this logic by defending the liberal principle of property. Contracts had been made with individuals and not between states. They were therefore binding regardless of war or political change for practical reasons—the failure to respect this principle would ensure that no foreigner would want to do business with Spain.[98] The most powerful retort to this line of reasoning was delivered by one of the leaders of the group of Spanish liberal deputies, Francisco Martínez de la Rosa: this was not a matter of liberal ideals, or economic interests, but of 'principles of international law'. These ideals were 'not subject to political vicissitudes, or the errors of governments'.[99] Those who failed to live by these doctrines and chose instead to 'cut the tree to pick a single fruit' would not find the resources they needed thereafter.[100] As the deputy José Canga Argüelles remarked, this was a contract between private citizens and a government. One could not deny Spanish individuals who had lent to the government their right to payment, and thus it was wrong to deny the Dutch their own.[101]

Lorenzo de Zavala, a representative for New Spain at the Cortes, took note of this exchange: he would later echo this argument in his defence of the need to repay colonial debts. Zavala's colleague, Miguel Ramos Arizpe, a former law professor and judge, asked his peers to remember that many debts in the Americas had yet to be paid; the people of New Spain had sacrificed themselves, acted in good faith, and taken on huge loans in order to fund the Spanish government's fight against Napoleon.[102] This was not the first time Arizpe had articulated this view. In 1811, after surviving a bout of yellow fever, Arizpe had participated in the Cádiz Cortes.

[96] *Diario de las actas*. Volume 11, p. 44; Volume 13, p. 376; Volume 18, p. 200.

[97] *Diario de las actas*. Legislatura. 1820/21 (1820). Volume 5, p. 156. For Argüelles' views on the Dutch debt see Juan Simal, 'José Canga Argüelles (1771–1842), la deuda pública española y el compromiso creíble: política y economía en tiempos de revolución y exilio', in Darina Martykánova and Juan Pan Montojo ed., *Misioneros del capitalismo: Aventureros, hombres de negocio y expertos transnacionales en el siglo XIX* (Granada: Comares, 2023), pp. 3–26.

[98] *Diario de las actas*. Volume 5, pp. 158–162.

[99] *Diario de las actas*. Volume 5, p. 162.

[100] *Diario de las actas*. Volume 5, p. 162.

[101] *Diario de las actas*. Volume 5, p. 164.

[102] *Diario de las actas*. Volume 10, pp. 50–53; Volume 17, p. 116. See Alberto Novales, *El Trienio Liberal* (Zaragoza: Prensas de la Universidad de Zaragoza, 2020), pp. 32–34.

During his interventions, he had made clear that the *castas*—the *pardos* and the *mulatos*—were the 'true builders and guardians of the Americas'; they bore the brunt of the Crown's taxation and they bled for the empire when they enrolled in its militias. They were therefore 'justly owed' equal political representation.[103] The Cortes ignored Arizpe's comments and, upon his return to power, Ferdinand imprisoned him for his views. Now, a decade after he defended the rights of the *castas*, Arizpe found himself, once again, trying to make it clear to his Spanish peers that Spain owed symbolic and financial debts to the Americas. In one of his interventions, Arizpe manifested his discontent towards the unwillingness of his peers to engage with the matter of Spanish American finances. He remarked that 'all that has been said' in these debates 'would incline me to suggest that the best thing with regard to this aspect of the public debt is for us Americans to be left to deal with it on our own'.[104] Peninsular officials, he continued, never considered including the ill-fated *vales* in discussions for the consolidation of the debt; these contracts 'had been happily ignored'.[105]

However, Arizpe made clear that New Spain understood its *deber*: it remained committed to financing the Spanish Empire so that 'it cannot be said that we back away from national charges, charges that with respect to America are still neglected'. He would therefore ensure that the province followed Spain and tried to make 'this system of public credit practicable in America'.[106] In spite of the peninsular disregard for Arizpe's views on debt, he was one of the signatories to a proposal put forward by the representatives from New Spain to create a monarchical confederation of states whereby each country would contribute to the financing of Spain's foreign debt. Arizpe even promised that New Spain would absorb and consolidate its own public debt—without the help of Spain.[107]

But it was not to be. As peninsular officials continued to ignore American affairs, the patience of some of the Spanish American representatives wore thin. Officials asked their representatives to return to America.[108] These deliberations on the

[103] Reprinted in Guillermo Durand Flórez, *El Perú en las Cortes de Cádiz*. Volume 1 (Lima: Comisión Nacional del Sesquicentenario de la Independencia del Perú, 1974), pp. 359–362. For an outline of debates on people of African descent at the Cortes see Herzog, *Defining Nations*, pp. 152–163.

[104] *Diario de las actas*. Volume 10, pp. 50–53.

[105] *Diario de las actas*. Volume 10, pp. 50–53; Volume 17, p. 116. On the broader economic ideas of the Mexican representatives at the Cortes see John H. Hann, 'The Role of the Mexican Deputies in the Proposal and Enactment of Measures of Economic Reform Applicable to Mexico', in Nettie Lee Benson, *Mexico and the Spanish Cortes, 1810–1822: Eight Essays* (Austin: University of Texas Press, 1966), pp. 153–184.

[106] *Diario de las actas*. Volume 10, pp. 50–53. On the broader proposal to contribute to the foreign debt see Anna, *Spain and the Loss of America*, p. 248.

[107] See articles 11 and 14 in *Exposición presentada a las Cortes por los diputados de ultramar en la sesión de 25 de junio de 1821: sobre el estado actual de las provincias de que son representantes, y medios convenientes para su definitiva pacificación, con una noticia de los trámites que la precedieron y motivaron* (Madrid: García y Campoy, 1821), pp. 15–16. See Jaime E. Rodríguez O., 'La transición de colonia a nación: Nueva España, 1820–1821', *Historia Mexicana* 43:2 (1993), pp. 265–322, p. 287.

[108] Anna, *Spain and the Loss of America*, p. 246.

repayment of Spanish American debts failed to deliver tangible reforms and provided fodder for Latin American authors to criticise Spanish liberalism for decades. In 1823, on the basis of the Troppau circular that stated that revolutionary governments in Europe were not legitimate, a French intervention in Spain reinstated Ferdinand VII as the King of Spain. Ferdinand repudiated the foreign debts of the Cortes while Spain continued to demand the payment of a share of its debts from its former imperial provinces.[109] As a Colombian envoy in London suggested, the King's obstinate repudiation of past debts was the only obstacle standing in the way of Spain raising a significant loan in London.[110] To the surprise of Colombian officials, who continued to sound the alarm on Spain's possible negotiation of a loan, the King did not yield.[111] On the other side of the Atlantic, Simón Bolívar was left befuddled by the behaviour of the Crown and wondered whether Spain would ever repay the owners of the *vales*.[112] Spain defaulted on its debts to America.

That same year, the United States made its first intervention in Latin American affairs. In response to the Troppau circular, James Monroe's secretary delivered before the United States Congress the speech that would become the basis of the Monroe Doctrine—the United States would treat European interventions in American affairs as hostile acts against the republic.[113] Spain fought back against the recognition of this doctrine: Argüelles invoked the Troppau circular to justify Spain's efforts to claw back the Spanish Americas.[114] Andrés Bello, the most important Latin American thinker of international law of his age, rejected its authority.[115] As one Colombian newspaper noted, Spain, a 'Don Quixote', continued 'to dream of empires!' but, after being repeatedly beaten to a pulp, Spain could only offer the exiguous resources of a small island estate, an *ínsula*, that Don Quixote had promised his sidekick, Sancho Panza, to entice him to assist the errant knight on his mad adventures.[116] In the aftermath of the failure to create a transatlantic

[109] Comín, *Las crisis*, p. 123.

[110] Archivo General de la Nación [henceforth AGN], Ministerio de Exteriores, DT2, t. 307, p. 28.

[111] AGN, Ministerio de Exteriores, DT2, t. 307, p. 48, p. 64.

[112] Bolívar may have reasoned that since the Cortes of 1811 transformed, as the decree stated, the 'consolidation of *vales reales*' into the 'national council of public credit', and the King had voided the contracts signed with *foreign* lenders by the Cortes, the repayment of the *vales* was still up in the air. Indeed, its payment may have fostered renewed support for the Crown. AGN, Ministerio de Exteriores, DT2, Box 15/508, F.101, p. 94; *Colección de los Decretos y Órdenes que han expedido las Cortes Generales y Extraordinarias desde su instalación de 24 de septiembre de 1811 hasta el 24 de mayo de 1812*. Volume 2 (Cadiz: Imprenta Real, 1813), pp. 2–3.

[113] Sexton, *Monroe*, p. 57.

[114] Argüelles, *Breve respuesta a la representación de los Comerciantes de Londres* (London: Caldero, 1829), p. 35.

[115] In his *Principios*, Bello would cite the example of the official British dispatch that rejected the congresses of Troppau and Laibach of 1821 to argue that intervention in a foreign nation was not licit once its sovereignty had been established, as noted in Alonso Gurmendi Dunkelberg, 'A Legal History of Consent and Intervention in Civil Wars in Latin America', *Journal on the Use of Force and International Law* 7:1 (2020), pp. 102–121, pp. 106–107.

[116] Sancho was eventually made governor of an island colony but gave up this position soon after because of his dislike of the cut-throat nature of politics; 'Chiste diplomático', in *La Miscelania*. Number 24, 26 February 1826.

Hispanic model of government, a new hemispheric order began to consolidate around Britain and the United States.

The responsibilities of bankrupt republics

Argüelles was one of the most important thinkers in the development of Spanish constitutional debates.[117] As the leading economic official at the Cádiz Cortes and the liberal Cortes of 1820–1823, Argüelles displayed a strategic ambiguity in American matters, initially going as far as to endorse the Spanish collaboration with Britain in the abolition of the slave trade.[118] Following Ferdinand VII's return to power in 1823, Argüelles went into exile in London.[119] There he collaborated closely with the Ecuadorian-born Mexican envoy Vicente Rocafuerte who, in an earlier work, had expressed his admiration for the Spaniard's political economic thought. Rocafuerte asked Argüelles to write a work that summarised the ideas of Smith, Jean-Baptiste Say, and David Ricardo, and which were not, he believed, sufficiently well known in the Spanish Americas.[120] In his own writings, Rocafuerte had been critical of Argüelles' constitutional legacy: he challenged the Cádiz consensus and argued that the political situation in Europe and the Americas was diametrically different; in Spain, 'to be a good patriot' was to be a defender of 'constitutional monarchy'.[121] In the Americas, a true patriot was a 'committed republican'. Burdened by debts and constantly breaching the law of nations, he continued, Europe was in no state to advance democracy. America, free from the burdens of the past, could implement a fair system of representation.[122]

[117] Juan Luis Simal, 'National Credit and the International Financial Market: The Spanish Debt and its Foreign Bondholders, 1820–1834', *Journal of Iberian and Latin American Studies* 25:3 (2019), pp. 381–402; Fernando López Castellano, 'Las Cortes de Cádiz y la implantación del buen orden económico (1810–1814)', *Historia Constitucional* 13 (2012), pp. 233–256; Marcello Carmagnani, 'De la economía política a la economía pública: José Canga Argüelles', *Iberian Journal of the History of Economic Thought* 2 (2016), pp. 221–238; Hamnett, *The End of Iberian Rule*, pp. 242–243.

[118] On his interventions on these matters in Cádiz see Rieu-Millan, *Los diputados*, pp. 274–285, pp. 296–299, pp. 316–318. On his views on slavery see Jesús Sanjurjo, *In the Blood of Our Brothers Abolitionism and the End of the Slave Trade in Spain's Atlantic Empire, 1800–1870* (Tuscaloosa: University of Alabama Press, 2021), pp. 16–17.

[119] Juan Pan-Montojo and Juan Luis Simal, 'Exil, finances internationales et construction de l'État: les libéraux et « josephins » espagnols (1813–1851)', *Revue d'histoire du XIXe siècle* 53 (2016), pp. 59–77.

[120] Berruezo León, *La lucha*, p. 512; See Vicente Rocafuerte, *Bosquejo ligerísimo de la revolución de Mégico: desde el grito de Iguala hasta la proclamación imperial de Iturbide* (Philadelphia: Teracrouef & Naroajeb, 1822), p. 1. On Rocafuerte see Jaime E. Rodríguez O., *The Emergence of Spanish America: Vicente Rocafuerte and Spanish Americanism, 1808–1832* (Berkeley: University of California Press, 1975). On Rocafuerte's views on Iturbide see Timothy Anna, *The Mexican Empire of Iturbide* (Lincoln: University of Nebraska Press, 1990), p. 15.

[121] Vicente Rocafuerte, *Ensayo politico: El sistema colombiano, popular, electivo, y representativo, es el que más conviene á la América independiente* (New York: A. Paul, 1823), p. 23.

[122] Rocafuerte, *Ensayo político*, pp. 24–25.

In London, surrounded by Rocafuerte and other Latin American intellectuals, Argüelles adjusted his views on political economy in response to changes in global affairs. In 1825, Argüelles published his *Elementos de la ciencia de hacienda*, dedicated to the Mexican President, Guadalupe Victoria.[123] In this book, he defended the establishment of liberal governments in the Americas and in Spain but fell short of declaring his support for independence.[124] In a section on Spain's public finances, he noted how 'fanaticism' and 'individual interests' stood in the way of the repayment of the national debt.[125] Argüelles provided a historical account of the early modern Spanish public debt: no king, he argued, had been able to relieve the empire of its debts: 'the nation', with the establishment of the Cortes of 1820–1823, had, he claimed, successfully kickstarted its reform. But the return of Ferdinand VII had driven Spain to bankruptcy.[126] While Argüelles discussed the matter of the American contributions to the Crown, he avoided engaging with the question of the American debt. Argüelles' text could be seen as a way to publicise and recommend his litany of reforms to the President of Mexico in the hope that, under a liberal administration, a reconciliation would be possible.

As one of the editors of the *Ocios de Españoles Emigrados*, a newspaper that published information about the Hispanic world in London, Argüelles provided information about the state of its politics and the value of government bonds in London.[127] The paper praised Rocafuerte's capacity to raise a loan for Colombia and increase the value of Mexico's stock.[128] Yet it also published articles about Mexico's financial struggles and remarked on how 'a country in its state' would lose or damage its credit if it was unable to 'recognise or pay its old debts'.[129] The Mexican Finance Minister, José Ignacio Esteva published a pamphlet in order to counter this charge, and refuted this claim by noting that Mexico had indeed promised to recognise its debts.[130] In the midst of this *querelle*, a vigorous debate about the nature of foreign loans, a nation's fiscal stability, and constitutionalism soon emerged in the pages of *The Times*, a newspaper over which Argüelles had little control. The editors of the newsprint had initially followed the British government's neutrality. But as support for the new Latin American states grew it began to publish letters in favour of independence.[131]

Towards the end of the 1820s, as the list of Latin American countries that had gained French or British recognition grew in size, Argüelles' views on the legacy

[123] José Canga Argüelles, *Elementos de la ciencia de hacienda* (London: Mackintosh, 1825).
[124] Berruezo León, *La lucha*, p. 456.
[125] Argüelles, *Elementos de la ciencia de hacienda*, p. 398.
[126] Argüelles, *Elementos de la ciencia de hacienda*, pp. 154–189.
[127] Berruezo León, *La lucha*, pp. 516–522.
[128] *Ocios de Españoles Emigrados*. Number 28, July 1826 (London: Dulan, 1826), p. 288.
[129] *Ocios de Españoles Emigrados*. Number 20, November 1824 (London: Dulan, 1825), p. 386.
[130] José Ignacio Esteva, *A los españoles ociosos en Londres. Un mexicano ocupado contestando al número 20 de su periódico* (Mexico City: Rivera, 1826); Richard J. Salvucci, *Politics, Markets, and Mexico's 'London Debt,' 1823–1887* (New York: Cambridge University Press, 2009), p. 108.
[131] Berruezo León, *La lucha*, p. 481.

of Cádiz soured.[132] It was an indictment of Argüelles' own failure to establish a clear definition of private property that could mollify sceptics and accommodate the political economic and legal dimensions of Spanish American political demands.[133] Eager to make a change, he yearned to return to Spain to take a more active role in political affairs and therefore sought to use his publications to ingratiate himself with Ferdinand VII.[134] He founded another newspaper, *El Emigrado Conservador*, which was critical of the economic management of Latin American governments.[135] An entire section was dedicated to their bankruptcies in London, likely in the hope of exposing the poor state of Latin American state finances.[136] In one of the issues, Argüelles wondered how Mexico could be expected to repay its debts to Britain when no silver was flowing from its mines.[137] In another issue, he made a farcical statement: British capitalists had a more lucrative market in Spain than in the Spanish Americas.[138] Gradually, however, he developed more sophisticated ideas and these came together in his *Breve Respuesta*. This pamphlet was a response to a range of articles published in the pages of *The Times* that defended the economic viability of Latin American independence. The *Breve Respuesta* was a radical departure from Argüelles' moderate stance: he not only questioned the solvency of Latin American governments but he also denigrated its peoples as uncivilised.[139]

One of the letters published in *The Times* claimed that Spain should enter 'the march of civilisation', end its threats to retake Peru, and recognise its independence; the new nation would then be able to lower its defence spending and would eventually find itself in a better position to pay back its foreign debts.[140] This was an argument that was commonly used by Latin American diplomats.[141] In response, Argüelles betrayed his earlier claim that a constitutionally bound liberal Spanish Empire would yield secure returns and greater profits for London's investors and ought therefore to be the preferable choice for Britain.[142] He now posited that

[132] Daniel Muñoz Sempere, 'Cultural Identity and Political Dissidence: The Periodicals of the Spanish Liberal Exile in London (1810–1841), in Constance Bantman and Ana Cláudia Suriani da Silva eds., *The Foreign Political Press in Nineteenth-Century London: Politics from a Distance* (London: Bloomsbury Publishing, 2017), pp. 33–50, pp. 45–47.

[133] See Botana, *Repúblicas y monarquías*, p. 49. Carlos Petit, *Un Código civil perfecto y bien calculado. El proyecto de 1821 en la historia de la codificación* (Madrid: Editorial Dykinson, 2019).

[134] On his publications in London during this period see Joaquín Varela Suanzes-Carpegna, *La monarquía doceañista (1810–1837). Avatares, encomios y denuestos de una extraña forma de gobierno* (Madrid: Marcial Pons, 2013), pp. 332–349.

[135] Berruezo León, *La lucha*, pp. 533–540.

[136] Berruezo León, *La lucha*, p. 535.

[137] *El Emigrado observador*. Number 3, 9/1828 (London: Calero, 1828), pp. 82–89.

[138] *El Emigrado observador*. Number 2, 2/1829 (London: Calero, 1829), pp. 41–51. See also Berruezo León, *La lucha*, pp. 541–542.

[139] Argüelles, *Breve respuesta*, p. 10.

[140] Argüelles, *Breve*, pp. 9–11.

[141] See AGN, Ministerio de Exteriores, DT2, t. 307, p. 260.

[142] *Ocios de Españoles Emigrados: periódico mensual*. Volume 7, January 1827 (London: Dulan et Comp, 1827), pp. 23–25.

the reunion of monarchical Spain with the Americas would put an end to the terms that 'desolate the Americas, make Europe poorer, and make investors desperate'.[143] Argüelles forcefully presented his strongest argument against his earlier claim: Latin American states did not have the necessary legal respect for private property, nor the financial means, to secure their freedom.[144] Latin Americans had shown, with their disregard for contracts and debt repayment, that 'they did not understand civilisation'. Civilisation, he continued, did not consist of paying back the huge loans they owed; it was built on the respect for liberal legal principles and institutions.[145] How could Latin Americans speak of a 'confederation' and formulate a 'foreign policy in line with this enlightened age' such that each state could assist the other when they were all unable to repay their debts to British financiers?[146] Driven by greed, British speculators, he reasoned, had mistakenly rushed to invest in the new republics because of the profits they seemed to offer, not out of any hope that these republics would gain recognition from Spain or Britain.[147] These monopolistic merchants should give up 'their ambitions for an exclusive dominance of the New World' and accept a new 'balance' of trade by following Ferdinand's wishes.[148] After all, the war over the Americas prevented Spain from paying back its debts to London.[149]

Latin American officials argued that sovereignty was not a matter of compensation. Bello understood that, in diplomatic negotiations with Spain, it was crucial to avoid quantifying the value of freedom. It was important not to ground the legitimacy of Latin American independence on finance. The right to nationhood had been won justly in war, Bello explained, and had not been—and could not be—bought. Hence it could not be sold. Spain sought to 'trade independence for the repayment of debt', explained Bello, to 'sell us rights we have wrested from their hands through force'.[150] Officials had to be cognisant of the broader racialised geopolitical redefinitions of sovereignty that set a high price for freedom: diplomats and journalists warned against accepting the 'manumission' of independence, and the example of Haiti not only fuelled Bolívar's fear of what he called '*pardocracia*', or 'rule by black people', but its indemnity debt cast a shadow over wishful hopes of buying independence.[151] Gran Colombia, Mexico, Chile, and Buenos Aires signed

[143] Argüelles, *Breve respuesta*, p. 43.
[144] Argüelles, *Breve respuesta*, p. 28.
[145] Argüelles, *Breve respuesta*, p. 10.
[146] Argüelles, *Breve respuesta*, pp. 29–30.
[147] Argüelles, *Breve respuesta*, pp. 13–15.
[148] Argüelles, *Breve respuesta*, p. 44.
[149] Argüelles, *Breve respuesta*, pp. 9–10.
[150] Originally published in *El Araucano* in 1834, see *Obras completas de don Andrés Bello*. Volume 10 (Santiago de Chile: Ramírez, 1886), pp. xxvi–xxvii n. *.
[151] AGN, Ministerio de Exteriores, DT2, t. 307, p. 92. Aline Helg, *Liberty and Equality in Caribbean Colombia, 1770–1835* (Chapel Hill: University of North Carolina Press, 2005), pp. 166–167; Daniel Gutiérrez Ardila, *El reconocimiento de Colombia: diplomacia y propaganda en la coyuntura de las restauraciones, 1819–1831* (Bogotá: Universidad Externado de Colombia, 2012), pp. 252–265. On Haiti's debt see Liliana Obregón, 'Empire, Racial Capitalism and International Law: The Case of

an accord to never enter into negotiations with Spain 'over indemnification' unless it agreed to pay damages for the unjust war it had waged on these states.[152]

The counterpoint of compensation was a term that emerged from negotiations in peace congresses in the 1810s and 1820s and which was adroitly harnessed by British officials: intervention. Haiti exemplified the feared outcome of the revolution. By contrast, Colombian diplomats drew extensively on the parallels between the Greek pursuit of freedom and Turkey's tyrannical rule and the Latin American struggle against Spanish oppression. Britain had developed its own doctrine of humanitarian intervention to advance the Greek cause, and Spain was, according to Colombian officials, 'The New Turkey'.[153] If a war that had lasted a few years, argued one Colombian diplomat, had summoned such sympathy among the British people, how could they overlook almost two decades of Spanish repression? The cause of humanity 'demanded' Britain's intervention in the conflict between Spain and the Latin American republics.[154] In response, British officials pointedly responded that they had shown their commitment to the cause of humanity in Latin America through their credit—the new Latin American republics, observed one British official, already owed a debt of gratitude to Britain for its support over two decades of war.[155] Financial intervention was an important form of intervention.[156] Liberty, insisted Bentham, was a form of security.[157] But it remained unclear whether Latin American states were safeguarded or threatened by the culture of security and securities that emerged in Europe in the 1820s.[158]

Manumitted Haiti and the Recognition Debt', *Leiden Journal of International Law* 31:3 (2018), pp. 597–615 and Joan DeJean, 'Les Capitalistes: The First Capitalists and the Debt Created by Haitian Slavery', *Capitalism: A Journal of History and Economics* 4:1 (2023), pp. 44–72. On Haiti and Cuba see Ada Ferrer, *Freedom's Mirror: Cuba and Haiti in the Age of Revolution* (Cambridge: Cambridge University Press, 2014), pp. 83–145

[152] Vicente Lecuna, *Relaciones diplomáticas de Bolívar con Chile y Buenos Aires: copiadas de los originales existentes en las secciones del Archivo del libertador denominadas de O'Leary y Juan de Francisco Martín*. Volume 1 (Caracas: Imprenta Nacional, 1954), pp. 8–36.

[153] AGN, Ministerio de Exteriores, DT2, t. 307, p. 201. On Greece and Latin America in debates about intervention see Mark Mazower, *The Greek Revolution: 1821 and the Making of Modern Europe* (London: Penguin, 2021), pp. 399–401. On the European uses of this analogy see Darina Martykánová and Juan Luis Simal, 'Ferdinand and the Sultan: The Metaphor of the Turk and the Crisis of the Spanish Monarchy in the Early Nineteenth Century', *Contributions to the History of Concepts* 10:1 (2015), pp. 1–26.

[154] AGN, Ministerio de Exteriores, DT2, t. 307, p. 201, pp. 221–222, p. 386.

[155] AGN, Ministerio de Exteriores, DT2, t. 307, pp. 221–222.

[156] Note the observation made by John Bew that during this period Britain evoked 'the spectre of intervention in defence of the principle of non-intervention'; see John Bew, '"From an Umpire to a Competitor": Castlereagh, Canning and the Issue of International Intervention in the Wake of the Napoleonic Wars', in Brendan Simms and D.J.B. Trim eds., *Humanitarian Intervention: A History* (Cambridge: Cambridge University Press, 2011), pp. 117–138, pp. 127–128.

[157] Frederick Rosen, *Bentham, Byron, and Greece: Constitutionalism, Nationalism, and Early Liberal Political Thought* (Oxford: Oxford University Press, 1992), pp. 33–37.

[158] On the rise of international debates of 'security' and 'securities' during this period see Glenda Sluga, 'Economic Insecurity, 'Securities' and a European Security Culture after the Napoleonic Wars', in Beatrice de Graaf, Ido de Haan, and Brian Vick ed., *Securing Europe after Napoleon: 1815 and the*

Compensation and indemnification fostered patriotism among the Latin American elites. The creole elites had a vested interest in protecting the contracts that upheld their rights to vast lands and slave labour. It was not clear whether the breach of contracts signed under Spanish rule served to establish new and durable private property laws or, as one Argentinian congressman put it, whether this default on past laws was nothing more than 'the canonization of fraud'.[159] There was no measure akin to the North American Northwest Ordinance, which settled who ought to be responsible for expansion or what terms justified the ownership of public land. Instead, the debate over property would increasingly focus on whether colonial laws over slavery and indigenous land ownership ought to remain in force. Indeed, this point of contention was first raised in the United States, and not in Latin America, as a result of the Congress of Panama: slaveholders understood that hemispheric commercial and legal reform threatened to promote abolition throughout the Americas.[160]

The lack of a resolution to these debates in Latin America ensured that the question of colonial debts remained permanently connected with the desire to establish a post-revolutionary liberal state. Latin American domestic justice systems remained heavily factional and the struggle for the homogenisation of national administrations across these war-torn and fissiparous territories remained a challenge. The price of reconciliation with Spain remained the repayment of colonial debts. The Holy See, in turn, provided little help and relations between many of the new nations and the Church remained tense as a result of the dispute over its rights and properties in the Americas.[161] Financial atonement would therefore arise from without. The fulfilment of foreign payments was portrayed as a way to signal respect for the principle of property rights abroad. But laws on property rights regarding enslaved peoples or land within these states remained undefined. In Mexico, congressional debates over the abolishment of the Spanish system of slavery were derailed, in part, by the fact that British financiers had purchased lands and hoped to harness slave labour therein. The Mexican government did not want to be seen breaching said contracts.[162]

New European Security Culture (Cambridge: Cambridge University Press, 2019), pp. 288–305. Graaf, *Fighting Terror after Napoleon*, pp. 302–356.

[159] Post-revolutionary France and the United States struggled with the same question. See chapter 6 in Rafe Blaufarb, *The Great Demarcation: The French Revolution and the Invention of Modern Property* (Oxford: Oxford University Press, 2006), pp. 175–207 and James Ely, *The Guardian of Every Other Right: A Constitutional History of Property Rights* (Oxford: Oxford University Press, 2007). On the origins of these questions in the foundational logic of the American Spanish Empire see Pagden, *Lords of all the World*, pp. 50–52.

[160] Sexton, *Monroe*, pp. 76–77.

[161] See, most recently, Elisa Cárdenas, *Roma: el descubrimiento de América* (Mexico City: El Colegio de México, 2018).

[162] José Luis Soberanes Fernández, 'La abolición de la esclavitud en México', *Ars Iuris* 50 (2015), pp. 247–259, p. 256 and John Lynch, *New Worlds: A Religious History of Latin America* (New Haven: Yale University Press, 2012), pp. 121–128.

These contracts ensured that the money kept flowing. In Mexico, the credit of foreign lenders and *agiotistas*, prosperous local private lenders, compensated for the absence of a national bank. Mexican statesmen tried to introduce paper money to consolidate the government's control over fiscal matters. But the constant change in government dampened the credit of patriotism.[163] In Argentina, the creation of a national bank only intensified the British domination of the nation's economy as British investors monopolised the bank's assets.[164] The Church remained the main creditor in many of the poorer areas of these new nations, particularly in Colombia, and thus to bet on an alternative banking system served to short the Catholic foundations of the community.[165] Some continued to invest on the assumption that the Spanish Crown would return. Others speculated in international markets on the basis that a protectorate would clear the nation's ever-growing debts.

As time passed, Argüelles and his writings provided few solutions and the foundations of Spain's public credit remained unstable.[166] Argüelles returned to Spain where he was named president of the Cortes and briefly served as tutor to Queen Isabella II.[167] Following his return to Spain, the nation sank into the first of three civil wars that ravaged the Iberian Peninsula in the nineteenth century. European investors sought to find ways to recover some of their investments or limit their losses. The British Bubble Act failed to discourage further investment in Spanish and Latin American enterprises. Yet British investors continued to purchase Spanish bonds which would only be renegotiated in 1848.[168] This generated a broader discussion on how to standardise the legal norms that should govern the settlement of unpaid British loans in Spain and in the new Latin American states.[169] War continued to complicate matters. Spain continued to refinance its

[163] Raymond Estep, *Lorenzo de Zavala: profeta del liberalismo mexicano*. Translated by Carlos A. Echánove Trujillo. Prologue by Carlos A. Castañeda (Mexico City: Porrúa, 1952), pp. 59–62.

[164] On the complex relationship between silver, paper currency, and elite interests in Buenos Aires see Tulio Halperín-Donghi, *Guerra y finanzas Guerra y finanzas en los orígenes del Estado argentino (1791 –1850)* (Buenos Aires: Belgrano, 1982), pp. 153–165.

[165] Salomón Kalmanovitz, 'Constituciones y crecimiento económico en la Colombia del siglo XIX', *Revista de Historia Economica—Journal of Iberian and Latin American Economic History* 26:2 (2008), pp. 205–241, p. 221. On its role in the broader Spanish Empire see, most recently, Regina Grafe, 'An Empire of Debts? Spain and Its Colonial Realm', Nicolas Barreyre and Nicolas Delalande eds., *A World of Public Debts* (London: Palgrave, 2020), pp. 5–35.

[166] Comín, *Las crisis de la deuda soberana en España*, pp. 145–205.

[167] Luis Sánchez Agesta, 'Introducción', in Agustín de Argüelles, *Discurso preliminar a la Constitución de 1812* (Madrid: Centro de Estudios Políticos y Constitucionales, 1987), p. 15. On his views in exile see Portillo, *Revolución de nación*, pp. 208–256.

[168] Boyd Hilton, *The Age of Atonement: The Influence of Evangelicalism on Social and Economic Thought, 1795–1865* (Oxford: Oxford University Press, 1988), p. 256. Charles Read, *Calming the Storms: The Carry Trade, the Banking School and British Financial Crises Since 1825* (Cham: Springer, 2023), pp. 113–117. One pamphlet noted that '[t]he only states that have been found to compete' with Spain in terms of bad faith and duplicity in their transactions with other nations 'are her ancient Colonies'. See *Spain, its government and policy, its loans and resources considered, with reference to the claims of its foreign creditors* (London: Ridgway, Piccadilly, 1839), p. 2.

[169] See Gemma Alonso Torres, 'Las relaciones hispano-británicas durante el reinado de Isabel II', *Espacio, Tiempo y Forma, Serie V* (1995), pp. 85–110; Marc Flandreau, 'Pari Passu Lost and Found: The

debts by mortgaging its assets, which decreased by the day, and included the mines of Almaden, once owned by the Fugger family, as collateral to raise a loan with the Rothschilds. Eventually, unable to draw on foreign credit due to the lack of faith in its capacity to repay its lenders, the Spanish government seized Cuban revenues to fund peninsular interests, a measure which fuelled unrest in Havana.[170] Therein would lie the origins of the US interpretation of odious debt. But Spanish officials originally hoped to use these resources to incentivise the negotiation of an alliance with the United States; perhaps, a number of Spanish ministers wondered, contracting a loan from the United States mortgaged against the proceeds from Cuba would encourage the United States to invest in the shared defence of Spanish sovereignty in the region.[171] Colombian officials worried that Spain would use this loan to fund a new invasion of Mexico.[172]

In this age of compensations, speculations of this sort were common and authors in Europe and America pondered who was responsible for the regulation of debts in national and international contexts.[173] In France, Proudhon and Frédéric Bastiat passionately debated the morality of interest rates.[174] In the United States, John O'Sullivan, writing in the *Democratic Review*, excoriated Europeans for suggesting, after a number of US states defaulted on their debts, that the United States could not pay back its creditors; not only had most of these state loans been accrued for the well-being of the nation, unlike in European monarchies, which used credit to pursue princely vanity projects, but many of the advances that states had defaulted on had been extended by irresponsible British bankers who were, in fact, at fault.[175] The extent of the economic reliance of the United States on Britain should not be overlooked: almost half of the mid-century United States' national debt was held in Britain, and London banks financed the Louisiana Purchase and the 1848 indemnity payment to Mexico.[176] An ever-expanding Britain provided the United States with generative loans. By contrast, a revanchist Spain sought to saddle Latin America with crippling debts.

Origins of Sovereign Bankruptcy 1798–1873', *Institute for New Economic Thinking Working Paper Series* 186 (2022), pp. 38–39. On British views on Mexican investments see Salvucci, *Politics*, p. 53.

[170] Comín, *Las crisis de la deuda soberana en España*, pp. 142–144; Susan J. Fernández, *Encumbered Cuba: Capital Markets and Revolt, 1878–1895* (Gainesville: University Press of Florida, 2002), pp. 22–36, pp. 88–115.

[171] Pérez Vejo, *3 de Julio*, p. 70, p. 74.

[172] AGN, Ministerio de Exteriores, DT2, t. 307, p. 251.

[173] The term 'age of compensations' was coined by Friedemann Pestel and Jan Jansen in their call for papers for the 'Compensations and Reparative Politics: A View from the Nineteenth Century' conference at the University of Heidelberg in November 2024.

[174] For the most entertaining account of this debate see Edward Chancellor, *The Price of Time: The Real Story of Interest* (London: Grove Press, 2022), pp. 1–5.

[175] John O'Sullivan, 'State debts', in *The Democratic Review*. Volume 14 (New York: Henry Langley, 1844), pp. 1–5, p. 1–16.

[176] Sexton, *Monroe*, p. 21.

In Britain, Bentham was one of the most ardent defenders of the introduction of the principle of limited liability in the United Kingdom, and the leaders of this overstretched empire wondered how to streamline bankruptcy.[177] Limiting financial loss abroad was, however, a diplomatic matter. In an 1848 circular, Palmerston, then Foreign Secretary, rejected the suggestion of a fellow member of parliament that force should be used to reclaim the payment of all British loans abroad. After all, investors had recently shown little interest in understanding the differences between Latin American nations.[178] This encouraged military adventurers and fraudsters like the Scottish soldier Gregor MacGregor to fake the existence of territories in the region only to defraud investors with his scheme.[179] In response to Palmerston's comments, an anonymous pamphlet was published by the printer of the Royal Exchange representing the interests of those bondholders who hoped to strengthen their claim for compensation on the loans they had extended to Spain—which remained unpaid. This text, while 'not written for the learned', offered an extensive legal argument which drew on the writings of property and debt of Locke, Grotius, Vattel, and William Blackstone. The reasoning was that a government had an obligation to enforce the respect of British property at home and abroad, to draw on reprisals if necessary, and, if this responsibility was abdicated, to compensate the investors who had incurred a loss as a result of the government's lack of intervention.[180]

But Palmerston had made his stern views on foreign debts and moralising bankruptcies clear in his circular: the 'losses of imprudent men' who had 'placed mistaken confidence in the good faith of foreign governments' would 'prove a salutary warning to others'. On the other hand, the 'loss' occasioned by the failure to pay the interest on the loan might 'become so great' that it would constitute 'too high a price for the nation to pay for such a warning as to the future'; in this case 'diplomatic negotiation' would be used to settle the matter.[181] Two years later, Palmerston clarified his view of the merits of diplomatic negotiation with Spain

[177] Hilton, *Age of Atonement*, p. 257; see Boyd Hilton, *A Mad, Bad, & Dangerous People? England 1783–1846* (Oxford: Oxford University Press, 2006), pp. 155–156.

[178] Frank Griffith Dawson, *The First Latin American Debt Crisis, The City of London and the 1822–25 Loan Bubble* (New Haven: Yale University Press, 1990), p. 74. In one of the last publications published during his lifetime, James Crawford studied the legal status of the 1814 indemnity debt and its relationship to Napoleon, providing an interesting source of comparison with Iturbide. See James Crawford, 'Napoleon 1814–1815: A Small Issue of Status' in Inge Van Hulle and Randall C. H. Lesaffer eds., *International Law in the Long Nineteenth Century (1776–1914)* (Leiden, Brill, 2019), pp. 3–19.

[179] See Damian Clavel, 'What's in a Fraud? The Many Worlds of Gregor MacGregor, 1817–1824', *Enterprise & Society* 22:4 (2021), pp. 997–1036.

[180] *The speech of Viscount Palmerston, in reply to the motion of Lord George Bentinck, M.P., for an address to Her Majesty, in favour of the Spanish Bondholders, tried and compared with the fundamental law of this country, as laid down by Blackstone and Locke, and with the principles and rules of Grotius and Vattel* (London: Royal Exchange, 1848), p. 92. See also the connections between this debate and Robert Phillimore's ideas of international law in Koskenniemi, *To the Uttermost*, pp. 791–793.

[181] Reprinted in Robert Phillimore, *Commentaries Upon International Law*. Volume 1 (Philadelphia: T. & J. Johnson, Law Booksellers, 1854), pp. 27–28.

and Latin America when he argued that 'these half-civilised governments, such as those of China, Portugal, Spanish America, require a dressing [down] every eight or ten years to keep them in order'.[182] It was harder, and, indeed, undesirable, for an overstretched empire like Britain to consistently apply the logic of limited liability to rogue investors or unstable states on an international stage. In his view, force, exercised responsibly, was justified when dealing with these governments and advancing civilisation. Indeed, quoting Ernest Renan, Alberdi noted that this was a period of history that had realised that the idea of 'responsibility' was at the heart of any moral reform.[183] But in an age of financialised morals, civilising missions, and gunboat diplomacy, quite what responsibility meant was not clear: were governments responsible for the management of the interests of foreign creditors or those of their citizens? Prior to the 1850s, when Spain fundamentally reformed its public debt, its government's response was disheartening: it defaulted on its debts to both foreign and national bankers.[184] Above all, it defaulted, as the Colombian revolutionary Camilo Torres noted, on its debts to those Americans who were 'descendants from those who gave their blood to acquire these new territories for the Crown' and who were therefore 'as deserving' of the same recognition and representation as peninsular Spaniards who 'descended from Don Pelayo', the medieval king associated with the rise of the Reconquista of Muslim Spain.[185] Creole elites, and all the other mixed peoples of Latin America, in turn inherited a heavy burden: to establish what they owed to the Crown of Spain.

[182] Quoted in Maeve Ryan, *Humanitarian Governance and the British Antislavery World System* (New Haven: Yale University Press, 2022), p. 163.

[183] Juan Bautista Alberdi, *El crimen de la guerra* (Buenos Aires: Cadal, 2020), p. 73.

[184] Comín, *Las crisis*, pp. 122–156.

[185] Camilo Torres, 'Memorial de Agravios' (1809), in *Boletín de la Sociedad Geográfica de Colombia* 66 (1960), pp. 1–23, p. 6. See also Herzog's use of this passage to illustrate the roots of this opposition between creoles and peninsular Spaniards in Herzog, *Defining Nations*, p. 151.

3

A History of Forgiveness

Moral Bankruptcy in Mexico

Moctezuma III and Cortés

What did Mexico owe the heirs of Moctezuma and Cortés? Once they left Cádiz, three of the Mexican representatives at the Cortes found themselves trying to decipher this question. In 1821, en route from Cádiz to Mexico City, Zavala and Arizpe travelled to Paris. In a hotel salon, they met Alfonso José Antonio Pedro Nolasco Nicolás Diego Manuel de Santa Gertrudis Marcilla de Teruel Moctezuma y García de Alcaraz, Count of Moctezuma—Moctezuma's heir. At this gathering, they conspired to crown the Count the new Aztec Emperor, Moctezuma III.[1]

The descendants of Moctezuma had skilfully exploited the rights conferred on them by the Crown as a result of their status as Indian royalty.[2] In the seventeenth century, these aristocrats had successfully sued the Crown to ensure their properties remained exempt from new forms of taxation. These nobles greatly benefited from the *encomienda* and harnessed indigenous labour to increase their wealth and expand their networks in Mexico and Spain.[3] In 1784, Alfonso Marcilla de Teruel was born in the small town of Lorca, in the southeast of Spain. He inherited the title of Count of Moctezuma and the estate of Francisco Jiménez de Cisneros, Cardinal Cisneros, the polyglot Grand Inquisitor who served twice as regent of Castile and was one of the most influential statesmen in Spanish history.[4] In 1802, he married Manuel Godoy's niece, María de los Dolores Álvarez de Faría.[5]

Marcilla de Teruel struggled to live up to expectations: he felt stuck in an unhappy marriage, fled Madrid as French troops marched into the city, and settled in

[1] Rafael Rojas, *La escritura de la independencia: el surgimiento de la opinión pública en México* (Mexico City: Taurus/CIDE, 2003), pp. 71–72.

[2] Donald E. Chipman, *Moctezuma's Children: Aztec Royalty under Spanish Rule, 1520–1700* (Austin: University of Texas Press, 2005); Sarah Albiez-Wieck, 'Indigenous Migrants Negotiating Belonging: *Peticiones de cambio de fuero* in Cajamarca, Peru, 17th–18th centuries', *Colonial Latin American Review* 26:4 (2017), pp. 483–508. On the blending of Spanish and indigenous 'republics' see Max Deardorff, *A Tale of Two Granadas: Custom, Community, and Citizenship in the Spanish Empire, 1568–1668* (Cambridge: Cambridge University Press, 2023), pp. 116–141.

[3] Chipman, *Moctezuma's Children*, pp. 119–142.

[4] Carlos Eire, *Reformations: The Early Modern World, 1450–1650* (New Haven: Yale University Press, 2016), pp. 95–98, pp. 118–120.

[5] José Ignacio Conde y Díaz-Rubín and Javier Sanchiz Ruiz, *Historia genealógica de los títulos y dignidades nobiliarias en Nueva España y México Volumen II. Casa de Austria (siglos XVI–XVII)* (Mexico City: UNAM, 2012), p. 124.

Odious Debt. Edward Jones Corredera, Oxford University Press. © Edward Jones Corredera 2024.
DOI: 10.1093/9780191982200.003.0004

Cádiz while the Cortes were underway. In Cádiz, he showed little interest in constitutional discussions but did donate a large sum to the Crown to demonstrate 'that he fulfilled his responsibilities as a good Spaniard and a good vassal of Ferdinand VII'.[6] When the King returned to the throne, he repaid the favour and made the Count of Moctezuma *corregidor*, or magistrate, of Madrid.[7] Moctezuma oversaw the installation of one of only two monuments in Madrid that celebrated the return of the King—and one of the few that survive to this day.[8] But it soon became clear that Moctezuma's morals were entirely questionable. Even though Moctezuma received a steady stream of income from his estates in Spain and New Spain, he was heavily in debt.

The King began to pay attention to his malfeasance when María de los Dolores wrote to Ferdinand and denounced her husband's domestic abuse and financial neglect. When asked to explain himself, Moctezuma wrote to the King and countered that he was heavily indebted and could only survive thanks to his mother's supply of money; he was in no position to cover the costs of his wife or pay back his creditors.[9] Ferdinand was not impressed. He told the Count to pay the Countess what she was owed and asked him to provide a list of his creditors. Moctezuma insisted that he could not pay his lenders because, as a result of the revolt in Mexico, his yearly funds from the Americas had not been delivered. He refused to give the names of his creditors, and, when pressed, drafted a list of lenders whose debts had been satisfied. But he failed to provide the documents to verify this claim. Ferdinand got tired of Moctezuma's farce and relieved him of his position as *corregidor*.[10] Hounded by creditors and lawyers, Moctezuma made his way to Paris. There he was crowned Emperor Moctezuma III.

Moctezuma was promptly summoned by the Spanish ambassador and asked to discuss the veracity of the scheme to make him Emperor of Mexico. Moctezuma responded that he was unaware of this scheme: he was simply passing through Paris on his way to London, where he hoped to negotiate a loan to service his sizeable debts.[11] But rumours emerged that suggested that Moctezuma was in fact hoping to travel to Mexico to take up the throne.[12] Arizpe sought to disavow his role in this coronation. According to the Spanish ambassador in Paris, upon hearing of the gathering between Zavala and Moctezuma, Arizpe denounced the Count not to

[6] Ángel González Palencia, 'El Conde de Moctezuma, Corregidor de Madrid' [Part 1], *Revista de la Biblioteca, Archivo y Museo* 57 (1948), pp. 373–422, p. 385.

[7] Palencia, 'El Conde de Moctezuma' [Part 1], p. 386.

[8] Emilio la Parra López, 'El Rey ante sus súbditos. Presencia de Fernando VII en el espacio público', *Revista de Historia Constitucional* 20 (2019), pp. 5–23, p. 12. The best biography of Ferdinand, and one of the best biographies written in the past 50 years, is Emilio la Parra López, *Fernando VII: un rey deseado y detestado* (Barcelona: Tusquets, 2018).

[9] Angel González Palencia, 'El Conde de Moctezuma, Corregidor de Madrid' [Part 2], *Revista de la Biblioteca, Archivo y Museo* 58 (1949), pp. 141–208, p. 149.

[10] González Palencia, 'El Conde de Moctezuma' [Part 2], pp. 154–158.

[11] González Palencia, 'El Conde de Moctezuma' [Part 2], pp. 169–170.

[12] González Palencia, 'El Conde de Moctezuma' [Part 2], pp. 173.

the Mexican authorities, but to the ambassador, in the hope that his titles and possessions in the Iberian Peninsula would be seized.[13]

As the King threatened to strip him of his properties and rights, Moctezuma remained in Paris, where he negotiated other loans.[14] As Mexican statesmen convened their constitutional assemblies, Zavala, a report would later claim, told his fellow congressmen that Spain was 'persecuting' Moctezuma for his support of Mexican independence, and forcing the Count to live in a state of penury in Paris.[15] Moctezuma benefited from the munificence of the Mexican government, which agreed to grant a pension to the 'descendants of Moctezuma the Second'. A few months later, Mexican statesmen were dismayed to hear that the police had imprisoned Moctezuma over his unpaid debts.[16] A motion was tabled in congress to debate whether 'Mr. Count of Moctezuma should not be considered a Mexican citizen' but it failed to gain traction.[17] Once he left prison, Moctezuma found that Mexico failed to consistently pay his pension, and the Count eventually escaped from the reach of his debtors by travelling to New Orleans. Broke and bitter, Moctezuma corresponded with countless Mexican statesmen to declare his support for the revolution and request his pension.[18] When he died penniless, the French government made it clear that the Countess should not bear the burden of his debts.[19] The men in the family had to renegotiate his loans—and received the outstanding pension funds that Moctezuma had been owed.[20]

In a letter to Lucas Alamán, Arizpe wrote that the worst aspect of Moctezuma's farce was that it seemed to have inspired a false hope among indigenous people, and those marginalised communities that Arizpe had defended at the Cortes, that the Emperor was returning to free them from the 'tyranny of the insurgent creoles'.[21] Lucas Alamán was a reluctant insurgent creole.[22] He had grown up in a family that had made and lost its wealth in the mining industry and had joined Zavala and Arizpe as a representative for New Spain at the Cortes. During his

[13] González Palencia, 'El Conde de Moctezuma' [Part 2], pp. 169–171. José María Tornel y Mendívil, *Breve reseña histórica de los acontecimientos más notables de la nación mexicana: desde el año de 1821 hasta nuestros días* (Mexico City: Cumplido, 1852), p. 44. Nothing came of this meeting. Lucas Alamán included Arizpe's remonstration in his seminal history of Mexico and recorded that the meeting may have been organised by Zavala, his unprincipled rival. Lucas Alamán, *Historia de Méjico desde los primeros movimientos que prepararon su independencia en el año 1808 hasta la época presente*. Volume 5 (Mexico City: Lara, 1852), pp. 576–578. See also page 66 of the appendix.

[14] González Palencia, 'El Conde de Moctezuma' [Part 2], pp. 185–186.

[15] Quoted in González Palencia, 'El Conde de Moctezuma' [Part 2], pp. 185–187.

[16] González Palencia, 'El Conde de Moctezuma' [Part 2], p. 188.

[17] Juan Antonio Mateos, *Historia parlamentaria de los congresos mexicanos*. Volume 4 (Mexico City: Imprenta de Villada, 1881), p. 21, p. 26.

[18] González Palencia, 'El Conde de Moctezuma' [Part 2], pp. 190–198.

[19] González Palencia, 'El Conde de Moctezuma' [Part 2], p. 197.

[20] González Palencia, 'El Conde de Moctezuma' [Part 2], p. 198.

[21] Francisco Javier Rodríguez Gutiérrez, *El Doctor José Miguel Ramos de Arizpe, de súbdito a ciudadano. Documentos, 1808–1822* (Saltillo: Congreso del Estado de Coahuila, 2008), p. 276.

[22] Joshua Simon, *The Ideology of Creole Revolution: Imperialism and Independence in American and Latin American Political Thought* (Cambridge: Cambridge University Press, 2017), pp. 128–167.

interventions at the Cortes, he had criticised the way that a range of mining taxes targeted indigenous peoples and argued they should be abolished.[23]

Upon his return to Mexico, Alamán accepted a peculiar job: he represented the interests of the heirs to Hernán Cortés' title, the Lucchesi-Palli family, minor Sicilian aristocrats who were hugely pleased with Alamán's efforts to extract revenues from these properties and thwart a number of government attempts to permanently seize their estate.[24] They were equally relieved when Alamán ensured that revolutionaries did not throw the remains of Cortés' grandson in the bin.[25] But some of Alamán's peers did not understand his defence of a set of rights that had emerged from conquest and tyranny. Some of the territories owned by the Lucchesi-Palli family had once belonged to Moctezuma II and, when his fellow congressmen pressed Alamán to explain his defence of the conquistador's inheritors, he reminded them that Mexicans were the 'heirs' of the Spanish Crown.[26] The seizure of these properties, which congressmen claimed was nothing more than the 'restitution' of private property to the nation, was in fact a 'usurpation' of rights.[27] It would be outrageous, continued Alamán, to absorb Spanish colonial debts and not accept its civil laws.[28]

Indeed, the resolution of the affairs of the heirs of Moctezuma and Cortés was consistent with the Mexican approach to Spain's colonial debts. Ours is not the story of the rise and fall of *caudillos*, the travails of federalism, or the social dynamics of the new state; ours is the story of how, in the eyes of the men who designed constitutional and diplomatic solutions to this historiographical and legal problem, this was a family feud—an inheritance dispute that began with the debates on whether the Americas were God's gift to the Crown.[29] The leading

[23] On his early life and on his contributions at the Cortes see Eric van Young, *A Life Together: Lucas Alamán and Mexico, 1792–1853* (New Haven: Yale University Press, 2021), pp. 13–64, pp. 89–90, p. 315.

[24] Jan Bazant, 'La familia Alamán y los descendientes del Conquistador: 1850–1907', *Historia Mexicana* 26:1 (1976), pp. 48–69, p. 48.

[25] Van Young, *A Life Together*, p. 316.

[26] On these buildings see Jan Bazant, 'Los bienes de la familia de Hernán Cortés y su venta por Lucas Alamán', *Historia Mexicana* 19:2 (1969), pp. 228–247, p. 229.

[27] Lucas Alamán, *Esposición que hace la Cámara de diputados del Congreso General el apoderado del Duque de Terranova y Monteleone, Sobre las proposiciones presentadas por los señores diputados Don Matías Quintana y Don Miguel Cañedo, relativas á las propiedades que dicho Duque tiene en esta República* (México: José Fernández, 1828), pp. 15–16. Charles Hale, *El liberalismo mexicano en la época de Mora.* Translated by Serio Fernández Bravo and Francisco González Aramburu (Mexico City: Siglo XXI, 2012), p. 123.

[28] Alamán, *Esposición*, p. 18.

[29] On these aspects see Michael T. Ducey, 'Gobierno, legitimidad y movilización: aspectos de la vida electoral en tiempos insurgentes', *Historia Mexicana* 68:4 (2019), pp. 1593–1638; Marco Antonio Landavazo, 'Para una historia social de la violencia insurgente: El odio al Gachupín', *Historia Mexicana* 59:1 (2009), pp. 195–225. The causes behind the revolutions throughout the Spanish Atlantic were varied and remain a subject of intense debate; see Brian R. Hamnett, *The End of Iberian Rule on the American Continent, 1770–1830* (Cambridge: Cambridge University Press, 2017); Leandro de la Escosura, 'The Economic Consequences of Independence in Latin America' in Victor Bulmer-Thomas, John Coatsworth, and Roberto Cortés Conde eds., *The Cambridge Economic History of Latin America* (Cambridge: Cambridge University Press, 2005), pp. 461–504. On Mexico see Eric van Young, *The Other Rebellion: Popular Violence, Ideology, and the Mexican Struggle for Independence* (Stanford: Stanford University Press, 2001), pp. 75–90.

revolutionary general in Mexico, Agustín de Iturbide, explained that Mexico was a son who had come of age, who wanted to be independent and start his own life, but had no intention of abandoning his family.[30] In his influential *Manifesto*, the cleric Manuel de la Bárcena, argued that the 'colonies are to the metropole what children are to their fathers' and asked the Spanish Crown to 'give us a King' who, like Abraham, would end the revolt in Mexico by conceding a share of the land to its people. In other words, the King could end the revolt by accepting the formation of a Mexican composite state within the Spanish monarchy.[31] When Spain refused and promised instead to reconquer the country, Mexico set up its own independent government. But, as Zavala remarked in his intervention on the settlement of the colonial debts, Mexicans were still the children of the conquerors and the conquered. The debts were entangled in broader questions of the succession of patrimonial crowns, a political model which Grotius had undermined and Vattel and Bentham had ridiculed. These debts ought to be a matter of inheritance; a matter for civil law—Spanish civil law—and not the law of nations. Women, in this vision, were seen through the lens of property and not citizenship: as Erika Pani has shown, in the nineteenth century Mexican nationality was an agnatic privilege for those children born abroad. Mexican nationality was only granted to the offspring of Mexican men.[32]

As Payno noted, '*Like father, like son*', Mexico's reformers faced the same challenges that Charles III' enlightened ministers had once encountered.[33] Bankruptcy and the threat of war, he observed, were crass manoeuvres that were used by merchants and tyrants: this was not how families, people 'who share the same blood', settled their disputes. It was no accident that the most famous Mexican novel of the century, his *Los Bandidos del Río Frío*, drew on a story about the inheritance of a fictional indigenous descendant of the Aztec Emperor, Moctezuma III, to structure a wide-ranging narrative about the culture and society of this era.[34] The history of Spain, as Alamán made clear, was as much a tale about New Spain's children as it was a chronicle of kings and queens who never set foot on the Americas. Spain could not end a bond that had united saints and sinners or the dead and the

[30] Tomás Pérez Vejo, *España en el debate público mexicano, 1836–1867: aportaciones para una historia de la nación* (Mexico City: El Colegio de México, 2008), p. 52. On the use of this term at the Cádiz Cortes see Marie-Laure Rieu-Millan, *Los diputados americanos en las Cortes de Cádiz (Igualdad o independencia)* (Madrid: CSIC, 1990), pp. 327–328. This was a recurrent metaphor throughout the century. See Vejo, *España en el debate público mexicano*, p. 111. Following his demise, Bolívar would lament that '[n]ations are like children, who soon throw away what they have wept to attain', see David Bushnell, *El Libertador: Writings of Simón Bolívar*. Translated by Frederick H. Fornoff (Oxford: Oxford University Press, 2013), p. xxiv.

[31] Manuel Bárcena, *Manifiesto al mundo la justicia y la necesidad de la independencia de la Nueva España* (Puebla: Imprenta Liberal de Moreno Hermanos, 1821), p. 7, p. 18.

[32] Erika Pani '"Ciudadana y Muy Ciudadana"? Women and the State in Independent Mexico, 1810–30', *Gender & History* 18:1 (2006), pp. 5–19, p. 9.

[33] Payno, *México y el Sr. Embajador*, p. 88.

[34] See, in particular, Manuel Payno, *Los bandidos del Río Frío* (Mexico City: Fundación Carlos Slim, n.s.), pp. 218–219.

living across time and space.[35] But by refusing to keep it in the family and failing to compromise on its position on Mexico's independence, Spain had made this into an affair that was to be settled by international law—the Spanish inheritance was, according to Payno, 'the first debt that burdened Mexico'.[36] It was now up to Mexico to decide how to distribute the inheritance of laws, lands, and debts of its forebears among the descendants of Moctezuma and Cortés. The colonial inheritance turned Mexico's congress into a seminary of lawsuits. Mexico would only find redemption by making peace with its Spanish past and correcting the crooked timber of international law.

In 1821, as news about the desultory results of the negotiations at the Cortes reached Mexico, the leading local political Spanish authority in Mexico, Juan O'Donojú, negotiated the Treaty of Córdoba with Iturbide, whereby he accepted the independence of the colony and its role as a constituent part of a confederation within the Spanish Crown.[37] But Spain had already rejected a similar proposal the Mexican representatives had put forward at the Cádiz Cortes and had never authorised O'Donojú to grant Mexico its independence.[38] As it became clear that Spain would never accept this course of action, a new emperor was found. In a dizzying sequence of events, Iturbide occupied the vacuum left by the absence of a Bourbon sovereign and declared himself 'the First Constitutional Emperor of Mexico' in a session of the Junta Provisional Gubernativa, the first Mexican congressional body.[39] His oath displayed his acceptance of the checks and balances imposed on sovereign power by the Cádiz Constitution.[40] Yet, within months, Iturbide's growing disregard for the nation's representative bodies became a source of tension in congress.[41] When elections were held the voters granted greater power to the legislature over the executive. In response, Iturbide expanded his own authority and dissolved the parliamentary institutions. After an initial coup against Iturbide failed, further unrest forced the Emperor to abdicate his throne. This instability triggered elections and generated difficult questions about the role of executive power at the heart of Mexican politics.[42]

[35] Eire, *Reformations*, p. 35.

[36] Manuel Payno, *México y sus cuestiones financieras con la Inglaterra, la España y la Francia* (Mexico City: Cumplido, 1862), p. 145.

[37] Barbara A. Tenenbaum, *The Politics of Penury: Debts and Taxes in Mexico, 1821–1856* (Alburquerque: University of New Mexico Press, 1986), pp. 18–19.

[38] Timothy Anna, *Spain and the Loss of America* (London: University of Nebraska Press, 1983), pp. 253–255; Rafael Rojas, *Las repúblicas de aire. Utopía y desencanto en la revolución de Hispanoamérica* (Madrid: Taurus, 2009), pp. 50–51.

[39] On the expansionist dimension behind the choice to refer to the polity as an empire see Timothy E. Anna, *Forging Mexico, 1821-7835* (Lincoln: University of Nebraska Press, 1998), p. 87.

[40] Timothy Anna, *The Mexican Empire of Iturbide* (Lincoln: University of Nebraska Press, 1990), pp. 76–78; Rojas, *La escritura*, p. 95.

[41] Its origins can be found in Anna, *The Mexican Empire of Iturbide*, pp. 68–71

[42] Roberto Breña, 'En torno al liberalismo hispánico aspectos del republicanismo, del federalismo y del liberalismo de los pueblos en la Independencia de México', in Izaskun Álvarez Cuartero and Julio Sánchez Gómez eds., *Visiones y revisiones de la independencia americana: México, Centroamérica y Haití* (Salamanca: Ediciones Universidad de Salamanca, 2005), pp. 179–204.

Arizpe seized control of the situation: he emerged as the flagbearer for a conciliatory federalism and helped to draft a new constitution.[43] In an effort to check the potential ambitions of another despotic figure, the provinces were granted greater control over the new constitutional levers of power.[44] Discussions over the concrete differences between confederalism and federalism gradually came to dominate Mexican political debate.[45] The government was made up of a federal bicameral government.[46] States controlled almost half of the tax sources that the colonial government had once managed; the national administration, by contrast, retained control of customs revenues and a number of monopolies.[47] Deputies drew on Vattel's writings to defend the motion to enshrine Catholicism as the nation's official religion in this new constitution.[48]

It was a fragile compromise. But this constitutional arrangement would allow Mexico to begin to resolve the question of its colonial debts. Arizpe, who years earlier had claimed that Spain owed to America countless debts had later watched his peers, through the rise and fall of Iturbide, debate what they owed to the Spanish Empire. As its statesmen sought to make peace with Spain, these discussions, spearheaded by Zavala, would influence the constitutional future of Mexico. Mexico's choice to forgive and forget Spain turned on a wide-ranging historiographical debate on the nature of colonial rule: as the rest of this chapter shows, deputies put forth conflicting visions of the past, with retroactive effect, to argue that the rights of creditors should mollify and trump the passions of the revolution, that Spain's rule in the Americas was entirely illegitimate, and that Grotius' and Vattel's reading of Philip II's moral bankruptcy did not correspond to Mexico's own view of its colonial past.

On the need for a history of Spain's debts to Mexico

On 9 October 1821, at one of the earliest gatherings of the Junta Provisional Gubernativa, representatives began to draft the *Acta de Independencia del Imperio*, a declaration of independence, a constitutional blueprint, and a political framework. The text, according to some of the deputies, should make clear that Mexico was 'not obliged to agree to pay any debts, but rather only those negotiated by

[43] Hale, *El liberalismo*, p. 81; Anna, *Forging Mexico*, pp. 127–129, pp. 142–144, p. 159.

[44] Rojas, *La escritura*, p. 95.

[45] Josefina Zoraida Vázquez, 'El federalismo mexicano, 1823–1847' in Marcello Carmagnani ed., *Federalismos Latinoamericanos: México/Brasil/Argentina* (Mexico City: Fondo de Cultura Económica, 1993), pp. 15–50.

[46] Rojas, *La escritura*, p. 100–101. Jaime E. Rodríguez O., *'We Are Now the True Spaniards': Sovereignty, Revolution, Independence, and the Emergence of the Federal Republic of Mexico, 1808–1824* (Stanford: Stanford University Press, 2012), pp. 306–308. On forced loans and other financial measures during this period see Anna, *The Mexican Empire of Iturbide*, pp. 127–136.

[47] Anna, *Forging Mexico*, pp. 188–190.

[48] *Constitución Federal de 1824: Crónicas*. Volume 1, p. 152.

a legitimate government', and that adding the word '*legitimate*' before '*debt*' would suffice to clarify this point.[49] Others believed this language was not strong enough: the commission established to assess Mexico's debts had 'distinguished between the debts contracted by Mexico and those contracted by Spain', and so the text should read that 'the government recognised the debt that is classified as legitimate'.[50] Mexico would ultimately define what debts were legitimate before it established what type of government was licit.

Zavala, then deputy for Yucatán, led congressional debates over Mexico's finances and drew on the liberal principles of Constant and Bentham.[51] But the more radical representatives thought the question of the colonial debts was intimately connected to the right to revolution. In his countless writings on the war of independence against Spain, the republican deputy and historian Carlos María de Bustamante proved to be one of the strongest defenders of the messianic view that Mexicans were the descendants of indigenous peoples. The revolution, he believed, should be seen as a restoration of the Aztec Empire. Cortés and his men had, in his view, usurped the rule of Emperor Moctezuma.[52] Hence the contracts signed under or by the usurping Spanish regime were null and void. Whatever he may have done in Paris, Zavala showed no inclination to support this view: he disagreed strongly with Bustamante, and their difference of opinion would set the terms of the debate over Mexico's debts to Spain.[53]

Bustamante radicalised the critique made by priests and officials against the Crown during the crisis of the *vales*: he argued that it was Spain who owed a debt of gratitude to Mexico. He began by drawing attention to the debt Spain owed Mexico for the American financial support to the empire in its war against Napoleon: once 'New Spain' heard the voice of the 'Spaniards' reclaiming their 'King' against France, countless Mexicans had eagerly sent funds to 'Old Spain' to finance its 'existential' struggle.[54] The propagation of the Enlightenment in Mexico during that time ensured that the 'nation awoke from its lethargy'. The nation

[49] On the debate in the 1810s see Carlos Marichal, *Bankruptcy of Empire: Mexican Silver and the Wars Between Spain, Britain and France, 1760–1810* (Cambridge: Cambridge University Press, 2009), pp. 237–254.

[50] Juan Mateos, *Historia parlamentaria de los congresos mexicanos de 1821 a 1857*. Volume 1 (Mexico City: Reyes), p. 78.

[51] See Barbara Tenenbaum, 'Banqueros sin bancos: el papel de los agiotistas en México', in Leonor Ludlow and Carlos Marichal eds., *Banca y poder en México* (1800–1925) (Mexico City: Grijalbo, 1985), pp. 75–98, p. 78. Raymond Estep, *Lorenzo de Zavala: profeta del liberalismo mexicano*. Translated by Carlos A. Echánove Trujillo. Prologue by Carlos A. Castañeda (Mexico City: Porrúa, 1952), pp. 61–68.

[52] This discourse would become associated with Bustamante, who would be blamed by its opponents for coining it; see Vejo, *España en el debate público mexicano*, p. 59. See Rojas, *La escritura*, pp. 69–70. Bustamante had made the same argument as early as 1810. See David Brading, *The First America: The Spanish Monarchy, Creole Patriots, and the Liberal State, 1492–1867* (Cambridge: Cambridge University Press, 1991), pp. 580–581 and, on his broader thought, Will Fowler, *Mexico in the Age of Proposals, 1821–1853* (London: Greenwood Press, 1998), pp. 101–128.

[53] On Bustamante's broader economic proposals see Elda de Jesús Moreno Acevedo, 'Génesis del sistema fiscal mexicano 1821–1824', *Documentos de Trabajo (IELAT)* 40 (2012), pp. 53–69, p. 60.

[54] Mateos, *Historia. (Appendix)*, p. 57.

manifested its desire for 'independence', an idea that was 'innate to the hearts of Americans'.[55] If the 'acquiescence' that Americans had shown towards Spain's colonial rule was a reason to 'accept the debt the Mexican nation has contracted', this tacit consent only lasted until '16 September of 1808', the date of the Cry of Dolores, when the American people expressed their true will. Any of the debts incurred thereafter were not the result of 'voluntary, but violent oblations', forced offerings to a deity.[56] What was required to settle these debts, explained Bustamante, was a history of the Mexican War of Independence. Deputies had 'to establish a distinction of epochs, quantities, and ways of demanding' the repayment of debt.[57] It just so happened that Bustamante had provided the basis for such a history in his *Cuadro histórico*, which sketched the various phases of the revolution, and he used his interventions on Mexico's colonial debts to promote the main themes of this work.

By contrast, Zavala drew on his memory of the Spanish Cortes, a government that Bustamante believed was illegitimate, as a virtuous example of liberal governance. The Spanish Cortes, he recalled, had 'recognised the Dutch debt from the time of Charles IV' because the 'honour and self-interest of nations' demanded it.[58] It was in Mexico's self-interest to follow the law of nations and repay these debts. This debate was 'not about the Mexican nation and the Spanish nation, but rather the individuals of the former gathering in the latter'. The law of nations could not be breached: the 'credit of these nations was one and the same, and its individuals lent sums under the guarantee of natural law and the law of nations'.[59] An investor, who had believed that a nation was on solid ground, should not lose their investment because of Mexico's 'right to independence'.[60]

Were Spaniards usurpers, tyrants, and conquerors in America or were they brothers and sisters in a congregation of American men and women? The settlement of Mexico's debts to Spain generated the most sophisticated debate on the nature of the Mexican War of Independence. The debate revealed that the right to revolution clashed with the principle of property rights.[61] Did the right of creditors trump the right of revolutionaries to sever their ties with their former occupiers? Was Spain nothing more than a colonising nation that ought to compensate Mexico or a glowing example of a liberal nation for others to follow? Mexican

[55] Mateos, *Historia. (Appendix)*, p. 57. On his view on taxation and Spanish law see Acevedo, 'Génesis', pp. 59–60.
[56] Mateos, *Historia. (Appendix)*, p. 58. It was only really during the Junta de Zitácuaro that 'in the eyes of the nations of the Old Continent the Mexican revolution took place', he argued. See Mateos, *Historia. (Appendix)*, p. 58.
[57] Mateos, *Historia. (Appendix)*, p. 58.
[58] Mateos, *Historia. (Appendix)*, p. 60.
[59] Mateos, *Historia. (Appendix)*, p. 59.
[60] Mateos, *Historia. (Appendix)*, p. 59.
[61] Zavala would also directly defend the repayment of the debt as a way of encouraging foreign investment; see Estep, *Zavala*, p. 65.

deputies turned to the law of nations to provide an answer to these questions and commenced Mexico's oral and operative history of Spain's odious debts.[62]

The odious sovereign: when was Spanish rule illegitimate?

Grotius and Vattel had established that the legitimacy of a kingdom's debts could be determined by studying the use of these public funds. Building on this principle, the republican deputy Juan Bautista Morales approached the topic by analysing whether colonial loans had benefited the American people. In his intervention, he suggested that the 'law of nations' had established as a 'type of royal charge' the debts of 'a nation when it changes its state', and thus Mexico ought to repay its 'public debt', even if its government had changed.[63] But the government had to 'carefully' separate each of these public debts, since, as he proceeded to make clear, each one was founded on a different set of rights. The 'Spanish nation', explained Morales, could have generated debt in a variety of ways: first, it could have drawn on funds from the Iberian Peninsula. 'America' had no responsibility for these loans. These funds were withdrawn abroad to meet peninsular needs. Spain could have taken on debts by 'mortgaging the Americas', which would have yielded no benefits to Spanish America, and which Americans therefore had 'no obligation to repay'. Finally, Spain could have taken out loans 'for the benefit of America' from Spanish financiers, which America, he contended, did not have to repay.

Indeed, Morales argued that only in those cases where Spain had borrowed 'for the utility of America and drawing funds from therein', that America had a duty to pay back. To wit, America only had to pay those debts that had been drawn in America and in order to improve its welfare. Where the Viceroy had taken out loans from local financiers to finance Spain's interests, Mexico had no duty to repay them, since the Viceroy had to be 'understood as an agent of the Spanish Government' at the time, and thus these were debts that belonged to the nation of Spain.[64] Morales further divided these loans into those that were used for the benefit of the 'American government' and those that were simply contracts the Crown had signed in the Americas, sometimes forcibly, to assist Spain during the Napoleonic invasion and for 'the utility of the peninsula'.[65] America—not just Mexico—could not pay 'more debts than it could have reasonably asked for'.[66]

The law of nations, and Morales' sharp distinctions, allowed Zavala to find a compromise that, he believed, would satisfy Bustamante. In May, a commission for

[62] On operative knowledge see John C. Rule and Ben S. Trotter, *A World of Paper: Louis XIV, Colbert de Torcy, and the Rise of the Information State* (Montreal: McGill-Queen's Press, 2014).
[63] Mateos, *Historia. (Appendix)*, p. 64.
[64] Mateos, *Historia. (Appendix)*, p. 65.
[65] Mateos, *Historia. (Appendix)*, p. 65.
[66] Mateos, *Historia. (Appendix)*, p. 65.

the reform of public credit led by Zavala produced its report on the nation's public debt. The report drew on Bustamante's suggestion to establish a timeline of the Mexican War of Independence: there were 'four periods' which were marked 'by the memorable events which have characterized our revolution, after a profound slumber of three centuries'.[67] Prior to the Cry of Dolores, the law of nations recognised Spain's sovereignty over the Americas. Mexicans, in turn, accepted the legitimacy of the Spanish Crown through 'their silence' and 'a tacit consent'. As such, it was clear that 'all the debts contracted by the nation during this period must be recognised'.[68]

But the report also drew on Zavala's experience in Spain. Regarding the debts incurred 'by insurgents' prior to 1810, the commission had followed 'the example of the Spanish Cortes', which, 'in the same circumstances', under assault from French troops, recognised the debts contracted by the popular *juntas* 'to sustain the nation's independence'. According to the commissioners, this was particularly 'just since that it was the creditors' patriotism which was in large part responsible for fostering the sacred fire which here and there', in Spain and Spanish America, 'saved our independence and the national honour'.[69] Those loans negotiated by the Cádiz insurgents had been incurred to secure the freedom of Spain and the Americas; these debts of honour had to be paid.

But there remained the question of what the status of Spain had been under French occupation, and what New Spain's role in Spain had been after the viceroyalty declared its independence. From the month of September of 1810, once the Cry of Dolores echoed across New Spain the 'right of the Spaniards over its colonies' became questionable. This controversy, as one deputy noted, was overshadowed by the invasion of Napoleon, and here the matter turned on a delicate question: 'should the government accept any of the debts incurred by the government after the cry of independence' but which were also used to defeat Napoleon?

Zavala's commission had concluded that Mexico had a responsibility to repay these debts. But the report distinguished between the voluntary and forced loans. Any 'merchant' or 'property-owning interested party' who had wished to support the Spanish government voluntarily should be punished since they had willingly financed Mexico's enemy. But when 'the Viceroy's government' used 'bayonets and ignored the law' and seized funds from 'well-meaning Americans who were addicted to the holy cause of liberty' it was clear that 'the nation was obliged to satisfy these credits, recognizing them as a sacred debt' not to Spain but to the victims of Spanish tyranny.[70]

67 Mateos, *Historia. (Appendix)*, pp. 314–315.
68 Mateos, *Historia. (Appendix)*, pp. 314–315.
69 Mateos, *Historia. (Appendix)*, pp. 316–317.
70 Mateos, *Historia. (Appendix)*, pp. 314–315.

Fray Mier and the right to default: what if Spain's rule was illegitimate?

The reading of the commission's proposals in the chamber caused a great deal of commotion. A number of representatives protested against the historical premises behind the proposals.[71] Since Spain had ruled by virtue of force and conquest, argued some deputies, it followed that Mexico ought to default on these debts.[72] The liberal Florentino Martínez endorsed the commission's conclusions and argued that this was a matter of fulfilling the demands of the future: Mexico had to demonstrate its 'public faith' to bolster its creditworthiness in negotiations with 'our compatriots and with learned nations'. Creditors were not responsible for a government's 'good or bad use' of its public debt.[73] To declare as much would be to close the door to the negotiation of other loans.[74] History showed that 'enlightened nations' had 'always recognised the debts contracted by their usurpers': Charles II recognised the loans contracted by Thomas Cromwell; France recognised Napoleon's liabilities. Hence Mexico should recognise Spain's debt.[75]

This, then, was the crux of the matter of Mexico's odious debts: paying the bills of a tyrant was the only way for a young nation to demonstrate its respect for private property and to encourage creditors to invest in the state. If Mexico were to stage 'the unprecedented spectacle of presenting before the world a people that has reunited to govern itself through the eternal principles of justice, and which began by not recognising the pacts of the previous government that had been made with our own compatriots' as private citizens, Martínez explained, 'who then would interest themselves' in the conservation of the Mexican government?[76]

Bustamante delivered the most scathing critique of the historical narrative of the report—and formulated a brilliant argument against the claim that Spaniards were nothing more than benign creditors in America. It was important, he argued in his intervention, to return to the foundations of Spain's colonisation of the Americas. Spain had exploited the Americas without their consent, for the Crown's profit, and by drawing on their mines to fund further conquests. Could it be said, he asked, that the 'obligations contracted by the Spaniards and the Americans had been legitimately contracted?' Bustamante then proceeded to deliver a 'sketch' of the Spanish 'conquest and usurpation' of Mexico, starting his tale with the travels of Christopher Columbus. Upon discovering 'a new world', the 'indigenous race' was exploited and destroyed in the pursuit of 'acquisition and profit'. Charles V, when exploiting the resources of Moctezuma, had failed

71 Mateos, *Historia. (Appendix)*, p. 318.
72 Mateos, *Historia. (Appendix)*, p. 318.
73 Mateos, *Historia. (Appendix)*, p. 321.
74 Mateos, *Historia. (Appendix)*, p. 321.
75 Mateos, *Historia. (Appendix)*, p. 321.
76 Mateos, *Historia. (Appendix)*, p. 322.

to 'spend a single cent' of Spain's funds, and those conquistadors who led the expedition were 'not from this territory'. Spaniards, Bustamante concluded, had no 'creditors' rights over us'.[77]

America's sacrifice, he argued, had preserved the Spanish Crown. The empire's debts had in turn never been used for the benefit of America. Bustamante noted that America had never 'needed the help of Spain to subsist'. America, in 'those times that politicians describe as dark', sacrificed 'its needs and delivered millions every year to the metropole'. Further to all of America's sacrifices, how could Spain try 'to demand from us the recognition of some debts that have not been used to our advantage?' And on what principles, he continued 'are we to base the claim that a man is a debtor to another, when we know that those funds that he received were the cause of his ruin and decline?' Was it not true, posited Bustamante, that most of the funds had served to finance the opulent demands of the Court rather than the well-being of the people?[78]

These principles, his fellow deputies replied, were drawn from international law. The consequences of declaring the former government illegitimate, countered the liberal Cayetano Ibarra, would be the 'disavowing [of] the judgements made by courts of justice'. He referred to Vattel's 'principle' that 'governments cannot draw debts without thinking of the known utility of the people, sanctioned by their will'. While Ibarra recognised the 'veracity of these principles', he believed it was 'from their wise or unwise applicability that we can infer favourable or negative consequences'.[79] The nation could not be free from past responsibilities, otherwise 'nations that had once been ruled despotically would not be obliged by any of the acts of the previous government [. . .] even if these have used their products against their expressed interests'. France 'could not have wished' for Napoleon to wage war on Europe but it had accepted the debts contracted by these governments.[80] Forswearing the contracts of previous governments, explained Ibarra, would 'destroy' the right to private property, 'that sacred right which is the soul of society', because this principle could not 'exist without laws and without a government which can authorise it'. If the Spanish government was illegitimate, it would follow that all contracts and property rights that derived from its norms would be null. Ibarra encouraged his colleagues to remember that Mexico was agreeing to recognise the debt. Mexico did not have 'a single peso' at that time. The proposed reform would only 'solemnly oblige' its officials to pay these debts once the government had the necessary resources.[81]

[77] Mateos, *Historia. (Appendix)*, p. 319. On the Mexican debates on the Spanish conquest of America see Tomás Pérez Vejo, 'Hispanófobos vs. Hispanófilos. La historia como arma de lucha política en México, 1821–1867' in Agustín Sánchez Andrés and Juan Carlos Pereira Castañares eds., *España y México. Doscientos años de relaciones, 1810–2010* (Morelia: UMSHN, 2010), pp. 125–166.

[78] Mateos, *Historia. (Appendix)*, p. 321.

[79] Mateos, *Historia. (Appendix)*, p. 342.

[80] Mateos, *Historia. (Appendix)*, p. 342.

[81] Mateos, *Historia. (Appendix)*, p. 343.

The most sophisticated intervention in this debate was delivered by Servando Teresa Mier. Mier was one of the most radical Mexican republicans—and an eclectic thinker. Mier had argued that Mexico did not owe its Catholic foundations to Spain: the term Mexico was the product of a creative pre-colonial translation of the Hebrew word for 'messiah'. This demonstrated that the indigenous assimilation of confessional beliefs predated the arrival of the conquistadors.[82] Mier had been twice imprisoned for his political views. He had participated in the Cádiz Cortes and had compared the tyranny of Spain over the Amerias to that of Napoleon over Spain. He was at once sceptical of confederations but hoped to create a single government for Latin America with three sub-departments.[83] His uncommon views contributed to the commercial success of his works: his *Historia de la Revolución de Nueva España*, a defence of Mexico's independence, was hugely popular in Mexico, Spain, and France.[84]

In his intervention on the matter of Mexico's colonial debts, he complained that in recognising both colonial debts and those of the insurgents, Mexico appeared to be taking on a schizophrenic identity; it was both paying and profiting from these loans.[85] Mexico, in other words, could not be both Spanish and Mexican. There was, he explained, a key difference between the periods before and after 1810: prior to 1810, the Spanish government, through the use of force, was in full possession of the Americas. Yet once the oppressed took arms against the government the legality of its rule was subject to interpretation.[86]

Mier explained that, by drawing on incontestable documents, he had demonstrated in his own 'history of the revolution of New Spain' that since 1810 the

[82] This was consistent with his broader views on Guadalupe, Saint Thomas, and the arrival of Catholicism in the Americas, opinions for which he was incarcerated: see the opening pages of his memoirs, written while he was in prison: Servando Teresa de Mier, *Memorias* (Mexico City: Secretaría de Cultura, 2016), pp. 11–85. Servando Teresa de Mier, *Carta de despedida a los mexicanos: 1821.* Prólogo, notas y cronología de Edmundo O'Gorman (Caracas: Biblioteca Ayacucho, 1978), pp. 7–13. On creole patriotic politics and questions of epistemology see Jorge Cañizares-Esguerra, *How to Write the History of the New World: Histories, Epistemologies, and Identities in the Eighteenth-Century Atlantic World* (Stanford: Stanford University Press, 2001).

[83] On changes and continuities in Mier's thought see the excellent studies Roberto Breña, 'Pensamiento político e ideología en la emancipación americana. Fray Servando Mier y la independencia absoluta de Nueva España', in Francisco Colom González ed., *Relatos de nación. La construcción de identidades nacionales en el mundo hispánico.* Volume 1 (Frankfurt: Vervuert, 2005), pp. 73–102 and Rafael Diego-Fernández Sotelo, 'Influencias y evolución del pensamiento político de fray Servando Teresa de Mier. *Historia Mexicana* 48:1 (1998), pp. 3–35. See also David Brading, *Los origenes del nacionalismo mexicano.* Translated by Soledad Loaeza Grave (México: Secretaría de Educación Pública, 1973), pp. 43–93.

[84] María Teresa Berruezo León, *La lucha de Hispanoamérica por su independencia en Inglaterra 1800–1830* (Madrid: Ediciones de Cultura Hispánica, 1989), p. 144

[85] Mateos, *Historia. (Appendix)*, p. 355.

[86] Mateos, *Historia. (Appendix)*, p. 355. On his views on Pufendorf and the reversion of power to the people following the abdication of a king see José Carlos Chiaramonte, *Nación y Estado en Iberoamérica. El lenguaje político en tiempos de la independencia* (Buenos Aires: Editorial Sudamericana, 2004), p. 116. In 1808, the Cabildo of Mexico had sought to gather the Cortes since the King's abdication had not followed the norms of the *Partidas*; see François-Xavier Guerra, *Modernidad e independencias: ensayos sobre las revoluciones hispánicas* (México: FCE, 2010), pp. 126–127.

viceroys' authority had been illegitimate and null.[87] Indeed, in his *Historia*, Mier had argued that, at the Cádiz Cortes, Spaniards had broken the true contract between Spanish Americans and the Spanish Crown.[88] While he was critical of Spanish colonial rule, and cited Bartolomé de las Casas' critique of the empire, he argued that the Cádiz Constitution, inspired by Jean-Jacques Rousseau's *Social Contract*, had ruptured the bond between America and the Spanish Crown that was based on the *pactismo*, the pact between the Crown and the people, that had been established since the arrival of Columbus.[89]

In his contribution to the debate on colonial debts, Mier elaborated on these views. In a state of 'anarchy' officials gathered at the Cádiz Cortes. They were not recognised by any of the Crown's councils—not even those in Cádiz. Hence the Cortes lacked the authority to name Francisco Javier Venegas de Saavedra as Viceroy of Mexico, which meant that he had not been a governor, either de facto or de jure. The Cry of Dolores therefore fought 'force with force'.[90] In the absence of a legitimate government, Mexico had simply resisted the forces of 'tyrants sent by others' and therefore did not have 'any obligation to recognise the debts contracted to wage war on us' and against principles of 'the law of nations'.[91] To be forced to pay for the actions of viceroys who were not legitimate rulers was wrong: these contracts were not binding because of the odious intentions of their signatories.[92]

Mier's rousing history of odious debt failed to convince his colleagues. Zavala's view that the debts of the 'children of the nation' ought to be paid won the day. The need to establish the nation's liberal adherence to property rights was more important than prolonging the historiographical litigation over the origins of the revolution.[93] In the debates that led to the drafting of the Federal Constitution, Mexico recognised the debts contracted by the viceregal government prior to 1810, as well as those incurred by the local colonial Spanish authorities between 1810 and the rise to power of Iturbide.[94] Yet the decision to state, in official government documents, that 'the Spanish government was a legitimate one' continued to elicit complaints.[95] This debate on the debt to Spain was, after all, nothing more

[87] See, in particular, the last volume of Servando Teresa de Mier's *Historia de la revolución de Nueva España* (Mexico City: CEMC, 1990).

[88] Mier, *Historia de la revolución*, pp. 555–556.

[89] Mier, *Historia de la revolución*, pp. 570–573. Mier himself had shown some interest in Rousseau's interpretation during the debates at Cádiz, see Rieu-Millan, *Los diputados*, pp. 15–16. See also Pagden, *Spanish Imperialism*, pp. 118–120 and José María Portillo, *Una historia atlántica de los orígenes de la nación y el Estado* (Madrid: Alianza, 2022), pp. 148–149.

[90] Mateos, *Historia. (Appendix)*, p. 356.

[91] Mateos, *Historia. (Appendix)*, pp. 357–358.

[92] Mateos, *Historia. (Appendix)*, pp. 356–357. Anna, *The Mexican Empire of Iturbide*, p. 88.

[93] See also the analysis of Pi-Suñer Llorens in Antonia Pi-Suñer Llorens, *La deuda española en México. Diplomacia y política en torno a un problema financiero, 1821–1890* (Mexico City: UNAM, 2006), pp. 42–43.

[94] Mateos, *Historia. (Appendix)*, p. 322. See also Estep, *Zavala*, pp. 66–67.

[95] Mateos, *Historia. (Appendix)*, p. 327.

than a revised draft of existing histories of the revolution, a first sketch of future chronicles of the rise of the Mexican state, and one of the first constitutional attempts to establish where Spain ended and Mexico began. Many of the histories of the revolution written in the 1830s were drafted by these deputies: most of them, including Zavala, followed the episodic history which framed these constitutional debates.[96]

Over the next two decades, countless governments harnessed the spirit of the revolution. In this time, 50 military governments ruled the nation.[97] General Vicente Guerrero, of Afro-Mexican descent, toppled the federal government before he was displaced by Anastasio Bustamante's coup. General Antonio López de Santa Anna would in turn overthrow Bustamante's government. By the middle of the century, Santa Anna would rise and fall from power 11 times.[98] Between 1821 and 1876, according to the historian Hilda Sabato, rebels launched over one thousand five hundred *pronunciamientos*: military threats to use violence to force the government's hand on a particular policy.[99] As noted by Antonia Pi-Suñer Llorens, the most important historian of Mexico's Spanish debt, a mid-century report on the nation's public credit observed that the rough figures of the colonial debt remained impossible to track down.[100] Constitutions would be drafted and discarded. International legal norms would be debated and contested. Treaties, in turn, would seek to consign old disputes to oblivion. Debts, however, remained outstanding and unpaid.

Who are the true Spaniards now?

As Mexican officials put an end to the debate over the nation's colonial debts, fiscal limitations encouraged Mexico to seek loans abroad. In 1824 and 1825, the Mexican government negotiated with two British firms, B.A. Goldschmidt & Company and the Barclay, Herring, Richardson Company, for the procurement of two loans. To secure these funds, the Mexican government promised to commit a third of its tariff duties towards the repayment of each loan.[101] One deputy who had been reluctant to pay the Spanish debt warned his peers that incurring these

[96] Hale, *El liberalismo*, p. 25. For Ocampo's periodisation see Anna, *Forging Mexico*, p. 90. On the influence of Bustamante on Alamán's thought see Eric van Young, 'Between Bustamante and Burke: Lucas Alamán's Historical Project', *Korpus* 21:1 (2021), pp. 395–418.

[97] Enrique Krauze, *Mexico: Biography of Power. A History of Modern Mexico, 1810–1996*. Translated by Hanz Heifetz (New York: Harper Collins, 1997), p. 133.

[98] Krauze, *Mexico*, pp. 137–139.

[99] Hilda Sabato, *Republics of the New World: The Revolutionary Political Experiment in Nineteenth-Century Latin America* (Princeton: Princeton University Press, 2018), p. 112.

[100] Pi-Suñer Llorens, *La deuda española*, p. 43.

[101] Tenenbaum, *The Politics*, p. 21.

foreign debts would lead Mexico into a 'tyranny of numbers' whereby 'a nation encircles another through loans by drawing on usury and mercantile calculations'. Like 'a fish that takes the bait', he continued, Mexico was close to falling into the hands of 'the Carthage of our time'.[102] Mexico would be unable to repay the loan and would be forced to declare bankruptcy. In his view, one only had to look at the experience of Buenos Aires to see how British products would flood the country and undermine any efforts at creating a national industry.[103] The Mexican population would take on the position that 'black people in Cuba occupy today'.[104] Mier in turn warned his colleagues about the risks of introducing a constitution based on foreign models of government while ignoring the nation's ethnic composition and its history.[105] Bustamante, by contrast, saw the negotiation of British loans as a way to demonstrate that Mexico was not Spain: the Bourbon dynasty, he argued, reneged on countless promises to repay its debts. Showing the world that Mexico, unlike the Spanish Crown, acted in good faith was the best way to 'start anew'.[106]

In the event, the government ensured its financial dependence on European networks when it reformed the constitution: foreign trade replaced colonial monopolies as the main source of the government's revenues.[107] Congress passed a decree that authorised the signing of a foreign loan that drew on the entirety of the national treasury as collateral. The measure bore fruit and foreign investments in Mexican mining companies grew exponentially.[108] The mounting authority of the provinces, in turn, offered hope that local governments would be able to generate more resources to fund the central government of the nation.[109] But constitutional reform did not resolve age-old questions: Mexico would soon have to confront, once again, what it meant to be different from Spain. Scholars have argued that Mexico's relative stability in the mid-1820s was premised on the fiscal stability brought about by the British loans.[110] Within a few years, however, the effects of the London stock market crash were felt. The British debt still had to be repaid

[102] Juan Mateos, *Historia parlamentaria de los congresos mexicanos de 1821 a 1857*. Volume 2 (Mexico City: Villada, 1878), p. 322
[103] Mateos, *Historia*. Volume 2, pp. 322–323.
[104] Mateos, *Historia*. Volume 2, p. 323.
[105] Brading, *First America*, p. 599; Brading, *Los origenes*, pp. 92–94.
[106] Mateos, *Historia*. Volume 2, pp. 324.
[107] Barbara A. Tenenbaum, 'The Early Republic and Santa Anna', in William Beezley ed., *The Oxford Handbook of Mexican History* (Oxford: Oxford University Press, 2021) (Online).
[108] Barbara A. Tenenbaum, 'Taxation and Tyranny; Public Finance during the Iturbide Regime, 1821–1823', in Jaime E. Rodríguez, *The Independence of México and the Creation of the New Nation* (Los Angeles: University of California Press, 1989), pp. 201–213, p. 208; for the most detailed analysis of the topic see Richard J. Salvucci, *Politics Markets, and Mexico's 'London Debt,' 1823–1887* (New York: Cambridge University Press, 2009), pp. 64–74. For an economic analysis of the fairness of the negotiation see Jan Bazant, *Historia de la deuda exterior de México, 1823–1946* (Mexico City: El Colegio de México, 1968), pp. 42–47.
[109] Rodríguez, *'We Are Now the True Spaniards'*, p. 325.
[110] Rojas, *La escritura*, pp. 105–106; Salvucci, *Politics*, p. 96.

and one eighth of customs revenue was assigned towards its repayment.[111] The Mexican government grew desperate to raise new funds.[112]

The government sought out credit from local lenders. Still haunted by the experience of the *vales*, Mexican financiers were reluctant to finance the new and unstable administration.[113] As a result of an increasingly desperate fiscal situation, the government created a legal quagmire that played into the hands of the Spanish government. Fears of disloyalty and financial speculation led Mexico to draft a decree expelling Spanish citizens from the country.[114] Given that some of these Spaniards were important investors, Mexican officials warned them of the implementation of this decree in advance. Many Spanish financiers sought to find new legal ways to retain their businesses.[115]

However, within weeks of the decree coming into effect, in need of funds, the government reformed its norms on internal borrowing: Spanish merchants who were willing to lend the government money in cash would now be allowed to remain in Mexico.[116] Eager to receive more funds, Mexico offered increasingly better terms to these creditors.[117] The legal status of these Spanish creditors at the time of the issuing of the loans generated a diplomatic dispute that lasted several decades. Spain weaponised this quagmire to argue that the debts of these men were in fact the debts of Spaniards and thus subject to treaty negotiation. Mexico, by contrast, would argue that these were private citizens dealing with a government and thus these loans were subject to municipal law.[118]

In 1829, Spanish officials, aware that many Mexicans were sceptical about the future prospects of their nation, having had five different presidents in the span of six years, tried and failed to reconquer Mexico.[119] The cost of the defence against this unsuccessful invasion was the least of Mexico's problems: Zavala's efforts to improve the state of Mexico's treasury failed and the reluctance of the government to banish all Spaniards from Mexico led to a constitutional crisis that was resolved

[111] Salvucci, *Politics*, p. 106.

[112] Ibarra Bellón, *El comercio y el poder*, pp. 94–96; Frank Griffith Dawson, *The First Latin American Debt Crisis: The City of London and the 1822–25 Loan Bubble* (New Haven: Yale University Press, 1990), p. 88.

[113] Anna, *Spain and the Loss of America*, pp. 56–57; Marichal, *Bankruptcy of Empire*, pp. 81–118; Salvucci, *Politics*, p. 37, p. 109.

[114] On the politics behind this measure see Anna, *Forging Mexico*, pp. 202–203.

[115] See Erika Pani, 'De coyotes y gallinas: Hispanidad, identidad nacional y comunidad política durante la expulsión de españoles', *Revista de Indias* 63:228 (2003), pp. 355–374; Van Young, *A Life Together*, p. 364.

[116] Rojas, *La escritura*, p. 106; Vejo, *España en el debate público mexicano*, pp. 389–390.

[117] The government even emulated the Habsburg Crown's practice of mortgaging government revenues, in this case tariffs, to create promissory notes for its lenders, see Tenenbaum, 'Banqueros sin bancos', pp. 80–81.

[118] Tenenbaum, 'Banqueros sin bancos', pp. 80–83. Tenenbaum, *The Politics*, pp. 31–32.

[119] Van Young, *A Life Together*, p. 357, p. 360; Edward Shawcross, *France, Mexico and Informal Empire in Latin America, 1820–1867: Equilibrium in the New World* (London: Springer, 2018), p. 92; Rojas, *Las repúblicas de aire*, pp. 261–262.

with the rise of General Vicente Guerrero to power.[120] After Guerrero's fall, Gómez Farías, during his brief tenure in power, sought to generate new revenue streams, and tensions with conservative officials and the Catholic Church over the potential disentailment and nationalisation of its patrimony intensified. These tensions would eventually lead to a civil war.[121]

Zavala grew disillusioned with Mexico's divisions. By the time Spain showed some willingness to recognise Mexico's independence, Zavala had lost hope in the future of Old Spain and New Spain. Once Ferdinand VII died in 1833, the Spanish Cortes passed a decree that allowed the government to discuss the recognition of the independence of Latin American states.[122] Zavala was sent to Paris to negotiate the Spanish and French recognition of Mexico. In a letter to the Colombian statesman Francisco de Paula Santander, he warned that Spain would continue to pressure the Latin American states into accepting a share of Spain's colonial debt. But this time, he noted, it was Spain and not Mexico that had to demonstrate that it was a liberal state by recognising Mexico's independence without demanding any kind of compensation.[123]

Manifest destiny did not wait for the children of Spain to redeem their debts to one another. A rebellion in Texas and the boundless ambitions of a rising empire allowed Zavala to abandon the lost cause of waiting for Spain to fulfil its potential liberality. Frustrated with the negotiations and the growth of despotism in the new government of Santa Anna, Zavala returned to Mexico and travelled to Texas. In 1836, Mexico and Spain signed, with haste and in the midst of the explosion of a revolution in Texas, the Santa María–Calatrava Treaty, a treaty of recognition: Mexico agreed to pay its colonial debts on the basis of the terms that Zavala had once defended during the debates around the Federal Constitution. But the treaty also included a number of clauses that generated diplomatic tensions for decades.[124] Zavala preferred to focus on the future rather than the past: he signed the Texan declaration of independence and served as the young nation's Vice-President.[125] Santa Anna, by contrast, led a charge against Texas. He was defeated, imprisoned, and forced to sign, in exchange for his life, the Treaty of Velasco that recognised the independence of Texas. Santa Anna was then sent to Washington DC to meet Andrew Jackson and assure him of his intention to abide by the terms of the accord. Mexico's government would later draw on the law of nations to dispute the validity of this treaty.[126]

120 Anna, *Forging Mexico*, p. 227.

121 Hale, *El liberalismo*, pp. 129–139.

122 Agustín Sánchez Andrés, 'México' in Carlos Daniel Malamud ed., *Ruptura y reconciliación España y el reconocimiento de las independencias latinoamericanas* (Madrid: Fundación Mapfre, 2012), pp. 37–52, p. 43.

123 Estep, *Zavala*, p. 271.

124 Sánchez Andrés, 'México', pp. 37–52.

125 Raymond Estep, 'Lorenzo de Zavala and the Texas Revolution', *The Southwestern Historical Quarterly* 57:3 (1954), pp. 322–335, pp. 329–331.

126 Krauze, *Mexico*, pp. 139–140.

But this new arbiter of American affairs made its own rules. As noted by Michel Chevalier, the French Saint-Simonian author who travelled the Americas, Anglo-Saxon morals were hard to reconcile with the Latin roots of Mexico and Cuba.[127] Zavala died a few months later, after advocating for the accession of Texas into the United States in the hope that this reconciliation of morals was possible.[128] In Texas, he noted, 'unlike their Spaniards and their imitators' like Mexico, a nation that had witnessed the execution of many of its deposed leaders, 'we do not execute [others]'. The North American colonisation of Texas, he hoped, would lead to the 'triumph of liberty'.[129] In the United States, by contrast, some congressmen hoped that the annexation of Texas would create a new home for slaves and thereby discourage their migration to northern cities.[130] It was vital to establish how the moral and legal sources of international obligations could bind the United States to a universal moral code. Bustamante characterised the United States as a new company of conquistadors: in the face of imperial aggression, it was crucial to master the law of nations that had served to vanquish past conquerors.[131] It was equally important to disabuse Chevalier of his view that, as part of the debts of 'solidarity' owed to their forefathers by the stronger states of the Latin race in the Old World, France ought to create a monarchy in Latin America that could redeem its nations and counter the advance of the Anglo-Saxon race.[132] As one radical Spanish author remarked, Chevalier treated the history of the independent nations of America like a 'dead letter'.[133] For Mexico, demonstrating that it could and would abide by the catechisms of international law, and showing that it could fulfil the nation's debts to the world, was an existential matter.

Manuel Payno's law of nations

One official was tasked with this monumental task. During the second half of the century, Manuel Payno would spearhead the reorganisation of Mexico's public and foreign debts. He was also one of the most important novelists of his age. As the author of a number of historical accounts which echoed his personal relationship to the nation's history, he understood the relationship between revolution and

[127] David Todd, 'A French Imperial Meridian, 1814–1870', *Past & Present* 210:1 (2011), pp. 155–186, p. 176.

[128] Estep, 'Lorenzo de Zavala and the Texas Revolution', pp. 329–331.

[129] Quoted in Estep, 'Lorenzo de Zavala and the Texas Revolution', p. 334 and Hale, *El liberalismo*, p. 209.

[130] On the complex relationship between the politics of US slavery, the annexation of Texas, and the US Civil War see Lars Schoultz, *Beneath the United States: A History of U.S. Policy Towards Latin America* (Cambridge: Harvard University Press, 2003), pp. 37–38.

[131] Carlos María de Bustamante, *El nuevo Bernal Díaz del Castillo: ó sea, Historia de la invasión de los Anglo-Americanos en México*. Volumes 1–2 (Mexico City: Vicente García Torres, 1847).

[132] Michel Chevalier, *Lettres sur l'Amérique du Nord*. Volume 2 (Paris: Charles Gosselin, 1836), pp. 397–422, p. 397.

[133] Pedro Pruneda, *Historia de la guerra de Méjico desde 1861 a 1867* (Madrid: Rojas, 1867), p. i.

private property: the construction of his school building had been financed with funds seized from the heirs of Moctezuma.[134] As a young man he 'read and re-read' Argüelles' writings.[135] He went on to work at the Department of Revenue and the Tariff Agency of Matamoros.[136] In 1842, he was assigned his first diplomatic role: to build on the treaties Mexico had signed 20 years earlier with Colombia and other Latin American countries in which these states swore not to sell their liberty to Spain in exchange for the repayment of colonial debts. But Payno turned this position down in order to pursue a more profitable position in the Tobacco Agency in Zacatecas.[137] He developed an interest in economic journalism and writing and achieved a certain fame that propelled him to the position of Finance Minister.[138]

Payno watched one empire after another draw on unpaid private debts in order to justify assaults on Mexican shores. In 1838, France carried out a blockade of Mexican ports over unpaid damages to French citizens.[139] Mexican forces successfully defeated the French navy and negotiated a treaty and an accord establishing how to pay these debts.[140] Mexico was, however, unable to overcome an attack by the United States.[141] When the United States harnessed the lamentations of a few of its citizens over a number of unpaid claims to declare war on Mexico, President Polk invaded much of Northern Mexico. Anxious European creditors, noted Bustamante, did not appear concerned that the United States invasion would obviously undermine Mexico's capacity to pay back its debts.[142] The North American victory in the Mexican–American War, as noted, led to the loss of half of Mexico's territory, an acquisition that was certified with the signing of the Treaty of Guadalupe Hidalgo.[143]

Payno regarded this territorial loss as the lesser of two evils: the treaty prevented the United States from conquering the entire country—although proposals in defence of this maximalist measure were indeed discussed during North American congressional sessions.[144] The North American indemnity payment for these

[134] Diana Irina Córdoba Ramírez, *Los derroteros del liberalismo. Las ideas políticas moderadas de Manuel Payno* (Published PhD Thesis) (Mexico City: UNAM, 2004), p. 23.

[135] Ramírez, *Los derroteros*, p. 16.

[136] Ramírez, *Los derroteros*, p. 28, p. 35.

[137] Ramírez, *Los derroteros*, pp. 43–45.

[138] Ramírez, *Los derroteros*, pp. 50–58, p. 98.

[139] Nancy Nichols Barker, *The French Experience in Mexico, 1821–1861: A History of Constant Misunderstanding* (Chapel Hill: UNC Press Books, 2018).

[140] With a number of terms subject to arbitration; see William Spence Robertson, 'French Intervention in Mexico in 1838', *Hispanic American Historical Review* 24:2 (1944), pp. 222–252, pp. 247–249; David Walker, *Kinship, Business, and Politics: The Martínez del Río Family in Mexico, 1823–1867* (Austin, Texas: University of Texas Press, 1987), pp. 6–7; Barbara A. Tenenbaum, 'Mexico's Money Market and the Internal Debt, 1821–1855', in Richard Liehr ed., *La deuda pública en América Latina en perspectiva histórica* (Frankfurt: Iberoamericana,1995), pp. 254–292, pp. 266–267.

[141] See Peter Guardino, *The Dead March: A History of the Mexican-American War.* (Cambridge: Harvard University Press, 2018), pp. 123–159.

[142] Bustamante, *El nuevo Bernal Díaz del Castillo*, pp. 204–205, p. 15.

[143] Schoultz, *Beneath*, pp. 26–40.

[144] Schoultz, *Beneath*, p. 65. On his narrative of the conflict in *El fistol del diablo* see Roberto Cantú, 'La guerra entre México y los Estados Unidos en la novela *El fistol del diablo*, de Manuel Payno', *Literatura Mexicana* 24:1 (2013), pp. 23–43.

territories as certified by the treaty offered a much-needed influx of capital to the Mexican state, free from the demands of greedy local lenders or from the risk of inflating interest on foreign loans. It was, Polk hoped, a way to stabilise Mexico.[145] Yet Mexico's past debts continued to haunt its administration. The British loans had yet to be resolved. The cost of the war with the United States had to be squared.[146]

Payno carried out some of the most important financial reforms of the period. He immediately recognised the value of allocating the funds towards financing the establishment of a railway along the Tehuantepec Isthmus, a passageway that rivalled the Panama strait.[147] While Payno proposed using the trade tariffs along this route to pay off the debt to Britain, Mexico had to rob Peter to pay Paul: Mexico granted the United States military and economic control of the Tehuantepec Isthmus to avoid a conquest.[148] Payno nonetheless continued to pursue the renegotiation of the British loans and Mexico's public debt. He ensured that, out of the indemnity payment, British bondholders received 60 per cent of what had been originally agreed.[149] But his most important reform was the consolidation of the public debt. This undermined the capacity of private lenders to request preferential treatment on the interest rates on the loan when negotiating with the government.[150] Foreign investors complained, however, that this reform flew in the face of the diplomatic conventions established with Britain and Spain.[151]

Payno also had to represent a disordered Mexican government: when he travelled to Europe to negotiate the matter of the debts to British banks, the Mexican administration separately sought to enhance its creditworthiness abroad and embarked on the settlement of its foreign debts with Spain, Britain, and France.[152] These conventions blurred the already tenuous divide between public and private finances and internal and foreign debts. Aware of the importance that the government assigned to the repayment of these debts, private financiers who had seen their claims ignored for years registered as a British corporation and successfully lobbied the British envoy to Mexico to include their claims in the diplomatic

[145] See Ibarra Bellón, *El comercio y el poder*, pp. 114–116 and Samantha Álvarez Macotela, *El peso de nuestro descontento: la diplomacia británica en torno al paso interoceánico por el istmo de Tehuantepec 1847–1858* (Mexico City: Instituto Mora, 2003), pp. 55–86. Sexton, *The Monroe Doctrine*, p. 111.

[146] Tenenbaum, 'Mexico's Money Market', pp. 282–287 and Salvucci, *Politics*, pp. 205–227.

[147] Ramírez, *Los derroteros*, p. 131.

[148] Manuel Payno and José Joaquín Pesado, *Cuestión de Tehuantepec* (Mexico City: Ignacio Cumplido, 1852), p. 15; Sexton, *Monroe*, p. 135. See also Rodolfo Ramírez Rodríguez, 'Manuel Payno y su polémica participación en las concesiones del Ferrocarril Mexicano'. *Relaciones. Estudios de Historia y Sociedad* 40:158 (2019), pp. 198–231.

[149] Nicole Giron, 'Manuel Payno, el ir y venir por la Secretaría de Hacienda' in Leonor Ludlow ed., *Los secretarios de Hacienda y sus proyectos (1821–1933)*. Volume 1 (Mexico City: UNAM, 2002), pp. 351–397, p. 362.

[150] Giron, 'Manuel Payno', p. 366.

[151] Giron, 'Manuel Payno', pp. 366–367.

[152] Antonia Pi-Suñer Llorens, *El General Prim y la "Cuestión de México"* (Published PhD Thesis) (Mexico City: Universidad Nacional Autónoma de México, 1991), p. 71.

negotiation.[153] In the words of Payno, this led to a paradoxical situation: the bulk of the '*domestic* debt' was 'as foreign as if it had been contracted directly with governments in Europe or North America' and the subject of intense disputes while Britain was always happy to let the Mexican government peacefully resolve matters regarding its 'foreign debt'.[154]

How, then, did Payno believe that international law could settle these debts? The problem with the Spanish debt was, at its core, the lack of clarity regarding the compatibility between the Federal Constitution, the terms of a number of diplomatic accords, and the status of Spanish financiers in Mexico. The treaty signalled Mexico's recognition of the debt contracted by the 'Spanish government' until 1821 as 'its own and national' debt. Indeed, article seven of the treaty was effectively a contradiction in terms: on the one hand it stated that Mexico recognised, on the basis of the federal constitutional debates, that the administration absorbed all of the debts contracted by the colonial Spanish government until 1821, and on the other asserted that property owners and their heirs would 'desist all reclamation or mutual pretension over these points' so that both 'contracting sides' were 'forever free and relieved from this responsibility'.[155] Mexico thus claimed to accept the responsibility for all the debts incurred by the Spanish Empire and denied those who owned said debts the capacity to reclaim their payment from Mexico.

However, Mexican and Spanish officials signed a new convention in 1847 and agreed that those who could prove they were owed money on the basis of Spanish loans could now make the Mexican government responsible for these debts.[156] Like their British compatriots, Mexican citizens who could trace their claims back to the colonial period sought out the support of Spanish authorities to demand the payment of their dues by the Mexican authorities. The 1847 convention between Spain and Mexico established a fund for the Spanish claims against Mexico which was to be managed by the Spanish ambassador in Mexico: these loans were now characterised as foreign debts.[157] While the treaty of recognition had categorised these loans as public debts, the convention now granted foreign investors a new diplomatic mechanism to appeal their claims.[158] This provoked further acrimony

[153] David Walker, *Kinship, Business, and Politics: The Martínez del Río Family in Mexico, 1823–1867* (Austin, Texas: University of Texas Press, 1987), pp. 164–216; Barbara Tenenbaum, 'Money, and Mischief the British in Mexico, 1821-1862', *The Americas* 35:3 (1979), pp. 317–339, p. 336; Bazant, *Historia*, pp. 95–97. On the various types of debt included under 'public debt' in mid-nineteenth-century Mexico see Barbara A. Tenenbaum and Sergio Negrete, 'Manuel Payno y los bandidos del erario mexicano, 1848–1873', *Historia Mexicana* 44:1 (1994), pp. 73–106, pp. 77–78.

[154] Manuel Payno and José Joaquín Pesado, *Cuestión de Tehuantepec* (Mexico City: Ignacio Cumplido, 1852), p. 18.

[155] As reprinted in Manuel Payno, *La Convención Española* (Mexico City: Ignacio Cumplido, 1857), p. 7.

[156] Pi-Suñer Llorens, *El General Prim*, pp. 68–69.

[157] Giron, 'Manuel Payno', p. 388.

[158] Most clearly summarised in Antonia Pi-Suñer Llorens, 'Mito y relación en la relación entre Juárez y Prim', in Zoraida Vázquez ed., *Juárez*, pp. 89–112.

between the two governments. Further renegotiations spurred concerns about the illegality of the arrangements, which prompted attacks against Spanish citizens and their properties. Spain threatened to respond by deploying its navy in their defence.[159] One of the members of a family of creditors seeking compensation was Spanish General Juan Prim, who would soon lead an expedition to Veracruz to force the repayment of these debts.[160]

Payno thought that Mexico and Spain were connected by something stronger than the bonds of international law: blood and race.[161] He praised the Santa María–Calatrava Treaty by noting how 'two peoples of the same race, the same religion, and the same traditions, shook hands to resolve this debt, which between merchants would have been a matter for noisy lawsuits'.[162] Payno repeatedly vindicated the historical merits of the Spanish race: those Mexicans who had fought against the United States had, in fact, breathed new life into the quixotic Spanish tradition of bravely engaging in a conflict where there was no chance of victory.[163] The historic ties between these two nations, in his view, generated mutual responsibilities and duties—the 'immortal sentiment of the race' could never 'be forgotten'.[164] International law, Payno explained, could not be used to advance the interests of naked colonialism among brotherly nations: 'colonies' suffered 'under the yoke of a metropolis' and 'conquering peoples impose harsh conditions on the conquered'. But Spain's relationship to Mexico was mediated by their shared history: to invoke a 'treaty of peace and reconciliation between two nations with the same tongue, religion, and customs' to 'humiliate' Mexico was unacceptable.[165]

Payno noted that Spain and Mexico had agreed to forgive one another when their representatives signed the treaty of recognition and 'the motherland was reconciled with her children'.[166] This was 'an agreement to forget that which happened between Mexicans and Spaniards' so that the terms declared that both parties were 'free from now and *forever* of all responsibility' regarding these debts.[167] In *La Convención*, Payno summarised a passage from the chapter on the interpretation of treaties and laws in Bello's *Principios*: 'according to all of the authors of international law', that which in 'changing from a present state leads to the benefits

[159] Barbara A. Tenenbaum, 'Manuel Payno, Financial Reform, and Foreign Intervention in Mexico, 1855–1880' in Vicente Peloso and Barbara A. Tenenbaum eds., *Liberals, Politics, and Power: State Formation in Nineteenth-Century Latin America* (Athens: University of Georgia Press, 1996), pp. 212–234, pp. 214–216.

[160] Pi-Suñer Llorens, 'Mito y realidad en la relación en la relación entre Juárez y Prim', pp. 89–112.

[161] Payno, *La Convención*, p. 28. Much more work needs to be done to understand Payno's views on race: the most detailed discussion on Payno's views on race is found in Ramírez, *Los derroteros*, pp. 60–65.

[162] Payno, *México y sus cuestiones*, p. 145.

[163] Payno, *México y sus cuestiones*, p. 64.

[164] Payno, *La Convención*, p. 28.

[165] Payno, *La Convención*, p. 14. In another convention, in 1853, Spain and Mexico agreed to mortgage 8 per cent of tariffs to repay the debt. See Bazant, *Historia*, pp. 106–107.

[166] Payno, *México y sus cuestiones*, p. 145.

[167] Payno, *La Convención*, pp. 6–7.

of some and to the losses of others: all that pretends to undermine a pact' and 'all that does not tend towards the equality and common utility of all contracting parties' was 'odious'.[168] The terms of the Constitution and the Santa María–Calatrava Treaty clearly demonstrated that the disputed claims were now a matter of internal Mexican sovereignty. Payno noted that treaties, as Bello had shown, had to respect national constitutions.[169] It therefore followed that the treaty of recognition and later conventions had been interpreted by Spain in bad faith and against 'the rules of the law of nations'.[170] Indeed, Payno drew attention to the fact that the 1847 convention had been negotiated and signed in the midst of a war with the United States; he entreated his Spanish readers to consider how they would have received foreign creditors who had chosen to demand repayment while Joseph Bonaparte occupied Spain and French troops advanced across the country.[171]

And yet, Spanish officials led by General Prim disregarded the bonds that emerged from their shared history with Mexico when, along with France and Britain, they sought to exploit the weaknesses of a nation that was recovering from war. Mexican political divisions had deepened in the aftermath of the Mexican–American War: Mexico's first indigenous President, Benito Juárez, implemented the liberal Constitution of 1857 that defended individual property rights; banned slavery, debtors' prisons, and monopolies; abolished hereditary titles; and forced the sale of Church properties. One of the intellectual leaders of these reforms, the Minister of Finance, Governance, and Foreign Affairs, Melchor Ocampo, compared the debt traps to which peons were subjected to a type of 'drug addiction' and called for the redistribution of lands.[172] Conservatives and Church officials fought back and fuelled the War of the Reform.[173] Juárez defeated his enemies and postponed the payment of its foreign debts to repair the damages caused by the war.[174] In response, Spanish, French, and British representatives signed the Convention of London, where they agreed to blockade the port of Veracruz to pressure the government into changing its course.[175]

In a letter to the French general in charge of the Mexican expedition, Payno questioned the senseless economic logic behind the war: why would 'such a

[168] Payno, *La Convención*, p. 11.
[169] Payno, *La Convención*, p. 22.
[170] Payno, *La Convención*, p. 11.
[171] Payno, *La Convención*, p. 17.
[172] Krause, *Mexico*, p. 155. Angel Pola ed., *Obras completas de Melchor Ocampo*. Volume 1 (Mexico City: F. Vázquez, 1900), pp. 110–118, n. 1.
[173] On his views on the internal tensions behind the response to the North American intervention see María Luna Argudín, 'La épica de la derrota: *Apuntes para la historia de la guerra entre México y los Estados Unidos*', *Fuentes Humanísticas* 54 (2017), pp. 131–145.
[174] On the government's logic see Brian R. Hamnett, 'Juárez: La verdadera significación de una presidencia controvertida', in Josefina Zoraida Vázquez ed., *Juárez: historia y mito* (Mexico City: El Colegio de México, 2010), pp. 17–32.
[175] Brian R. Hamnett, *Juárez. El benemérito de las Américas* (Madrid: Biblioteca Nueva, 2006), p. 172; Silvestre Villegas Revueltas, *Deuda y diplomacia. La relación México-Gran Bretaña, 1824–1884* (Mexico City: UNAM, 2005), pp. 75–122.

powerful and large nation wage war over such a miserable sum of money'? The war would only deprive Mexico of a year's worth of revenues, he reasoned, that could have been used to repay the foreign debt: 'why was *the book of the law of nations*', whereby reconciliation had to be pursued before engaging in open conflict, and which was 'open to and served to support the rest of the world, closed to Mexico?'[176] Payno urgently drafted an analysis of Mexico's debts with Spain, Britain, and France. He invoked the principle of *force majeure* to argue that if Mexico had been unable to repay debts it had been as a result of 'revolution', war, and civil war.[177] His greatest concern was the ever-growing interest payments on the debts: for every year that Mexico was unable to summon the necessary revenues to repay it as a result of war, the sum swelled.[178]

The liberal government hurriedly renegotiated the debt repayment with Britain and Spain through the Treaty of Soledad: General Prim, after successfully resolving his family's fiscal disputes with the government, believed Mexico could still be 'saved' through this peaceful resolution, one which ensured that Spain's reputation in America would improve more than it would by waging 'a hundred battles'.[179] As Payno remarked, Prim 'reconciled all Spaniards and Mexicans' and 'demonstrated the unique and singular character of the ancient race of Castille' when he made the unilateral decision to withdraw his troops, a measure which sparked fury in Spain.[180]

Payno noted that Mexico had never thought of defaulting on its debts to Spain: 'even though the motherland remained bitter' about Mexico's independence, even though Spain waged war on Mexico, even if these types of claims were used to 'shed the blood of our children, and those who started to bleed centuries earlier in Cholula', even if 'in the end this credit belongs to the enemies of our liberty and our independence', reflected Payno, 'this does not matter, for we recognise these debts'.[181] Payno responded to Spanish diplomatic reports that Mexican conservatives were the Catholic descendants of the Spanish settlers while the liberals were the children of 'barbaric' *mulatos* and mestizos: Mexicans were the product of creolisation. Liberals, countered Payno, had carried out the same reforms as enlightened Spanish officials and liberals. Far from constituting a barbaric administration, the liberals had simply implemented 'Enlightenment' reforms in Mexico to improve its finances. As a result, its government was heavily indebted, much like those of 'all civilised nations'.[182] The disentailment of Church properties

[176] Manuel Payno, *Carta que sobre los asuntos de México dirige al Sr. General Forey comandante en gefe de las tropas francesas* (Mexico City: Imprenta de Vicente García Torres, 1862), p. 36.
[177] Payno, *México y sus cuestiones financieras*, p. 26, p. 32.
[178] Payno, *México y sus cuestiones financieras*, p. 11.
[179] Quoted in Pi-Suñer Llorens, 'Mito y realidad', pp. 100–112.
[180] Manuel Payno, *Cuentas, gastos, acreedores y otros asuntos del tiempo de la intervención francesa y del imperio. De 1861 a 1867* (Mexico City: Imprenta de Ignacio Cumplido, 1868), p. 919.
[181] Payno, *Mexico y sus cuestiones financieras*, pp. 144–145.
[182] Payno, *México y el Sr. Embajador*, pp. 50–52.

and other such policies had generated the same revolution in Mexico and in Spain, a nation torn by civil wars over the property rights of the Church.[183] '*Like father, like son*', concluded Payno.[184] Mexico's future lay in its Spanish past. Payno was not drawn to North American offers to foster Mexico's economic growth through continental unity: this was an impossible prospect because of the variety of 'races' that populated the continent. Stronger powers, like the United States, would always seek to erase weaker powers. There was only one race that could 'take hold' in Mexico and coexist with the other ethnicities: 'the Spanish race'.[185]

Mexican conservatives sought to overturn Juárez's reforms and approached the Habsburg Viceroy of Lombardy-Venetia, Ferdinand Maximilian Josef Maria von Habsburg-Lothringen, to discuss the possibility of making him Emperor of Mexico.[186] Ferdinand Maximilian welcomed the idea. When presented with this scheme and the request for his military support for the intervention, Napoleon III hesitated.[187] But conscious that the Civil War in the United States would erode Washington's capacity to defend the Monroe Doctrine, and aware that the conflict could create in the Confederacy a buffer state between Abraham Lincoln's North and Mexico, Napoleon and his officials saw this plan as an opportunity to counter the expansion of North American interests in the region, establish a French military and banking presence in the Americas, and improve the silver reserves of the Latin Monetary Union.[188] Napoleon promised to protect Mexico from the United States. But he also sought to profit from Ferdinand Maximilian's tenure in power before the Habsburg prince set foot in the Americas: the two men negotiated, at the Treaty of Miramar, that Ferdinand Maximilian would indemnify France for its military expenses, the maintenance of its troops, and any French 'claims' motivated by the expedition.[189] A French loan would be negotiated in order to fulfil these obligations and another one would be needed to satisfy the needs of Ferdinand Maximilian's court.[190] Foreign diplomats believed that France would absorb and

[183] Payno, *México y el Sr. Embajador*, p. 29, p. 88.

[184] Payno, *México y el Sr. Embajador*, p. 88. He reiterated this argument in other writings, including his *La reforma social en España y México: apuntes históricos* (Mexico City: Pámpano Servicios Editoriales, 2013) and his *Tratado de la propiedad: ensayo de un estudio del derecho romano y del derecho público y constitucional en lo relativo a la propiedad* (Mexico City: I. Cumplido, 1869).

[185] Payno, *Tratado de la propiedad*, p. 193; Payno, *México y el Sr. Embajador*, pp. 66–67.

[186] Erika Pani, *Para mexicanizar el segundo imperio: el imaginario político de los imperialistas* (Mexico City: El Colegio de México, 2001), pp. 189–242; Patricia Galeana, *Las relaciones iglesia-estado durante el Segundo Imperio* (Mexico City: UNAM, 1991). For recent insights on Maximilian, including how the development of the Castle of Miramar was financed, see Konrad Ratz, *Tras las huellas de un desconocido: nuevos datos y aspectos de Maximiliano de Habsburgo*. Prólogo de Patricia Galeana de Valadés (Mexico City: Siglo XXI, 2008).

[187] Egon Conte Corti, *Maximiliano y Carlota* (Mexico City: FDCE, 1997), pp. 58–65.

[188] Stève Sainlaude, *France and the American Civil War: A Diplomatic History* (Oxford: Oxford University Press, 2019), pp. 110–126.

[189] Bazant, *Historia*, pp. 102–103; Arnold Blumberg, 'The Diplomacy of the Mexican Empire, 1863–1867', *Transactions of the American Philosophical Society* 61:8 (1971), pp. 1–152, pp. 12–13; Hamnett, *Juárez*, p. 178. For an overview see Shawcross, *France, Mexico and Informal Empire*, pp. 197–236.

[190] Blumberg, 'The Diplomacy', p. 13.

repay Mexico's debts.[191] Instead, Napoleon saddled Ferdinand Maximilian with unredeemable bills. Only 20 per cent of the grand total of these loans was designed to address Mexico's needs.[192]

Maximilian I: the martyr

As Napoleon III's troops took control of the nation's administration, Payno was arrested and imprisoned for the contents of his letter to the French general.[193] In prison, he made the difficult decision to collaborate with the regime.[194] As Emperor, Maximilian I sought to deliver a number of initiatives that were far more liberal than progressives or conservatives expected: the *Ley de Trabajo*, or labour law, for example, sought to end the practice of debt peonage and corporal punishment.[195] Maximilian spearheaded urban reforms in Mexico City, paid particular attention to indigenous concerns, and engaged in many charitable initiatives towards the poor.[196] Napoleon III suggested that he should establish a 'liberal dictatorship' but, instead, Maximilian sought to reaffirm the right to private property and the preservation of religious freedom in a way that was compatible with Mexico's Catholicism.[197] He defended the freedom of the press: one of the most controversial articles of the century, drafted by the atheist journalist Ignacio Ramírez, was published during this time. In *La Desespañolización*, or 'The Dehispanisation', Ramírez countered accusations that Mexicans were wrong to 'renege' on their Spanish past. Ramírez argued that Spain had contributed little to Latin America; Columbus had 'tripped' in the Americas on his way to the 'Oriental Indies', and the Spanish had robbed the locals of their resources ever since.[198]

[191] Agustín Sánchez Andrés, 'La diplomacia hispano-mexicana: de la intervención tripartita a la caída del imperio', in Clara E. Lida and Andrés Lira eds., *España y el imperio de Maximiliano: finanzas, diplomacia, cultura e inmigración* (Mexico City: El Colegio de México, 1999), pp. 105–178, p. 132.

[192] Patricia Galeana, *La disputa por la soberanía (1821–1876)* (Mexico City: El Colegio de México, 2010), p. 165

[193] Tenenbaum, 'Manuel Payno, Financial Reform', p. 220; Hammnett, *Juárez*, p. 176.

[194] Tenenbaum, 'Manuel Payno, Financial Reform', p. 221.

[195] Robert H. Duncan, 'Maximilian and the Construction of the Liberal State, 1863–1866' in Jaime E. Rodríguez ed., *The Divine Charter: Constitutionalism and Liberalism in Nineteenth-Century Mexico* (Lanham: Rowland & Littlefield Publishers, 2005), p. 156 and Michael Hogan, 'Juárez, Maximilian, and the French Occupation of Mexico', in Beezley ed., *The Oxford Handbook of Mexican History* (Online).

[196] Robert H. Duncan, 'Political Legitimation and Maximilian's Second Empire in Mexico, 1864–1867', *Mexican Studies/Estudios Mexicanos* 12:1 (1996), pp. 27–66, pp. 64–65.

[197] Duncan, 'Maximilian and the Construction of the Liberal State', p. 143.

[198] Ignacio Ramírez, *Obras de Ignacio Ramírez*. Volume 1 (Mexico City: Secretaría de Fomento, 1889), p. 318. For a summary of his broader thought see Víctor Manuel Torres, 'El pensamiento político de Ignacio Ramírez', *Historia Mexicana* 12:2 (1962), pp. 190–228. See also Corinna Zeltsman, *Ink under the Fingernails: Printing Politics in Nineteenth-Century Mexico* (Berkeley: University of California Press, 2021), pp. 157–162. Historians have shown how Britons and Americans waged these debates in the context of the American Revolution. Americans harnessed and militarised the culture of sensibility, while British authors rejected this legacy of the Enlightenment ahead of the development of the stiff upper lip in the nineteenth century. See Sarah Knott, 'Sensibility and the American War for Independence', *American Historical Review* 109:1 (2004), pp. 19–40.

He described Charles II as 'a type of Maximilian' who had allowed rival contenders to tear the Spanish Empire to pieces.[199]

This historical comparison was all too accurate: under Maximilian's rule, competing powers from within and without threatened to tear Mexico asunder. To fight the counterinsurgence led by Juárez and carry out his ambitious reforms, Maximilian financed his government by tripling Mexico's debt through foreign loans in the course of a single year.[200] The price of the British recognition of his regime was the capitalisation of interests on the outstanding loans: an increase of the size of the debt.[201] Once the US Civil War ended and the new administration began to support Mexican rebels, Napoleon decided to withdraw his forces from the country. Foreign diplomats noted that Maximilian's regime was bankrupt. Tensions with other powers grew when Maximilian drew on forced loans and tariffs, mortgaged to pay foreign loans, to wage war against the insurgents.[202] In 1867, Maximilian's army was defeated and Juárez and his troops arrived in Mexico City. The rebellion against Maximilian was complete and a military tribunal decreed the execution of the Emperor. After a firing squad executed Maximilian, Juárez justified this measure by arguing that the Emperor had sought to end the ancient Anahuac peoples. The deposed leader was the last emperor who sought to perpetuate the tyrannical traditions of the early modern Habsburg Spanish Empire. An indigenous Mexican president brought centuries of Spanish tyranny to an end.[203]

Officials in the Juárez administration granted a general amnesty to those who had collaborated with Maximilian's regime and requested Payno's help in the hope of harnessing his knowledge of financial affairs.[204] The new administration cited his studies on the national debt to justify its repudiation of the debts that Maximilian had incurred and disavow earlier diplomatic conventions.[205] This experience of foreign intervention led to a number of other legal reforms in Mexico: a new criminal code was established in order to incorporate humanitarian approaches to the law of war into domestic legislation.[206] One of the Mexican generals who routed

[199] Ramírez, *Obras de Ignacio Ramírez*, p. 318. Payno in turn recovered, edited, and printed Mier's memoirs. See Manuel Payno, *Vida, aventuras, escritos y viajes del doctor don Servando Teresa de Mier, precedidos de un ensayo histórico por Manuel Payno* (Mexico City: Imprenta de Juan Abadiano, 1865).

[200] Bazant, *Historia*, p. 103. Steven C. Topik, 'When Mexico Had the Blues: A Transatlantic Tale of Bonds, Bankers, and Nationalists, 1862–1910', *The American Historical Review* 105:3 (2000), pp. 714–738, p. 714.

[201] Galeana, 'La disputa', p. 174.

[202] Sánchez Andrés, 'La diplomacia hispano-mexicana', pp. 162–163.

[203] Hamnett, *Juárez*, p. 199.

[204] The general amnesty included some exceptions: see Amaro Valencia Alejandro de Jesús, '¿Memoria, olvido y perdón? Vaivenes discursivos en la construcción de la historia oficial sobre la Intervención Francesa y el Segundo Imperio Mexicano', *Estudios de historia moderna y contemporánea de México* 64 (2022), pp. 43–68. Tenenbaum, 'Manuel Payno, Financial Reform', p. 222.

[205] Bazant, *Historia*, p. 106; Tenenbaum, 'Manuel Payno, Financial Reform', p. 223.

[206] See Tania Ixchel Atilano, 'The 1871 Mexican Criminal Code as the missing piece in the history of criminalising violations of the laws of war', *International Review of the Red Cross* 104 (2022), pp. 1650–1683.

Maximilian's forces, Porfirio Díaz, would one day oversee the modernisation of the country.

Maximilian's rule complicated the logic behind the repayment of Mexico's foreign and public debt. As Ramírez noted, 'our debts would lead us to jail if nations were liable for fraud'.[207] Yet the potential wardens of the law of nations had sought to tyrannise Mexico: Spain and Britain had recognised the regime of Maximilian and financial institutions in London had bankrolled his government.[208] The United States, by contrast, had firmly rejected his authority.[209] A range of Latin Americans saw this as a reaffirmation of the Monroe Doctrine. But, as Payno noted, the doctrine was an admirable principle that President Lincoln had specifically avoided drawing on to defend his approach towards Maximilian.[210] Indeed, the United States had 'watched on unaffected as European troops disembarked on our shores'.[211] The United States had not yet 'sanctioned' this doctrine and, as far as Payno was concerned, the principles and the actions of the United States posed clear 'dangers' for Latin America.[212]

The categories of private interests and the public authority were blurred by Maximilian's rule. Public debt had to be ordered swiftly: tens of thousands of soldiers who had fought for Mexico's freedom had yet to be paid. But Mexico's debt had ballooned under the Emperor's rule.[213] In his *Cuentas*, a nine-hundred-page report on Mexico's finances, Payno established a clear standard to determine the legitimacy of debts. This report was a collection of decrees and statistics on a number of old debts, the terms of diplomatic negotiations, administrative branches, and, above all, the costs incurred in the struggle against, and the government led by, Maximilian I. In this account, he rejected his earlier views on the legality of the bulk of the foreign debts owed to Spain and Britain.[214] It was 'debatable' whether it was licit, according to the law of nations, to pay back these debts given that the invasion had been used to seize the nation's rents, slow down Mexico's march 'in the race towards civilisation and peace', and to burden its treasury with huge costs.[215]

In his earlier texts, Payno had drawn on the high-minded principles of international lawyers like Bello or Henry Wheaton. The weight of legal principles

[207] Ramírez, *Obras de Ignacio Ramírez*, p. 366.

[208] Duncan, 'Political Legitimation', p. 36; Pi-Suñer Llorens, *La deuda española*, p. 214.

[209] Bazant, *Historia*, p. 110; Ernesto de la Torre Villar, 'La política americana durante la Intervención Francesa en México. Notas para su estudio', *Revista de Historia de América* 63–64 (1967), pp. 13–67.

[210] Payno, *México y el Sr. Embajador*, p. 67. On Lincoln's reluctance to use the term see Jay Sexton, 'The Monroe Doctrine in an Age of Global History', *Diplomatic History* 47:5 (2023), pp. 845–870, p. 866; On the Mexican response to the mid-century North American use of the term see Paolo Riguzzi, 'Mexico and the Monroe Doctrines, 1863–1920: From Appropriation to Rejection', *Diplomatic History* 47:5 (2023), pp. 785–792.

[211] Payno, *México y el Sr. Embajador*, p. 66.

[212] Payno, *México y el Sr. Embajador*, pp. 66–67.

[213] Tenenbaum and Negrete. 'Manuel Payno y los bandidos', p. 99.

[214] Pi-Suñer Llorens, *La deuda española*, p. 249.

[215] As noted by Pi-Suñer Llorens, *La deuda española*, p. 249, n. 32.

in this text, compared to his other writings, was greatly diminished.[216] It was clear to Payno that money, not the law of nations, ruled the world. Citing Henry Thomas Buckle, he proposed that the way to write 'accurate and faithful history' was through 'Arithmetic, Statistics, and Political Economy'. He concluded that Mexico had never been independent because of the way that foreign powers had used their foreign loans to control its destiny—at least, he reflected, 'during the time of Spanish domination the name of the motherland and its colonies was respected' by foreign powers.[217] For over 50 years, argued Payno, foreign states had considered Mexico's pursuit of freedom as a crime, a 'deicide' which 'nations that call themselves civilised' had used to proscribe and invade the young nation. Lady Credit spoke a foreign tongue: a 'single note' written by a foreign minister served to destroy treasury reforms.[218] Unjust claims were satisfied, murky debts were paid, a new convention was convened, all while troops went unpaid, a few cents were granted to widows who had failed to receive their pensions, and contracts were signed before the money was available; nothing, continued Payno, was enough.[219] An unforgiving system of international law had brought Mexico to its knees. Only Mexico could absolve its people.

No system of government—not even Maximilian's empire—could survive the financial threats posed by the changing whims of foreign sovereigns.[220] The alliance of Britain, France, and Spain which aimed to force Mexico to pay its foreign debts was nothing more than a 'collaboration of creditors who descended upon the skeleton, the scarce bread, and the pain of the poor'.[221] While the British and the Spanish forces had soon realised the folly of this effort to 'imprison a nation over its debts', French officials had cooked the books and lied to their government about the state of Mexico's finances.[222]

Payno carefully laid the ground for the argument that Mexico should repudiate the debts incurred in the war and during Maximiliam's tenure in power.[223] The most jarring aspect of the invasion was Napoleon's demand that Mexico should absorb the costs of the war: 'Juárez did not provoke the war' and Maximilian had not granted the French administration a reason to demand such a payment. Charging the Emperor and the nation with this debt was nothing more than a 'punishment, an injustice, a hostile act' and the creation of an 'insurmountable obstacle for the establishment of the treasury'.[224] Maximillian himself realised that the sums he

[216] He was also sceptical about debates on 'legality', emphasising the need for expediency in politics instead; see Ramírez, *Los derroteros*, pp. 186–187.
[217] Payno, *Cuentas*, p. 915.
[218] Payno, *Cuentas*, p. 915.
[219] Payno, *Cuentas*, p. 916.
[220] Payno, *Cuentas*, p. 916.
[221] Payno, *Cuentas*, p. 918.
[222] Payno, *Cuentas*, pp. 918–919.
[223] On the broader 'Mexicanisation' of the French intervention see Shawcross, *France, Mexico, and Informal Empire*, pp. 238–242.
[224] Payno, *Cuentas*, p. 923.

had negotiated in Paris had never been delivered; Napoleon, not Juárez, was his greatest enemy.[225] Yet Napoleon's government continued to argue that it had spilt 'French blood' to protect Mexico and regenerate the 'Latin race'.[226] Payno reasoned that even if Juárez's revolt had failed, and the support of the United States had never arrived, Mexico, under Maximilian's rule, would never have been able to repay its French debt.[227] Payno warned his French readers that Napoleon's morally bankrupt monarchy, which had disgraced its people by abandoning Maximilian and dismissing Juárez's authority, would undermine its own officials: a nation as great as France ought instead to embrace its Republican roots.[228] With its legitimacy and its economy weakened by the intervention in Mexico, France was unable to quash Prussia: the French defeat in the Franco-Prussian War led to the collapse of Napoleon's government and the rise of the Third Republic.[229]

Payno, moreover, alluded to the parallels between Maximilian and Moctezuma: Maximilian, 'of good and gentlemanly character', abandoned by Napoleon, chose to stay in Mexico and 'die valiantly and heroically, to avoid tarnishing the traditions of his house, nor the origins of the warrior princes of his bloodline'.[230] In this reading, Payno cast Maximilian as a martyr like Moctezuma whose sacrifice was a way of showing respect to the traditions of his dynasty.[231] It was a remarkable narrative that honoured Maximilian's '*política indigenista*': it rendered Napoleon III as a tyrannical emperor advised by covetous Cortés-like officials and Maximilian as a well-intentioned statesman overwhelmed by circumstances; a ruler who was ready to renege on his debts to a tyrant to save his family's ancestral honour.[232] History repeated itself: Juárez's revolution had been nothing more than an inevitable act, another turn of the wheel of history, since men were guided by an 'invisible and unknown power' as shown by the mathematical precision of Buckle's historical tradition.[233]

This manifest destiny would be disastrous for Mexico's prospective conquerors: those who led a blockade against Mexico would find that this measure harmed the commercial interests in silver of two powerful nations, Britain

[225] Payno, *Cuentas*, p. 926.
[226] Payno, *Cuentas*, p. 923.
[227] Payno, *Cuentas*, p. 927.
[228] Payno, *Cuentas*, pp. 932–933.
[229] Jerome Greenfield, 'The Mexican Expedition of 1862–1867 and the end of the French Second Empire', *Historical Journal* 63:3 (2020), pp. 660–685.
[230] Payno, *Cuentas*, p. 924, pp. 927–928.
[231] Payno, *Cuentas*, p. 928.
[232] Payno, *Cuentas*, p. 928 and p. 927. This reflected Maximilian's efforts to present himself as Moctezuma's heir. See Érika Pani, '¿"Verdaderas Figuras de Cooper" o 'Pobres Inditos Infelices'? La Política Indigenista de Maximiliano', *Historia Mexicana* 47:3 (1998), pp. 571–604. On mid-nineteenth-century reinventions of Moctezuma see part one of Matthew Restall, *When Montezuma Met Cortés: The True Story of the Meeting that Changed History* (New York: Harper Collins, 2018).
[233] Payno, *Cuentas*, p. 928. On Buckle's influence on Alberdi see Natalio Botana, *La tradición republicana: Alberdi, Sarmiento y las ideas políticas de su tiempo* (Buenos Aires: Sudamericana, 1984), pp. 423–425.

and the United States. An invasion of Mexico would require so many men that it would bankrupt the wealthiest nation in the world. A conquest—what was the point of a conquest? Payno surveyed the parties that might have an interest in the matter: Britain had India and France had Argelia. If the United States were to invade Mexico, other nations might challenge this conquest. The costs of fighting the Mexican resistance would be too high and hinder North American interests in the region.[234] A hard-nosed Payno continued to vindicate his belief in enlightened values: a nation that 'opened its doors to the whole world' and sought to lead all others by following the century's 'moral philosophy' would always generate international support for its cause. Morality contributed to the 'equilibrium of societies'.[235]

Mexico, he concluded, had to be rebuilt. This meant improving the state of the treasury to build infrastructure and liquidate the internal debt.[236] Mexico, he reasoned, was in no state to pay 'a single cent of the foreign debt'. The peace would be preserved and the government would last 'until the day when the last peso has been spent'. This was, in Payno's view, 'an evangelical truth'.[237] It was questionable whether, according to the law of nations, Mexico ought ever to repay its foreign debt. It was those who invaded its territory, seized its rents, and slowed its march in the race towards civilisation and peace who should feel the pain of the consequences of their actions.[238] Maximilian's empire did little in 'moral or material terms' that was worth mentioning; Mexico's 'redeemers' had been poor rulers, far worse than its autochthonous leaders.[239] On the basis of these writings, the Mexican administration argued that Britain's support of Maximilian nullified previous accords.[240] Juárez developed what was known as the Juárez Doctrine: he defaulted on all existing treaties with the parties who had supported the rise of Maximilian I. Mexico's focus in signing new treaties, he made clear, should be the acquisition of economic, not diplomatic or political, advantages.[241]

The 1884 debate

In 1884, inequality was rampant, debt peonage served as a widespread source of labour, and the "London debt", as Mexico's British debt became known, remained

[234] Payno, *Cuentas*, p. 929.
[235] Payno, *Cuentas*, p. 930.
[236] Payno, *Cuentas*, p. 930.
[237] Payno, *Cuentas*, pp. 930–931.
[238] Payno, *Cuentas*, p. 930.
[239] Payno, *Cuentas*, p. 931.
[240] Bazant, *Historia*, p. 112. On the idea that mid-century liberal governments appropriated the earlier republican tradition of the revolution see Rojas, *Las repúblicas*, pp. 143–184.
[241] Daniel Cosío Villegas, 'La Doctrina Juárez', *Historia Mexicana* 11:4 (1962), pp. 527–545, pp. 530–531.

unpaid.[242] New periodicals and platforms emerged to counter old inequalities: the journals *El álbum de la mujer*, *El correo de las señoras*, and *Violetas del Anáhuac* demanded greater rights for women.[243] Yet the early years of Porfirio Díaz's rule are typically remembered for the exponential growth experienced by Mexico's economy thanks to the government's investment in trade, infrastructure, and mining, and the rise of US investment in railway lines. The prospective payment of the British debt was seen by Díaz and his modernising administrators as a practical measure: it would help to improve the status of Mexico's credit in the European markets and allow the government to leverage subsequent financial offers from the Old World in negotiations with North American financiers.[244] Instead, a congressional debate on the matter descended into a two-week discussion about the symbolic debts Mexico owed Spain and Britain: the memory of Spain, the motherland and the first usurper of Mexico, continued to generate debates, disputes, and violence.

At one of the sessions, the poet and parliamentarian Salvador Díaz Mirón argued that if anyone ought to be repaid it was the Spanish government 'whose generous blood runs through us' and which had given Mexico its 'magnificent language'.[245] The author and historian Justo Sierra Méndez, by contrast, argued that Britain had been the first and perhaps the only friend of Mexico in Europe. The 'British debt' had been contracted 'by virtue of the political sights which honour our ancestors', both to provide resources to the Mexican government but also to generate an 'indirect alliance' with Britain in Europe; Mexico, argued another deputy, owed Britain a 'debt of gratitude'.[246] Díaz Mirón, as if echoing the warnings of Bustamante towards Mexico's reliance on a great empire, favoured using this measure to bolster ties with Europe and cautioned against fostering Mexico's financial dependence on the United States: 'We know what this would lead to: this would hold us to an irremediable economic tutelage which could never be shaken off'.[247]

Some focused on the more recent history of European imperialism. Parliamentarians like Fernando Duret argued that to repay Britain was to

[242] On the debates of the 1870s see Tenenbaum, 'Manuel Payno, Financial Reform', pp. 225–228. Payno continued to provide his advice to the government and worked as a foreign envoy in Europe during this period; see Ramírez, *Los derroteros*, pp. 255–260. On the complexities of debt peonage see Alan Knight, 'Debt Bondage in Latin America', in Léonie Archer ed., *Slavery: And Other Forms of Unfree Labour* (New York: Routledge, 2013), pp. 102–117.

[243] Elvira Hernández Carballido, 'Un recorrido por las publicaciones de mujeres en el siglo XIX', in Patricia Galeana ed., *Historia de las mujeres en México* (Mexico City: INEHRM, 2015), pp. 157–180, pp. 168–176.

[244] Bazant, *Historia*, pp. 128–134; Javier Pérez Siller, 'Razones, pasiones y violencia en México. El reconocimiento de la deuda inglesa en 1884', *Nuevo Mundo Mundos Nuevos* (Online).

[245] *Diario de los debates de la cámara de diputados. Duodécima legislatura constitucional de la Unión.* Volume 1 (Mexico City: Horcasitas, 1884), p. 216.

[246] *Diario de los debates*, p. 221, p. 269.

[247] *Diario de los debates*, p. 223.

'place a price on the heroic blood of those who died for the sacred cause of our country'; Britain's colonial ambitions in the region made it 'shameful' to consider indemnifying its government.[248] Others focused on the future. Simón Sarlat Nova, who had fostered the exploitation of oil in Mexico, noted that it was undignified to indemnify a nation that had previously used force in order to enforce a payment.[249] Yet repaying the British debt would generate greater foreign investment; train lines could be established by Mexican companies so the wealth remained in the nation and contributed to its well-being.[250] The historian Hilario Gabilondo seconded this view and cited how the indemnification payments of the United States had enabled the building of 'railways that, with their webs of steel, cut across from one extreme of the republic to another' and encouraged American investment in Mexico.[251] He noted that the future of 'the Latin Race' depended on the preservation of Mexican-Spanish friendship, which was that of a mother and a daughter.[252] Both of these debts, he argued, ought to be paid.

This was a historiographical mêlée over whether the country's future was to be shaped by the virtuous cycles of foreign investment or by the law of nations that had influenced their forebears. Manuel Jauregui argued that following Maximilian's fall, 'our public law' had established that no debts would be recognised other than those that belonged to the nation.[253] Eduardo Viñas went one step further: given that Juárez had established that the British debt should be paid only after mutual concessions were granted, why should Mexico, which had negotiated 'exceptions founded in international law and civil law towards our creditors', not create a precedent out of these negotiations, and argue, whenever a foreign government demanded the repayment of a debt, that without mutual concessions the original loan was annulled?[254]

When the public heard that the government was considering compensating lenders half a world away instead of fulfilling its obligations to communities in need, protesters gathered outside Congress. A session was interrupted by the noise of the crowds, which entered the building, and by quarrelling deputies in the chamber. As the shouts grew louder, Díaz Mirón cited the rights of man and made a powerful argument: should Mexico not focus on the Mexican lenders who as 'servants of the nation, are dying of hunger?' This remark received the effusive applause of his peers.[255] As the vote on the measure commenced the police began to remove the public from the gallery and postpone the session.[256] Tensions boiled

[248] *Diario de los debates*, p. 226.
[249] *Diario de los debates*, p. 259.
[250] *Diario de los debates*, p. 261.
[251] *Diario de los debates*, p. 271.
[252] *Diario de los debates*, p. 269.
[253] *Diario de los debates*, p. 288.
[254] *Diario de los debates*, p. 338.
[255] *Diario de los debates*, p. 343.
[256] *Diario de los debates*, p. 351.

over outside the chamber when policemen opened fire on protesters and caused several casualties.[257] At the next session, shots were once again heard outside the chamber.[258] There was no choice but to reject the motion and postpone the discussion of the repayment.

Under the rule of Porfirio Díaz, the Mexican government eventually leveraged offers from North American bankers in negotiations with European financiers.[259] The "London debt" was thus resolved in the only way it could be fixed: through further borrowing. In this case, Otto von Bismarck's private banker provided the Mexican government with a loan in the hope of fostering German trade in the region.[260] In the 1880s and 1890s, Germany would become Mexico's fourth largest exporter.[261] The resolution of the Spanish debt, in turn, followed soon after, and the Mexican administration made sure that the legacy of Spanish obstructionism and lawfare was noted in the resolution, ensuring, as the diplomat in charge of the negotiation told Congress, 'that the basis for fixing the bonds of the "Spanish Convention" should be lower than those adopted for the "British Convention" '.[262] Efforts to settle Maximilian's debts generated heated popular protests and arrests. In 1904, these bills were quietly paid off thanks to a loan from the banking house in the United States that first fostered the North American investment in Mexican railroads. The following year, Mexico adopted the gold standard and thus connected the peso to the fate of the dollar.[263]

Indeed, once these debts to Britain, Spain, and France were settled, Mexico had to establish what it owed to the United States. The administration developed the Díaz Doctrine, which rejected the right of unilateral intervention and sought to reinforce the principles of the Monroe Doctrine.[264] Yet, in 1910, the civil war that would become known as the Mexican Revolution exploded as a result of the government's inability to address popular complaints about the unequal and irregular distribution of land and property in the country: the United States intervened twice in the conflict. It was important, according to Woodrow Wilson, who spearheaded the highest number of interventions in this era, to protect North American oil interests and 'to teach the South American republics to elect good men'.[265] Instead, the 1917 Mexican Constitution established the state's ownership over all underground minerals, the right of Mexicans to receive land grants for

257 *Diario de los debates*, p. 353. See Pérez Siller, 'Razones, pasiones y violencia en México'.
258 *Diario de los debates*, p. 366.
259 Leonardo Weller, 'Government versus Bankers: Sovereign Debt Negotiations in Porfirian Mexico, 1888–1910', *The Journal of Economic History* 75:4 (2015), pp. 1030–1057.
260 Salvucci, *Politics*, p. 285–286; Carlos Marichal, 'Foreign Loans, Banks and Capital Markets in Mexico, 1880–1910' in Liehr ed., *La deuda pública*, pp. 337–374, p. 363; Bazant, *Historia*, pp. 134–136.
261 Jürgen Buchenau, 'The Life Cycle of a Trade Diaspora: The German "Colony" in Mexico City, 1821–present', *Jahrbuch für Geschichte Lateinamerikas* 39 (2002), pp. 275–297, p. 281.
262 Pi-Suñer Llorens, *La deuda española*, p. 309.
263 Topik, 'When Mexico Had the Blues', pp. 734–735.
264 Sexton, 'The Monroe Doctrine in an Age of Global History', p. 866.
265 Sexton, *Monroe*, p. 234. Quoted in Schoultz, *Beneath*, p. 244.

the mining of the subsoil, and the conditional award of these rights to foreign citizens who surrendered their claims to invoke protection from their respective governments.[266] The purpose of this constitutional reform, emboldened by the use of the Calvo Clause, was to prevent foreign intervention. Instead, it triggered intense protests from board members of North American oil companies, whose profits had soared on the basis of booming US demand for cars and were not at risk.[267] In the 1920s, Mexican representatives would craft new arguments in favour of the rights of debtor nations in the face of opposition from the United States.[268]

In the 1930s, the radical presidents Venustiano Carranza and Lázaro Cárdenas scaled up this constitution into a doctrine of non-intervention known as the Carranza Doctrine.[269] This was a doctrine that sought to redefine the meaning of non-intervention and disentangle it from the United States.[270] Mexican officials drew on these ideas to criticise the League of Nations' reluctance to engage in the Spanish Civil War.[271] Mexico spearheaded international efforts to deliver relief and aid to the war-torn nation and host its refugees.[272] As Mexican jurists explained, there was a moral obligation to help the Spanish Republic, but there was also a practical incentive behind this exercise in solidarity: the victory of General Francisco Franco, after all, could embolden Mexican conservatives to pursue a similar insurrection against Mexico's revolutionary government.[273] The concept of the Spanish race continued to elicit hopes and fears of closer cooperation between Mexico and Spain.[274] As Mexican diplomats explained, at stake was the defence

[266] Quoted in Schoultz, *Beneath*, pp. 272–273.

[267] Schoultz, *Beneath*, pp. 273–280.

[268] Christy Thornton, *Revolution in Development Mexico and the Governance of the Global Economy* (Berkeley, University of California Press, 2021), pp. 18–57; Kathryn Greenman, 'The Mexican Revolution: Alien Protection and International Economic Order', in Kathryn Greenman, Anne Orford, Anna Saunders, and Ntina Tzouvala eds., *Revolutions in International Law: The Legacies of 1917* (Cambridge: Cambridge University Press, 2021), pp. 339–364; Juan Pablo Scarfi, *The Hidden History of International Law in the Americas: Empire and Legal Networks* (Oxford: Oxford University Press, 2017), pp. 67–68.

[269] Juan Pablo Scarfi, 'Mexican Revolutionary Constituencies and the Latin American Critique of US Intervention', in Greenman, Orford, Saunders, and Tzouvala eds., *Revolutions in International Law*, pp. 218–241.

[270] Juan Pablo Scarfi, 'Denaturalizing the Monroe Doctrine: The Rise of Latin American Legal Anti-Imperialism in the Face of the Modern US and Hemispheric Redefinition of the Monroe Doctrine', *Leiden Journal of International Law* 33:3 (2020), pp. 541–555; Agustín Sánchez Andrés and Fabrián Herrera León, *Contra todo y contra todos: la diplomacia Mexicana y la cuestión española en la Sociedad de Naciones, 1936–1939* (Las Palmas: Ediciones Idea, 2011), pp. 205–324.

[271] Fabia Fernandes Carvalho Veçoso, 'Mexican Post-Revolutionary Foreign Policy and the Spanish Civil War: Legal Struggles over Intervention at the League of Nations', in Greenman, Orford, Saunders, and Tzouvala eds., *Revolutions in International Law*, pp. 242–268.

[272] Mario Ojeda Revah, *México y la guerra civil española* (Madrid: Turner, 2005), pp. 139–184; Sánchez Andrés and Herrera León, *Contra todo*, pp. 191–204.

[273] Ojeda Revah, *México y la guerra civil española*, pp. 215–254; Carvalho Veçoso, 'Mexican Post-Revolutionary Foreign Policy', pp. 264–265.

[274] On Mexican cultural attitudes towards the reception of these refugees see Tomás Pérez Vejo, 'España en el imaginario mexicano: el choque del exilio', in Agustín Sánchez Andrés and Silvia Figueroa Zamudio eds., *De Madrid a México. El exilio español y su impacto sobre el pensamiento, la ciencia y el sistema educativo mexicano* (Morelia: Universidad Michoacana de San Nicolás de Hidalgo, 2001), pp. 23–93.

of the bonds that unite nations, a vindication of the morality of international law through the reaffirmation of the connections that united the Spanish-speaking world. As Cárdenas' Foreign Minister, Isidro Fabela, made clear in his correspondence on the negotiations at the League of Nations and Franco's insurgency: 'were destiny to temporarily undermine the cause of the true Spanish people, one which we uphold with such constancy and courage, we would then, and forever, remain convinced that we defended with the greatest generosity of spirit an ideal which will, by necessity, triumph in Spain'.[275]

[275] Isidro Fabela, *Cartas al Presidente Cárdenas* (Mexico City: Offset Altamira, 1947), pp. 12–27, p. 27.

4
Fratricide and Redemption
Gran Colombia's Debt to Simón Bolívar

Pay the tyrant

In 1819, at the Congress of Angostura, where the Colombian Republic was founded, Bolívar laid out the soteriological political economy of independence when he praised the 'philanthropic principles' of British financiers, who were 'friends of humanity' for lending money to Latin America.[1] He characterised Latin American citizens as 'debtors of an eternal recognition, and a religious fulfilment, of the sacred obligations we have contracted with them'. He compared the 'national debt' to the '*Arca Santa*', or 'Holy Ark'. Bolívar drew on this metaphor to remind his citizens of the obligation to repay this debt: it would be better for Colombia 'to perish before we default on the loan that has saved our *Patria* and the lives of its children'.[2] Bolívar would grow to rue the day he spoke these words.

By 1822, Bolívar's state had grown into Gran Colombia. Its borders were surrounded by enemies. According to Bolívar, it was flanked by 'floating fortresses' from Europe, the 'most powerful nation' in the United States, the 'vast' Mexican Empire, the 'ambitious' Portuguese Crown in Brazil; and Peru, 'with its millions', remained an enemy of Gran Colombia and a friend to its rivals, Buenos Aires and Chile. To establish a new balance of power in the region, Bolívar had to continue to rid the Andes of the Spanish military presence and harness liberation campaigns to galvanise support for his leadership. He first united New Granada—then the world's largest producer of gold—Venezuela, Panama, and Quito into Gran Colombia.[3] He then favoured the expansion of Gran Colombia into an Andean confederation, a union of states comprising of Gran Colombia, Peru, and Bolivia, a landlocked territory which contained the mines of Potosí. Embraced as the

[1] 'Discurso pronunciado por Simón Bolívar ante el Congreso de Venezuela en Angostura, 15 de febrero de 1819'. *Correo del Orinoco*. Number 19, Saturday 20 February 1819. Reprinted in *Co-herencia* 16 (2019), pp. 397–424, p. 404. On soteriological economics see Boyd Hilton, *The Age of Atonement: The Influence of Evangelicalism on Social and Economic Thought, 1795–1865* (Oxford: Oxford University Press, 1988), p. 6.

[2] 'Discurso', p. 404.

[3] Quoted in Ivan Jaksic, *Andrés Bello: Scholarship and Nation-Building in Nineteenth-Century Latin America* (Cambridge: Cambridge University Press, 2006), p. 58. On New Granada's gold production see Reinhard Liehr, 'La deuda exterior de la Gran Colombia frente a Gran Bretaña, 1820–1860', in Reinhard Liehr ed., *América Latina en la época de Simón Bolívar. La formación de las economías nacionales y los intereses económicos europeos 1800–1850* (Berlin: Colloquium-Verlag, 1989), p. 485.

Odious Debt. Edward Jones Corredera, Oxford University Press. © Edward Jones Corredera 2024.
DOI: 10.1093/9780191982200.003.0005

Libertador in Gran Colombia, Bolívar was eyed with suspicion in Peru.[4] Finding a binding element that could consolidate this union was a challenge: this federation, according to Bolívar, ought to be more closely bound than the United States or the Holy Alliance. But the use of the word 'federation', he continued, should be avoided to prevent fragmentation.[5] This union built on strategic ambiguity was therefore subject to similar challenges around the principles of *aeque principaliter* and usufructuary government that the Spanish Crown had once faced: Panama's representatives reminded Bolívar that their state had entered into this 'family', voluntarily, freely, but on the condition that the terms of its declaration of independence would be acknowledged and accepted.[6] As one *Panameño* official remarked, Vattel's principles which 'have become well known', showed that a change in government did not alter the obligation to repay a nation's past debts—Gran Colombia had to settle Panama's revolutionary debt.[7] The legal nature of the association of this union was never established—it would therefore be subject to intense retroactive debates over the succession of states in international law.

Once it was unified, the question remained as to how the interests of this union could be represented abroad. Gran Colombia's first treaties were signed with Mexico and Buenos Aires in order to prevent any of the parties from signing a peace treaty in exchange for monetary compensation.[8] Across the ideological spectrum, thinkers like Alamán and Bolívar hoped that a reunion of Latin American officials at the Congress of Panama would generate 'our law of nations', a code to consistently resolve common problems of the region.[9] The Colombian author Rufino Cuervo and a number of other liberal writers were the editors of the periodical *La Miscelania* and, as the negotiations in Panama were underway, they published an erudite article titled *España y Colombia*.[10] The column considered whether Gran Colombia should pay a 'financial indemnification' to Spain 'for the loss it will incur in recognising our independence'. There were two ways of approaching

[4] David Brading, *The First America: The Spanish Monarchy, Creole Patriots, and the Liberal State, 1492–1867* (Cambridge: Cambridge University Press, 1991), p. 608.

[5] Quoted in Jaksic, *Bello*, p. 57. On the bonds that united the Holy Alliance see Isaac Nakhimovsky, *The Holy Alliance: Liberalism and the Politics of Federation* (Princeton: Princeton University Press, 2024), pp. 18–58.

[6] Anonymous, 'Introducción', *Debates de la Cámara del Senado de la República de Colombia del día 4 de febrero del año décimo quinto* (Cartagena, Juan Antonio Calvo, 1826), pp. iii–vii, p. vi; see also Corredera, 'The End of Composite Monarchies'.

[7] Anonymous, 'Introducción', p. vii.

[8] On how Bernardino Rivadavia threatened to thwart this effort see Ricardo R. Caillet-Bois, 'La Convención Preliminar de Paz celebrada con España en 1823 y las Misiones de Alzaga y Las Heras', *Revista de Historia de América* 6 (1939), pp. 5–46.

[9] This was, in Rafael Rojas' view, accompanied by a turn from 'constitutions of war' towards the establishment of virtuous citizens; see Rafael Rojas, *Las repúblicas de aire. Utopía y desencanto en la revolución de Hispanoamérica* (Madrid: Taurus, 2009), pp. 12–13.

[10] 'España y Colombia', in *La Miscelania*. Number 24, 26 February 1826. On *La Miscelania* see David Bushnell, 'The Development of the Press in Great Colombia', *The Hispanic American Historical Review* 30:4 (1950), pp. 432–452, pp. 437–438. See also Eduardo Posada-Carbó, 'Newspapers, Politics, and Elections in Colombia, 1830–1930', *The Historical Journal* 53:4 (2010), pp. 939–962.

the question: law or utilitarianism. In terms of justice, Spain had waged an unjust war against Gran Colombia for 16 years and therefore the Crown was not owed anything; instead, it had a duty to 'repair the harms and damages' it had caused.[11] But the question of the expediency of Gran Colombia's repayment constituted 'the crux of the matter'.[12] The editors then estimated that Spain might continue to wage war for years on end. They considered the military cost and the loss of life this would entail, along with the 'demoralising aspect of the war' which would undermine the 'liberal and philanthropic' principles of its politics. They concluded that the most useful option was for Gran Colombia to pay Spain to avoid further loss of life. Spain would recognise Gran Colombia, other countries would follow suit, and this process would unlock its economic development through immigration and investment in roads, factories, and navigation.

International law, argued the editors of *La Miscelania*, generated trust within and between nations. To overcome the Hobbesian state of nature which continued to afflict Gran Colombia, the editors explained, officials had to follow Vattel's principle that nations who were at peace with one another could fulfil the mutual, reciprocal, and 'sacred duties' that nature had imposed on them. There was no need to rely on Monroe's promises: at the Congress of Panama, these states would find that 'a common organ of intelligence has been created among all the new states for the settlement of the great interests that are common in America'. There, the editors hoped, 'we will see a definitive solution' to war.[13] Indeed, the representatives of the Holy Alliance stepped up the pace in reclaiming payment from the new republics since many worried that the Congress would declare all debts owed to the Spanish Crown null.[14] Yet rival interests, recurrent rebellions, and the burst of the Latin American bubble at the London Stock Exchange undermined these negotiations. Bello sought to build on the important work of his peers: in his *Principios*, he explained that his purpose in writing the book was to remedy the 'uncertainty and doubt' that the 'lack of a code of international law' produced and which 'the powerful states never cease to interpret in their favour'.[15]

Bolívar by contrast hoped that an ever-expanding system of confederations would compensate for the fiscal shortcomings of each member state.[16] The story of Gran Colombia is a tale about the collapse of one of the most ambitious federative

[11] 'España y Colombia', in *La Miscelania*.

[12] 'España y Colombia', in *La Miscelania*.

[13] 'España y Colombia', in *La Miscelania*.

[14] Santos Rodulfo Corté, 'La creación de Bolivia y la Santa Alianza', *Boletín de la Academia Nacional de la Historia* 84 (2001), pp. 109–124, p. 123.

[15] Liliana Obregón, 'Construyendo la Región Americana: Andrés Bello y el Derecho Internacional', *Universidad de Los Andes. Revista de Derecho Público* 24 (2010), pp. 1–22, p. 9.

[16] Daniel Gutiérrez Ardila, *El reconocimiento de Colombia: diplomacia y propaganda en la coyuntura de las restauraciones, 1819–1831* (Bogotá: Universidad Externado de Colombia, 2012) and 'Un Sistema para la América independiente', in Alfredo Ávila, Jordana Dym, and Erika Pani eds., *Las declaraciones de Independencia: Los textos fundamentales de las independencias americanas* (Mexico City: Colegio de México, 2013), pp. 441–478.

and international schemes in history. The Holy Roman Empire inspired Saint-Pierre's vision of perpetual peace, which Bolívar praised, and Benjamin Franklin's model for the United States. But, in the absence of a Diet in Panama, Bolívar's supranational state was an unholy Roman Empire that lacked a higher purpose than unity.[17] Bolívar's warning to his citizens that it was better for the nation to perish before it defaulted on the debts that had saved the state and the lives of its children became a millstone around his neck. Bolívar listened to Bentham's writings on the law of nations but disregarded the philosopher's recommendation that Gran Colombia should default on its British debts—eventually, he was forced to declare bankruptcy. He also defaulted on his debt of gratitude to Haiti's President Alexandre Pétion after he failed to abolish slavery, as he had promised Pétion, in an expression of appreciation for Haiti's military assistance during his struggle for independence against Spain.[18] Bolívar initially ignored the suggestions of the editors of *La Miscelania*: in his 'Decree of War to the Death' and a number of other declarations, Bolívar defended the war against Spain and the seizure of enemy properties as a 'reprisal' authorised both by divine law and the law of nations.[19]

The promise to pay Gran Colombia's British agents of redemption did not absolve Bolívar from the sin of defaulting on the property rights of the Spanish Crown. As the composite parts of his empire rebelled against Bolívar, he watched as his enemies changed the terms of the debate: virtuous debts incurred for independence were depicted by secessionists as odious debts owed to a tyrannical state. Bolívar repeatedly deployed ideas of forgiveness and oblivion for political ends: he exonerated royalist priests, amnestied his enemies, and sought to use members of the clergy as couriers for his pardons. But he did not forgive revolutionary debts.[20] Rebels in Peru would counter that Bolívar's demands of debt repayment were tyrannical requests condemning them to a perpetual penance, similar to French demands on Haiti or Spain's claims on its former colonies. Bolívar's officials despaired: in the words of a Colombian diplomat, the rebellions were nothing short of acts of 'parricide'.[21]

Bolívar's model of absolution from without—through the establishment of a British protectorate or the protection of a praetorian ruler, in his own words, like

[17] Jürgen Overhoff, 'Benjamin Franklin, Student of the Holy Roman Empire: His Summer Journey to Germany in 1766 and His Interest in the Empire's Federal Constitution', *German Studies Review* 34:2 (2011), pp. 277–286. On the influence of the Holy Roman Empire on Vattel's ideas see Nakhimovsky, *Holy Alliance*, pp. 167–186.

[18] Sibylle Fischer, 'Bolívar in Haiti: Republicanism in the Revolutionary Atlantic', in Carla Calarge et al eds., *Haiti and the Americas* (Jackson: University Press of Mississippi, 2013), pp. 25–53, pp. 40–41.

[19] Tomás Cipriano de Mosquera ed., *Memorias sobre la vida del Libertador Simon Bolívar* (New York: S.W. Benedict, 1853), pp. 48–54; 'Angostura octubre 24 de 1818', *Correo del Orinoco*, Number 14, 24 October 1818; 'Decreto de Bolívar', *Correo del Orinoco*, Number 11, 18 August 1821.

[20] Fernando Cruz Kronfly ed., *Adictos a mí. Cartas a Tomás Cipriano de Mosquera (1826–1830)* (Bogotá: Universidad Nacional de Colombia, 2022), p. 260.

[21] AGN, Ministerio de Exteriores, DT2, t. 307, p. 401.

'Caesar in Gaul'—offered obligation without redemption.[22] Above all, it clashed with the principle of consent: Bolívar justified his decision to disregard the wishes of Congress and amnesty the insubordinate Venezuelan General José Antonio Páez Herrera by claiming the General had, by choosing to avoid a civil war, 'saved the tables [of the law] from the shipwreck of war', noting that it was 'the people who owe him gratitude and admiration'. Like Cicero's Scipio, he continued, it was time to 'thank the Heavens' and ignore 'complaints and lamentations'.[23] But these spiritual readings of obligation were incompatible with the logic of electoral politics, Bolívar's own concerns with Páez's separatist tendencies, and the *Libertador*'s libertarian views on religion.[24]

In 1828, when a threat was made against his life, Bolívar intensified his authoritarian control over the government, reaffirmed Catholic values, and struck Bentham's writings from the law curriculums in universities.[25] He then asked one of his envoys to gauge the Spanish Crown's interest in accepting compensation in exchange for the recognition of the independence of all Latin American nations.[26] The response of the British mediator was politely discouraging: there were some doubts about Gran Colombia's capacity to pay the promised sum 'on time'.[27] It was the beginning of the end for the enlightened statesman. For Bolívar, dissenting officials and the increasingly rebellious parts of Gran Colombia were guilty of fratricide: he lambasted his peers for betraying the thrift of those revolutionaries who had failed to incur any debts and taking on endless 'shameful debts' once peace had been secured.[28]

Towards the end of his life, Bolívar was not granted a debt of gratitude by what he described as his 'ungrateful *patria*'.[29] The *Libertador* believed his citizens had defaulted on their mutual obligations and their debts to their redeemers. In one intervention, he noted how the Latin American political experience showed that there was no 'good faith' in America: 'treaties are scraps of paper, our constitutions are empty texts'.[30] Yet he continued to promise to 'religiously indemnify' British lenders and, in his last major speech, pronounced months before his death, he

[22] David Bushnell, 'The Last Dictatorship: Betrayal or Consummation?', *Hispanic American Historical Review* 63:1 (1983), pp. 65–105, p. 82; Jaksic, *Bello*, p. 55;

[23] *Autobiografía del general José Antonio Páez*. Volume 1 (New York: Impr. Ponce de León, 1878), p. 369.

[24] See chapter 10 in John Lynch, *Simón Bolívar: A Life* (New Haven: Yale University Press, 2006).

[25] Victor M. Uribe-Uran, *Honorable Lives: Lawyers, Family, and Politics in Colombia, 1780–1850* (Pittsburgh: Pittsburgh University Press, 2000), p. 109.

[26] As noted by Daniel Gutiérrez Ardila, 'Colombia y Haití: historia de un desencuentro (1819–1831)', *Secuencia* 81 (2011), pp. 67–93, p. 74.

[27] See in particular the documents in AGN. Ministerio de Relaciones Exteriores. DT2. Box: 731. File 233. Fol. 84, Number 443, and File 234, Fol. 457.

[28] Simón Bolívar, *Mensaje del Libertador Presidente de la República de Colombia a la Gran Convención, en el año de 1828* (Bogotá: Impreso por J. A. Cualla, 1826), p. 2.

[29] Kronfly ed., *Adictos a mí*, p. 260. The same language was used by his officials; see AGN. Ministerio de Relaciones Exteriores. DT2. File 234, Fol. 419.

[30] Bushnell ed., *El Libertador*, p. 101.

declared that public debt was 'Colombia's cancer', one which 'cries out for you to honour its sacred obligations'.[31] Treaties and constitutions were disavowed and discarded but debts remained unpaid. One of Bello's tasks as an envoy in the service of Gran Colombia in London was the negotiation of these loans.[32] These debts outlasted Bolívar's republican ambitions: Bello, Constant, and the abbé de Pradt all tried to make sense of Bolívar's dictatorship as European authors debated whether the fate of republicanism and monarchism would be decided in the New World.[33]

Following Bolívar's death, Bolivia was in debt to Peru, Peru was in debt to Gran Colombia and Chile, and Gran Colombia was beholden to both Mexico and Britain. Gran Colombia, in turn, hoped to pay back the British debt with the money that Peru owed it. None of the revolutionary debts were forgotten or forgiven: as former deputies in service of one nation now met as diplomats representing different states, unifying national debts of gratitude born of the heat of revolution were transformed into fractious foreign debts of tyrants and usurpers. Some of these states resolved the debts they owed to Spain and Britain before they established what they owed to one another. Officials warned that their agents of financial redemption in Britain would pressure the government to use its naval power to force the repayment of their loans.[34] Foreign and fratricidal debts weighed like a nightmare on the brains of those who sought to ensure the survival of Bolívar's dream.

Why not default?

Like Bolívar and Bello, after the fall of the Spanish Empire, Jeremy Bentham struggled to reconstitute the Hispanic World through international law. Bentham offered Bolívar two answers to the question of Gran Colombia's diplomatic role in Europe: 'ambo-national representation' and a declaration of bankruptcy. In a letter written on 4 June 1823, Bentham castigated Simón Bolívar: 'Intrusive as this address can scarce fail to appear' in the choice of Colombian 'Diplomatic Agents in this country yours has, from first to last, been most unfortunate'.[35] Bentham was

[31] AGN. Ministerio de Relaciones Exteriores. DT2. File 234, Fol. 340. Bushnell, *El Libertador*, p. 108.

[32] Eduardo Plaza Alfonso, 'Las fuentes del derecho internacional de Bello de su periodo londinense; la experiencia y los estudios', in *Bello y Londres: Segundo Congreso Del Bicentenario*. Volume 2 (Caracas: La Casa de Bello, 1980), pp. 263–282, pp. 272–274.

[33] Rojas, Las repúblicas de aire, pp. 352–359; Mark Mazower, *The Greek Revolution: 1821 and the Making of Modern Europe* (London: Penguin, 2021), pp. 399–410.

[34] *Discurso pronunciado por el ciudadano Manuel de Vidaurre, presidente de la Corte Suprema de Justicia y del Soberano Congreso Nacional de la República del Perú, en el mes de julio, sobre la base de la Constitución* (Lima, 1827). Reprinted in Grover Paúl Morales Cama and Joan Manuel Morales Cama, 'El magistrado Manuel Lorenzo de Vidaurre y el nacimiento de la República', *Revista Del Archivo General De La Nación* 31:1 (2016), pp. 123–189, pp. 166–175; see pp. 169–171.

[35] Jeremy Bentham to Simón Bolívar, 4 June 1823, in Catherine Fuller ed., *The Collected Works of Jeremy Bentham: The Correspondence of Jeremy Bentham*. Volume 11: January 1822 to June 1824 (Oxford: Oxford University Press, 2000), pp. 238–265, p. 239.

referring to the fateful negotiations of the diplomat and natural scientist Francisco Antonio Zea and his compatriots.

Zea had served as Vice-President of Gran Colombia.[36] When news arrived that a number of officials from the territories that formed part of Gran Colombia had negotiated loans in their capacity as diplomatic envoys, Zea was sent to London to clarify the matter and ensure the financial credibility of the union. After Zea arrived in London, constitutional amendments were made to guarantee that the Congress had the last word on the approval of all foreign debts. While Congress sent a letter to Zea to inform him of this constitutional change, the news arrived in London after Zea had negotiated a loan on behalf of his country with the Herring, Graham and Powles banking house.[37] Zea died before he could remedy this mishap and Gran Colombia initially refused to acknowledge any of his debts. However, the government was soon forced to assume its payment and to fund this reimbursement through the negotiation of another British loan with the firm B.A. Goldschmidt & Company.[38]

This, then, was the background to Bentham's assessment of the situation. Bentham's frustration must also be understood in the broader context of his relationship with key political figures of the Hispanic World. On the whole, the trials and tribulations of the rump Spanish Empire proved too much for Bentham, who must have been disappointed at the results of his efforts. The codifier of international law had once held high hopes for the Hispanic world: he had contributed to the development of constitutional debates in Spain, Buenos Aires, and Gran Colombia. Had he achieved the homogenisation of nascent countries around his principles it would have been easier to convince the rest of the world of their merits—after all, he was already advising statesmen in Greece and Russia, and his followers were pushing for a utilitarian reform of the government in India.[39] By 1823, his influence on the Hispanic world was waning: José María Queipo de Llano, Count of Toreno, a prominent figure in Spanish politics, had, in spite of his initial praise and his

[36] Zea even argued that American independence, and the establishment of a representative government and a confederate alliance, was in the interest of Spain. See his 'Mediación entre España y América', in *Correo del Orinoco*. Number 7, Angostura, 8 August 1818, pp. i–ii. The text can be found in full in Francisco Antonio Zea, 'Mediación entre España y América', in Diaz, Pedro Pablo, José Luis Ramos, and Domingo Navas Spinola eds., *Varios discursos del ciudadano Francisco Antonio Zea* (Caracas: Spinola, 1825), pp. 1–80.

[37] David Bushnell, *The Santander Regime in Gran Colombia* (Newark: University of Delaware Press, 1954), pp. 96–124.

[38] This is a mere summary of the situation. For a full discussion of the debts incurred during this period see Bushnell, *Santander*, pp. 112–118. María Teresa Berruezo León, *La lucha de Hispanoamérica por su independencia en Inglaterra 1800–1830* (Madrid: Ediciones de Cultura Hispánica, 1989), pp. 247–255; Frank Griffith Dawson, *The First Latin American Debt Crisis: The City of London and the 1822–25 Loan Bubble* (New Haven: Yale University Press, 1990), pp. 22–46.

[39] Bentham sent Rivadavia's letter where the Argentinian statesman showed how he had applied the British jurist's principles in Buenos Aires to his Greek correspondents, likely with a view to further expanding them to the rest of the Mediterranean. Bentham to the Greek Legislature. 21 September 1824. Catherine Fuller et al. eds., *The Correspondence of Jeremy Bentham*. Volume 12: July 1824 to June 1828 (Oxford: Oxford University Press, 2006), pp. 48–51.

insistence on including Bentham's ideas in Spanish constitutional schemes, gradually learned to ignore his letters. Bentham's friendship with Miranda and Bolívar had not borne fruit.[40] Rivadavia's reputation had been tarnished once his commercial ambitions in London had been exposed. Perhaps he could use the issue of Gran Colombia's mishandling of its foreign loans to change the tide.[41]

After all, the world was in a state of flux, and Bentham found himself negotiating a loan for Greece and watching London's financiers bolster financial aid to Spanish liberals.[42] Bentham had been developing his idea of 'official aptitude' in his writings on Spain, and on the basis of these ideas he suggested that the solution to Colombia's reputation problems was not a renegotiation of the debts but an improvement of its administration: 'So low has been the reputation of Colombia in this country, for some time past, that whatever benefit depends upon reputation, will be necessarily lost to her, unless some better system of Agency for her can be framed'.[43] Instead, the young nation ought to establish an 'ambonational mode of agency' of diplomatic representation that would foster the country's technological development.[44] But Bolívar's Gran Colombia was not just ambonational but multinational; it was a combination of multiple sovereign republics that had united under one entity, with a variety of debts as guaranteed by their foundational constitutional texts which were at odds with one another.

Bentham overstated the failure of Bolívar's diplomacy. British officials showed a keen interest in recognising Gran Colombia's independence: in negotiations over the terms of the first treaty of friendship with Britain, British diplomats agreed to draw on the terms of the Jay Treaty to mediate peace negotiations between Spain and Colombia. The goal was to prevent the Crown of Spain from demanding an 'outsized indemnification' in exchange for the recognition of independence of the new nation.[45] But British officials also tried to ensure that a treaty of recognition did not generate tensions with Spain. When the Colombian ambassador, Pedro Gual, questioned the draft's use of the term 'state' and not 'republic' to characterise Colombia, his British counterpart pulled a dictionary out of his book collection

[40] Bolívar drew on and praised Bentham's ideas but he was never dogmatic about them. On Bolívar's political thought see Lynch, *Bolívar*, pp. 257–252; Carolina Guerrero, *Liberalismo y Republicanismo en Bolívar* (Caracas: Universidad Central Venezuela, 2005); Brading, *First America*, pp. 610–611; José Chiaramonte, *Nación y Estado en Iberoamérica. El lenguaje político en tiempos de la independencia* (Buenos Aires: Editorial Sudamericana, 2004), pp. 167–172; Ángel Rafael Almarza Villalobos, 'Rousseau, Bolívar y las revoluciones de Venezuela', in Gabriel Entin ed., *Rousseau en Iberoamérica* (Buenos Aires: SB Editores, 2018), pp. 121–136.

[41] On Bentham's broader designs during this period see Nakhimovsky, *The Holy Alliance*, pp. 193–209.

[42] On Bentham's negotiations of a Greek loan and his comparative analyses of Greece and Latin America see Rosen, *Bentham, Byron, and Greece*, pp. 96–146.

[43] Bentham to Bolívar, 4 June 1823, p. 239. On the impact of Bentham's work on Spain and the rise of his idea of 'official aptitude' see Philip Schofield, *Utility and Democracy: The Political Thought of Jeremy Bentham* (Oxford: Oxford University Press, 2006), p. 275.

[44] Bentham to Bolívar, 4 June 1823, p. 246.

[45] AGN. Ministerio de Relaciones Exteriores. Legación de la Gran Bretaña. 1824–1828. DT2. 304. 13 April 1825.

and showed him that in English the terms carried the same meaning. Gual, however, wisely insisted that the Spanish draft of the treaty carried the word 'republic'. George Canning, after all, still believed the creation of monarchies in the Americas was possible, and instructed his officials to avoid the use of 'republic'.[46] The treaty was signed in 1825. When the historian José Manuel Restrepo authored the first chronicle of Colombia's revolution and published it in Paris, he made a note of this debate and titled his book *Historia de La Revolución de la República de Colombia.*[47]

Colombian officials hoped that greater awareness of the revolution would improve the nation's credit.[48] But disaster struck when the London Panic of 1825 led to the demise of B.A. Goldschmidt & Company Bolívar now had to confront the more pressing question that Bentham had posed to him in another letter on Gran Colombia's diplomatic prospects:

> As to actual payment, whether in money or money's worth, it must, in this case as in every other, depend upon possession of the means; and where that possession is wanting, and power to obtain it wanting also, all reproach is useless, and, in so far as that event has taken place without blame on the part of the debtor, groundless.

Would it not be simpler, continued Bentham, for Gran Colombia to declare bankruptcy in London?[49]

'The credit of the *libertadores* of Colombia must be paid': Property rights and slavery

At the Congress of Angostura, The Fundamental Law, a constitutional charter, stated that the debts of Venezuela and New Granada, incurred after the Caracas Cabildo

[46] Ardila, *El reconocimiento de Colombia*, pp. 247–248. This was a recurrent concern. See AGN, Ministerio de Exteriores, DT2, t. 307, p. 112. See also Antonio Nariño's careful observation of the etymology of independence in José María Portillo, *Crisis Atlántica; Autonomía e independencia en la crisis de la monarquía hispana* (Madrid: Marcial Pons, 2016), p. 137. Not only was there a 'crisis of language', as Fernández Sebastián has noted, but there was a crisis of the translatability of both the colonial and Spanish pasts into discourses set from without. See Javier Fernández Sebastián, *Historia conceptual en el Atlántico ibérico: Lenguajes, tiempos, revoluciones* (Madrid: FCEE, 2021), pp. 217–228, the 'querelle of dictionaries' at pp. 234–241, pp. 268–278, and the transformation of concepts at pp. 256–257.

[47] José Manuel Restrepo, *Historia de la Revolución de la República de Colombia* (Paris: Lib. Americana, 1827).

[48] AGN, Ministerio de Exteriores, DT2, t. 307, p. 72.

[49] Bentham to Bolívar, 4 June 1823, p. 242, n. 17. As David Armitage has noted, in 1830, when Bentham hoped to design an 'international law' based on 'happiness', he turned to Jabez Henry, a barrister who had first caught Bentham's attention through his analysis of the tensions generated by international bankruptcies, and who designed an international bankruptcy code which he sent to Bentham. See David Armitage, *Foundations of Modern International Thought* (Cambridge: Cambridge University Press), pp. 185-186; Jabez Henry, *Outline of a Plan of an International Bankrupt Code for the Different Commercial States of Europe* (London, n.d).

established the Junta Suprema Conservadora de los Derechos de Fernando VII (1810), a year before the declaration of independence was formally declared, would be recognised *in solidum*.[50] But to establish its public credit, Gran Colombia would first have to choose what internal loans to default on. At the Congress of Cucuta (1821), where the new constitution was drafted, the then leading Colombian diplomat and parliamentarian, Pedro Gual, explained to his fellow congressmen that, in establishing legal norms to arrange Gran Colombia's loans, the government would not exactly be establishing its national debt. Rather, it would be declaring 'bankruptcy' and defaulting on some of its debts.[51] Yet this too was an oversimplification: its constituent representatives could not agree on what debts they were willing to recognise and repudiate. The Congress of Cucuta had to establish how best to address the question of war debts of its constituent states, including Panama and Ecuador. Panama's representatives had made the recognition of its war debts a condition of the state joining the union.[52] Gran Colombian authorities, however, had dismissed the idea of repaying Spain.[53] The situation quickly grew more complex. For every territory that was assimilated and annexed into the new state of Gran Colombia, the question of whether or not to absorb its debts arose, all while costly wars raged on multiple fronts. Deputies considered the competing demands of *jus postliminii*, economic growth, and regional interests.[54] In the event, the representatives agreed to restate the terms agreed at Angostura: the debts of Venezuela and New Granada were 'recognized *in solidum*' as 'Colombian national debt'. All 'goods and properties of the state' were thereby mortgaged for its repayment, and a commission was set up to recognise and liquidate the national debt.[55] The decree did not resolve the matter of just where the money to repay the debt would come from, or how the debts of the other composite parts would be settled.[56]

Desperate for funds, the Congress passed a decree authorising the government to negotiate and accept a loan of three million pesos 'in Europe or elsewhere', where it could mortgage any of the rents of the state in order to achieve it. The loan was to be used to finance the bulk of the state's spending, to 'repay the interests on the national debt, or to pay off part or the whole of the debt, and to cover the deficit in civil and military affairs that the rents of 1822 cannot cover'.[57] The following year some of the salaries of public officials—including soldiers—were seized and

[50] See Acta 253: *Actas del Congreso de Angostura 1819–1820* (Bogotá: Biblioteca de la Presidencia de la República, 1988), pp. 380–385.

[51] Carlos Restrepo Piedrahita, *Actas del Congreso de Cúcuta: 1821* (Bogotá: Fundación Francisco de Paula Santander, 1990) Volume 1, p. 162.

[52] Ecuador's representatives, in turn, failed to consult the people on the matter of its accession to the confederation. Bushnell, *Santander*, p. 23, p. 14.

[53] Bushnell, *Santander*, p. 23.

[54] Piedrahita, *Actas*, p. 89, pp. 131–132.

[55] Piedrahita, *Actas*, pp. 65–66.

[56] Piedrahita, *Actas*, p. 198.

[57] Piedrahita, *Actas*, p. 765.

these employees were granted promissory notes.[58] Legislators speculated with these notes for their own private gain while they debated the establishment of a Colombian civil code.[59] These disordered fiscal arrangements overshadowed some of the progress made during the Congress: Bolívar and Francisco de Paula Santander were elected President and Vice-President, a clear set of voting norms was established which limited the electorate to literate citizens, the Inquisition was abolished, freedom of expression was recognised, and an ambitious system of public education was created.[60] The difficulty in establishing an income tax without a reliable population census meant that most taxes had to be placed on foreign trade.[61] The Congress successfully reformed internal customs duties and abolished the *alcabala*, the Indian tribute, and a number of monopolies.[62]

A sense of euphoria characterised many of these congressional sessions: Jerónimo Torres closed the final gathering of 1823 by asking his peers to remember the lessons of Bentham: 'remember and repeat often with Bentham: "What a thing is law! How many things in a law!"'[63] Indeed, Bentham could not have imagined Torres and Joaquín Mosquera would use his ideas on interests and utility to defend fulfilling the repayments to the Spanish Crown, in contradiction of the ideas he had put forward in *Rid Yourselves of Ultramarina*.[64] Latin American officials understood that under the velvet glove of Bentham's ideas lay the iron fist of Cicero's regressive politics, a type of governance that praised a Roman model of virtue while its government was falling apart; one that drew on terms like virtue and duty to forestall Catiline's policies of debt forgiveness and land reform.[65] Officials like Torres and Mosquera would depict the repayment of debt as a type of love of country: they defended its legitimacy, and the preservation of slavery, as a way of protecting property rights, as Cicero, in *De Officiis*, had defended the need for *fides*, or trust, to ensure the payment of public debt, protect property rights, and secure the well-being of the republic.[66]

This defence of the legitimacy of the rights imposed by a vanquished empire had been entirely disavowed by Bolívar. But by the mid-1820s, officials in this composite empire were reminding Bolívar of the global struggle to show that republics could be as creditworthy as monarchies: Louis XVIII, explained one official, was

[58] Bushnell, *Santander*, pp. 105–108. A policy that Caesar himself drew on; see M. W. Frederiksen, 'Caesar, Cicero and the Problem of Debt', *The Journal of Roman Studies* 56 (1966), p. 132.

[59] Liehr, 'La deuda exterior', p. 473.

[60] Frank Safford, *Historia de Colombia: País fragmentado, sociedad dividida*. Translated by Marco Palacios and Ángela García (Bogotá: Ediciones Uniandes, 2011), pp. 182–183.

[61] Lynch, *Bolívar*, p. 163.

[62] Bushnell, *Santander*, p. 77.

[63] Quoted in Theodora Louise McKennan, *Santander and the Vogue of Benthamism in Colombia and Nueva Granada* (Unpublished PhD thesis) (Chicago: Loyola University, 1970), p. 155.

[64] Bartolomé Clavero, '"Libraos de Ultramarina!" El fruto podrido de Cádiz', *Revista de Estudios Políticos* 97 (1997), pp. 109–116, pp. 109–137.

[65] See Frederiksen, 'Caesar', pp. 128–141.

[66] Frederiksen, 'Caesar', p. 139.

forced to indemnify creditors and pay Napoleonic War reparations, and Prussia, Russia, and Austria had paid for Poland's partition. Kings that 'enslaved others' could not be seen to be 'fairer' than representative governments.[67] Military leaders of the process of independence like Ignacio de Herrera y Vergara were submitting letters to the official newspaper, the *Gaceta de Colombia*, complaining that Spanish goods had rightly been sequestered on the basis of reprisal and the law of nations—but these resources had not been used to pay the nation's soldiers. Gran Colombia 'founded its law in the law of nations that is observed in all learned nations', but by not satisfying the claims of its military revolutionary leaders for their services it was flying in the face of international law: 'the credit of the *libertadores* must be paid'.[68] In a speech to the Congress, Santander lamented that claimants came forward every day asking for repayment for their military services.[69] The Vice President reminded his peers that this debt was 'sacred'.[70]

Yet discussions about the sanctity of debt had to be reconciled with hard facts: military expenditure accounted for three quarters of the state's revenue.[71] Faced with the prospect of bankruptcy, the three communities with the greatest political power—lawyers, soldiers, and the clergy—clashed over the management of the nation. Lawyers suggested cutting spending on the costly army, soldiers opposed the lawyers' constitutional framework, and the Church remained opposed to educational reforms which threatened to erode its influence over day-to-day life in the provinces.[72] New territories were added to Gran Colombia while efforts to wrestle Peru away from Spain's control continued to deplete the treasury of resources.[73] Earlier reforms were reconsidered: the monopoly on alcohol and tobacco was re-established.[74] Small loans contracted in London, including one negotiated by the Ecuadorian-born Mexican envoy, Vicente Rocafuerte, allowed Gran Colombia to cover past military expenses and repay private loans owed to foreign merchants, which were now helpfully included under the umbrella of the state debt, but delivered few economic benefits to the general public.[75]

67 Anonymous, 'Introducción', p. vii; Thomas Gauchet and Christine Haynes, 'Restoring Credit in Post-Napoleonic France: Settling French War Claims', *War in History* 27:3 (2020), pp. 433–455; Simon Hinrichsen, *When Nations Can't Default* (Cambridge: Cambridge University Press, 2023), pp. 86–99; George E. Munro, 'Paying for Poland's Partitions', *Journal of Baltic Studies* 20:4 (1989), pp. 327–336.

68 'Vista Fiscal', in *Suplemento a la Gaceta de Colombia*. Number 246, 2 July 1826. On this gazette see Lina del Castillo, *La invención republicana del legado colonial. Ciencia, historia y geografía de la vanguardia política colombiana en el siglo XIX* (Bogotá: Universidad de los Andes, 2018), pp. 23–30. A response to Herrera's claims was published in the *Gaceta de Cartagena*. 30 July 1826. Number 16.

69 'El Vicepresidente de la República encargado del poder executivo al excmo. Presidente de la Cámara', in *Gaceta de Colombia*. Number 17, 15 May 1825. Bushnell, *Santander*, pp. 275–286.

70 'El Vicepresidente de la República encargado'.

71 Lynch, *Simón Bolívar*, p. 159.

72 Bushnell, *Santander*, pp. 101–104; Safford, *Historia*, pp. 187–190.

73 Safford, *Historia*, p. 193. On the socio-economic dynamics of Alto Peru during this period see Jeremy Adelman, *Republic of Capital: Buenos Aires and the Legal Transformation of the Atlantic World* (Stanford: Stanford University Press, 1999), p. 84.

74 Lynch, *Simón Bolívar*, pp. 162–163.

75 Liehr, 'La deuda exterior', p. 481.

It was in this context that Church officials and former soldiers intensified their pressure on the government to resolve the question of what Gran Colombia owed to Spain. Spanish colonial treasuries, or *cajas*, had been earmarked for the pensions of revolutionary soldiers.[76] It was not clear whether Spain ought to be compensated for these losses. Conservative officials used this quagmire to generate a reconsideration of the status of all colonial debts. The matter of Gran Colombia's debt to Spain and Spanish citizens was further complicated by a revolutionary measure: the memory of the violent expulsion of Spaniards and the confiscation of properties that belonged to Spanish families.[77] The congressional debate on the Spanish debt was broadly shaped by two legal ideas: respect for property rights and the right of reprisal.

The representative Santiago Pérez Arroyo explained that if the nation declared that the Spanish Crown had not been a legitimate government, contract laws upon which private property was established would be void and the government would have to deem the Spanish distribution of land illegitimate. The state would have to 'take possession of all that is enjoyed by the Nation and the people by virtue of usurpation or an unjust title'.[78] Torres, a centralist who had been involved in earlier efforts at educational reform, pointed to the interests of those who had in good faith entered into these contracts and their descendants: the government had no right to ruin the lives of these individuals, 'arbitrarily depriving them of property'. Undermining these contracts would render the government of Gran Colombia a 'despotic and tyrannical government' and would damage its own foundations, built on the 'vote of the people'.[79] This would be a betrayal of the debt owed to those who suffered to achieve independence: 'is this the government full of rectitude, humanity, and philanthropy which we so anxiously desired and for the sacrifice of which so much blood and sacrifices have been made?'. This duplicity, warned Torres, would even encourage some to consider the benefits of 'returning' to the old 'regime'.[80]

By contrast, Francisco Soto, another centralist deputy, appealed to the logic of expediency: it was crucial to establish the identity of these creditors. Otherwise Gran Colombia would find itself 'with a huge debt and who knows what dukes, counts, and marquises, who perhaps would have contributed to the preservation of our slavery, engrossing the vaults of the King with the same funds'.[81] If the 'legitimacy' of repayment was to be based on the idea that 'a government had been needed to preserve the security of property and public rents', Gran Colombia

[76] Bushnell, *Santander*, pp. 101–104.
[77] Lynch, *Simón Bolívar*, p. 189.
[78] Roberto Cortázar and Luis Augusto Cuervo, *Congreso de 1825. Senado. Actas* (Bogotá: Imprenta Nacional, 1902), p. 98.
[79] Cortázar and Cuervo, *Congreso de 1825*, pp. 98–99.
[80] Cortázar and Cuervo, *Congreso de 1825*, p. 99.
[81] Cortázar and Cuervo, *Congreso de 1825*, p. 100.

would be forced to recognise Philip II's debts and other obligations dating back to the 'burial ceremony of the Zipa', the leader of the Zipazgo power that governed the bulk of Colombia's territory at the time of the Spanish invasion.[82] The measure ought to clarify the 'conditions' under which the colonial payments which made up the bulk of the debt had been made.[83]

The logic of reprisal was one way to justify defaulting on the sums owed to Spaniards while repaying Colombians. Torres argued that since the government had already confiscated Spanish properties it should be clear that the recognition of debts would only be made in favour of Colombians.[84] This was about recognising a 'debt owed to Colombians' based on 'the private property of individuals'.[85] Torres drew on Bentham's discussion of 'the suppression of employment' and 'the injustice which is committed in wanting to sacrifice the property of particulars for the sake of a pretended general interest'.[86] Interpolating his reading of the text with his own comments, Torres claimed that the sacrifice of individual property would undermine the general interest and provide 'no utility' to society; divided into unclear parts, it would threaten all property rights, because if individual property was not protected the general right to property would be impossible to uphold.[87] The legislature would thus establish itself with this 'predatory act over foreign property', he continued, 'like the beast that Lucan had referenced in an extract cited by Bentham in this section'.[88] Torres had drawn on the same extract of Bentham's writings once before in order to argue against the special provision in a law on entailed Church land, whereby the estates that had under Spanish legislation been provided for the Church, had to be granted to their de facto holders, along with their ownership rights.[89]

Joaquín Mosquera, then an experienced diplomat who had negotiated Gran Colombia's treaties with Chile, Peru, and Buenos Aires, claimed that the question of Gran Colombia's succession from Spain had been resolved. There was no doubt that just as it succeeded from the Crown in its 'rights it had succeeded in its obligations'. Gran Colombia had merely separated itself 'from the person who was last in charge' and replaced 'this arrangement with a government of a different kind'.[90] The 'Nation had never ceased to exist'. Mosquera reiterated the idea that the law on the sequestration of Spanish properties resolved the question of whether 'we owe

[82] Cortázar and Cuervo, *Congreso de 1825*, p. 101; David Bushnell, *The Making of Modern Colombia: A Nation in Spite of Itself* (Berkeley: University of California Press, 1993), p. 6.
[83] Cortázar and Cuervo, *Congreso de 1825*, p. 101.
[84] Cortázar and Cuervo, *Congreso de 1825*, p. 101.
[85] Cortázar and Cuervo, *Congreso de 1825*, p. 101.
[86] Cortázar and Cuervo, *Congreso de 1825*, p. 101 and Jeremy Bentham, *Theory of Legislation*. Translated from the French of Etienne Dumont (London: Trübner & Co, 1864), pp. 143–148.
[87] Cortázar and Cuervo, *Congreso de 1825*, pp. 101–102.
[88] Cortázar and Cuervo, *Congreso de 1825*, p. 102.
[89] McKennan, *Vogue of Benthanism*, p. 165.
[90] Cortázar and Cuervo, *Congreso de 1825*, p. 102. Marcela Revollo Rueda, *Epistolario de Joaquín Mosquera (1845–1874)* (Chía: Universidad de la Sabana, 2018), p. 17.

or we don't owe' money to the Spaniards'.[91] Yet others argued that 'many territories which now compose the Republic' had not only lived under Spanish domination but had waged war against those who had declared independence.[92]

The solution was, therefore, to establish a clear standard by which to rule on the matter of the odiousness of debts. Diego Fernando Gómez, a jurist who had participated in the government's project to develop a penal and civil code, noted the ambiguities of odious debts: he argued that 'as Bentham explained' all obligation 'created a right' but it remained to be established whether the government had controlled these funds, and whether it had found in them monies from which it had benefited; but since the government had found these coffers empty, it was not obliged to recognise these loans. Given that it never benefited from these funds, continued Gómez, it followed that it did not make sense to recognise them.[93] Establishing that 'the King of Spain had bound the Colombians to a perpetual contribution' would lead to terrible consequences, so that the government would be forced to finance its own troops and the conservation and security of Spain; this would be to perpetuate the old injustices only because Spain had once mortgaged the treasuries of the Americas to pay for its debts.[94] It was, moreover, wrong to declare that 'the Republic was inherited from the Government of Spain': instead, Gran Colombia had merely recovered 'the rights which' Spain 'had usurped'.[95] The debt should thus go unpaid. Congress approved the repayment of the funds owed to the soldiers but Santander vetoed the measure on the basis of the nation's financial difficulties.[96] The *libertadores* awaited their payment and the government sought new loans abroad.

Slaveowners used the debate on colonial and foreign debts to bolster their commercial interests. Mosquera and Torres, the two patrician representatives for Cauca, an important mining region that had undergone a severe economic downturn in the early years of the nineteenth century, made the most important interventions in debates over the morality of colonial and foreign debts in more extensive pamphlets.[97] Mosquera and Torres had been involved in a decade-long campaign to overturn another measure that deprived its former owners of their property: abolitionism. Mosquera and Torres opposed the project to create a Free Womb Law that nominally freed the offspring of enslaved mothers but in

[91] Cortázar and Cuervo, *Congreso de 1825*, p. 103.
[92] Cortázar and Cuervo, *Congreso de 1825*, p. 104.
[93] Cortázar and Cuervo, *Congreso de 1825*, pp. 104–105.
[94] Cortázar and Cuervo, *Congreso de 1825*, p. 105.
[95] Cortázar and Cuervo, *Congreso de 1825*, p. 106.
[96] Bushnell, *The Making of Modern Colombia*, pp. 60–61.
[97] See Willian Alfredo Chapman-Quevedo, 'La red sociofamiliar Mosquera y sus relaciones de poder en Popayán, 1832–1836', *Memoria y Sociedad* 14:29 (2010), pp. 37–54; Safford, *Historia*, pp. 267–268. Pilar López-Bejarano, *Un Estado a crédito. Deudas y configuración estatal de la Nueva Granada en la primera mitad del siglo XIX* (Bogotá: Editorial de la Pontificia Universidad Javeriana, 2015), pp. 197–204; Safford, *Historia*, p. 94, p. 269.

fact bound these children to their mothers, and their enslavers, until they grew of age.[98] Bolívar hoped, by contrast, that the Free Womb Law reconciled 'property rights, political rights, and natural rights'.[99] Mosquera and Torres, who provided the most sophisticated analyses of the colonial debt, fervently fought the abolitionist reform. Torres suggested that the state would have to compensate the slaveowners for the freedom of their slaves – this was a 'national debt'.[100] Abolitionist legislation, Torres and Mosquera agreed, deprived their owners of their property.[101] In the event, the law would not prove particularly successful in reforming the system of unfree labour. The benefits of the approval of a manumission law for those who served in the military were further hampered by a government amendment to the law that ensured that slaveowners had to be indemnified.[102]

As this debate over women's rights, slavery, and war raged on, Mosquera and Torres served on the congressional commission on public credit. Its report suggested that all of the nation's debts ought to be recognised and consolidated—foreign debts were to be paid according to the terms of each individual contract.[103] Torres addressed the question of the repayment of the colonial debts in his *Opinión*.[104] During the war against Spain, he had sided against fellow revolutionaries to defend the right of the *cabildo* of Popayan to embargo the goods and revenues of Quito following its revolt against the Spanish Empire; the people of Quito had committed the crime of high treason and it did not follow from 'reason nor the law of nations' that a 'sovereign was deprived of the indemnification they deserved, or of the innate right of the Sovereign to punish insurgents with the deprivation of their properties'.[105]

In his *Opinión*, Torres studied how 'the legitimacy of this debt, and the responsibility that the republic has over it' had been challenged. He argued that the Spanish Crown was not an invader or a usurper: it had laid the foundation for the nation, which was made up of the children of the conquistadors, and not indigenous

[98] Yesenia Barragan, Freedom's Captives: *Slavery and Gradual Emancipation on the Colombian Black Pacific* (Cambridge: Cambridge University Press, 2021), pp. 123–157, pp. 142–155. Aline Helg, Liberty and Equality *in Caribbean Colombia, 1770–1835* (Chapel Hill: University of North Carolina Press, 2005), pp. 170–171.

[99] Quoted in Peter Blanchard, *Under the Flags of Freedom: Slave Soldiers and the Wars of Independence in Spanish South America* (Pittsburgh: University of Pittsburgh, 2008), p. 81.

[100] Barragan, *Freedom's Captives*, pp. 150–152.

[101] Barragan, *Freedom's Captives*, p. 156.

[102] Blanchard, *Under the Flags of Freedom*, pp. 81–82. Barragan, *Freedom's Captives*, pp. 124–127; Marcela Echeverri, *Indian and Slave Royalists in the Age of Revolution* (Cambridge: Cambridge University Press, 2015), pp. 229–230.

[103] 'Deuda Colombiana'. AGN. Hacienda Pública: SR.8, V.9, R.40, pp. 18–25.

[104] Torres, *Opinión*. See also the analysis in López-Bejarano, *Un Estado*, pp. 61–64.

[105] Armando Martínez Garnica, *Historia de la primera República de Colombia, , 1819–1831. 'Decid Colombia sea, y Colombia será'* (Bogotá: Editorial Universidad del Rosario, 2018), p. 33. Torres had participated in Santander's early efforts to consolidate a unified state and his views on the importance of ensuring that the Constitution guaranteed property rights had been consistent. See Bushnell, *Santander*, p. 64.

peoples. The descendants of the conquerors could not be defrauded.[106] He cited Vattel and Pufendorf to argue that the moral responsibility to deliver on contracts with private creditors did not change with succession.[107] It would, moreover, be wise for Gran Colombia to avoid repeating the mistakes of the Habsburg Crown in mishandling such commitments to its creditors.[108] Failing to follow the 'sacred law of contracts' would only mean that the people would be less willing to fund wars. It would allow Spain to argue that Gran Colombia was depriving its people of an essential right. Money would leave the country; this would constitute the ruin of universities, schools, hospitals, and religious communities that provided for widows and orphans.[109] The United States' recognition of its share of the British debt in the Jay Treaty, Mexico's decision to recognise its colonial debts, and the Cádiz Cortes' choice to recognise the obligation to pay the Crown's *juros*, all testified to widespread recognition that inherited debts ought to be disbursed.[110] In a passage that was likely inspired by his reading of Bentham, Torres argued that 'the more one respects self-interest, the more the public spirit is strengthened'.[111] Torres argued that the nation was leaving an honourable inheritance to future generations: 'the prosperity that will flow from our present sacrifices grants this current generation the right to make those who are yet to be born participate in these debts'.[112] The debt had to be repaid.

The fragmentation of Gran Colombia

The question of Gran Colombia's British loans quickly displaced the debate over the nation's debt to Spain. The London Panic of 1825 weakened international trade, the main source of revenue for the new Latin American states, and the British government began to study measures to curb corporate greed.[113] Over the next two years, Gran Colombia and Mexico defaulted on their loans. The editors of the government-sponsored *Gaceta de Colombia* defended the administration's negotiations of British loans by maintaining that its goal had not been to 'carry out a conquest of foreign lands', 'to liberate the Holy Land from the Turks', to 'carry out a tour around the world in search of new colonies', or in pursuit of retaliation, all of which would have been unjust. The government's goal had been to provide for the welfare of the Colombian people and compensate creditors who had 'lent their

[106] Torres, *Opinión*, p. 7.
[107] Torres, *Opinión*, p. 8.
[108] Torres, *Opinión*, p. 10.
[109] Torres, *Opinión*, pp. 3–4.
[110] Torres, *Opinión*, p. 6.
[111] Torres, *Opinión*, p. 7.
[112] Torres, *Opinión*, p. 13.
[113] Hilton, *Age of Atonement*, p. 256. See, however, a critique of the effectiveness of these reforms in Trevor Jackson, *Impunity and Capitalism: The Afterlives of European Financial Crises, 1690–1830* (Cambridge: Cambridge University Press, 2022).

fortunes to the preservation of independence'.[114] These were debts, they noted, of 'honour, good faith, and gratitude'.[115]

The failure of the Congress of Panama to deliver any substantial agreements further undermined Bolívar's supranational ambitions. Unrest in Venezuela and Peru soon transformed into open revolt. Bolívar assumed dictatorial powers, suspended the repayment of loans in order to increase military spending and, a year later, Gran Colombia declared war on Peru, citing the Peruvian government's reluctance to pay its debts to Colombia as one of the reasons for the conflict.[116] Gran Colombia's Vice-President, Francisco de Paula Santander, publicly criticised Bolívar, whose authoritarian turn he despised, and was promptly exiled. Others pursued conciliatory measures: Mosquera convinced Bolívar that redrafting the Constitution of Gran Colombia in light of Bolivia's own would be counterproductive.[117] Torres justified Bolívar's authoritarianism by arguing that order would fix that which federalism had broken: in emulating the United States, Gran Colombian officials had failed to realise that the Spanish cultural influence in Latin America prevented the people from understanding their true interests.[118] Despotism would enlighten them.

In light of the failure of the confederate model, and faced with a Venezuelan declaration of independence, Colombian officials were forced to argue, like their Spanish predecessors, that debts were commutative obligations that binded nations together.[119] The editors of the *Gaceta* noted that Venezuela's taxes on the tobacco monopoly were key to Gran Colombia's capacity to repay its foreign loans and dividing up these debts would lead to 'interminable disagreements'.[120] The erudite deputy José María Vargas argued against treating the declaration of Venezuelan pursuit of independence as a declaration of war: the political representation of Gran Colombia did 'not allow for its fragmentation' because in regards to 'debts and loans the union of Colombia and foreign peoples and societies has been recognised'.[121] 'Military costs, indemnifications, and seizures' had ensured the 'mixture' of the citizens of Venezuela, New Granada, and Quito. The dismemberment of Gran Colombia, he warned, would lead to a discussion about how to share the debt which would prove impossible to resolve. Vargas framed the union as a way to 'preserve the integrity of the conditions of these contracts and deals

[114] 'Concluye artículo sobre el empobrecimiento y ruina de la nación', *Gaceta de Colombia*. Number 278, 11 February 1827.
[115] 'Concluye artículo sobre el empobrecimiento y ruina de la nación', *Gaceta de Colombia*. Number 278, 11 February 1827.
[116] Bushnell, *The Making of Modern Colombia*, pp. 68–70.
[117] Safford, *Historia*, p. 202.
[118] Jerónimo Torres, *Observaciones políticas dirijidas a la gran Convención de Colombia, por el ciudadano que las subscribe* (Bogotá: Imprenta de Nicomedes Lora, 1828), pp. 1–2.
[119] Bushnell, *Santander*, p. 124.
[120] 'Editorial', in *Gaceta de Colombia*. Number 487, 24 October 1830.
[121] 'Discurso pronunciado por J. Vargas, diputado de Caracas en el congreso constituyente', in *Gaceta de Colombia*. Number 446, 3 January 1830.

and the mandatory effect of their stipulations'. Division would render the various fragmented parts weaker and expose the nation to 'a Caesar preparing his chains in Gaul', and thereby exacerbate Bolívar's authoritarian tendencies.[122]

To further complicate matters, Santander decided to mortgage the money that Peru owed Gran Colombia to repay the interests on its British loans to avoid 'losing our standing abroad'.[123] Peruvian representatives committed to repaying the debt but declared that the people had been impoverished by the war and thus were in no state to pay at the time. Peru in turn pressed Bolivia to pay a share of its debts: as one official noted, Peru recognised Bolivia's right to independence 'on the condition that the government they belong to should indemnify Peru with the costs of emancipating her'.[124] Peru had 'not asked for a favour; it has reclaimed the payment of a sacred debt'.[125] Bolivian officials countered that the only debt that it had with Peru was the one contracted in the expeditions that had protected the region from a Spanish invasion. Bolivia had, however, made considerable sacrifices to free Peru in the early stages of the revolution, as part of the generous efforts extended to its brethren as a result of belonging to the 'American family'.[126] Indeed, Bolivian officials argued that Peru had not repaid Bolivia for its military assistance in liberating it from the Spaniards.[127] Officials denied that Bolivia 'owed its existence to Peru' and declared that it would never 'recognise this debt'.[128] Peru's claim amounted to 'right by conquest': following the tyrannical example of 'the King of France in Haiti' it was now demanding compensation for its recognition.[129]

As Gran Colombia waged war on Peru to enforce the repayment of these debts, officials who defended the merits of aggression had to represent the original burden which it hoped to impose on the former constituent parts of the empire in a new light. The government-sponsored *Gaceta* offered its readers a counterfactual history: it considered the prospect of remaining part of the Spanish Empire and calculated what each individual in the region would owe the Crown. Drawing on a report on Spain's debts and an estimate of the population size of Gran Colombia,

[122] 'Discurso pronunciado por J. Vargas'. On other uses of Roman tropes to characterise Bolívar's leadership see Francisco Ortega, 'Tiempo precario y tiempo eterno: República y moral en la primera mitad del siglo XIX neogranadino', in Fabio Wasserman ed., *Tiempos Críticos: Historia, revolución y temporalidad en el mundo iberoamericano* (siglos XVIII y XIX) (Buenos Aires: Prometeo, 2010), pp. 197–222, pp. 204–207.

[123] Bushnell, *Santander*, p. 125. *Gaceta de Colombia*, 14 May 1826, Number 16.

[124] Quoted in Patricio A. Alvarado Luna, 'Reorganizando las nuevas fronteras republicanas: Perú y Bolivia (1826–1836)', *Revista Ciencia y Cultura* 24:44 (2020), pp. 37–62, p. 59.

[125] Fernán Altuve Febres-Lores, *La monarquía sin corona: Obras de José María de Pando (1787–1840)* (Lima: Fondo Editorial del Congreso del Perú, 2015), p. 73.

[126] Carlos Ortiz de Zevallos, *Misiones Peruanas 1820–1826*. Volume 1 (Lima: Comisión Nacional del Sesquicentenario de la independencia del Perú, 1975), p. 568.

[127] Zevallos, *Misiones Peruanas*, pp. 568–569.

[128] Zevallos, *Misiones Peruanas*, p. 569.

[129] Zevallos, *Misiones Peruanas*, p. 574. On the broader economic history of Bolivia's debt see Thomas Millington, *Debt Politics After Independence: The Funding Conflict in Bolivia* (Gainesville: University Press of Florida, 1992).

the editors of the *Gaceta* explained to their readers that their bills would have been considerably greater. Since the start of the revolution in Gran Colombia, the Crown's borrowing had only grown larger: 'Are we debtors today of a larger sum than there would have been if we had continued as Spanish *colonos* or members of the Spanish nation?'[130] Public debt remained the best way to 'unite citizens and the government' and harmonise 'individual interests'. A 'disunited Colombia' would find that this debt would become a source of 'perpetual discord' and likely encourage 'a foreign intervention'.[131]

In 1830, Bolívar renounced his presidency, and the fragmentation of Gran Colombia into three states—Venezuela, New Granada, and Ecuador—was formalised. Mosquera was made President of New Granada.[132] In December, Bolívar died and left behind a broken Gran Colombia. The threat of further fragmentation haunted New Granada as Panama debated the merits of independence.[133] It was still not clear which colonial or foreign debts had been absorbed within Gran Colombia's national debt. Three years later, representatives of New Granada and Venezuela gathered to discuss how to divide up the foreign debt. Santander, who had returned from exile to assume his role as President of New Granada, argued it should be divided equally; Mosquera, then Vice President, thought wealth and population size should be considered. This would mean that Venezuela would be responsible for a greater share of the payment. The final accord was based on the population figures of the three republics: New Granada was to shoulder half of the debt. But New Granada's congress reviewed this treaty and promptly disavowed it.[134] This only exacerbated tensions between Santander and Mosquera. Mosquera attacked Bentham's influence on the region and led the charge against the treaty that settled the debt of Gran Colombia in order to undermine Santander's authority.[135]

Mosquera argued that wealth ought to contribute towards the common good. He published a pamphlet on the division of the debt, which selectively drew on Thomas Robert Malthus' studies and principles that were 'observed in Britain'.[136] Malthus' studies of Ireland, he argued, demonstrated that a nation could be relatively poor and still generate population growth through the expansion of agricultural production.[137] He studied the size, and the commercial potential, of the land

[130] 'Deuda pública de Colombia', in *Gaceta de Colombia*. Number 297, 24 June 1827.
[131] *Gaceta de Colombia*. Number 46, 11 April 1830.
[132] Safford, *Historia*, p. 208.
[133] Safford, *Historia*, pp. 211–212.
[134] Clímaco Calderón Reyes, *Elementos de Hacienda* (Bogotá: La Luz, 1911), pp. 229–231. López-Berajano, *Un Estado*, p. 75. On the division of indigenous lands in New Granada see Castillo, *La invención*, pp. 105–127.
[135] Safford, *Historia*, pp. 223–224.
[136] Joaquín Mosquera, *Opinión de un granadino sobre la división de la deuda colombiana entre los tres Estados de Nueva Granada, Venezuela y Ecuador* (Popayán: Manuel Córdoba, 1836).
[137] Mosquera, *Opinión*, p. 2.

managed by Venezuela and he argued that an 'English capitalist' could repay the outstanding debts in exchange for the acquisition of public lands in the Orinoco and 'the privilege of navigation' in Venezuela's rivers.[138] New Granada, by contrast, would be forced to declare bankruptcy because it simply lacked the resources to repay the debt.[139] It thus followed that foreign creditors should divide the debt on the basis of each nation's economic 'strength' and not its population.[140]

Mosquera then posited that New Granada was not responsible for this debt. After Venezuela separated from New Granada it violated the 'fundamental law' of 1821. New Granada, explained Mosquera, had no debts when it first entered into an alliance with Venezuela, and agreed to contribute to the repayment of the latter's burden on the basis of 'the perpetual union' of the two states.[141] It followed, then, that Venezuela's breach of the terms of the union meant that New Granada was not obliged to repay its debts.[142] Drawing on Roman law, Mosquera argued that the debts owed to the farmers of the three republics had to be repaid because of the principle of *Nemo locupletari debet cum aliena iactura*, the notion that a claimant cannot be granted greater rewards than what they lost and one cannot profit from the misfortune of another.[143] An anonymous response appeared soon after the publication of Mosquera's text.[144] Where Mosquera had tried to argue that Venezuela's breach of the fundamental law freed New Granada from its obligations, this author noted that the sacrifices of war from 1810 onwards had delivered benefits to many citizens.[145] War debts would not be forgotten.

In the event, Santander ignored Mosquera's proposal for default. New Granada shouldered half of Gran Colombia's debt but the repayment was subject to constant renegotiations. Three of the constituent parts of Bolívar's empire agreed to settle their debts with Spain before they paid off their revolutionary debts to one another.[146] In the 1840s, Bolivia, Ecuador, and Venezuela all signed treaties of recognition with Spain. Many of the officials involved in these negotiations had a great deal of experience with debt diplomacy: Gual, who had represented Gran Colombia at the Congress of Panama, represented Ecuador, then governed by Rocafuerte, in negotiations with Spain. The salience of the question of debts in these negotiations varied. Venezuela leveraged Spain's interest in fostering commercial relations in the Caribbean to reject the assumption of colonial debts, and

138 Mosquera, *Opinión*, p. 5.
139 Mosquera, *Opinión*, p. 6.
140 Mosquera, *Opinión*, p. 6.
141 Mosquera, *Opinión*, p. 7.
142 Mosquera, *Opinión*, p. 8.
143 Mosquera, *Opinión*, p. 7.
144 *Breve examen del cuaderno publicado en Popayán con el título de Opinión de un granadino sobre la división de la deuda colombiana etc.* (Bogotá: J.A. Cualla, 1836).
145 *Breve examen del cuaderno publicado en Popayán*, pp. 3–4.
146 Venezuela took on 28.5 per cent of the debt and Ecuador assumed 21.5 per cent of the payment. See Liehr, 'La deuda exterior', p. 486.

the conclusion of the treaty of recognition took seven years. The final accord only established the shared resolve to settle the matters in future conventions.[147] By contrast, in discussions with his Bolivian counterpart, the Spanish ambassador explained that most of the outstanding debts owed to the Crown were in fact owed to Bolivian citizens.[148] Bolivia agreed to pay debts incurred by the Spanish government in Alto Peru before 1824.[149] In Ecuador, the acceptance of viceregal debts in the treaty of recognition was seen as a way to enrich the local elites who owned the bulk of these bonds.[150]

Santander also rejected Mosquera's criticisms of Bentham: university syllabi were to include those writings of the British jurist that did not contradict the dogmas of Christian ethics.[151] The matter of Bentham's influence over the country continued to elicit intense debate: the leading conservative historian of his age, José Manuel Groot, noted that Montesquieu had already warned that epicureanism had once corrupted the Roman Republic and suggested that Bentham's thought was undermining Colombia's politics.[152] By contrast, Catholic principles, he reasoned, would continue to foster the growth of civilisation in the Spanish Americas.[153]

Whose utility? Bolívar's legacy

In the mid-nineteenth century, New Granada's tobacco exports boomed and its public sphere expanded: the author María Josefa Acevedo de Gómez, separated from her husband, Diego Fernando Gómez, the deputy who proposed coming up with a clear definition of odious debt, drew attention to the importance of the duties of husbands to their wives in a work that proved popular in New York and Paris.[154] But divisions over social reform, the administration of

[147] Francisco Alfaro Pareja, 'Capacidades para la paz en las negociaciones para el reconocimiento de la Independencia de Venezuela por parte de España (1833 y 1846)', *Revista de Paz y Conflictos* 7 (2014), pp. 175–194, p. 188.

[148] Enrique Guerrero Balfagón, 'El reconocimiento de la independencia de Bolivia por España', *Revista de estudios políticos* 135–136 (1964), pp. 181–234, p. 220.

[149] Guerrero Balfagón, 'El reconocimiento', p. 218.

[150] Agustín Sánchez Andrés, 'Las dificultades del reinicio. Las relaciones entre España y Ecuador durante la minoridad de Isabel II, 1834–1843', in Agustín Sánchez Andrés y Marco Antonio Landavazo eds., *Conflicto y reconciliación. España y las naciones hispanoamericanas en el siglo XIX* (Madrid: Marcial Pons, 2021), pp. 275–308, p. 279.

[151] Diana Paola Herrera Arroyave, 'Sobre la Querella Benthamista en Colombia', *Telos* 15:2 (2009), pp. 9–29, p. 20.

[152] Luis Horacio López Domínguez, *Obra educativa: la querella benthamista, 1748–1832* (Bogotá: Fundación para la Conmemoración del Bicentenario del Natalicio y el Sesquicentenario de la Muerte del General Francisco de Paula Santander, 1993), pp. 74–75.

[153] See Sergio Andrés Mejía Macía, *El pasado como refugio y esperanza: La historia eclesiástica y civil de Nueva Granada de José Manuel Groot* (Bogotá: Universidad de los Andes, 2010).

[154] Its success was noted in the fifth edition of the text: see María Josefa Acevedo Sánchez, *Ensayo sobre los Deberes de los Casados* (Bogotá: Torres Amaya, 1857), p. i. On her broader thought see Catherine

Church properties, and the abolition of slavery led to a civil war and a revolution.[155] Political parties emerged as a result of this division.[156] The Conservative Party drew support from the slaveholders of Cauca and the Liberal Party featured radical and moderate wings which benefited from the support of the black population.[157] The lawyer Ezequiel Rojas was seen as a leading Benthamite and the founder of the ideology of the Colombian Liberal Party. Rojas had studied law and travelled with the exiled Santander to Europe, where he had met Say and Bentham.[158] Upon his return to New Granada, Rojas opened a law firm in Bogotá and was elected as a parliamentarian in the House of Representatives for the Province of Tunja.[159] In the 1850s, Ezequiel Rojas served as a diplomat in Europe. Following the end of his diplomatic efforts, Rojas returned to New Granada and contributed to mid-century political debates that shaped the Constitution of 1853.[160]

The Constitution abolished slavery and the ecclesiastical *fueros*.[161] Slaveowners were indemnified with public debt certificates, certificates that were eventually deemed worthless.[162] This charter sought to limit executive power and consolidate the separation between Church and state. Forced loans were used to finance these reforms. As these constitutional debates were underway, Rojas chose to defend one principle above all: the establishment of the principles of *pari passu*, the principle of equality of national and foreign creditors. As in Mexico and Argentina, one of the best ways to ensure that contracts were respected in the aftermath of civil wars was to establish a corporation with a foreigner, or to generate foreign interest in one's investments.[163] Rojas argued that foreigners had the means to 'compel the government to repay debts', while nationals had to 'suffer at the hands

Davies, 'La familia republicana: Josefa Acevedo politiza lo doméstico', in Sara Beatriz Guardia ed., *Escritoras del Siglo XIX en América Latina* (Lima, Centro de Estudios la Mujer en la Historia de América Latina, 2012), pp. 153–163; Josefa Acevedo, *A Treatise on Domestic Economy, For the Use of Mothers and Housewives*. Translated by Catherine Davies and Sarah Sánchez (Nottingham: CCCP, 2007).

155 Bushnell, *The Making of Modern Colombia*, p. 105.

156 Safford, *Historia*, pp. 236–238.

157 Bushnell, *The Making of Modern Colombia*, p. 107. As López-Bejarano has noted, 10 of the 15 presidents that ruled between 1830 and 1867 were born in Cauca. See López-Bejarano, *Un Estado*, p. 198.

158 Carlos Gabriel Salazar Cáceres, *Ezequiel Rojas: vida y pensamiento* (Boyacá: Academia Boyacense de Historia, 2006), p. 40; Uribe-Uran, *Honorable Lives*, p. 113.

159 Cáceres, *Ezequiel Rojas*, p. 47.

160 Jimena Hurtado, 'La economía política en los estudios superiores en la segunda mitad del siglo XIX en Colombia: Ezequiel Rojas, sus influencias y programas', in Andrés Álvarez and Juan Santiago Correa eds., *Ideas y políticas económicas En Colombia durante el primer siglo republicano* (Bogotá: Universidad de los Andes, Colombia, 2016), pp. 35–68.

161 Safford, *Historia*, pp. 302–303. On the swell of support for emancipation see Jason McGraw, *The Work of Recognition: Caribbean Colombia and the Postemancipation Struggle for Citizenship* (Chapel Hill: University of North Carolina Press, 2014), pp. 20–50. On broader administrative and civic changes brought about by mid-century constitutional reforms see Castillo, *La invención*, pp. 229–270.

162 López-Bejarano, *Un Estado*, pp. 201–202.

163 López-Bejarano, *Un Estado*, p. 207, n. 27.

of the law'.[164] To grant 'guarantees' to foreigners while depriving the nationals was a 'monstrous injustice'.[165] In his *Filosofía Moral*, he argued that state bankruptcies and forced loans were simply illegal because they required mortgaging the private property of individuals.[166] He cited Bentham's views on the Roman expropriation of private funds to defend his view that the state had to repay its debts, and avoid seizing the funds of its citizens, to demonstrate that the right to property was respected.[167] Rojas defended the *agiotistas* by arguing they were no better or worse than a standard national bank and rejected the view that there were two types of credit, public and private, just as there were not two types of morality.[168]

Manuel Murillo Toro argued that Rojas' opinions on debt were compromised by his own financial interests as creditor to the government—and by his own views on utilitarianism.[169] Murillo Toro was a journalist and a radical liberal thinker who twice served as President of the nation, then named the United States of Colombia.[170] Murillo Toro believed it was licit to default on odious debts. He blamed Spain's fight against Colombia's independence for 'ruining the country and leaving behind this immense debt that weighs over our treasury'.[171] Murillo Toro argued that as long as most of the nation's land remained in the possession of a few owners, as it had during the colonial period, true equality would never flourish: a fair redistribution of property should trump and override existing property rights.[172]

Murillo Toro argued that the debts incurred in the process of independence had given the nation its freedom and thus had to be paid.[173] However, the repayment of those debts which went into the pockets of the wealthy, like Rojas, could be consolidated into a floating debt, fundamentally altering their value without the consent of the investors, while the nation developed its industry and generated the required profits to repay it.[174] Did Bentham's utilitarian principles, he asked, not

[164] Ezequiel Rojas, Teoría *del crédito público i privado con su aplicación al de los Estados Unidos de Colombia* (Funza: Imprenta del Estado, 1863), p. 37.

[165] Rojas, *Teoría*, p. 37.

[166] Ezequiel Rojas, *Filosofía Moral* (Bogotá: Imprenta de la Nación, 1868), pp. 136–137.

[167] Rojas, *Filosofia Moral*, pp. 121–122.

[168] Ezequiel Rojas, 'Una Defensa' (1872), in Camilo González, Carlos Arturo López, Rusbel Martínez, María Cristina Conforti Rojas, and Marcela Forero Rey eds., *Textos filosóficos de Ezequiel Rojas: compilación y presentaciones* (Bogotá: Portal Pontificia Universidad Javeriana, 2017), pp. 294–346, pp. 335–337.

[169] On the broader debates see Malcolm Deas, 'The Fiscal Problems of Nineteenth-Century Colombia', *Journal of Latin American Studies* 14:2 (1982), pp. 287–328, 319–321. On the ideological dimensions behind these political divisions see Helen Delpar, *Red Against Blue: The Liberal Party in Colombian Politics, 1863–1899* (Tuscaloosa: University of Alabama Press, 1981), pp. 63–70.

[170] On these divisions and on his broader reforms see Safford, *Historia*, pp. 301–302, pp. 317–329.

[171] Jorge Mario Eastman, *Obras selectas: Manuel Murillo Toro* (Bogotá: Cámara de Representantes, 1979), p. 143. Repeated again in 1852; see Eastman, *Obras selectas*, p. 229.

[172] Salomón Kalmanovitz, *La idea federal en Colombia durante el siglo XIX* (Bogotá: Banco de la República, Mimeo, 2003), pp. 17–19; Eastman, *Obras selectas* pp. 71–72.

[173] Eastman, *Obras selectas* p. 179, p. 230.

[174] Eastman, *Obras selectas*, pp. 9–11, p. 23, p. 319, pp. 360–361; Deas, 'The Fiscal Problems', p. 320.

dictate that politics and law should focus on the benefit of the largest number of people?[175] The Colombian legacy of Bentham's writings lived on: who determined the nature of utility for the greatest number? Could the state truly reshape property rights according to its needs? Were all states, like their Roman predecessors, founded on theft? In the second half of the century, four civil wars would be fought over the control of the Colombian state and the legitimation of its rulers.

Obligations of solidarity and Gran Colombia's redeemers

Colombia, Ecuador, and Venezuela carried the shared burden of the dreams of Bolívar and Bentham. In response to Bentham's legacy, a strong Colombian conservative cultural movement would draw attention to the nation's cultural debt to its colonial past and exalt the Hispanic civilisation to counter xenophobic European attitudes towards Latin America: the descendants of Rufino Cuervo, the editor of *La Miscelania*, recovered the journal's proposal for a literary federation, developed Bello's studies of Spanish grammar, emphasised the potential of the Spanish language to unify Latin America, and defended of the Spanish Catholic heritage as the basis of civilisation.[176]

Britain, in turn, did not redeem Bolívar's empire. Gran Colombia's debts to Britain remained subject to constant fragmentation and renegotiation into the twentieth century.[177] Britain rejected a variety of Colombian proposals for repayment which included turning Colombia into a British protectorate, the cession of Panama to Her Majesty's Government, or the concession of the tobacco monopoly to British lenders.[178] Britain instead secured a mortgage on the nation's tariffs for the repayment of its debts and employed the threat of a blockade to ensure the renegotiation of the Colombian payment of a private debt, "the Mackintosh Debt".[179]

Ecuador, in turn, leveraged Gran Colombia's debt to Mexico to recover the ambitions of the founders of the Congress of Panama. Following its independence from Gran Colombia, a 15-year period of conflict came to an end with the rise to power

[175] González, López, Martínez, Rojas, and Rey eds., *Textos*, p. 142.

[176] Ángel Cuervo y Rufino José Cuervo, *Vida de Rufino Cuervo y noticias de su época.* Two volumes (Paris: Roger and Chernoviz, 1892). Andrés Jiménez Ángel, 'Ciencia, lengua e hispanidad en la construcción de la cultura nacional en Colombia, 1867–1880', *Iberoamericana* 13:50 (2013), pp. 85–99.

[177] Liehr, 'La deuda exterior', p. 487.

[178] Rafat Ghotme, *De la debilidad al acomodamiento: la diplomacia de la Nueva Granada frente a Gran Bretaña y Estados Unidos, 1832–1857* (Published PhD Thesis) (Barcelona: Universidad Autónoma de Barcelona, 2016), pp. 128–140.

[179] López-Bejarano, *Un Estado*, pp. 208–209. Ghotme, *De la debilidad al acomodamiento*, p. 141. The Mackintosh debt was renegotiated but would not be repaid for a number of decades. See Malcolm Deas, 'Weapons of the Weak?' Colombia and Foreign Powers in the Nineteenth Century' in Matthew Brown ed., *Informal Empire in Latin America: Culture, Commerce and Capital* (London: Wiley, 2008), pp. 173–186, pp. 176–177 and *Cuestión Mackintosh* (Bogotá: Imprenta de Neo Granadina, 1852).

of the conservative strongman Gabriel García Moreno.[180] In 1895, the liberal Eloy Alfaro overthrew Moreno's regime and declared himself President of Ecuador.[181] While national divisions endured, Alfaro sought to establish a new congress for Latin American nations and create a regional system of international law.[182] Alfaro also carried out the economic modernisation of Ecuador by enhancing its gold reserves and boosting exports by lowering tariffs.[183] Alfaro's political thought was informed by his views on the problem of the foreign debt; he was the author of a pamphlet titled *Deuda Gordiana*, or 'Gordian Debt', one of the best contemporary studies of the distribution of the British debt among the former constituent parts of Gran Colombia.[184] Alfaro evoked the biblical image of Daniel at Belshazzar's feast to note that, after decades of inequality, he would follow the patriotic calls to stabilise Ecuador's public debt.[185]

Alfaro saw in the debt diplomacy of Ecuador's diplomat and president, Vicente Rocafuerte, the basis of future Latin American unity. In his autobiography, Rocafuerte had recalled how he had looked beyond the borders of Mexico and Gran Colombia and risked his own career when he had negotiated a loan on behalf of Bolívar because 'at that time the whole of Spanish America was like my motherland' and the loan was 'an act of fraternity which bound the New World together and created a financial alliance'.[186] Alfaro believed that a Latin American 'cordial union' would deliver peace: it would be 'an irresistible force against our foreign enemies and the basis of a new political system that does not require the use of bayonets'.[187] Inspired by Rocafuerte and the 'perennial memory of Bolívar', Alfaro sought to bind Latin America together. Under Alfaro's administration, Ecuador took responsibility for the payment of the loan on behalf of 'the three states that once formed the old Colombia' in order to foster closer regional cooperation.[188]

In negotiations with Mexico, echoing Rocafuerte's spirit, he proposed an alliance between the two countries and the newly founded Central American Union, made up of Nicaragua, Salvador, and Honduras. Together these states would

[180] Linda Alexander Rodríguez, The Search for Public Policy: *Regional Politics and Government Finances in Ecuador, 1830–1940* (Berkeley: University of California Press, 1985), pp. 78–87.

[181] Juan José Paz y Miño Cepeda, *Eloy Alfaro: Políticas económicas* (Quito: Ministerio de Coordinación de la Política Económica, 2012); A. Kim Clark, *The Redemptive Work: Railway and Nation in Ecuador, 1895–1930* (Lanham: Rowman & Littlefield, 1998), pp. 24–37.

[182] Germán Rodas Chaves, *Eloy Alfaro y Cuba en el siglo XIX* (Havana: Fondo Editorial Casa de las Américas, 2013).

[183] Paul Henderson, 'Cocoa, Finance and the State in Ecuador, 1895–1925', *Bulletin of Latin American Research* 16:2 (1997) pp. 169–186, p. 177.

[184] Eloy Alfaro, *Ecuador: Deuda Gordiana* (Panama: Imprenta Ramos, 1891); *Deuda Goridiana* (Quito: Imprenta Nacional, 1896). This is the edition used henceforth.

[185] *Deuda Goridiana*, p. 83.

[186] *Deuda Goridiana*, pp. 22–23.

[187] Alfaro, *Deuda Gordiana*, p. 10; this required overlooking the tense negotiations around the debt in the mid-nineteenth century; see Walker, *Kinship*, pp. 208–209.

[188] Joaquín Ramírez Cabañas, *El empréstito de México a Colombia: recopilación de documentos con una introducción y notas* (Mexico City: Publicaciones de la Secretaría de relaciones exteriores, 1930), p. 226.

constitute a Continental Confederation.[189] At the 1896 International American Congress in Mexico, Alfaro and other officials hoped to form a public law for America which could expand the reach of the Monroe Doctrine.[190] The Congress failed to deliver on the high expectations of Alfaro, who continued to foster the growth of the economy and, above all, the cocoa trade, in order to finance the development of Ecuador's public infrastructure.[191]

Yet Alfaro and his administration did not extend such bonds of solidarity to Britain. Rocafuerte's loan, like Gran Colombia's debt to the *libertadores*, would eventually be renegotiated in London. Emilio María Terna, one of Alfaro's leading economic officials, produced a study of the foreign debt where he discussed the 'common glories' and the 'obligations of solidarity' between the nations that once constituted Bolívar's empire. Britain, however, was depicted as a predatory power. Terna cited the idea of eminent domain and drew on the principles of the Calvo Clause: 'according to the law of nations' contracts signed in Ecuador regarding local goods remained subject to autochthonous laws and needs.[192] Since foreign creditors ignored conventions, showed no patience towards a country in turmoil, or assumed Ecuador's leaders were acting in bad faith, Ecuador should focus on its own interests when negotiating the debt. Inspired by these ideas, Alfaro suspended repayments on 'that foreign debt known as the British debt'.[193] Yet when the opportunity arose to construct a trainline from Guayaquil to Quito, Alfaro sought to renew the promise of repayment to raise funds in London in order to both clear the debt and generate investment in this enterprise.[194]

Following his father's death, Alfaro's son, Colón Eloy Alfaro, who served as Ecuador's ambassador to the United States, harnessed the memory of these efforts in a number of meetings with James Brown Scott to encourage the creation of the Inter-American Tribunal of International Justice, the predecessor to the Inter-American Court of Human Rights. James Brown Scott was considered one of the most important North American international lawyers of the early twentieth century and fostered the growth of interest in international law in the United States. A technical delegate at the second Hague Convention of 1907 and a legal advisor

[189] Colón Eloy Alfaro, *Eloy Alfaro y el Derecho público de América* (Bogotá: Imprenta de J. V. Barón, 1935), p. 77.

[190] Eloy Alfaro, *Eloy Alfaro*, p. 80.

[191] Henderson, 'Cocoa, Finance and the State in Ecuador, p. 177.

[192] Emilio María Teran, *Informe al jefe supremo general Eloy Alfaro sobre la deuda anglo-ecuatoriana extendido* (Quito: Imprenta Nacional, 1899), pp. 808–809; Alberto Acosta, *La deuda eterna: una historia de la deuda externa ecuatoriana* (Quito: Libresa, 1990), pp. 109–110. See Rodríguez, *The Search for Public Policy*, pp. 106–107.

[193] Acosta, *La deuda eterna*, pp. 111–112.

[194] This measure would deliver underwhelming results but would soon be overshadowed by concerns over North American debts. Acosta, *La deuda eterna*, pp. 113–114. Alfaro had warned against this kind of policy; see *Deuda Gordiana*, pp. 15–16. See also his views on the enterprise in Eloy Alfaro, *El ferrocarril trasandino: cartas del Gral. Don Eloy Alfaro* (Quito: Imprenta de 'El Tiempo', 1903); Clark, *The Redemptive Work*, pp. 31–37.

to Elihu Root, he later served as Secretary of the Carnegie Institute in Washington DC.[195] He used his influence as editor of the *American Journal of International Law* to publish the writings of Latin American authors and developed initiatives through the American Institute of International Law, which Scott helped to develop to assuage Latin American fears about North American intervention in the region.[196] In the 1920s, Scott started to foster other ways to counter Latin American apathy towards the United States and used the occasion of the commemorations of the colonisation of America to reflect on the Spanish origins of international law.[197] Scott pursued a number of other strategies to fulfil this goal: he fostered the participation of Latin American officials in international congresses and sought to make Cuba a base of American international law.[198] But, above all, he sought to rewrite the history of international law. He believed that the reconciliation of the history of Spanish colonialism and Protestant international law that had proven so elusive to Latin American thinkers turned on a simple rhetorical move: casting the Spanish Scholastics as the founders of modern international law.[199] He edited and published his *The Spanish Origin of International Law: Francisco de Vitoria and his Law of Nations*, where Scott drew on the ideas of Francisco de Vitoria to develop a view of international law that would allow the United States to shape American international law.[200] Little did it matter that Latin Americans had repudiated the imperial norms these Scholastic thinkers had once hailed by drawing on the works of Grotius and Vattel.

Scott was nonetheless more than happy to acknowledge that Bolívar and Alfaro's father had also played a role in the construction of the law of nations. In the 1930s, Scott invited Colón Eloy Alfaro to a meeting at New York City's Metropolitan

[195] Juan Pablo Scarfi, El imperio de la ley. James Brown Scott y la construcción de un orden jurídico interamericano (Buenos Aires: FCE 2014), p. 181; Juan Pablo Scarfi, *The Hidden History of International Law in the Americas: Empire and Legal Networks* (Oxford: Oxford University Press, 2017), p. 2. On the role of the Spanish–American War of 1898 in the construction of Scott's ideas of international law see Paolo Amorosa, *Rewriting the History of the Law of Nations: How James Brown Scott Made Francisco de Vitoria the Founder of International Law* (Oxford: Oxford University Press, 2019), pp. 57–86.

[196] Scarfi, *Hidden History*, p. 37–44.

[197] Mark Somos and Joshua Smeltzer, 'Vitoria, Suárez, and Grotius: James Brown Scott's Enduring Revival', *Grotiana* 41:1 (2020), pp. 137–162, p. 150; Joshua Smeltzer, 'On the Use and Abuse of Francisco de Vitoria: James Brown Scott and Carl Schmitt', *Journal of the History of International Law* 20 (2018), pp. 345–372, pp. 347–354; James Brown Scott, 'Asociación Francisco de Vitoria', *The American Journal of International Law* 22:1 (1928), pp. 136–139.

[198] Scarfi, *Hidden History*, p. 189.

[199] Ignacio de la Rasilla del Moral, 'Francisco de Vitoria's Unexpected Transformations and Reinterpretations for International Law', *International Community Law Review* 15:3 (2013), pp. 287–318; Somos and Smeltzer, 'Vitoria', pp. 150–159.

[200] Scarfi, *El imperio de la ley*, p. 187. p. 205. Scott's *Sovereign States and Suits* began with a quote and a reflection on William Prescott's *Conquest of Mexico*, a work that fostered the myth of the Black Legend; see James Brown Scott, *Sovereign States and Suits before Arbitral Tribunals and Courts of Justice* (New York: New York City, 1925) and William Prescott, *History of the Conquest of Mexico*. Three volumes (New York: Harper and Brothers, 1843). On the role of Prescott in disseminating the ideas associated with the Black Legend see Richard L. Kagan, 'Prescott's Paradigm: American Historical Scholarship and the Decline of Spain', *The American Historical Review* 101:2 (1996), pp. 423–446.

Club.[201] There, according to Alfaro's account of events, the conversation focused on how early twentieth-century Pan American conventions were still influenced by Bolívar's ideas.[202] According to Alfaro, at a meeting at the Carnegie Institute attended by both men, participants recognised that any tribunal of justice that was to be 'permanently established' in America would have to embrace the Central American Court of Justice as its most important antecedent.[203] On the basis of these steps, a number of representatives had written to American governments to gauge the interest in establishing a new Interamerican International Tribunal of Justice. It was then that Colón Eloy Alfaro had taken the decision to compile for Scott a collection of documents on his father's initiative.[204] 'American public law must rest on the inviolability of the autonomous American continent', Alfaro argued. This required the establishment of a 'Continental Code'. This charter would recommend the autonomy of those American states still under the hold of foreign powers. War between American countries would, moreover, 'be outlawed'.[205] Scott praised the efforts carried out by Alfaro's father to further 'Bolívar's dream' and acknowledged the value of his initiative. But he disregarded the rest of Alfaro's suggestions. Scott, after all, believed that the representation of interests in international congresses should be based on the population and economic power of each nation.[206] A year later, Scott published a note in the *American Journal of International Law*, titled 'The Good Neighbor Policy'.[207] He rejected the view that the United States had breached the terms of treaties established with states in Latin and Central America. He cited the praise of a number of Latin American officials of the Monroe Doctrine and concluded his defence of the good neighbour policy with a declaration of things to come: 'We have tried neighborliness on a continental scale. Let us try it on the rest of the world'.[208]

The United States soon developed new forms of financial intervention in Central America that circumvented international legal norms.[209] In the resolution of the disputes that emerged from the foreign abuses of the composite parts of Bolívar's rump empire, Britain accepted that the United States—an empire the *Libertador* never trusted—was the new redeemer of Latin America.[210] Britain's

[201] Alfaro, *Eloy Alfaro*, p. 7. Martha Finnemore, *The Purpose of Intervention: Changing Beliefs About the Use of Force* (Ithaca: Cornell University Press, 2013), p. 34, n. 27.
[202] A contradiction of Scott's earlier ideas, see Scarfi, *Hidden History*, p. 50.
[203] Alfaro, *Eloy Alfaro*, p. 7. Scarfi, *Hidden History*, pp. 29–30. See also Charles Ripley, 'The Central American Court of Justice (1907–1918): Rethinking the World's First Court', *Diálogos: Revista Electrónica de Historia* 19:1 (2018), pp. 47–68.
[204] Alfaro, *Eloy Alfaro*, p. 9.
[205] Alfaro, *Eloy Alfaro*, p. 12.
[206] Scarfi, *Hidden History*, p. 28.
[207] James Brown Scott, 'The Good Neighbor Policy', *American Journal of International Law* 30:2 (1936), pp. 287–290.
[208] Scott, 'The Good Neighbor Policy', p. 290.
[209] Peter James Hudson, *Bankers and Empire: How Wall Street Colonized the Caribbean* (Chicago: Chicago University Press, 2017).
[210] David Bushnell, 'Introduction', in David Bushnell ed., *El Libertador: El Libertador: Writings of Simón Bolívar*. Translated by Frederick H. Fornoff (Oxford: Oxford University Press, 2013), pp. xli–xliv.

attitude towards Venezuela's debts shaped the future of international law. In order to repay its foreign debt, Venezuela sold bonds to its creditors.[211] Yet the intensification of conflict prevented the government from delivering on these bonds and led to the destruction of foreign property.[212] Under General Cipriano Castro, the Venezuelan government invoked the Calvo Doctrine to reject arbitration regarding unpaid claims, a doctrine which the United States did not recognise.[213] Tensions rose as Germany and the United states vied for greater influence in Latin America, and Germany, along with Britain and Italy, enforced a blockade on Venezuela over its refusal to accept the settlement through arbitration over unpaid debts to their citizens.[214] This affair overlapped with ongoing negotiations regarding the Venezuelan boundary dispute with Britain regarding British Guyana, an issue that was settled when Britain accepted the Monroe Doctrine as a norm and, in exchange, the United States promised to exclude from arbitration any lands that had been settled by British subjects for more than 50 years.[215] Britain acknowledged there was a new regional redeemer in exchange for the preservation of a territorial acquisition. The United States once again abandoned one of its southern neighbours in its fight against a European power. After referring the matter of these unpaid claims to The Hague Tribunal, the Court favoured the claimants of those nations which had participated in the blockade.[216] It was in this context that the Argentinian jurist Luis María Drago, drawing on his nation's own engagement with foreign debt and the history of interventionism in Latin America, wrote his famous note where he stated that war could not be used to force the payment of public debt.

[211] Alfredo N. Vivot and Alberto A. Conil Paz, *Homenaje al doctor Luis M. Drago* (Caracas: Oficina Central de Información, 1976), pp. 14–16.

[212] Matthias Maass, 'Catalyst for the Roosevelt Corollary: Arbitrating the 1902–1903 Venezuela Crisis and Its Impact on the Development of the Roosevelt Corollary to the Monroe Doctrine', *Diplomacy & Statecraft* 20:3 (2009), pp. 383–402, p. 386.

[213] Embert J. Hendrickson, 'Roosevelt's Second Venezuelan Controversy', *Hispanic American Historical Review* 50:3 (1970), pp. 482–498, pp. 485–486.

[214] Dawson, *The First Latin American Debt Crisis*, pp. 230–231. For a summary of the broader background see Nancy Mitchell, 'The Height of the German Challenge: The Venezuela Blockade, 1902–3', *Diplomatic History* 20:2 (1996), pp. 185–210.

[215] Sexton, *Monroe*, pp. 208–209.

[216] Sexton, *Monroe*, p. 227.

5
The Armed Debtor
The Utility of Bankruptcy in Argentina

'Debt destroys itself'

In 1826, the government of Buenos Aires should, in the words of its Finance Minister, Manuel José García, move at 'the speed of lightning'.[1] It was time to 'seize the moment': encircled by states pressed by a 'feeling of vertigo', ministers spurred on the Buenos Aires revolutionary government to advance headlong into the future until its Spanish past was nowhere to be seen.[2] There was no need to 'waste time', the deputy Julián Segundo de Agüero repeatedly exhorted his colleagues, and 'good politicians' understood the need to ignore calls for prudence and '*Omnia tempus habent*'—everything has its season—and instead had to 'bring forth time'.[3] Credit, with its raids on the future, would wrest profit away from the hands of the future for the benefit of the present: the nation had 'no interest in drawing rents from the product of its lands', its focus should be 'to build rents in proportion to the loan advances from emphyteusis'.[4] Credit had allowed France, 'devastated by twenty years of war' and burdened with a heavy debt, to discharge its payments.[5] Britain had proved David Hume wrong: the dictum that either 'the public credit will destroy the nation, or the state destroys it', as claimed by the representative Bernardino Rivadavia, had been shown to be incorrect; instead, he argued, 'debt destroys itself'.[6] According to the first professor of civil law in Buenos Aires, Pedro Alcántara de Somellera, while 'Pufendorf, Bourlamaque, Vattel, Locke, and Rousseau' had 'done little else' other than study how obligations emerged from natural law to no

[1] Uladislao Frias, *Trabajos legislativos de las primeras Asambleas arjentinas desde la junta de 1811 hasta la disolución del Congreso en 1827: Enero á abril de 1826*. Volume 3 (Buenos Aires: Compañía sud-americana de billetes de banco, 1889), p. 490.

[2] *Diario de sesiones de la Junta de Representantes de la Provincia de Buenos Aires* (1 May–23 December 1822) (Buenos Aires: Imprenta de la Independencia, 1823), pp. 2–3. See also how the idea of vertigo was used to describe contemporary global affairs in Natalio Botana, Repúblicas y monarquías. *La encrucijada de la independencia* (Buenos Aires: Edhasa, 2016), p. 139.

[3] *Diario de sesiones de la Junta de Representantes*, p. 123. On Agüero and the establishment of public credit see Jeremy Adelman, Republic of Capital: *Buenos Aires and the Legal Transformation of the Atlantic World* (Stanford: Stanford University Press, 1999), pp. 99–101.

[4] Quoted in Sergio Bagú, *El plan económico del grupo Rivadaviano (1811–1827). Su sentido y sus contradicciones, sus proyecciones sociales, sus enemigos* (Santa Fé: Universidad Nacional del Litoral, 1966), p. 36.

[5] *Diario de sesiones de la Junta de Representantes*, p. 129.

[6] *Diario de sesiones de la Junta de Representantes*, p. 697. Reversing Hume's original phrasing.

Odious Debt. Edward Jones Corredera, Oxford University Press. © Edward Jones Corredera 2024.
DOI: 10.1093/9780191982200.003.0006

avail, Bentham had shown that utility was the true source of obligation.[7] There was no need to resolve the tensions between the legacy of Roman law and Bentham's thought for analysing 'that which jurists have written on the meaning of the word *dominium* and the word *property*' could take up 'several books' but 'we must not waste time on such useless questions'.[8] If utilitarians like Bentham, as Leslie Stephen once suggested, were contradictory in their commitment to experience and their indifference to history, Rivadavia and other Argentine revolutionaries hoped to reshape European history into a compressed historical experience that could help Argentina resolve the perennial challenges embedded in public credit.[9] It was no accident that, when he took over the Governorship of Buenos Aires, Juan Gregorio de Las Heras coined a term that is still used to describe Rivadavia's tenure in power, the 'Happy Experience'.[10]

What was the cause of this sense of haste? Officials in the Banda Oriental had been pursuing the establishment of a stable government for over a decade.[11] In the eighteenth century, thanks to a relatively weak colonial administrative presence in the city, Buenos Aires had benefited from the growth of smuggling.[12] Labourers and *gauchos* populated the hinterland while merchants shaped the social life of the port cities.[13] During the first two decades of the nineteenth century, Buenos Aires' victory over British forces and its internecine conflict with its neighbours put some distance between the Banda Oriental and the memory of its Spanish inheritance.[14] During the May Revolution, the *cabildo* of Buenos Aires, a government-sponsored guild, defeated British troops, fostered a revolution against Spanish rule, and

[7] Pedro Alcántara de Somellera, *Principios de Derecho Civil.* Noticia preliminar de Jesús H. Paz (Buenos Aires: Instituto de Historia del Derecho Argentino, 1939), pp. 186–187.

[8] Somellera, *Principios de Derecho Civil*, p. 115.

[9] On Stephen and Bentham's historicism see Callum Barrel, *History and Historiography in Classical Utilitarianism, 1800–1865* (Cambridge: Cambridge University Press, 2021), pp. 29–30

[10] Klaus Gallo, 'Reformismo tardo-ilustrado y utilitario. La "feliz experiencia" y su dimensión europea. 1776–1824', *Trabajos y Comunicaciones* 54 (2021) (Online).

[11] On these earlier debates see Juan Antonio González Calderón, *Derecho constitucional argentino, historia, teoría y jurisprudencia de la Constitución.* Volume 1 (Buenos Aires: Lajouane, 1923), pp. 1–77; José Carlos Chiaramonte, 'El federalismo argentino en la primera mitad del siglo XIX', in Marcello Carmagnani ed., *Federalismos Latinoamericanos: México/Brasil/Argentina* (Mexico City: Fondo de Cultura Económica, 1993), pp. 81–132, pp. 105–109. See also Fabio Wasserman, 'De la revolución al historicismo romántico: experiencias de tiempo y política en el Río de la Plata (1780–1850)' in Wasserman ed., *Tiempos Críticos: Historia, revolución y temporalidad en el mundo iberoamericano* (siglos XVIII y XIX) (Buenos Aires: Prometeo, 2010), pp. 169–196, p. 187. On the urgency of the need for order see Enrique Gandía, *Las ideas políticas de la independencia americana* (Buenos Aires: Depalma, 1968), p. 696.

[12] Tulio Halperín-Donghi, *Politics, Economics and Society in Argentina in the Revolutionary Period.* Translated by Richard Southern (Cambridge: Cambridge University Press, 1975), p. 4.

[13] Nicolas Shumway, *The Invention of Argentina* (Berkeley: University of California Press, 1991), p. 10; Halperín-Donghi, *Politics*, pp. 101–104; Mark D. Szuchman, 'From Imperial Hinterland to Growth Pole: Revolution, Change, and Restoration in the Río de la Plata', in Mark D. Szuchman and Jonathan Charles Brown, *Revolution and Restoration: The Rearrangement of Power in Argentina, 1776–1860* (Lincoln: University of Nebraska Press, 1994), pp. 1–26, pp. 4–5.

[14] Adelman, *Republic of Capital*, p. 106.

sought to establish a robust constitutional arrangement for the Banda Oriental.[15] But the revolutionary leader José Gervasio Artigas led a number of provinces to unite against Buenos Aires.[16] Artigas established the Liga Litoral. Artigas encouraged the state-led distribution of land to all indigenous peoples and the expropriation of properties owned by European residents, but was eventually defeated by Portuguese forces.[17]

Others sought to create a new order. To defend against Spanish attacks from Montevideo, General José de San Martín seized a range of funds and took out a loan from financiers in Buenos Aires in the hope of uniting Argentina, Chile, and Peru, an extension of land that, as the historian Enrique de Gandía noted, it formed one of the largest territorial political units in the world.[18] San Martín declared the independence of Peru and committed the new state to repay all debts that had been incurred for the benefit of its people, but not those that had been used to oppress it. British diplomats, however, noted his interest in indemnifying the Spanish Crown with monetary and commercial benefits in exchange for the independence of the Americas.[19] In a famous meeting with Bolívar in the port city of Guayaquil, the two men sought to unite their respective territories. San Martín expressed his desire to step down from his role as general once a government had been established. Like Bolívar, he endorsed the model of a constitutional monarchy. However, following their meeting, San Martín grew resentful of Bolívar's actions. Bolívar failed to supply San Martín with an adequate number of troops and, more importantly, the *Libertador* seized Guayaquil for Gran Colombia without first consulting its people.[20] In a move that has puzzled historians and intellectuals like José Luis Borges ever since, San Martín retired to Europe and allowed Bolívar to expand his praetorian empire.

Buenos Aires emerged as a counterweight to Bolívar's ever-expanding federation. Yet the tension between Buenos Aires and the other provinces of the region, which were constituted as sovereign states, would shape the future of Argentina's constitutional politics. The Congress of Tucuman was an itinerant constituent assembly spearheaded by Buenos Aires that first gathered in 1815, approved a declaration of independence in 1816, and promulgated the Constitution of the United

[15] Shumway, *Invention*, p. 17; Miron Burgin, *Aspectos económicos del federalismo argentino* (Buenos Aires: Hachette, 1960), pp. 36–37. On debts and economic experiments that emerged during this time see Adelman, *Republic of Capital*, pp. 94–96.

[16] Adelman, *Republic of Capital*, pp. 87–88.

[17] Shumway, *Invention*, pp. 59–60; Jeremy Adelman, *Sovereignty and Revolution in the Iberian Atlantic* (Princeton: Princeton University Press, 2006), pp. 281–283.

[18] Gandía, *Rivadavia y su tiempo*, pp. 43–44. The correspondence around these loans and resources was reprinted by Bartolomé Mitre; see his *Historia de San Martín y de la emancipación Sud-Americana*. Volume 4 (Paris: Bouret, 1890), pp. 451–501.

[19] Gandía, *Las ideas* [1968], p. 213.

[20] Javier Pérez Valdivia, César Puerta Villagaray, and Daniel Morán, '"Dos soles no pueden brillar bajo el mismo cielo". La entrevista de Guayaquil entre José de San Martín y Simón Bolívar (1822)', *Desde el Sur* 13(3) (2021) (Online).

Provinces of South America in 1819.[21] At the Battle of Cepeda of 1 February 1820, federalist provincial forces defeated the unitary forces led by Buenos Aires and consolidated the emergence of 13 Provinces.[22] This was reaffirmed by the Treaty of Pilar of 1820, which guaranteed the organisation of the state as a federation.[23] In the evocative words of a scholar, this accord led to the establishment of 'an archipelago of independent sovereign states'.[24] Buenos Aires' officials were forced to acknowledge that the United Provinces based their independence and their sovereignty on international law. Experienced federalist parliamentarians like Juan José Paso, who a decade earlier had drawn on the principle of *negotiorum gestio* and the right to revolution to justify the war of independence against Spain, would never let them forget it.[25] Divisions between Buenos Aires and the Provinces slowed down change: throughout this period, Spanish colonial laws were still used to settle bankruptcies and crimes.[26]

An assembly set up in 1821 by Buenos Aires established a number of laws, including the basis for an electoral law, the law of emphyteusis, the creation of a bank, the Banco de Descuentos, and the study of the regulation of debt.[27] It lacked a constitutional code and the effort to establish one floundered.[28] Yet Britain, the model that many of Rivadavia's officials followed, had fared well without one and Bentham had been critical of the way declarations of rights limited the right of assemblies to draft future laws.[29] Ideas of consent and sovereignty in Buenos

[21] On the complex and unresolved dilemmas that emerged from the 1816 Congress see Botana, *Repúblicas y monarquías*, pp. 27–64. Marcela Ternavasio, 'La revolución y sus silencios' in Marco Palacios ed., *Las independencias hispanamericanas. Interpretaciones 200 años después* (Bogotá: Norma, 2009), pp. 157–181.

[22] Adelman, *Republic of Capital*, p. 91; Marcela Ternavasio, 'Las reformas rivadavianas en Buenos Aires y en el Congreso General Constituyente (1820–1827)', in Noemí Goldman ed., *Nueva Historia de Argentina. Revolución, República, Confederación (1806–1852).* Volume 3 (Buenos Aires: Editorial Sudamericana, 2001), pp. 159–198, pp. 161–162.

[23] Ternavasio, 'Las reformas rivadavianas', pp. 161–162

[24] Beatriz Bragoni as quoted in Luis Iriarte, 'Crisis del año XX', in Fontán ed., *Alberdi*, pp. 193–212, p. 195.

[25] Rodolfo Antonio Iribarne, 'La cuestión capital en 1826', *Universidad de Buenos Aires. Facultad de Derecho. Departamento de Publicaciones* (1970), pp. 185–221, p. 196. See also Botana's insightful analysis of Paso's use, in 1810, of the Bonapartist phrase 'end of the revolution, start of order'. See Botana, *Repúblicas y monarquías*, p. 135. On the principle of *negotiorum gestor* and the pursuit of independence see Elias Palti, *El tiempo de la política. Lenguaje e historia en el siglo XIX* (Buenos Aires: Siglo XXI, 2007), pp. 133–140.

[26] Even if they were increasingly contested. See Magdalena Candioti and Melina Yangilevich, 'La justicia en la construcción del orden estatal', in Marcela Ternavasio ed., *Historia de la Provincia de Buenos Aires.* Volume 3: De la organización provincial a la federalización de Buenos Aires (1821–1880) (Buenos Aires: UNIPE, 2013), pp. 179–204, p. 182.

[27] Marcela Ternavasio, *Historia de la Argentina. 1806–1852* (Buenos Aires: Siglo XXI, 2009), pp. 141–145; Marcela Ternavasio, *La revolución del voto: Política y elecciones en Buenos Aires, 1810–1852* (Buenos Aires: Siglo XXI, 2016), pp. 79–98. On the state of the internal debt at this time see Burgin, *Aspectos*, pp. 84–87.

[28] Marcela Ternavasio, 'Construir poder y dividir poderes. Buenos Aires durante la "feliz experiencia" rivadaviana', *Boletín del Instituto de Historia Argentina y Americana "Dr. Emilio Ravignani"* 26 (2004), pp. 7–43, p. 12.

[29] Woodbine Parish informed Rivadavia in a letter that he did not much appreciate constitutions that were drafted in a hurry; they seemed to have little practical use. See Ternavasio, 'Construir

Aires were interpreted through the moral writings of Jean-Jacques Rousseau and Bentham; two leaders of the revolution, Mariano Moreno, who translated the *Contrat Social*, and Manuel Belgrano, cited the Swiss author's conclusion that 'according to Grotius a people is a people before it gives itself to a King'.[30] As Rivadavia explained to Bentham, he hoped to use the jurist's utilitarian works to ensure that 'peoples who are too lazy to appreciate these principles march towards civilisation with the steps of a giant'.[31] The design of the building which housed the Congress of Buenos Aires was based on Bentham's *Tactics of the Legislative Assembly*.[32]

Mexican congressmen studied Spain's political history to create a constitutional framework for the repayment of its debts that emphasised responsibility and restraint. By contrast, Buenos Aires' statesmen fostered a triumphalist historical reading of Britain's public debt to avoid responsibility and restraint. A fanciful vision of British financial history shaped Buenos Aires' decision to pursue loans abroad. Inspired by William Pitt's Sinking Fund, García argued that in order to reach this self-sufficiency and build infrastructure that would generate further revenue, it was necessary to draw on British loans and establish paper money.[33] It was a way to avoid overtaxing industry while stimulating financial investment—and the best way to prepare for war.[34] When Paso tried to suggest that perhaps the language of the law should feature a passage that would encourage the investment of other Latin American nations, as a way to generate the 'ties' to neighbouring territories, García argued with breezy indifference that declaring that the sales of bonds would happen 'abroad' was general enough; it made little difference whether the trading took place in London, Amsterdam, or Lima.[35] The measure was approved and Argentina entered the race to secure its loans from 'abroad'. In 1824, the Baring House granted Rivadavia a loan mortgaged against the public rents and lands of the state.[36]

poder', p. 14, n. 15; Philip Schofield, *Utility and Democracy: The Political Thought of Jeremy Bentham* (Oxford: Oxford University Press, 2006), p. 58.

[30] Some officials, like Juan Ignacio de Gorriti, did however reject Rousseau's views on representative democracy; see Juan Ignacio de Gorriti, *Reflecciones sobre las causas morales de las convulsiones interiores en los nuevos estados americanos y examen de los medios eficaces para reprimirlas: Precedidas de un compendio de la vida pública del autor* (Valparaíso: Imprenta del Mercurio, 1836), pp. 32–36. See also Adam Sharman, *Deconstructing the Enlightenment in Spanish America: Margins of Modernity* (London: Routledge, 2020), pp. 151–200, pp. 167–168.

[31] Quoted in Marcela Ternavasio, 'Construir poder', p. 21.

[32] Ternavasio, 'Las reformas rivadavianas', p. 3; Ternavasio, 'Construir poder', p. 21.

[33] For an overview of the economic approach of Rivadavia's circle see Mariano di Pasquale, 'Entre la experimentación política y la circulación de saberes: la gestión de Bernardino Rivadavia en Buenos Aires, 1821–1827', *Secuencia* 87 (2013), pp. 51–65; Bagú, *El plan económico del grupo Rivadaviano*, pp. 21–22.

[34] *Diario de sesiones de la Junta de Representantes*, pp. 697–698.

[35] *Diario de sesiones de la Junta de Representantes*, pp. 702–703.

[36] Shumway, *Invention*, p. 97.

Failing to achieve escape velocity, the revolutionary model of the state fell into the gravitational pull of the ancient cycle of rise and decline that characterised Habsburg Spain: land turned into a speculative asset and foreign financiers acquired the majority of the shares of its first bank.[37] The Provinces rebelled against these changes by pointing to past treaties and drawing on the principle of consent and international law.[38] Buenos Aires, drawing on Bentham's own apathy towards retroactivity, saw no value in rummaging through the dustbin of history. Instead of making a nation Buenos Aires pursued a project of nationalisation and wealth extraction for the elites. 'Nationalisation', as Agüero, a close ally of Rivadavia, explained, meant, in this case, to default on Argentina's revolutionary loans: 'the way to pay these debts is a type of bankruptcy'; after all, the state had the 'dominion over society on individual interests' and could 'force' the people 'to subordinate them to the general interest'. In this regard, 'The Nation' was not 'using violence, but using its rights'.[39] The utility of bankruptcy, the representatives of Buenos Aires would argue, would deliver greater benefits to the people than the adherence to the principles of consent and sovereignty.

The nationalisation of the revolutionary debt

In 1825, Buenos Aires signed a treaty of friendship with Britain which guaranteed its merchants favourable terms of trade. Its leaders gathered representatives from the United Provinces to form a new constituent assembly.[40] These Provinces had, as noted, declared their self-government and were sovereign states.[41] This

[37] Raúl Scalabrini Ortiz, *Política británica en el Río de la Plata* (Barcelona: Editorial del Sol, 2001), p. 61; Halperín-Donghi, *Guerra y finanzas en los orígenes del Estado argentino (1791 –1850)* (Buenos Aires: Belgrano, 1982), p. 157–164; On the debts accumulated since 1810 see Adelman, *Republic of Capital*, pp. 95–97. On the economic impact of emphyteusis see Burgin, *Aspectos*, pp. 136–141. On later British efforts to draw on escape velocity through industry rather than credit, and for the origins of the term, see Duncan Bell, 'Escape Velocity: Ancient History and the Empire of Time', in *Reordering the World: Essays on Liberalism and Empire* (Princeton: Princeton University Press, 2016), pp. 119–147.

[38] A point that is often overlooked in narratives about state formation; see Fabio Wasserman, 'El concepto de nación y las transformaciones del orden político en Iberoamérica, 1750–1850', *Jahrbuch für Geschichte Lateinamerikas* 45 (2008), pp. 215–216; Botana, *Repúblicas y monarquías*, p. 21, pp. 67–69, p. 74.

[39] Frias, *Trabajos legislativos*, p. 247.

[40] On how the treaty undermined Argentinian industry see Shumway, *Invention*, p. 99.

[41] Charles Jones, 'Constituting Argentina, 1810–1860', in Stephen G. H. Roberts and Adam Sharman eds., *1812 Echoes: The Cádiz Constitution in Hispanic History* (Newcastle: Cambridge Scholars, 2013), pp. 264–281, p. 275; On the similarities in the economic thought of both sides see Burgin, *Aspectos* 186–187; On this ambiguity see José Carlos Chiaramonte, 'El federalismo argentino en la primera mitad del siglo XIX', in 'El federalismo argentino en la primera mitad del siglo XIX', in Marcello Carmagnani ed., *Federalismos Latinoamericanos: México/Brasil/Argentina* (Mexico City: Fondo de Cultura Económica, 1993), pp. 81–132, pp. 94–95; Alejandro Agüero, '¿Provincias o estados? El concepto de provincia y el primer constitucionalismo provincial rioplatense: Un enfoque ius-histórico', *Revista de Historia Americana y Argentina* 54:1 (2019), pp. 137–175, pp. 152–155, Marie-Laure Rieu-Millan, 'Presencia Americana en Cádiz y en las Cortes. Encuentros y desencuentros', in Scarlett O'Phelan Godoy y Georges Lomné eds., *Voces americanas en las Cortes de Cádiz: 1810–1814* (Lima: Institut

association of the term province with statehood was reinforced by a number of other historical factors: the deliberations of the status of the provinces at Cádiz, the initial pursuit of greater autonomy without independence from the Spanish Empire, and James Monroe's use of the term 'Spanish provinces' in his defence of the recognition of their independence.[42]

During these congressional sessions, Rivadavia was named President of the Congress, Agüero was named Home Minister, and García was named Minister for Foreign Affairs.[43] The Fundamental Law, a constitutional code, decreed that the Provinces would govern over their territories and only provisionally granted executive powers to the government of Buenos Aires.[44] The question of war debts and foreign loans was discussed with some urgency. The matter of what to do with the norms established in 1821—which had not been approved with the consent of the representatives of a number of regions now present—lurked in the background. On 7 October 1825, the assembly met to discuss the consolidation of the national debt. The government had put forth a motion to discuss a decree which established the consolidation of debt prior to 1820 that could be proven with adequate documentation, the commitment to fulfil the terms of the various laws established in 1821 for the repayment of debt, and the 'mortgaging' of 'public land and other goods' for the 'payment of capital and interests on the national debt'.[45] A treasury commission which featured both Agüero and Dalmacio Vélez had studied the debts prior to 1820 that still had to be repaid. Public credit, its report read, would be like an 'inexhaustible spring well' that would provide the means to face the costs of 'our situation'.[46]

It was important to repay the debt, the commission's report continued, since it proceeded from 'loans that we were forced to sign in order to conquer our independence with a war as long as it was obstinate'. It followed then that 'our liberty ought to be seen as the result and the priceless fruit of the sacrifices' that 'in the course of revolution all of the classes in our society have endured'.[47] The United Provinces would, the report read, commit to the terms of the laws established by Buenos Aires in 1821 for the repayment of debt since the United Provinces would

Français d'Études Andines, 2014), p. 35; on the overlap between pueblos and provincias see Palti, *El tiempo de la política*, pp. 123–129. On the relationship between the Cádiz Constitution and these debates see José María Portillo, *Crisis Atlántica: Autonomía e independencia en la crisis de la monarquía hispana* (Madrid: Marcial Pons, 2016), p. 34 and p. 87.

[42] Gabriella Chiaramonti, 'El primer constitucionalismo peruano: de Cádiz al primer congreso constituyente', in Antonio Annino and Marcela Ternavasio eds., *El laboratório constitucional iberoamericano: 1807/1808–1830* (Madrid: Iberoamericana, 2012), pp. 135–156, pp. 145–153; Agüero, '¿Provincias o estados?', pp. 152–155. See also Chiaramonte, 'El primer federalismo', pp. 94–97.

[43] Ternavasio, *Historia*, p. 152.

[44] Ternavasio, *Historia*, p. 150. See Gandía, *Rivadavia y su tiempo*, pp. 190–204.

[45] Frias, *Trabajos legislativos*, p. 224.

[46] Frias, *Trabajos legislativos*, p. 224.

[47] Frias, *Trabajos legislativos*, p. 224.

'always recognise' the service given by Buenos Aires to the nation by establishing the 'National Credit'.[48]

The report generated a difficult question: was the consolidation and nationalisation of the debts of Buenos Aires and the rest of the Provinces consistent with the logic of consent? Representatives from the Provinces argued that their people had never consented to the loans signed by Buenos Aires. Somellera explained that there was a difficulty when describing the debt as contracted 'by the whole State', and questioned whether by 'State', one was to understand its composition and its laws as reflecting the terms of the 1821 congress. It was not clear whether the lenders from Bolivia, the 'Republic of Alto Peru, which belonged to the Provinces of Potosí, Charcas, Cochamaba and la Paz' would be 'seen as creditors whose debts have to be consolidated'.[49]

In other words, it was not clear who was to bear the costs of independence. General Lucio Norberto Mansilla, who had fought against Artigas' army and carried out a number of diplomatic missions to stabilise tensions in the region, represented the province of Entre Ríos.[50] Mansilla argued that it was not equitable to 'charge the Nation with the debts that some Provinces had taken on'.[51] However, following the 'dissolution of the state' as a result of Artigas' invasion, the role of Entre Ríos had been to guarantee the defence of the nation against attacks from Uruguay and Brazil, and it was thus incumbent on 'the Nation' to 'recompense' their efforts and expenses during the war.[52]

Yet, unity had surely been the ultimate goal of the wars of independence: Juan Ignacio de Gorriti was another revolutionary leader who had defended the Latin American wars of independence on the basis of international law. Gorriti rejected Agüero's view that the nation was already established.[53] As a long-standing representative of the Province of Salta, he argued instead that the nation had yet to be established on the basis of principles of law, and as the discussions went on he embraced a staunch federalist position.[54] In this intervention on the question of debt, he sought to establish the province's 'precedence' over others, since it had resisted and defeated 'the Spanish Army' in recent years and, as a result, its 'sons' had been too busy 'wielding weapons' and were now unable to 'engage in productive jobs'.[55]

[48] Frias, *Trabajos legislativos*, p. 224.
[49] Frias, *Trabajos legislativos*, p. 239.
[50] On the federalist ambitions of Entre Ríos see Adelman, *Republic of Capital*, pp. 87–88.
[51] Frias, *Trabajos legislativos*, p. 225
[52] Frias, *Trabajos legislativos*, p. 226. On these efforts see Botana, *Repúblicas y monarquías*, p. 208. On Entre Ríos' pursuit of independence see Gandía, *Rivadavia y su tiempo*, pp. 1–15. On the political situation in Entre Ríos between 1816 and 1820 see Rosario Janet Leriche, 'La política de Entre Ríos en el marco de la crisis directorial y el tratado del Pilar', *Claves* 7:13 (2021), pp. 189–212. See also Portillo, *Crisis Atlántica*, pp. 120–121.
[53] José Chiaramonte, *Ciudades, provincias, Estados: Orígenes de la Nación Argentina (1800–1846)* (Buenos Aires: Ariel Historia, 1997), p. 218.
[54] Ternavasio, 'Las reformas rivadavianas', p. 183.
[55] Frias, *Trabajos legislativos*, p. 226.

If 'all of these sacrifices' had been made for the 'common cause', why would they not be recognised, 'and the Nation not be obliged to pay them?'[56] In protecting the nation, the Province of Salta had 'economised the loss of blood of the sister provinces'.[57] The objective of the legal decree, Gorriti continued, should be the recognition of the costs that had been incurred 'without national authorisation, but for the general good of the Nation'.[58]

Buenos Aires' model of national unity clashed with the communitarian principles of the Provinces. The representative Dalmacio Vélez Sarsfield, professor of political economy in Buenos Aires, argued that there was no doubt that different Provinces had made different kinds of sacrifices, and Buenos Aires was right to include the immense debt for services it had carried out for the Nation that were not related to the war. However, it was important for the deputies to realise that there simply were not enough funds to repay all of these debts, and so the most urgent matters had to be addressed first, which were the debts incurred by the national government, and thereafter those incurred during the war. If constituted as a centralised rather than a federalist government, he continued, 'everything will be paid by the Nation: there will be no national debt or provincial debt'.[59] This session and legal decree could, he believed, serve to establish the consolidation and recognition of the debt, not the means of its repayment.[60] Gorriti was concerned that this was an evasive response. He replied that this amounted to the logic of 'figuring out how much I owe, and then deciding whether I pay or not'.[61] All the debts had to be repaid in full, since failure to pay a nation's debt that 'morality declares legitimate' far from 'establishing its credit, will ruin it'.[62]

The moral bankruptcy of the armed debtor

Unbridled optimism defeated caution. Agüero won the day by once again drawing on the example of Britain. Agüero explained that debt 'consolidation' was a 'foreign word' which British authors had adopted to discuss financial matters. When Britain consolidated its debt for the first time, it provided an example for other nations to follow: Britain did not take on loans without first establishing a special tax to cover the interests and the repayment of the debt. It thereby brought together all its debts. This was, as Agüero remarked, a separate matter from their

[56] Frias, *Trabajos legislativos*, p. 226.
[57] Frias, *Trabajos legislativos*, p. 226.
[58] Frias, *Trabajos legislativos*, p. 226.
[59] Frias, *Trabajos legislativos*, p. 227. On his life and thought see Sandro Schipani ed., *Dalmacio Vélez Sarsfield e il diritto latinoamericano* (Padova: CEDAM, 1991).
[60] Frias, *Trabajos legislativos*, p. 227.
[61] Frias, *Trabajos legislativos*, p. 227.
[62] Frias, *Trabajos legislativos*, p. 228.

actual repayment.[63] Since the Argentine nation had been dissolved with the Battle of Cepeda of 1 February 1820, since there was no national authority, and since the means to present the original contract were not available, the law could only focus on this later period.[64] Article one of the decree was approved and featured the following terms: 'all internal State debts, prior to 1 February 1820, proceeding from supplements or services for national ends, accredited with original documents granted in time and correctly, are now consolidated; regarding the debts of later times, the Congress will provide other measures'.[65]

In 1826, Buenos Aires would use the outbreak of war with Brazil to defend the speedy resolution of constitutional debates. A project for the establishment of a national bank was authorised and, in February, the Congress debated the proposal for the establishment of the capitalisation of Buenos Aires, which entrenched its authority over the rest of the region and granted it control of the management of tariff duties.[66] It also breached the compromise and the terms that the Congress was based on.[67] Tensions between federalists and representatives who supported the consolidation of executive authority around Buenos Aires boiled over.[68] The proposed capitalisation generated protests from the commercial elites, Gorriti, Moreno, and other deputies, and fractured the fragile consensus that held the Congress together.[69] Gorriti accused the representatives of Buenos Aires of rushing through reforms without acknowledging the impact they had on earlier agreements or considering the needs of the people. The government had to establish a clear timeframe for citizens from far-flung areas to present their private debts for consideration as part of the consolidation of the national debt. Buenos Aires was steamrolling over its moral obligations: 'The State' Gorriti observed, 'is an armed debtor, which seizes [goods] with force, and perhaps against the will of the contributor, at times taking more than they can or should contribute, and through these violent it can reduce some citizens to extreme misery'.[70] A hasty consolidation threatened the poorest creditors, those who did not have the means to make their claims, and those who had suffered from violence; widows and orphans of 'servants of the state' who first lost their fortune and then their lives 'defending the liberty which we enjoy, leaving their family in ruin and with a thick pile of outstanding debts'.[71] These widows, invalids, and orphans who lived in far-flung

[63] Frias, *Trabajos legislativos*, p. 228.
[64] Frias, *Trabajos legislativos*, p. 229.
[65] Frias, *Trabajos legislativos*, p. 240.
[66] Ternavasio, *Historia*, pp. 153–4; Burgin, *Aspectos*, p. 120. Gandía, *Rivadavia y su tiempo*, pp. 314–326.
[67] Burgin, *Aspectos*, pp. 187–188.
[68] See the seeds of this dispute in Gandía, *Rivadavia y su tiempo*, pp. 250–259. Nora Souto, 'El debate en torno a la "capitalización" de Buenos Aires de 1826 y la cuestión de la soberanía', *IX Jornadas Interescuelas/Departamentos de Historia, Córdoba: Universidad Nacional de Córdoba* (2003), pp. 1–12, p. 3, n. 5.
[69] On the social identity of the federalists see Burgin, *Aspectos*, pp. 151–152.
[70] Frias, *Trabajos legislativos*, p. 246.
[71] Frias, *Trabajos legislativos*, p. 246.

territories and who did not know how to make these claims would suffer the most from the consolidation of the national debt.[72]

Agüero did not understand his colleagues' reluctance to see 'things for what they really are'. The nation, moreover, had a right to exercise its authority through bankruptcy:

> [T]he way to pay our debts is through a type of bankruptcy: given that the Nation cannot pay as it should, it pays the only way it can, with whatever it has, drawing on the advantages that the authority it has, or not the authority, but the dominion it has over society and over individual interests, to force them and to subordinate them to the general interest, when it is necessary for the public health and the tranquillity and happiness of the Nation. In this the Nation is not drawing on violence, but employing a right, which it eminently possesses, and to which all particular interest must be subordinated.[73]

Gorriti was undeterred. The mountainous territory of the Province of Salta, after all, would make it harder for claimants to file their claims before their regional representatives or in Buenos Aires. Gorriti depicted the government's attitude to declaring a moratorium on the filing of these claims as nothing more than 'the canonization of fraud'. The state had 'an obligation to pay all of its creditors'; it could not 'seize the property of citizens' and deny the demands of those who had supported it during its time of greatest need.[74] The state was 'defrauding' its people.[75] The Agüero-Gorriti debate reflected broader trends caused by the centrifugal ambitions of the revolutionaries in Buenos Aires. Economic dynamics that shaped the economy of the interior, and were far less dependent on foreign trade, were fundamentally disrupted.[76] The only way for provincial representatives to defend their rights, then, was to turn to international law and the principles of their war of independence.

An empire of speed: reversion and private property

Was the pursuit of the common good determined by the morality of its prospective ends or by the ethics of its means? The problem with Buenos Aires' disregard for existing property rights was not just that Rivadavia's government threatened to disavow private debts incurred for the good of the nation. Its officials also hoped to harness the public land of the Provinces to negotiate further loans. Manuel

72 Frias, *Trabajos legislativos*, p. 246.
73 Frias, *Trabajos legislativos*, p. 247.
74 Frias, *Trabajos legislativos*, p. 248.
75 Frias, *Trabajos legislativos*, p. 248.
76 Burgin, *Aspectos*, pp. 163–167.

Moreno, the strongest defender of federalism at the Congress, built on the ideas of his brother, the intellectual leader of the May Revolution, Mariano Moreno. Mariano Moreno had noted the importance of consent in establishing new social contracts across the region.[77] Manuel Moreno, in turn, argued that the land actually belonged to the various provinces that formed 'the union'.[78] The Congress drew its legitimacy from the consent of the people.[79] Moreno cited the example of the United States in order to remind his peers that both nations shared the view that states had 'rights over their lands' and 'dominion over them'.[80] These territories were 'not just provinces, but real States, as ours are now', and the land of each state belonged to each of them— Argentina's Congress never had a claim to it.[81] The nation, he continued, might mortgage this land to repay the national debt but it could not seize it without the consent of the various Provinces. Moreno noted how the United States had chosen instead to establish that public lands were a 'patrimony for the provision of the Nation's emergencies'.[82]

Agüero countered by defending the status of Buenos Aires as *primus inter pares*: if an Argentine Congress had authorised a foreign loan on the back of mortgaged public lands without the consent of the Provinces once, it could do so again now.[83] The lands had been 'deposited' in the hands of the Provinces during the period of 'anarchy' that followed the dissolution of the government of Buenos Aires, but the lands had never belonged to the Provinces. This was a question of expediency: the nation had to be able to finance its needs and could not demand heavier taxes from the people.[84] The example of the United States was unsuitable; for decades, its officials had been able to calculate the revenues of each of their ports and raise tariffs and taxes accordingly. The United Provinces only had two ports.[85] The Provinces, he continued, had to 'subordinate themselves to that which is just'.[86] Threatened by Brazil's monarchical ambitions, there was little point in drafting laws if there was no recourse to implement them and defend the nation.[87]

Moreno showed how Agüero's application of the logic of utility clashed with the law of nations: based on the right of conquest, Argentine lands had once belonged to the Crown of Spain. Following the revolution, these domains were then transferred to the national government after Spain lost its claim to these territories.

[77] Chiaramonte, *Ciudades*, pp.131–132.
[78] Burgin, *Aspectos*, pp. 152–153.
[79] Frias, *Trabajos legislativos*, p. 254.
[80] Frias, *Trabajos legislativos*, p. 254.
[81] Frias, *Trabajos legislativos*, p. 254.
[82] Frias, *Trabajos legislativos*, p. 255. See also the brief analysis of Moreno's view on this matter in Juan Antonio González Calderon, *Derecho constitucional argentino, historia, teoría y jurisprudencia de la Constitución*. Volume 1 (Buenos Aires: Lajouane, 1923), pp. 120–121.
[83] Frias, *Trabajos legislativos*, p. 255.
[84] Frias, *Trabajos legislativos*, p. 258.
[85] Frias, *Trabajos legislativos*, pp. 260–261.
[86] Frias, *Trabajos legislativos*, p. 258.
[87] Frias, *Trabajos legislativos*, p. 259.

This sovereignty was concentrated under a general government and was then subdivided in the Provinces, so that each Province retained the right to its land. Mortgaging the lands of the Provinces would constitute a violation of the rights they had reserved for themselves. Since states had control over their territories, they had ceded these spaces for the payment of national debts, and the Congress had gained the means to impose tributes and direct contributions over the Provinces. Congress thus had certain assigned rights. But it had no right to occupy the Provinces' lands. Moreno urged caution: 'as a result of running too fast, we must be careful not to fall behind, or not even arrive where we ought to'.[88]

Moreno's most compelling argument was that the Provinces had in fact inherited their rights; they were 'successors' to the Crown of Spain. Congress, however, had not inherited any powers from past constituent assemblies set up by Buenos Aires and the Provinces. Overruling 'sovereign bodies ruled by their own institutions that raised taxes and gathered contributions in the Provinces' and seizing their properties would constitute 'the dissolution of the state'.[89] The very term consolidation was a 'legal confusion' because property rights were conflated with the rights of a creditor. The term liquidation was the more apposite word.[90] Moreno defended the establishment of another body, a senate, to check the impulses of the Congress.[91] He concluded his intervention by explaining that the problem of sovereignty over public lands would remain an issue unless the constitution was reformed: the state could 'in constitutional terms not be said to own these lands'.[92] Since the law would take time to be implemented, it was 'necessary for these lands to remain unused' before signing any further loans.[93]

Yet the nation's war with Brazil allowed Buenos Aires' leaders to defend the most expedient course of action on the basis of reason of state: 'Will we be forced to ask the enemy', quipped Rivadavia, 'to wait until these two Chambers are established so that we can debate our laws?'[94] Unless officials were ready to go looking for territories 'on the moon' these public lands were the only ones that could be mortgaged.[95] Agüero reminded his peers that this process amounted to a kind of reasonable bankruptcy. It meant 'making a rational and indispensable transaction among all the partial interests, with everyone sacrificing a piece, for the sake of the national interest'.[96] Buenos Aires had already established laws that safeguarded property, protected the people, and defended freedom of thought.[97]

[88] Frias, *Trabajos legislativos*, p. 265.
[89] Frias, *Trabajos legislativos*, p. 268.
[90] Frias, *Trabajos legislativos*, p. 268.
[91] On earlier debates in the region on the political benefits of the senate see Botana, *Repúblicas y monarquías*, p. 161.
[92] Frias, *Trabajos legislativos*, p. 268.
[93] Frias, *Trabajos legislativos*, p. 269.
[94] Frias, *Trabajos legislativos*, p. 270.
[95] Frias, *Trabajos legislativos*, p. 271.
[96] Frias, *Trabajos legislativos*, p. 363.
[97] Frias, *Trabajos legislativos*, p. 365.

These principles had shaped the 'laws that have established and founded the public law of the Province of Buenos Aires'.[98] Nationalisation was a way to ensure that everyone recognised the authority of 'a centre' that could then disseminate reason, liberty, and prosperity.[99] As his words elicited the jeers of his peers, he responded with his most blunt statement yet: nationalisation could happen through a number of means: through 'the power of principles, or through the power or force' or, 'to use a vulgar phrase: through blows'.[100] If a nation could not be formed in this way, it would be formed by another type of force—'a foreign force'.[101] These words elicited loud protests from congressmen: Gorriti accused Agüero of 'usurping' rights and establishing 'an arbitrary superiority' of Buenos Aires 'to impose duties and remove rights without the consent, and even against the will, of the people'.[102]

Buenos Aires' representatives ensured a majority approval for their measures but Rivadavia's government fell within a matter of months. The 1826 constitutional experiment only served to widen the divide between the Provinces and Buenos Aires. Following the failure of the Congress to establish a clear relationship between these states, those who had once served together as deputies became diplomats on opposing sides.[103] Sovereignty remained undefined: the pages of *El Lucero*, a newspaper with a wide readership among the Buenos Aires elite and edited by one of the earliest historians of Argentina, the Neapolitan Pedro de Angelis, witnessed debates over the coherence of Somellera's law course and the way it reconciled Roman law with Bentham's ideas.[104] War with Brazil undermined Buenos Aires' trade, its main source of revenue.[105] The peace between the two powers led to the independence of Paraguay and further internecine conflicts.[106] In this context of fiscal difficulties and territorial losses, General Juan Manuel de Rosas was named Governor of Buenos Aires. He was granted extraordinary powers and named García as his Finance Minister. Manuel Moreno would later serve as Rosas' ambassador in London, where he sought to resolve Argentina's outstanding debts and its disputes with Britain over the Falkland Islands. Rosas would eventually assume dictatorial authority and govern a confederation until 1852.[107]

[98] Frias, *Trabajos legislativos*, p. 366.
[99] Frias, *Trabajos legislativos*, p. 363. Gandía, *Rivadavia y su tiempo*, p. 195.
[100] Frias, *Trabajos legislativos*, p. 363.
[101] Frias, *Trabajos legislativos*, p. 364. On this see Iribarne, 'La cuestión capital', p. 193.
[102] Frias, *Trabajos legislativos*, p. 387.
[103] As noted in Chiaramonte, *Ciudades*, p. 166, pp. 225–228; Chiaramonte, 'El primer federalismo', p. 118.
[104] Abelardo Levaggi, 'El derecho romano en la formación de los abogados argentinos del ochocientos', *Revista de Estudios Histórico-Jurídicos* 10 (1985), pp. 16–33. On Pedro de Angelis and *El Lucero* see Hernán Pas, 'Prensa periódica y cultura popular en el Río de la Plata durante el siglo XIX', *Perífrasis. Revista de Literatura, Teoría y Crítica* 9:18 (2018), pp. 11–29.
[105] Roberto Schmitt, 'Finanzas públicas, Puerto y recursos financieros', in Ternavasio ed., *Historia de la provincia*, pp. 205–224, p. 216.
[106] Burgin, *Aspectos*, pp. 48–49.
[107] On the contradictions of this scheme see González Calderón, *Derecho constitucional*, pp. 188–197.

Succession and the armed debtor

In 1830, the federalists of the Provinces of the interior created a Unitarian League and excluded Buenos Aires from the new federal arrangement; Buenos Aires led the establishment of the rival Federal League with the coastal provinces of Santa Fé and Entre Ríos. The Federal Pact, a treaty signed in 1831, guaranteed the terms of its union, although the separation between the domain of the law of nations and constitutional matters remained inconsistent. Indeed, Pedro Ferré, the Governor of Corrientes, pushed for the nationalisation of tariff revenues and, faced with Rosas' rejection of his proposals, walked away from the negotiations.[108] The accord guaranteed a defensive alliance, created free trade within the region's rivers between the peoples of the three states, and eliminated trade tariffs. It included an invitation to the other provinces to join in this 'federal administration' and granted Buenos Aires the responsibility to direct the foreign affairs of the federation.[109] Ferré returned to the negotiating table in order to defend the need to establish a 'right of intervention' among the provinces. Rosas rejected this proposal because he argued it would create a 'general confusion'. Over the next few decades, however, Rosas would frequently deploy this policy of intervention to generate greater unity and consolidate his authority.[110]

Ferré eventually agreed to Buenos Aires' terms and Corrientes adhered to the Federal Pact. As Corrientes became part of Rosas' League many of the issues at the core of Ferré's dispute with Rosas remained unresolved. In these early negotiations between the composite parts of the federation, the matter of debt and its distribution played a key structuring role in their unification. José María Roxas, who had served as the director of the Banco de Descuentos, and later as Buenos Aires' diplomatic representative at the negotiations for the Federal Pact, argued in a memorandum addressed to Ferré that its allies were asking Buenos Aires to give up its benefits from exports that made their way towards the interior and to increase tariffs on foreign trade.[111] Roxas noted that Buenos Aires' wealth contributed to the financing of the revolutionary wars and the recent war with Brazil with 'countless debts of honour'.[112] Pedro Ferré replied to Roxas' proposal in another memorandum. He claimed that Buenos Aires' approach to free trade was destroying the nascent industries of the provinces. Allowing the provinces to retain some of the revenues from trade and fostering their industry would allow them to

[108] Burgin, *Aspectos*, pp. 198–199.

[109] Luis Iriarte, 'Del centralismo al confederacionismo', in Fontán ed., *Alberdi*, pp. 213– 240, pp. 220–221.

[110] Víctor Tau Anzoátegui, *Formación del Estado Federal Argentino, 1829–1852: la intervención del gobierno de Buenos Aires en los asuntos nacionales* (Buenos Aires: Perrot, 1965), pp. 87–92.

[111] José Chiaramonte, *Ciudades, provincias, Estados: Orígenes de la Nación Argentina (1800–1846)* (Buenos Aires: Ariel Historia, 1997), p. 376. On these debates see Burgin, *Aspectos*, pp. 294–297. Roxas occupied other roles in government; see Gandía, *Rivadavia y su tiempo*, p. 235.

[112] Chiaramonte, *Ciudades*, p. 376.

repay the debt.[113] The division of this burden on the basis of the size of the population, Ferré continued, would generate an unequal society.[114] These projected fiscal reforms would undoubtedly generate a 'debt' for posterity, which present officials had no 'right to cast' on future generations since it was in no way connected to 'the price of independence'.[115]

In a pamphlet titled *Cuestiones Nacionales*, Ferré echoed Manuel Moreno's views on debt and defended the principles of international law. It was wrong to suggest, as Rosas' officials had done, that trade in the region had emerged with the rise of the nation of Buenos Aires. It was part of the Spanish inheritance and was thus subject to the law of nations. The state had come to manage, and profit from, these rents 'on the basis of the powers it wrested from the hands of the former Kings' so that the question of the national rents was 'born of a legal qualm'. Citing examples of secession, including the separation of the 'House of Braganza' from the Crown of Spain, Ferré noted how the new governments preserved 'the rights and taxes that constituted the treasury and the rents of the Princes that stopped ruling them'. The law of nations, continued Ferré, ensured that the right of conquest guaranteed these 'immense benefits' to the victor; the variation of titles did not alter the 'essential right by conquest'.[116] The acquisition of these rents entailed the assumption of certain responsibilities, including the right to self-preservation.[117]

Rosas had little interest in the law of nations but he understood how to use coercion and the interests of the region's elites to his advantage.[118] Political instability had led Buenos Aires to grant Rosas extraordinary powers. Order, he believed, would allow him to retain them. Contemporaries suggested that Rosas ruled the confederation as the head of a landed estate.[119] Yet, prior to becoming the ruler of Argentina, he had been a coloniser, the head of a trading company, and an investor who speculated on the changing value of land as it was seized from indigenous peoples.[120] A descendant of a family that belonged in the constellation of the colonial elite, he praised the stability of the Spanish colonial system and sought to promote Catholic values and institutions.[121] He understood that, in the aftermath of the revolution, Buenos Aires' tradesmen had connected their business interests

[113] Chiaramonte, *Ciudades*, p. 382.

[114] Chiaramonte, *Ciudades*, p. 382.

[115] Chiaramonte, *Ciudades*, p. 385.

[116] Pedro Ferré, Cuestiones Nacionales: *Contestación al 'Lucero', ò, Los falsos y peligrosos principios en descubierto: con la refutación a los autores escondidos bajo el título de 'Cosmopolita' y 'Porteño'* (Imprenta del Estado, 1832/1833), p. 17.

[117] Ferré, *Cuestiones Nacionales*, pp. 17–18.

[118] Ricardo D. Salvatore, *Wandering Paysanos. State Order and Subaltern Experience in Buenos Aires During the Rosas Era* (Durham: Duke University Press, 2003), pp. 161–196.

[119] John Lynch, *Argentine Dictator: Juan Manuel de Rosas 1829–1852* (Oxford: Clarendon Press, 1981), pp. 1–2. See also José Ingenieros, *La evolución de las ideas argentinas*. Volume 1 (Buenos Aires: La Revolución, Talleres Gráficos Argentinos, 1918), pp. 89–133.

[120] Lynch, *Argentine Dictator*, p. 24.

[121] Lynch, *Argentine Dictator*, p. 13, pp. 184–185.

to the development of agricultural production in the hinterland; efforts to splinter the country or redraw its boundaries could therefore threaten their profits.[122] As leader, he colonised indigenous lands through a set of raids that became known as his 'Desert Campaign' and granted these territories as favours to his supporters.[123] Even though Rosas enhanced Buenos Aires' control of tariffs, British officials noted that the economy was simply unable to generate enough wealth to repay the nation's foreign debt. British diplomats prioritised instead securing the privileged access of British merchants to the markets of Buenos Aires.[124] Rosas nonetheless agreed to repay the original loan of 1824 and its interests. Investors would have to wait another two decades before the payments started.[125]

Rosas continued Buenos Aires' nationalisation of Argentina without the consent of the other regions.[126] In his *Memoirs*, Ferré would capture the historical connotation of Rosas' lack of interest in the consent of the provinces: the *caudillo* was the heir to the Spanish Crown. Rosas, he argued, believed he had 'a right to dominate the peoples of the old viceroyalty and to treat the national wealth as his own'. Rosas, Ferré continued, thought he had a right to 'contract great debts on behalf of the peoples, without their knowledge of these promises or where the [funds] will be invested'. It followed that 'this government seems to believe it is the sole and universal heir of Ferdinand VII'.[127]

Others followed this logic to a plausible conclusion: it was lawful to kill a tyrant. Under Rosas' rule, the young Alberdi and a number of other intellectuals that became known as the Generation of 1837 met and discussed how to 'emancipate' Latin American culture from Spain. This second generation of revolutionaries would develop a 'literary revolution' that would complete the unfinished revolution of the founding fathers of Latin American independence.[128] But they also thought of ways to end Rosas' rule. Following an altercation between two French citizens and the police, France registered a small complaint that its people should not be subject to excessive police force or enlistment in the army. Argentinian representatives countered that their constitution granted the nation the authority to enrol foreigners in the army. France used this as a justification to block the port of Buenos Aires and claim indemnification for the losses of their citizens. Britain,

[122] Lynch, *Argentine Dictator*, p. 32. See also Tulio Halperín-Donghi, *Guerra y finanzas en los orígenes del Estado argentino (1791 –1850)* (Buenos Aires: Belgrano, 1982), pp. 215–249.

[123] Lynch, *Argentine Dictator*, pp. 57–60.

[124] Lynch, *Argentine Dictator*, pp. 256–257.

[125] Henry Stanley Ferns, *Britain and Argentina in the Nineteenth Century* (Oxford: Clarendon Press, 1960), p. 292.

[126] Lynch, *Argentine Dictator*, p. 177.

[127] Pedro Ferré, *Memoria del brigadier general Pedro Ferré. Octubre 1821 a diciembre 1842* (Buenos Aires: Coni, 1921), pp. 54–55.

[128] See Juan María Gutiérrez, 'Fisonomía del saber español; cual deba ser entre nosotros'in *Discursos pronunciados el día de la apertura del salón literario* (Buenos Aires: Imprenta de la Independencia, 1837), pp. 43–61, p. 56; Ingenieros, *La evolución*, pp. 605–753.

as part of its rapprochement with France, contributed its naval support to the blockade.[129] In a book titled *Rosas y sus opositores*, one of Alberdi's peers, the author José Rivera Indarte, in collaboration with the writer Florencio Varela, drew on the ideas of Mariana, Grotius, Pufendorf, and Vattel on the right to revolution to defend a European intervention in Argentine politics.[130]

Indarte and Varela hoped to paint a grim picture of Rosas' rule, one which would encourage the Anglo-French alliance to deliver regime change in Argentina. In this book, Indarte accused Rosas of being responsible for the deaths caused by the region's divisions. He argued that Rosas had increased Argentina's public debt and its reliance on foreign lenders. Indarte noted that Grotius had defended the right to 'depose and kill a usurper' and quoted an extract where the Dutch jurist considered how Roman law allowed the people to castigate their leader.[131] The law of nations, Indarte concluded, showed that it was a licit and 'holy action to kill Rosas'.[132] The 'doctrine of democracy' was 'that of tyrannicide' and there was 'not a single nation in Europe that has not founded its public law on one or many examples of tyrannicide'.[133]

Varela, in turn, tried to use other ideas in international law to generate foreign interest in intervention. He argued that as a result of the knots of treaties that the various provinces had signed in the process of constituting the nation, contradictions and inconsistencies had frayed the fabric of the state. There was therefore no official representative institution that was based on the consent of the people: the nation of Argentina, concluded Varela, did not exist.[134] When rivals countered that much like in the United States, there was a singular presidential figure who ruled over the composite parts of the state, Varela responded that said president rose to power precisely thanks to the consent and approval of the people; Rosas could claim no such authority—he was nothing more than a usurper.[135] Indarte and Varela's texts were distributed in London and in Paris in order to foster

[129] Jorge Mayer, *Alberdi y su tiempo* (Buenos Aires: Editorial Universitaria de Buenos Aires, 1963), pp. 199–200.

[130] José Rivera Indarte, *Rosas y sus opositores* (Montevideo: Imprenta del Nacional, 1843). On the broader political backdrop see Edward Shawcross, 'When Montevideo Was French: European Civilization and French Imperial Ambitions in the River Plate, 1838–1852', *European History Quarterly* 45:4 (2015), pp. 638–661, pp. 649–650.

[131] Indarte, *Rosas*, pp. xxxiv–xxxvi. Decades earlier, Artigas had worried that the failure to establish a state that was recognisable by outside powers would lead other nations to accuse the revolutionaries of being 'usurpers' of Spanish power; see Botana, *Repúblicas y monarquías*, p. 97.

[132] Indarte, *Rosas*, pp. xxii, xxxiv–xxxv, and 'Appendix', p. 1.

[133] Indarte, *Rosas*, pp. xxxviii–xxxix.

[134] Félix Weinberg, *Florencio Varela y 'El Comercio del Plata'* (Bahía Blanca: Instituto de Humanidades Universidad Nacional del Sur, 1970), pp. 42–44. An anxiety about the existence of the nation that was echoed in Spanish debates among liberals in 1839; see Tomás Pérez Vejo, 'El imperio que quiso ser una nación', in Roberto Breña ed., *Cádiz a debate: Actualidad, contexto y legado* (Mexico City: Colegio de México, 2014), pp. 69–71, and, in Mexico, see Charles Hale, *El liberalismo mexicano en la época de Mora*. Translated by Serio Fernández Bravo and Francisco González Aramburu (Mexico City: Siglo XXI, 2012), p. 17. On these treaties see Ingenieros, *La evolución*, pp. 319–392.

[135] Weinberg, *Florencio Varela*, p. 45.

Anglo-French support for regime change.[136] The French statesman Adolphe Thiers met Varela and drew on his writings when drafting his speeches on the blockade.[137]

Britain soon reaffirmed its support for Rosas and France remained reluctant to intervene any further. Yet the origins of the blockade had a lasting impact on the political thought of the Generation of 1837. For Argentina, a country that depended entirely on the exports delivered through the port, the French blockade had severe economic effects. Some, like Alberdi, would never forget the precedent whereby the rights of foreigners had been used as a justification for foreign intervention.[138] He would build his constitution by defending the establishment of separate rights and privileges for migrants as a way to prevent war and foster the integration of European values and interests in the region.[139]

A constitution for foreigners

One of the most outstanding aspects of Alberdi's thought is how it captured the historical relationship between the law of nations and property rights in Latin American constitutional debates.[140] Born in Tucuman, he learned about economics through his work at a trading house and later studied jurisprudence.[141] In 1837, inspired by the writings of François Guizot and Friedrich Carl von Savigny, he drafted an important text, the *Fragmento*, where he defended Rosas' rule and cautioned against rushing progressive political developments.[142] He argued that, for modern democracy to work, the people first had to be educated and enlightened.[143] Yet when Rosas sought to reinforce his authority through a number of authoritarian measures Alberdi fled first to Uruguay and then to Chile. Alberdi then championed the idea of harnessing foreign intervention in Argentina to topple Rosas: he published a number of articles on this theme and praised Varela's

[136] On the French strategy in Latin America during this period see Iwan Morgan, 'French Policy in Spanish America: 1830–48', *Journal of Latin American Studies* 10:2 (1978), pp. 309–328; Edward Shawcross, *France, Mexico and Informal Empire in Latin America, 1820–1867: Equilibrium in the New World* (London: Springer, 2018), pp. 65–80.

[137] Shawcross, 'When Montevideo Was French', pp. 649–650.

[138] Mayer, *Alberdi*, p. 151.

[139] On alternative ideas of citizenship in the '37 Group see Adelman, *Republic of Capital*, pp. 177–178.

[140] Ingenieros described his thought as a combination of Bentham's economics, Leroux's humanitarian socialism, and the juridical thought of Savigny and Lerminier; see Ingenieros, *La evolución*, p. 653; Natalio Botana, *La tradición republicana: Alberdi, Sarmiento y las ideas políticas de su tiempo* (Buenos Aires: Sudamericana, 1984), pp. 295–298, Adelman, *Republic of Capital*, p. 180.

[141] Mayer, *Alberdi*, pp. 45–46, p. 88.

[142] Juan Bautista Alberdi, 'Fragmento preliminar al estudio del derecho', in *Obras completas*. Volume 1 (Buenos Aires: La Tribuna Nacional, 1886), pp. 103-142, pp. 114–116. On the broader logic behind this view see Botana, *La tradición republicana*, p. 296; Adelman, *Republic of Capital*, pp. 182–183.

[143] Alberdi, 'Fragmento', p. 115. On the influence of contemporary French thought on Alberdi see Daniel Schwartz, 'Juan Bautista Alberdi and the Mutation of French Doctrinaire Liberalism in Argentina', *History of Political Thought* 30:1 (2009), pp. 140–165, pp. 143–146; Bernardo Canal Feijóo, *Alberdi y la proyección sistemática del espíritu de mayo* (Buenos Aires: Losada, 1961), pp. 37–39.

character.[144] In 1838, Alberdi called on his compatriots to 'brandish their swords' and recall that the May Revolution had sought to liberate the nation from 'tyrants from within and from without'.[145]

In Chile, he gained a degree from the University of Santiago de Chile by submitting a memoir on the need for a general American congress. In this text he drew on the ideas of the abbé de Pradt, Bolívar's efforts to create a 'holy alliance of South American states', and Germany's *Zollverein* to defend the need to establish a tariff-free continental union.[146] One of the benefits of such a customs union would be that 'bills of exchange' would be valid across the continent and would become a type of 'paper money' that could be backed by the establishment of a continental bank and a common system of public credit.[147] On this basis, civil and penal laws could be scaled up and homogenised across the region. Latin America would be ruled by a singular 'commercial law'.[148] As proposals for the establishment of a railway in Panama gained traction, a congress could connect all of America through a single road. Latin America would then witness the growth of its populations and its economies.[149]

Once he learned of Rosas' fall in 1852, he quickly drafted his *Bases y puntos de partida para la organización política de la República de Argentina*, a book he later described as 'a plan of action' for Argentina.[150] There was, however, a distinctive dimension to Alberdi's text, a peculiar reading of the history of Latin American countries like Argentina, Peru, and Chile. The state, Alberdi argued, could not be trusted to protect the most important type of rights: the property rights of foreigners.[151] Alberdi suggested the establishment of an entirely separate public law for North American and European immigrants and investors. Indeed, in the section on the 'public law deferred to foreigners', Alberdi built not on earlier constitutions, but on the terms of a most favoured nation. Argentina had granted Britain this status with the 1825 treaty of friendship, and France had sought to acquire these same privileges with its blockade. Foreigners were to be exempted from 'forced loans and

[144] Mayer, *Alberdi*, pp. 181–182. Luis Iriarte, 'Alberdi por Alberdi: Luces y sombras de su pensamiento y accionar político', in Fontán ed., *Alberdi*, pp. 389–456, pp. 416–423.

[145] Quoted in Mayer, *Alberdi*, p. 185. In his later writings, he would depict Rosas' rule as a broader restoration by strongmen in Latin America of 'the old colonial regime'; see 'Escritos económicos' in Juan Bautista Alberdi, *Escritos póstumos*. Volume 1 (Buenos Aires: Imprenta Europa, Moreno, y Defensa, 1895), p. 129, a point noted by Ingenieros, *La evolución*, p. 13.

[146] On the influence of German thought on Alberdi see Feijóo, *Alberdi*, pp. 50–52, pp. 64–70.

[147] Juan Bautista Alberdi, *Sobre la conveniencia de un congreso general americano* (Mexico City: UNAM, 1979), pp. 5–6, p. 11, p. 14.

[148] Alberdi, *Sobre la conveniencia*, p. 14.

[149] Alberdi, *Sobre la conveniencia*, p. 19.

[150] Botana, *La tradición republicana*, pp. 386–387. Carmen Fontán, 'Las "Bases" y su influencia en la constitución de 1853', in Fontán ed., *Alberdi*, pp. 259–283, p. 277. On the sources that inspired his mid-nineteenth-century works see Mayer, *Alberdi*, pp. 132–134.

[151] Juan Bautista Alberdi, *Bases y puntos de partida para la organización política de la República Argentina*. Prólogo de Matías Farías (Buenos Aires: Biblioteca del Congreso de la Nación, 2017), pp. 66–67.

military demands or requisitions'. In awe of the migratory waves prompted by the Gold Rush, Alberdi suggested that this 'calculated system' would inspire European populations who, 'thrown out by Europe because of civil war or industrial crises', travelled to California in search of wealth 'they could find here with greater ease and fewer risks'.[152] European and North American migration and capital would foster the growth of Argentina. Alberdi sought to shield these commercial interests from political turmoil: freedom of trade should be permanent so that the 'unstable hand of our governments cannot derogate today that which it agreed yesterday'. In this respect, it was important to avoid reading 'Vattel or Martens'.[153] Private law, he believed, could secure the interests that public law could not be trusted to safeguard. Utility was the law of the land: women were to show honour, modesty, and take care of the home: 'we need *señoras* and not artists'.[154]

Rights, he believed, should be used to attract European migration and investment.[155] The constitution was to be a 'type of merchant contract of collective societies' that would serve to stimulate the construction of railways that would serve to establish an indivisible unity in Argentina.[156] Indeed, Alberdi hoped that foreign trade could remedy the profoundly harmful effects of the Spanish legacy in the region. The expansion of railways was the best way to 'reverse' the effects of the Spanish Crown on the law of Latin America; it would do what 'all congresses could not do' and 'innovate, reform, and change the most difficult things without decrees or riots'.[157]

Alberdi's *Bases* would have a profound influence on the Argentine Confederation's Constitution of 1853.[158] This was a practical code for a federal state; article 67, for instance, granted the Congress the capacity to stimulate industry or

> the power to provide for all that conduces to the prosperity of the country, to the advancement and welfare of all the provinces, and to the advancement of the people by prescribing plans for general and university instruction and by promoting industrial enterprise, immigration, the construction of railways and navigable canals, the colonisation of public lands, the introduction and establishment of new industries, the importation of foreign capital, by laws which protect these ends and by temporary concessions of privileges and rewards.[159]

[152] As noted in González Calderón, *Derecho constitucional*, pp. 387–388.
[153] Alberdi, *Bases*, p. 106.
[154] Alberdi, *Bases*, p. 90.
[155] Adelman, *Republic of Capital*, p. 204, p. 207.
[156] Adelman, *Republic of Capital*, p. 204; Alberdi, *Bases*, p. 80.
[157] Alberdi, *Bases*, p. 103.
[158] Fontán, 'Las "Bases"', pp. 276–281; On other sources see Adelman, *Republic of Capital*, p. 205.
[159] As noted in Winthrop Wright, *British-Owned Railways in Argentina: Their Effect on the Growth of Economic Nationalism, 1854–1948* (Austin: University of Texas Press, 1974), p. 67. See also Dante Mirra, 'La perdurabilidad de la Constitución en las "Bases" de Alberdi', in Fontán ed., *Alberdi*, pp. 323–339.

A powerful executive was granted extensive powers. The right of intervention of one province in the affairs of another, a norm that, as noted, Rosas had harnessed to entrench his rule, was enshrined in the constitution as a means to secure the nation's 'republican principles'.[160]

In line with Alberdi's ideas, the Constitution also granted foreigners the right to remain citizens of another nation: they were not 'obliged to recognise citizenship nor pay forceful and extraordinary contributions'.[161] His rivals, including Domingo Sarmiento, immediately drew attention to the problems this could cause: foreigners could profit from, and monopolise, local trade. Sarmiento turned Alberdi's reading of the causes of the French blockade on its head: when foreign governments asked for indemnifications over a firm's bankruptcy, Argentina would lack the authority to settle the matter and the resources to pay these claims, and blockades would follow.[162]

Argentina remained deeply divided: the government of Buenos Aires refused to participate in the Argentine Confederation or adhere to the constitution upon which it was based. Alberdi published his *Sistema económico* and his *Elementos del derecho público* in order to develop his ideas on the constitutional arrangement of the nation.[163] He reminded his readers that tariffs and prohibitions on trade of the kind favoured by Buenos Aires were a legacy of the failed Spanish ambitions of Charles V and Philip II.[164] His experience as a diplomat would only serve to reaffirm his convictions.

Alberdi's diplomacy

In 1856, Alberdi was sent as an envoy to Europe to foster support for the Confederation of Argentina against Buenos Aires and Brazil, a state he saw as a perpetual threat to the rest of Latin America on account of its monarchism.[165] He spent the bulk of his time in London, where he met Rosas for the first time and encouraged the former ruler to write a biographical account of his tenure in power.[166]

160 Adelman, *Republic of Capital*, pp. 207–208.

161 See Article 20 in *Constitución de 1853*. Reprinted and digitised by the Biblioteca Virtual Miguel de Cervantes (Online).

162 Domingo Sarmiento, *La condición del extranjero en América* (Buenos Aires: La Facultad, 1928), pp. 37–41. On Sarmiento's changing views on migration see Samuel L. Baily, 'Sarmiento and Immigration: Changing Views on the Role of Immigration in the Development of Argentina', in Joseph T. Criscenti ed., *Sarmiento and his Argentina* (London: Lynne Rienner Publishers, 1993), pp. 131–142.

163 Botana, *La tradición republicana*, pp. 309–310.

164 Juan Bautista Alberdi, *Sistema económico y rentístico de la confederación argentina según su Constitución de 1853* (Valparaíso: Mercurio, 1854), p. viii, pp. 51–52, pp. 114–115; Juan Bautista Alberdi, *Elementos del derecho público provincial para la República Argentina* (Valparaíso: Mercurio 1853), p. 368; Luis Iriarte, 'Alberdi por Alberdi', p. 394.

165 Mayer, *Alberdi*, 498.

166 Lynch, *Argentine Dictator*, pp. 356–357. Alberdi would confess that, upon meeting Rosas, he saw the *caudillo* as a product, and not as the cause, of Buenos Aires' audacity.

In meetings with representatives from the Baring House, he explained that the payment of the 1824 debts was contingent on Buenos Aires forming a part of the Confederation; Argentina would otherwise not take responsibility for these payments.[167] In the face of an international economic crisis, Argentina renegotiated its debts to the Baring House by promising to repay them in full by 1860 and committing the sale of public land as its basis.[168] This prompted a renewed wave of British investment in Argentina: one of the financiers who participated in this round of speculation was one Friedrich Engels.[169]

Upon his arrival in Spain, Alberdi found that the Spanish government continued to draw on the favourable terms established by past treaties with certain Latin American nations to dictate the terms of the negotiations. Spanish diplomats demanded the repayment of debts from the colonial era and, prompted by the crisis in Mexico over the contested nationality of Spanish lenders, they sought to resolve the matter of the naturalisation of the children of Spanish citizens in Argentina. The question of what determined what made one Argentinian or Spanish, or the nature of citizenship, was the subject of the *guerre de plume* between Alberdi and his Spanish counterpart, Jacinto Albistur.[170] Alberdi argued that citizenship depended on one's lineage, a principle known as *ius sanguinis*, while Albistur defended the logic of *ius solis*, or citizenship based on the site of one's birth.[171] Alberdi believed *ius sanguinis* would safeguard the individual's economic interests and prevent the government from enlisting them into the army or seizing their properties.[172] It would further undermine the international support for Buenos Aires, since its government did in fact oblige the children of foreigners to participate in the army.[173] Foreign governments, he believed, would prefer the treatment afforded by these terms.[174]

[167] Feijóo, *Alberdi*, p. 527. Part of a broader economic aspect of the dispute between both sides; see Adelman, *Republic of Capital*, pp. 255–257.

[168] The Baring House continued to supply Argentina with credit until the explosion of the banking crisis. D. C. M. Platt, 'Foreign Finance in Argentina for the First Half-Century of Independence', *Journal of Latin American Studies* 15:1 (1983), pp. 23–47, p. 32; Adelman, *Republic of Capital*, p. 264.

[169] As shown in a brilliant article by Eduardo Elena, 'Spinsters, Gamblers, and Friedrich Engels: The Social Worlds of Money and Expansionism in Argentina, 1860s–1900s', *Hispanic American Historical Review* 102:1 (2022), pp. 61–94, pp. 68–70.

[170] Iván Pastoriza Martínez, 'Nacionalidad y soberanía. El debate entre Alberdi y Albistur sobre el estatus de los hijos de españoles en la construcción de la extranjería en el Río de la Plata (c. 1852–1869)', *Revista de historia del derecho* 62 (2021), pp. 51–81, See also Isidoro Ruíz Moreno, *Relaciones hispano-argentinas de la guerra a los tratados* (Buenos Aires: R.J. Pellegrini, 1981), pp. 285–288.

[171] Moreno, *Relaciones hispano-argentinas*, p. 174. Albistur's attitude built on the Cádiz Constitution, which had sought to resolve the question of nationhood in much the same way; see Tomás Pérez Vejo, 'El imperio que quiso ser una nación', in Roberto Breña ed., *Cádiz a debate: Actualidad, contexto y legado* (Mexico City: Colegio de México, 2014), pp. 63–84, p. 81.

[172] Martínez, 'Nacionalidad y soberanía', p. 66; See also Juan Bautista Alberdi, 'Estudios sobre la colección de tratados de D. Carlos Calvo', in *Escritos póstumos de J. B. Alberdi*. Volume 3 (Buenos Aires: Imprenta Europea, Moreno, y Defensa, 1896), pp. 201–280, pp. 243–244.

[173] Moreno, *Relaciones hispano-argentinas*, p. 158; Adelman, *Republic of Capital*, pp. 211–212.

[174] A point developed by the Argentinian statesman Estanislao S. Zeballos, who developed a theory of international private law; see John William Cooke, *Acción parlamentaria*. Compilation by Eduardo Luis Duhalde (Buenos Aires: Colihue, 2007), pp. 209–211.

Earlier negotiations had been suspended over disagreements regarding the matter of debts. The Spanish government had proposed that Argentina would 'recognise' all debts based on loans or contracts that emerged from 'direct orders of the Spanish Government', and asked for the funds from the *cajas*, the colonial provincial treasuries, to be repaid. The Argentine government, in turn, corrected the article in the draft treaty to note that claimants could 'corroborate and justify' their claims before its courts, and noted that Argentina had no interest in paying debts incurred to fight the cause of independence.[175] Negotiations collapsed. Congress considered the merits of determining future indemnifications on the basis of narrower terms, based on the damages caused by the actions of employees of the state.[176]

Yet, when Alberdi was asked to lead a second round of negotiations the territorial integrity of Argentina came into question, as tensions between the various constituent parts grew; Buenos Aires considered how to unite all sides and integrate its interests within the Confederation of Argentina.[177] Spain's recognition of the Confederation of Argentina could therefore harm Buenos Aires' cause. Faced with a fractured nation, the treaty with Spain was an opportunity for Argentina to reconcile itself with its past: as Alberdi noted, given that Argentina was willing to absorb the debt Buenos Aires 'contracted to attack our Nation, how could we refuse to recognise the debt to the country that gave us our entire identity?'[178] Recognising the Spanish debt, Alberdi reasoned, 'would favour Argentinians, that is to say, the heirs of the seized goods'.[179] Before signing the treaty, Alberdi met Isabella II, Queen of Spain. He later noted that in this meeting he had been treated 'like a foreigner, even though the treaty of recognition had not been signed before today. I did not kiss her hand'.[180] This was a significant gesture for Alberdi because, as he would later note, the great share of European nations, along with Spain, saw those Latin American states that were yet to be recognised by the 'mother nation' as 'insurrectionary colonies of Spain' on the basis of the 'forms and terms of the law of nations'.[181] The Queen's reception was a tacit acknowledgement of the nation's independence.

While he worried about the possible repudiation of this treaty by his own government, once Alberdi successfully negotiated this accord it became clear his diplomatic mission had been a victory for Argentina. Pedro Pidal, one of his Spanish counterparts, nominated Alberdi as a corresponding member of the Royal Academy of History.[182] Alberdi hoped that the terms of this treaty, built on his own

[175] Moreno, *Relaciones hispano-argentinas*, pp. 103–104.
[176] Feijóo, *Alberdi*, p. 592.
[177] Adelman, *Republic of Capital*, pp. 216–217.
[178] Quoted in Moreno, *Relaciones hispano-argentinas*, p. 140.
[179] Quoted in Moreno, *Relaciones hispano-argentinas*, p. 140.
[180] Quoted in Moreno, *Relaciones hispano-argentinas*, p. 143.
[181] Juan Bautista Alberdi, *España y las repúblicas de la América del Sur* (Paris: J. Kugelmann, 1861), p. 6.
[182] Moreno, *Relaciones hispano-argentinas*, p. 148, n. 174.

constitutional and international schemes, would lay the basis for the negotiation of 'indemnifications' with Britain and France.[183] The treaty signalled the 'end of the war of independence and the completion of the May Revolution of 1810'. Where the 'Government of Argentina' had drawn its sovereignty from 'natural law and victory', it now acquired through the treaty the authority and sanction of 'traditional law': the law of nations. Its 'legitimacy' was as 'regularised and well established as that of the American governments of the United States, Brazil, Chile, etc.'.[184] In a letter to the Foreign Ministry, he noted how the 'difficulties over the debt and the nationality of Spaniards I have resolved according to the Law of Nations sanctioned by all of the Republics of South America and the Private Law of Nations of the absolute majority of the States of Europe'.[185] The date of independence recognised in the treaty by virtue of the periodisation of the debts owed to the Spanish Empire—1810—marked the earliest date of independence featured in any accord signed between Spain and a Latin American country; this was a Spanish recognition of the 'initiative' played by Argentina in this 'American glory'.[186]

In a curious reinvention of history, Alberdi assumed Buenos Aires had once acted entirely in line with the law of nations. He cited the decrees 'inspired by Rivadavia' that were approved in the 1820s which 'accepted' Spain's debt and, in his view, repaid the bulk thereof.[187] This policy responded to a matter of principle, Alberdi went on, since the most 'respectable' writers of international law, 'Grotius, Puffendorf, Wheaton, Heffter, and G. F. Martens' had shown that a change in the 'debtor government' did not alter the obligation of said state to repay past debts, as the new administration remained bound by the obligations of the administration that preceded it.[188] Buenos Aires' imposition of obligations on the Provinces in the debates of 1826 was reconfigured, in Alberdi's writings, into a demonstration of the adherence to international law. There could, Alberdi assumed, not be that many outstanding colonial debts. In recognising these debts in the treaty Argentina was merely 'recognising the principles' behind a 'purely hypothetical debt'.[189]

By the time news of the treaty reached Argentina, a new civil war had led to the establishment of a new government. Buenos Aires emerged victorious and established its authority as the core of the nation.[190] The new administration, spearheaded by Alberdi's adversary, Bartolomé Mitre, rejected the terms of the treaty, disavowed Alberdi, and began renegotiations with Spain. The final treaty signed

[183] Quoted in Moreno, *Relaciones hispano-argentinas*, pp. 187–188.
[184] Quoted in Moreno, *Relaciones hispano-argentinas*, p. 205.
[185] Quoted in Moreno, *Relaciones hispano-argentinas*, p. 146.
[186] As noted by Moreno, *Relaciones hispano-argentinas*, p. 205.
[187] Juan Bautista Alberdi, 'Memoria en que el Ministro de la Confederación Argentina en las cortes de Inglaterra: Francia y España da cuenta a su gobierno de los trabajos de su misión, desde 1855 hasta 1860', in Juan Bautista Alberdi, *Obras completas*. Volume 6 (Buenos Aires: La Tribuna Nacional, 1886), pp. 5–150, p. 111.
[188] Alberdi, 'Memoria', pp. 111–112.
[189] Alberdi, 'Memoria', p. 113.
[190] Adelman, *Republic of Capital*, p. 220.

by Mitre's representatives was a carbon copy of the one negotiated by Alberdi, with the exception of the norms on citizenship, which were now determined by *ius sanguinis* and not *ius solis*.[191] Alberdi responded by publishing his *Diplomacia*, where he outlined the parallels between the two texts. He noted how his own decision to use citizenship to attract investment and migration was consistent with the law of nations, political economy, and the 1853 Constitution, which declared, in its preamble, that the nation was constituted for the benefit of 'all of those men around the world who may wish to settle in Argentine soil'.[192] Citizenship was a 'title, not a burden'.[193] Under the new treaty, foreigners would continue to arrive as invaders, not as prospective citizens.[194] The new treaty transferred 'the permanent turmoil of the interior politics to the serious terrain of external transactions, which are the anchor of salvation for the civilisation of these countries'.[195]

Alberdi repeatedly clashed with the new administration. He was forced to beg for his remuneration and endured some of the most difficult years of his life in Paris. Argentina changed while Alberdi remained in exile but debates on *ius solis*, *ius sanguinis*, and the relationship between citizenship, revolution, and rights, continued to divide its politics.[196] Indeed, the memorialisation of the revolution generated new political visions: when the Congress awarded pensions to the children of the nation's founding fathers, one of those awarded with an annuity was Juana Manuela Gorriti, the daughter of the spirited congressman, who would become one of the most important authors of the period. Her writings explored the relationship between profit and patriotism. She lamented that her father and his peers had squandered their private wealth and the 'future of their children' for 'a dream nation' which forced its citizens to pray for a share of their nation's wealth.[197] In a number of publications, she collaborated with Eduarda Mansilla de García, the daughter of another founding father of the nation, Lucio Norberto Mansilla, and another popular author of her age.[198] Both authors reconsidered the memory of

[191] Alberdi further noted that the provincial treasury of Buenos Aires was not obliged to repay the debt in this treaty, which would harm Spanish interests; see Juan Bautista Alberdi, *Diplomacia de Buenos Aires y los intereses americanos y europeos en el Plata con motivo del reciente tratado entre España y la República Argentina* (Buenos Aires: Imprenta Hispanoamericana de Cosson, 1864), p. 44.

[192] Alberdi, *Diplomacia*, pp. 25–29. Something he would do repeatedly; see Juan Bautista Alberdi, *La crisis de 1866, ó, Los efectos de la guerra de los aliados en el órden económico y político de las repúblicas del Plata* (Paris: Impr. de Dubuisson, 1866), p. 53.

[193] Alberdi, 'Memoria', p. 16. See also Moreno, *Relaciones hispano-argentinas*, p. 158.

[194] Alberdi, *Diplomacia*, p. 31.

[195] Alberdi, *Diplomacia*, p. 44.

[196] Pilar González Bernaldo, 'Estanislao Zeballos and the Argentine Doctrine of Human Private Law: A Micro-Social Approach to the History of Private International Law', *Jus Gentium. Journal of International Legal History* 2:5 (2021), pp. 529–564.

[197] Quoted in Miriam Bucuré, 'Militancia y compromiso de Juana Manuela Gorriti', *Quaderns de Filologia. Estudis literaris* 27 (2012) 13–25, p. 19; Francine Masiello, *Between Civilization and Barbarism: Women, Nation, and Literary Culture in Modern Argentina* (Lincoln: University of Nebraska Press, 1992), pp. 125–129; Sergio Waisman, *Dreams and Realities: Selected Fiction of Juana Manuela Gorriti* (New York: Oxford University Press, 2003), p. xxxiv.

[198] Waisman, *Dreams*, pp. xxx–xxxi.

the revolution, the Spanish colonial past, and the inequalities that continued to shape Latin America: Gorriti's *El Tesoro de los Incas* was a tale of colonial creolisation, dispossession, love. Above all, it was a denunciation of greed and the allure of the extraction of guano and gold.[199]

When Calvo wrote to Alberdi

In 1861, Alberdi received a letter from Carlos Calvo. Calvo, born in Montevideo when the city was the capital of the United Provinces, had accepted a job as representative for Paraguay in Europe and had been asked to settle the Canstatt affair.[200] Santiago Canstatt was an individual who had claimed to be a British subject after he had been jailed for participating in an effort to overthrow the President of Paraguay. Britain had retaliated through the use of force to demand his release. When Calvo approached Alberdi for his opinion on the matter, Alberdi explained that political questions could not be considered in the abstract. Paraguay, he reasoned, would benefit from collaborating with Britain and negotiating a favourable treaty of commerce; there was not much point in appealing to the principles of international law to reject its claims. This was, he explained, what he had recommended for his own country in his *Bases*. Paraguay should demonstrate its 'respect for foreigners' and their interests to entice international financiers to invest in its nascent industry.[201]

Calvo, in response, criticised Alberdi's attitude towards Paraguay and sublimated his views, as expressed in his *Bases*, into a 'doctrine', one that suggested that 'South-American states stand to *gain* more than they may lose by submitting themselves to the exigencies of the powerful nations of Europe through the concessions they may make.'[202] This would be, in Calvo's reading, to abdicate the very rights that resulted from the 'processes of independence.'[203] Calvo documented this exchange and his broader efforts to achieve a peaceful and fair resolution to the affair in his *Una página de derecho internacional*. Published the year Maximilian was crowned Emperor of Mexico, it featured a preface written by Paul Pradier-Fodéré which defended Napoleon III's foreign policy and praised his Foreign Minister, Drouyn de Lhuys. Pradier-Fodéré applauded the French vision for Latin America whereby, as he described, this 'nascent America' was reaching out for help, and European 'intervention', through the 'generosity' of France, had charitably responded to this call and

[199] Lisa Burner, 'Tales of Incan Gold in an Era of Guano: Juana Manuela Gorriti's Precious Metal Melodramas', *Hispanic Review* 86:3 (2018), pp. 353–376, p. 366.

[200] Eduardo Ricardo Pérez Calvo, *Vida y trabajos de Carlos Calvo* (Buenos Aires: Dunken, 1996), p. 21.

[201] Carlos Calvo, *Una página de derecho internacional: o La América del Sur ante la ciencia del derecho de gentes moderno* (Paris; Durand, 1864), p. 253, pp. 249–251.

[202] Calvo, *Una página*, p. 251, p. 254.

[203] Calvo, *Una página*, p. 255.

diffused arts and industry throughout the region.[204] Calvo praised Drouyn de Lhuys in terms that he would later use to extol the Monroe Doctrine: 'Latin America, and in general any weak state that has been oppressed by the violence of the strongest, has found in him, wherever his aid has been sought out, the most eloquent defender of its rights'. 'South America', he continued, 'and in particular Paraguay, owe a great gratitude to Mr. Drouyn de Lhuys'.[205] Calvo noted how international law could solve the 'mistake' made by leaders of Latin American independence who had 'fractured their peoples' and subdivided them among 'pompous denominations like *Confederation*, *United States*, etc., parodying in that way the Anglo-Americans'.[206]

For Alberdi, the most painful aspect of Calvo's writings, however, was his use of the memory of Rosas' rule. In his letter to Alberdi, Calvo argued that an example of a weaker power fighting against a more powerful state was, in fact, the 'astute Argentinian tyrant', Rosas, since 'the firmness of his foreign policy' had served as the 'barrier' against the law of force in the River Plate, in reference to Rosas' 'Desert Campaign' and his struggle against indigenous peoples.[207] Calvo ended his *Una página* by praising the authoritarian leader of Paraguay for his management of negotiations with Britain. Calvo repeated and adapted the view he had expressed in his letter to Alberdi: he noted that the resolution of the issue demonstrated that 'the application of international law to all civilised countries establishes barriers in Latin America that prevent the rise of unscrupulous governments'.[208]

This, then, would allow Alberdi to note that Calvo's international law was that of the tyrant Rosas.[209] It was a damning indictment of Calvo, who four years later would defend a new type of barrier, set by the United States, as a way to protect Latin America. Indeed, one of the rhetorical devices used by the French defenders of the establishment of Maximilian I was the creation of a border wall to check North American power.[210] Calvo therefore equivocated and defended both of the dominant mid-century foreign visions of Latin America, one where the continent was controlled by France and the other where it was administered by the United States. The history of interventions and debt in Argentina and Latin America suggested, in Alberdi's view, that international law was nothing more than the

[204] Calvo, *Una página*, p. xi. Stève Sainlaude, *France and the American Civil War: A Diplomatic History* (Oxford: Oxford University Press, 2019), pp. 16–65. See Maike Thier, 'The View from Paris: "Latinity", "Anglo-Saxonism", and the Americas, as Discussed in the "Revue Des Races Latines", 1857–64', *The International History Review* 33:4 (2011), pp. 627–644.

[205] Calvo, *Una página*, p. 264.

[206] Calvo, *Una página*, pp. 1–2.

[207] Calvo did note that 'this constituted the only lesson from this otherwise ruinous episode in the region's history'. Calvo, *Una página*, p. 255. An internal colonising logic he would later develop; see Teresa Davis, 'The Ricardian State: Carlos Calvo and Latin America's Ambivalent Origin Story for the Age of Decolonization', *Journal of the History of International Law* 23:1 (2020), pp. 40–42.

[208] Calvo, *Una página*, p. 300.

[209] Alberdi, 'Notas', pp. 241–242.

[210] William Spence Robertson, 'The Tripartite Treaty of London', *The Hispanic American Historical Review* 20:2 (1940), pp. 167–189, p. 177.

justification of an imperial sphere of influence. Political economy, by contrast, strengthened the bonds that connected peoples and nations.

Alberdi believed he had formulated the basis for an alternative system of foreign relations for Latin America: the Argentine Constitution that emerged from his design had, he explained, been praised by European authors and could be scaled up to a system of international law: 'a real revolution in international law is embedded within the great and fruitful innovations introduced [. . .] by the Constitution of the Argentine Republic, on the basis of which there already exist a number of perpetual treaties on navigation and trade which elevate its constitutional doctrine to the rank of international law'.[211] Money united citizens and nations where international law, by turning war into an 'element of civilisation', tore them asunder.[212] Political economy would show foreign investors 'that there are cases where he who gives the most receives the most, that foreign wealth is part of our own'.[213]

The psychology of the armed debtor

In the final years of his life, Alberdi noted that many Western countries had abolished the 'barbaric practice' of capital punishment over bankruptcy: there was a need, he argued, to outlaw its international parallel: war over outstanding loans.[214] Warfare, moreover, exacerbated fiscal difficulties: it increased public debt and the reliance on foreign lending with high interest rates. This increased the tax burden on citizens and indebted future generations.[215] These demands on people's income stalled 'the birth of a nation's wealth and progress'.[216] By 'lending to the soil, and not to the man, Europe has studied the land but not the person and the life of its debtor'. 'Universal exhibitions' and 'thousands of European books' focused on the animals, the minerals, and the crops of the region: the loans followed 'these exhibitions' and 'omitted' the study of the 'man and the society of South America, that is to say, the origins and causes of human wealth, which are labour and thrift or, more correctly, the worker, and not any worker, but the modern, intelligent worker, educated to understand labour and thriftiness'.[217] This economic dynamic generated economic misunderstandings: Europe's mortgage over America was 'the most ruinous of all' because it was 'inexecutable': nobody could imagine 'the public destruction' of 'sixteen nations, all at once'.[218] The use of war and intervention to force

211 Alberdi, 'Notas', p. 254.
212 Alberdi, 'Notas', p. 251.
213 Alberdi, 'Estudios económicos, p. 462.
214 Juan Bautista Alberdi, *El crimen de la Guerra* (Buenos Aires: Cadal, 2020), p. 44.
215 Alberdi, *El crimen de la guerra*, p. 83.
216 Alberdi, *El crimen de la guerra*, p. 185.
217 Alberdi, 'Estudios económicos', pp. 83–84. This was also another swipe at Sarmiento's history in his *Facundo o civilización y barbarie en las pampas argentinas* (Santiago: Imprenta del Progreso, 1845).
218 Alberdi, 'Estudios económicos', p. 83.

a state to honour a debt compelled a nation to fulfil its obligation to the creditor. But it also undermined the purpose of the debt: to fulfil the needs of its citizens.

Alberdi saw his homeland as an example of this economic trend. Divisions between Buenos Aires and the Argentine Confederation continued throughout the century. A particularly difficult source of disagreement was how to distribute the foreign debts of the two states. In the absence of a stable unified government, Alberdi argued that the River Plate would continue to be 'the open gateway' for any 'retrograde European nation' which retained 'papers and old titles of putative property and dominium' with hopes to reclaim their rights.[219] Alberdi considered the matter of how to manage the foreign debts of Buenos Aires and Argentina. Buenos Aires had monopolised the wealth of the Provinces and signed loans with Britain, with which it then hoped to saddle the rest of the Argentine territories.[220] Buenos Aires, he explained, had not used these funds for the good of the nation: it had used the British loan of 1825 to wage a war against Brazil. Not only was the war a waste of money but it further resulted in territorial losses.[221] In agreeing to contribute to the resolution of this payment, the Argentine Confederation would be paying a debt that was not its own—and which would not be its own 'even if it had been used for its own good'. In letting Buenos Aires retain the control of tariffs, the Argentine Confederation had paid its neighbours more than what was owed to Britain.[222] The Argentine Confederation should only absorb Buenos Aires' debt if it was awarded control of the port tariffs.[223]

In 1879, after 40 years spent away from his country, Alberdi returned to Argentina. A year later, the Argentine Republic and Buenos Aires fought another civil war which resulted in the latter's federalisation and the final unification of the Argentine nation. Concerned for his health, Alberdi returned to Europe. He did not live to witness the most significant sovereign debt crisis of the nineteenth century: the Baring Crisis.[224]

Alberdi, Drago, and the Baring Crisis

When the Baring Crisis decimated the nation's finances, it was not clear whether the province of Buenos Aires ought to be accountable to the Argentine Supreme

219 Juan Bautista Alberdi, *Diplomacia argentina y americana* (Buenos Aires: Librería 'La Facultad', 1920), p. 214.
220 Alberdi, *Diplomacia argentina*, p. 150.
221 Alberdi, *Diplomacia argentina*, p. 213.
222 Alberdi, *Diplomacia argentina*, p. 213.
223 Juan Bautista Alberdi, *Condiciones de la unión y consolidación de la República Argentina* (Besançon: José Jacquin, 1862), pp. 29–30.
224 For a summary of the crisis see Kris James Mitchener and Marc D. Weidenmier, 'The Baring Crisis and the Great Latin American Meltdown of the 1890s', *The Journal of Economic History* 68:2 (2008), pp. 462–500; Juan Flores Zendejas, 'Crying on Lombard Street: Fixing Sovereign Defaults in the 1890s', *European Review of History: Revue Européenne d'histoire* 19:6 (2012), pp. 979–997, pp. 988–991.

Court.[225] The responsibility, administration, and consolidation of the debts incurred by each state remained a source of contention. Mitre's grandson, Luis María Drago, then Attorney General of Buenos Aires, was asked to make the case to the Court that public debt was a matter of national sovereignty and Buenos Aires remained, in fact, a separate sovereign state from Argentina. On matters of public debt payment and default, it was therefore unaccountable to the Supreme Court of Argentina; the Argentine Supreme Court, in other words, could not decide what debts Buenos Aires ought to pay.

Drago's intellectual formation has received less attention than the ideas he defended. Yet his principles emerged directly from nineteenth-century debates he had contributed to as a journalist, a translator of British classics, a pioneering criminologist, and a lawyer. He edited articles for *La Nación*, the newspaper that Alberdi had helped to establish; acted as a founding member of the Sociedad de Antropología Jurídica Argentina, which sought to study the sociological origins of crime, and served as Attorney General and congressman in Buenos Aires. A consistent source of interest was the subject of his doctoral thesis: the juridical dimensions of divorce and the rights of women in marital relations.[226]

By the time he was named Foreign Minister and turned his attention to international law, Drago had developed a persuasive style of writing and was interested in a wide array of topics, including legal history and the psychological backgrounds of criminals.[227] As Foreign Minister, Drago hoped to contribute to the development of the codification of the international law of war that crystallised at the Hague conventions of 1899 and 1907.[228] His background in criminology would, however, allow him to formulate a response to Roosevelt's foreign policy: when he was faced with accusations that US policies violated international law, Roosevelt would vindicate the role of the United States as an international police force.[229] As Drago noted, this was 'nothing more than one of the many applications of the Darwinian Theory of the survival of the fittest'.[230]

In his intervention on Buenos Aires' public debt, titled '*Los estados federales no son ejecutables*', or 'The federal states cannot be sued over debts by the executive branch', Drago cited Alberdi's *Bases*, and examples from the constitutional

[225] Henry Stanley Ferns, 'The Baring Crisis Revisited', Journal of Latin American Studies, 24:2 (1992), pp. 241–273; Carlos Marichal, A Century *of Debt Crises in Latin America, from Independence to the Great Depression, 1820–1930* (Princeton: Princeton University Press, 1989), pp. 118–136.

[226] Luis María Drago, *El poder marital* (Buenos Aires: El Diario, 1882); see Drago's speech on the matter in 'Discurso del ex Diputado Nacional Dr. Luis María Drago', in Miguel J. Font ed., *La mujer: encuesta feminista argentina* (Buenos Aires: Imp. Costa Hnos., 1921), pp. 189–194.

[227] Alfredo N. Vivot and Alberto A. Conil Paz, *Homenaje al doctor Luis M. Drago* (Caracas: Oficina Central de Información, 1976), p. 11.

[228] Evgeny Roshchin, 'The Hague Conferences and "International Community": A Politics of Conceptual Innovation', *Review of International Studies* 43:1 (2017), pp. 177–198.

[229] Stephen G. Rabe, 'Theodore Roosevelt, the Panama Canal, and the Roosevelt Corollary to the Monroe Doctrine', *IdeAs. Idées d'Amériques* 22 (2023) (Online).

[230] Luis Maria Drago, 'State Loans in Their Relation to International Policy', *American Journal of International Law* 1:3 (1907), p. 707.

histories of Argentina and the United States, to argue that all Argentine territories, including Buenos Aires, retained the right to self-government as sovereign states. The management of public debt was the prerogative of any government. As such, Argentina's Supreme Court could only give advisory opinions on matters related to Buenos Aires' treasury.[231] To undermine a state's capacity to manage its public debt would be to intervene in, and undermine, its management of public services.[232] A Supreme Court could not, moreover, serve as an arbiter in this matter because, as Drago noted Calvo had argued, it lacked enforcement mechanisms.[233] Crucially, since Buenos Aires also held 'foreign debt', it was important to avoid a defence of the principle that its repayment could be acquired through 'coercive means' by appealing to the Supreme Court.[234]

Drago's key rhetorical move was to explain that a sovereign state which managed its public debt wisely would eventually generate enough wealth to pay its loans: as 'difficult circumstances end, things become clearer and, sooner or later' the nation's 'obligations are fulfilled'.[235] No outside force, neither the Supreme Court nor any other institution, could force the state of Buenos Aires to change the way it administered its public debt. Public debt was simply one aspect of the state's pursuit of the common good. On the basis of this commutative view of debt, intervention in the administration of a nation's affairs was never justified. Drago employed the arguments that Alberdi and the United Provinces had traditionally used to curb Buenos Aires' exceptionalist power over the rest of the region to the benefit of the capital. As Foreign Minister, he would try to scale up this principle into a doctrine of international law. He would face, in his engagement with the United States, an entirely different form of exceptionalism.

[231] Luis M. Drago, *Cobro coercitivo de deudas* (Buenos Aires: Hermanos Coni, 1906), pp. 51–53.
[232] Drago, *Cobro*, p. 57.
[233] Drago, *Cobro*, p. 42.
[234] Drago, *Cobro*, p. 59.
[235] Drago, *Cobro*, p. 73.

6

Sacred Debt and Just War

Moral Economy beyond International Law

The end of revolutionary credit

The world of nineteenth-century Latin American high politics was dominated by men who were largely interested in grammar, literature, and science; in the absence of a formal diplomatic service, writers were still asked to serve as diplomats.[1] Their bookish analyses of international law contrasted strongly with the reality of most of their fellow citizens. Once Bustamante started his history of Mexico's odious debt by referring to Hernán Cortés, his fellow deputies asked him to return to the matter at hand and avoid engaging in pedantry. But Bustamante refused to yield.[2] Debates in constituent bodies could last weeks. Leaders with absolute power, like Rivadavia, could spend two daily sessions reading a speech that exceeded four hundred pages.[3] The decrees passed on the basis of their debates and their correspondence were, however, binding, carried legal and political weight, and shaped future political fault lines in the region and in international law.

In their eyes, foreign credit promised to catalyse the pace of political, diplomatic, and economic change. An optimism bias with providentialist overtones encouraged Latin American officials to see credit as a demiurgic force, and to hope that, thanks to *vacatio legis*, interest payments would be manageable 'within a few years' since foreign credit would accelerate the growth of industry.[4] The pursuit of revolutionary credit predated the rise of national banking.

Officials in Mexico, Colombia, and Argentina took out foreign loans before they established how to pay for them; ministers removed the main sources of revenue, including the *alcabala*, deemed a source of Spanish oppression since

[1] On the ideas of 'hombres de bien' and 'gente decente' see Hilda Sabato, *Republics of the New World: The Revolutionary Political Experiment in Nineteenth-Century Latin America* (Princeton: Princeton University Press, 2018), pp. 170–177.

[2] Juan Antonio, Mateos, *Historia Parlamentaria De Los Congresos Mexicanos de 1821 A 1857*. Appendix to Volume 2 (Mexico City: J. V. Villada, 1882), p. 319.

[3] John Lynch, *Argentine Dictator: Juan Manuel de Rosas 1829–1852* (Oxford: Clarendon Press, 1981), p. 302.

[4] Echoed in constitutional visions, or what Hale described as 'constitutional determinism', see Charles Hale, *El liberalismo mexicano en la época de Mora*. Translated by Serio Fernández Bravo and Francisco González Aramburu (Mexico City: Siglo XXI, 2012), p. 76. Foreign debt contributed to the sense of temporal dislocation studied by Sebastián in Javier Fernández Sebastián, *Historia conceptual en el Atlántico ibérico: Lenguajes, tiempos, revoluciones* (Madrid: FCEE, 2021), p. 312.

Odious Debt. Edward Jones Corredera, Oxford University Press.
DOI: 10.1093/9780191982200.003.0007

the seventeenth century, along with other streams associated with Spanish colonial policies, such as tributes, and monopolies. In an effort to foster free trade with Britain, tariffs were reduced or abolished.[5] Associating the revolution with freedom from taxes and tributes came at a cost: no politician wanted to be tasked with the mission of imposing and enforcing the collection of taxes on a war-torn country.[6] Government efforts to reintroduce these tributes for the practical purpose of bolstering the economy fostered tensions or floundered because they were depicted by the government's opposition as a return to colonial tyranny.[7]

Foreign debt and exports therefore continued to fuel economic growth in the region. Predating and unresolved by constitutions, the settlement of foreign debt was, as we have seen, frequently outsourced to international legal spaces.[8] Latin American authors like Bello, Alberdi, Payno, or Calvo showed that there was nothing benign about this shift: drawing on international law, they argued that matters of debt remained the subject of municipal law—their constitutional reforms were binding and retroactive, and they had to be respected abroad. Arbitration shifted the terms of the debate so the resolution of unpaid claims was favourable to Europe and the United States.[9] As José Gustavo Prieto Muñoz has noted, Latin American states were involved in almost half of all mixed claims commissions from 1794 to 1934.[10]

[5] Henry Stanley Ferns, *Britain and Argentina in the Nineteenth Century* (Oxford: Clarendon Press, 1960), p. 103, David Bushnell, *The Santander Regime in Gran Colombia* (Newark: University of Delaware Press, 1954), p. 77; David Bushnell, *The Making of Modern Colombia: A Nation in Spite of Itself* (Berkeley: University of California Press, 1993), pp. 53–54; Hale, *El liberalismo*, pp. 260–265. Many of these taxes would have to be reinstated soon after their abolition. See Barbara A. Tenenbaum, 'Taxation and Tyranny; Public Finance during the Iturbide Regime, 1821–1823', in Jaime E. Rodríguez, *The Independence of México and the Creation of the New Nation* (Los Angeles: University of California Press, 1989), pp. 201–213, p. 205; Bushnell, *Santander*, p. 29.

[6] Bushnell, *Santander*, p. 84.

[7] Joaquín Mosquera, *Examen de las observaciones del señor senador Joaquín Mozquera sobre el empréstito decretado por la Cámara de Representantes en 28 de abril de 1825* (Bogotá: Impreso por F.M. Stokes, 1826), p. 24. In the 1880s, officials commented on how revolutionaries had tried to foster popular support for the revolution through these measures, and noted the ironies of abolishing the very sources of revenues that the revolutionaries would need the most; see Joaquín Demetrio Casasús, *Historia de la deuda contraída en Londres* (Mexico City: Imprenta del Gobierno federal, 1885), pp. 12–13.

[8] Barbara A. Tenenbaum, *México en la época de los agiotistas, 1821–1857* (Mexico City: Fondo de Cultura Económica, 1985). For the economics of this dynamic see Juan Flores Zendejas, 'The Entanglements of Domestic Polities: Public Debt and European Interventions in Latin America', in Nicolas Barreyre and Nicolas Delalande eds., *A World of Public Debts* (London: Palgrave, 2020), pp. 111–235.

[9] Kathryn Greenman, *State Responsibility and Rebels: The History and Legacy of Protecting Investment Against Revolution* (Cambridge: Cambridge University Press, 2021), pp. 40–43. For an alternative interpretation see Steven M. Harris, 'The Global Construction of International Law in the Nineteenth Century: The Case of Arbitration', *Journal of World History* 27:2 (2016), pp. 303–325, p. 316. Frank Griffith Dawson, *The First Latin American Debt Crisis: The City of London and the 1822–25 Loan Bubble* (New Haven: Yale University Press, 1990), pp. 234–235.

[10] José Gustavo Prieto Muñoz, 'Mixed Claims Commissions in Latin America during the 19th and 20th Centuries: The Development of International Law in between Caudillos and Revolutions', in Raphael Schäfer and Anne Peters eds., *Politics and the Histories of International Law: The Quest for Knowledge and Justice* (Leiden: Brill, 2021), pp. 250–269, p. 259.

Was arbitration a fair way to resolve international trade disputes or was it a means of dispossession? What, after all, was the difference between arbitration and intervention? Was the moral code of international law that Latin American officials had studied to the letter nothing more than another apology for empire? If so, reasoned Calvo, Latin America should choose its imperial protector. In response, Alberdi accused Calvo of trying to emulate Napoleon Bonaparte in his hope of creating a 'code for the world' rather than a moral system of international law.[11]

The Calvo–Alberdi debate: intervention and imperialism

By the late nineteenth century, debt, the catalyst of the foreign recognition of Latin American independence, the putative source of economic and cultural development, and the connecting tissue of citizens and nations, had been transformed into the cause of endless wars and invasions in the region.[12] According to Alberdi, 'the war that generated its liberty' from Spain 'shackled' Latin America 'with debts'.[13] To 'escape the debts created by war, what does an overdrawn America do? It searches for the means to pay off its debts through war'.[14] The sanctity of contracts was used to legitimate conflict but the use of violence undermined the sacred purpose of debt: to fulfil the state's obligations to the community. The three themes that had shaped discussions over the 'sacred debt' of independence—the ethics of repayment, the need for violence and revolution to overthrow a tyrant, and the liberal emphasis on the respect for private property—all had to be reconsidered in light of the rise of a new empire: the United States.

Latin America had twice overcome the imperial impositions of a moral international order on the basis of unpaid debts: it had undermined Spain's claim to its empire and it had exposed the imperial uses of international law by European powers. It now faced a new moral arbiter in the form of the United States. If Latin America could not honour its debts to its own and the wider world, would its fate forever be determined by foreign empires?

Depressed, defeated, and discarded by the nation he had once served, Alberdi faced some of the toughest years of his life in Paris: he even considered whether monarchical rule in Latin America would stabilise the region.[15] But Alberdi harboured too much hatred towards the legacy of the Spanish Crown in Latin America to consistently endorse this position. As he considered the merits of the Pan-Americanism

[11] Alberdi, 'Estudios sobre la Colección de Tratados de D. Carlos Calvo', p. 213, p. 218, pp. 237–238, pp. 249–250.
[12] Alberdi, *Escritos económicos*, p. 224.
[13] Alberdi, *Escritos económicos*, p. 407.
[14] Alberdi, *Escritos económicos*, p. 408.
[15] Faced with Maximilian's rule over Mexico, Alberdi did also contemplate the monarchical model for Latin America: see Horacio Crespo, 'La tentación monárquica de Alberdi', *Historia Mexicana* 65:2 (2015), pp. 599–628.

outlined in Calvo's *Derecho internacional*, Alberdi transformed this critique of monarchy into a critique of empire. Alberdi vehemently disagreed with Calvo's defence of the United States as an agent of progress in Latin America: 'Should the South American law of nations be known as the *Monroe doctrine*? One might say that [Carlos] Calvo believes so. Yet this doctrine is not American'.[16] While he noted that Britain had first developed this concept, he was keen to emphasise that the North American uses of this doctrine were redolent of Spain's imperial foundations. Alberdi observed that 'Monroe's Americanism resembles that of [Pope] Alexander VI'.[17] Alexander's providential papal bulls had, after all, excluded other powers from intervening in the region's affairs, redefined just war, and recognised the rights of the Spanish Crown over those territories. The United States' claim to moral authority was nothing new: it was based on the same set of principles once used by Spain, the empire which, in Alberdi's view, had ruined Latin America.

Alberdi believed that the law of nations of each country responded to its history and its culture: it could not be imposed from afar on the basis of foreign principles. As he continued to review Calvo's text, Alberdi claimed that the Monroe Doctrine was 'misunderstood'; it was harmful towards Latin America since it undermined its 'natural guarantees'.[18] This doctrine failed to speak about '*intervention* or *influence*' and only addressed '*colonisation*'. It was, he continued, 'poorly understood and poorly applied to questions that are not about conquest nor colonisation'.[19] History shed some light on the matter: Calvo portrayed the North American opposition to the Mexican Empire of Maximilian I as a reaffirmation of the doctrine. Alberdi, by contrast, believed that the United States had made it clear that this policy was 'circumstantial': after all, it was used to justify the annexation of Texas and, as a result of the Mexican–American War, '[t]hose who boasted about teaching Europe by example to not intervene in South America are now the owners of half of Mexico'.[20] Perhaps, Alberdi ventured, the establishment of the Panama Canal would unite Europe and the Americas through the laws of commerce and ultimately lead to the 'tacit derogation' of the Monroe Doctrine.[21]

At the core of their disagreement was the ambivalent association of foreign intervention with ideas of war, 'satellite', to use Alberdi's term, or 'mediation', to use Calvo's own, colonisation, culture, civilisation, or what the Argentinian jurist Luis María Drago would later call 'financial intervention'. This debate between

[16] Alberdi, 'Notas', p. 236.
[17] Alberdi, 'Notas', p. 250.
[18] Alberdi, 'Notas', p. 237.
[19] Alberdi, 'Notas', p. 236.
[20] Alberdi, 'Notas', p. 236. On Lincoln's reluctance to use the term see Jay Sexton, 'The Monroe Doctrine in an Age of Global History', *Diplomatic History* 47:5 (2023), pp. 845–870, p. 866. On the popularisation of this analysis of the cynical North American approach to Mexican affairs see Gretchen Murphy, *Hemispheric Imaginings: The Monroe Doctrine and Narratives of U.S. Empire* (Durham: Duke University Press, 2005), p. 147.
[21] Alberdi, *Escritos póstumos*. Volume 3 (Buenos Aires: Imprenta Europea, 1895–1896), p. 124.

Argentinian lawyers turned on conflicting readings of the history of foreign intervention in Argentina and Latin America. These three men shared a profound concern about the way that foreign powers had deployed debts to advance their interests in Latin America—indeed those few paragraphs in Calvo's *Derecho internacional* which discussed indemnification and intervention were part of a broader commentary on non-interference and the Monroe Doctrine.[22]

In the nineteenth century, as Alberdi noted, the meaning of the Monroe Doctrine proved mutable and subject to interpretation. It was based on the sections in Monroe's speech formulated by John Adams, who did not think Latin American governments were sufficiently stable, and who rejected the notion that there was any 'community of interests or principles between North and South America', but saw the defence of non-intervention in the Americas as a way to stave off European and Russian claims to these lands.[23] By the middle of the century, Latin Americans conflated it with a range of interventionist ideas, including the concept of Manifest Destiny, a central rhetorical device in the Mexican–American War.[24] It was only in the 1850s, with the rise of filibusterism and the signing of the treaties of Guadalupe Hidalgo and Mesilla, that the United States government embraced Monroe's ideals and sublimated his speech into a doctrine.[25]

Manifest Destiny and the idea of Latin America emerged at the same time to illuminate the ethics of intervention. The same decade saw the intensification of debates regarding the label of 'Latin America' to describe the southern and central regions of the Americas. French authors drew on the term in order to bolster Napoleon III's intervention in Mexico and depict their nation as the head of the 'Latin race'. Calvo would later describe this use of the term Latin America as nothing less than a dangerous 'doctrine'.[26] And yet Calvo had been one of the first Hispanic authors to use the words 'Latin America'.[27] As part of his initial effort to

[22] Carlos Calvo, *Derecho internacional teórico y práctico de Europa y América*. Volume 1 (Paris: Durand et Pedone-Lauriel, 1868), p. 92. For a valuable contextualisation of his thought see Teresa Davis, 'The Ricardian State: Carlos Calvo and Latin America's Ambivalent Origin Story for the Age of Decolonization', *Journal of the History of International Law* 23:1 (2020), pp. 32–51.

[23] Sexton, *Monroe*, pp. 40–53.

[24] See Marcos Reguera, *El imperio de la democracia en América. John O'Sullivan y la formación del concepto de Destino Manifiesto* (Mexico City: Fondo de Cultura Económica) (Forthcoming) and Sexton, *Monroe*, p. 99–103.

[25] Sexton, 'The Monroe Doctrine in an Age of Global History', p. 852. The term 'South America' gained traction in North American political debates through the writings of critics of the United States' participation in the Congress of Panama, who used the expression to establish and foster a clear division between the United States and the Latin American republics. See Sexton, *Monroe*, p. 79.

[26] Calvo, *Derecho*, pp. 90–91.

[27] Carlos Marichal: 'El Nacimiento de los estudios internacionales: Comentarios a las obras de José María Caicedo y Carlos Calvo a mediados del siglo XIX', *Foro Internacional* 221 (2015), pp. 707–736, p. 710. Michel Gobat, in turn, has argued that the term emerged in order to undermine the North American endorsement of 'Manifest Destiny' and the emergence of filibustering, both of which relied on the view that the 'Spanish' element of the Americas was backward, reactionary, and zealous, and thus ought to be civilised. See Michel Gobat, 'The Invention of Latin America: A Transnational History of Anti-Imperialism, Democracy, and Race', *The American Historical Review* 118:5 (2013), pp. 1345–1375.

endorse Napoleon's project for the region, he dedicated his *Colección completa de los tratados*, a collection of treaties negotiated by the Spanish Empire and Latin American countries, to the Emperor.[28] Alberdi was critical of Calvo's decision to endorse French imperial visions and include, in a guide about Latin American diplomacy, early modern treaties and documents that had once been used to 'tyrannise' these states: the inclusion of these texts appeared to imply, in Alberdi's view, that Latin America was still beholden to the 'fulfilment of the obligations' that Spain once had towards other nations.[29]

Alberdi's aversion to international law only grew more intense the more he analysed Calvo's work. After all, Calvo's *Derecho internacional* was published the year that French forces ensured that Maximilian I was crowned Emperor of Mexico—the same year that witnessed the start of one of the bloodiest wars in the nineteenth century, the Paraguayan War. Argentina, Brazil, and Uruguay, in the hope of establishing a favourable 'equilibrium' in the River Plate, waged war against Paraguay: there was not a single mention, Alberdi noted, of the word 'equilibrium' in the writings of the erstwhile representative of Paraguay in Europe.[30]

By contrast, Calvo saw the French and North American imperial spheres of influence as benign mechanisms that served to correct Latin American international law: the opening paragraph of his *Derecho* was a carbon copy of the first passages of Bello's own *Principios*. It noted that 'the lack of a code' that could be applied to the resolution of international conflicts allowed might to trample right.[31] However, Calvo was critical of earlier efforts to harness the law of nations to bind Latin American nations together.[32] The goal of this publication was nothing like Bello's own: Calvo hoped to show Europeans how international law could protect their investments in Latin America.[33]

Bello, the voice of an earlier generation, responded with the publication of a new edition of his *Principios* in Valparaíso and Paris. This edition presented two variants: the Valparaíso edition featured a long section on debts and acknowledged Bello's debt to Calvo's works.[34] In this variant, Bello expanded the section on intervention and clarified his views on loans: debts contracted for the service of the

[28] Marichal, 'El Nacimiento de los estudios internacionales', pp. 723–724.

[29] Juan Bautista Alberdi, 'Estudios', pp. 167–168.

[30] Alberdi, 'Notas', p. 238. The Monroe Doctrine was originally depicted as a way to transcend the European logic of the balance of power; see Sexton, *Monroe*, p. 107. The debate around the Paraguayan War will be discussed in a separate article: see Jones Corredera, in 'The Laws of Debt: The Paraguayan War (1864–1870) and the Drago Doctrine', in Cahen, Castellanos-Jankiewicz, and Simon eds., *The Monroe Doctrine: History, Interpretations, Legacy* (Under review).

[31] Calvo, *Derecho*, pp. i–ii.

[32] Carlos Calvo, *Una página de derecho internacional: o La América del Sur ante la ciencia del derecho de gentes moderno* (Paris: Durand, 1864), pp. 1–2.

[33] Calvo, *Una página*, p. 4.

[34] The Paris edition, by contrast, was an amended version of the 1844 edition and did not include the passages on debts and intervention. Andrés Bello, *Principios de derecho internacional* (Valparaíso: Imprenta de la Capital, 1864) and Andrés Bello, *Principios de derecho internacional* (Paris: Librería de Garnier hermanos, 1864).

state were binding whether or not the funds had been invested in its betterment or squandered. Palmerston's circular, he noted, supported this view.[35] Even the dissolution or colonisation of a nation did not absolve its people from paying 'national debts'.[36]

Like Calvo, Bello continued to argue that disputes had to be settled through local procedures.[37] Unlike Calvo, Bello did acknowledge the role of 'equilibrium' in justifying intervention: he noted that this 'doctrine' could not curtail the territorial expansion of another territory. When said expansion threatened another state, he continued, it would be easy to establish the injustice of aggression. But the finer points on intervention and balance of power remained within 'the sphere of politics and not the Law of Nations'.[38] Bello died a year later: Alberdi, Calvo, and Drago would have to establish the reach of international law and its limits in the face of national politics.

Latin America's debt to European interventions

In his *Derecho internacional*, Calvo discussed the ethics of intervention over debts and indemnifications: he claimed that international law did not legitimise the use of violence to enforce the payment of private claims in America, and claimed that European states had never used this reasoning to legitimate their intervention in one another's affairs. Why, he continued, should European powers act in a different way with regard to American states?[39] It was important, he cautioned, to distinguish between 'intervention' and 'mediation', which was rather like 'arbitration'.[40] Alberdi countered that the only way to remedy the 'insecurity' a dictator like Rosas caused to international investments was through foreign intervention. Hence to deny, on the basis of the Monroe Doctrine, 'the principle that a Europe that fills us with its people, its riches, its commerce cannot intervene in America is practically a frivolity'.[41] As Argentina's history showed, where governments were 'lacking', foreign interventions were 'transformed into a permanent dynamic' that established law and order.[42] The alliance of Rosas' enemies with France had not been a European imperialist initiative, but a local one: Argentina, he explained, stood to gain more than France from the fall of this tyrant.[43] Thanks to the blockade, the

35 Bello, *Principios* pp. 32–33.
36 Bello, *Principios*, p. 140.
37 Frank Griffith Dawson, 'The Influence of Andrés Bello on Latin-American Perceptions of Non-Intervention and State Responsibility', *British Yearbook of International Law* 57:1 (1986), pp. 253–315.
38 Bello, *Principios*, p. 30.
39 Alberdi, 'Notas', p. 92.
40 Calvo, *Derecho*, pp. 92–93.
41 Alberdi, 'Notas', p. 245.
42 Alberdi, 'Notas', p. 245.
43 Alberdi, 'Notas', p. 247.

rights of foreigners were established in South America. In other words, 'the right of the law of nations' was upheld, 'to the degree that' the right of foreign investors 'is the guarantee of progress in that part of the world'.[44]

By the end of his life, Alberdi held a hardened view of the weight of economic interests in international relations.[45] 'Had the modern leaders' of 'South America' studied 'the natural history' of the region instead of 'studying the civil and administrative history of colonial America' they would have realised that '*political economy* and not *international law*' ought to resolve the territorial problems that threatened 'the poor and insolvent states with new wars'.[46] In response to his disenchantment with the law of nations, Alberdi furthered the dissemination of the ideas of the French economist Jean Gustave Courcelle-Seneuil, who fertilised the study of laissez-faire and neoliberal economics in Latin America.[47] Where Alberdi had once hoped that the establishment of the Panama Canal would unite Europe and the Americas through the laws of commerce and lead to the 'tacit derogation' of the Monroe Doctrine, the United States' administration of the canal fostered the escalation of financial intervention in the region.[48] Indeed, interventions associated with the Panama Canal catalysed the development of a new North American foreign policy: 'Dollar Diplomacy'.[49]

Was Calvo's approach the right one? Could international law really protect the weak against the financial interests of the strong? On the one hand, Calvo would prepare a dictionary of international law for the Congress of Berlin, where he betrayed his principles, defended Portugal's imperial interests, and contributed to racialised civilising efforts of colonisation.[50] On the other hand, even during his lifetime, countless Latin American statesmen deployed the Calvo Clause, with mixed results, in defence of their nation's rights. In his later years, Calvo would participate in The Hague Convention of 1899. He then ensured that Drago's writings were discussed by leading authorities in Paris through the publication of their opinions on the topic in the *Revue de Droit International* in 1903.[51] In his commentary

[44] Alberdi, 'Notas', p. 248.

[45] Although Calvo, Payno, and Alberdi had a keen interest in migration; Payno would serve as a Mexican agent of colonisation in Europe. Diana Irina Córdoba Ramírez, *Los derroteros del liberalismo. Las ideas políticas moderadas de Manuel Payno* (Published PhD Thesis) (Mexico City: UNAM, 2004), p. 150.

[46] Alberdi, 'Estudios económicos', p. 462. An issue he had lamented earlier in his life: see Jeremy Adelman, 'Between Order and Liberty: Juan Bautista Alberdi and the Intellectual Origins of Argentine Constitutionalism', *Latin American Research Review* 42:2 (2007), pp. 86-110, p. 92.

[47] See Oscar Mac-Clure, 'El economista Courcelle-Seneuil en el período fundacional de la economía como disciplina en Chile', *Universum (Talca)* 26:1 (2011), pp. 93–108.

[48] Alberdi, *Escritos póstumos*. Volume 3, p. 124.

[49] Lars Schoultz, Beneath *the United States: A History of U.S. Policy Towards Latin America* (Cambridge: Harvard University Press, 2003), p. 209.

[50] Pilar Bernaldo, 'Estanislao Zeballos and the Argentine Doctrine of Human Private Law: A Micro-Social Approach to the History of Private International Law', *Jus Gentium. Journal of International Legal History* 2:5 (2021), p. 5.

[51] Amos S. Hershey, 'The Calvo and Drago Doctrines', *American Journal of International Law* 1:1 (1907), pp. 26–45, p. 37, n. 34. See also Greenman, *State Responsibility and Rebels*, pp. 109–111.

on the Venezuelan debt crisis, formulated during his time as an Argentinian plenipotentiary minister in Paris, Calvo would deliver a message that could have been formulated by Alberdi: Argentina could not assist the United States to the detriment of Europe since European migration and capital fostered the development of Argentina's industry.[52]

Bankruptcy and financial intervention: Drago and Roosevelt

In 1906, in response to disputes over foreign debt in Venezuela, Cuba, and Santo Domingo, and in the aftermath of a number of controversial North American interventions in Central America which aimed to strengthen North American control of the Panama Canal, President Theodore Roosevelt established the Roosevelt Corollary to the Monroe Doctrine.[53] The Corollary stated that the United States would mediate the resolution of disputes between European private creditors and American states.[54] Roosevelt hoped this policy would quiet criticisms that his interventions in the region breached international law.[55] The Corollary granted the United States the capacity to intervene, 'however reluctantly', in states where the ties of 'civilised society' were weakened and private contracts were neglected.[56]

In the midst of the Venezuela debt crisis, Drago wrote a note to Martín García Mérou, Argentina's ambassador in the United States and an admirer of Alberdi, with his views on the blockade that was being used to force Venezuela's repayment of foreign debts.[57] Drago hoped that the publication of his note would serve to

[52] Luis María Drago, *La República Argentina y el caso de Venezuela: Documentos, juicios y comentarios relacionados con la nota pasada al ministro argentino en Washington* (Buenos Aires: Hermanos Coni, 1903), p. 17. Drago and other authors sought to reconcile the ideas of these two men. The Colombian diplomat José María Torres Caicedo, for example, was another influential author and statesman, known today as one of the earliest Latin American officials to use the term Latin America. Adopted by the Mosquera family, he was not just an admirer of Alberdi—he was Alberdi's first biographer, who did not appreciate Caicedo's praise of Calvo—and he reconciled his ambitions for a *Zollverein*, and Calvo's own early criticism of the Monroe Doctrine, in his influential work, *Unión Latino-Americana*. Torres Caicedo's writings and political initiatives would in turn foster a Colombian rapprochement with Spain in the final decades of the century. See Emilio Carilla, 'El primer biógrafo de Alberdi (José María Torres Caicedo), *Boletín del Instituto Caro y Cuervo* 53:1 (1988), pp. 1–11.

[53] On the context behind this reform see Schoultz, *Beneath*, pp. 183–185.

[54] Christopher R. Rossi, *Whiggish International Law: Elihu Root, the Monroe Doctrine, and International Law in the Americas* (Leiden: Brill, 2019), pp. 102–106, p. 147.

[55] Sexton, *Monroe*, pp. 200–208

[56] See Einer David Tah Ayala, 'El principio de no intervención en América Latina: el corolario Roosevelt y la Doctrina Drago', *Intersticios sociales* 21 (2021), pp. 173–195; Matthias Maass, 'Catalyst for the Roosevelt Corollary: Arbitrating the 1902–1903 Venezuela Crisis and Its Impact on the Development of the Roosevelt Corollary to the Monroe Doctrine', *Diplomacy & Statecraft* 20:3 (2009), p. 397; Juan Pablo Scarfi, *The Hidden History of International Law in the Americas: Empire and Legal Networks* (Oxford: Oxford University Press, 2017), p. 72; Alejandro Romagnoli, 'El proyecto historiográfico de Martín García Mérou: Sus lecturas de Alberdi, Echeverría y Sarmiento', *Prismas* 27 (2023), pp. 89–108, pp. 95–98.

[57] Alfredo N. Vivot and Alberto A. Conil Paz, *Homenaje al doctor Luis M. Drago* (Caracas: Oficina Central de Información, 1976), pp. 14–16.

unite American continental interests and counter the demonisation and agglomeration of countries under the banner of 'South America'.[58] The note repeated, word for word, many of the statements Drago had made as Attorney General of Buenos Aires: Drago clarified that there was no need to demand the immediate repayment of a debt at any price and through violent means because 'bleak situations will be resolved, the resources will grow, the common aspirations of equity and justice will prevail and the delayed compromises are fulfilled'.[59] He drew attention to the constitutional history of Argentina and the United States, and explained that the 'compulsive and immediate' demand of debt repayment ruined 'the weakest nations' and led to their loss of sovereignty.[60] In a comment that overlooked the profound tensions between Buenos Aires and the Argentine Confederation, he cited the example of Argentina's repayment of the 1824 British debt throughout the nineteenth century, through the endurance of 'great sacrifices', as a demonstration that there was no need to use intervention to prompt a nation's fulfilment of its foreign dues.[61]

Officials in the United States reacted coldly to his note.[62] In an effort to expand awareness of his ideas in North America, Drago developed his views in an article published in the first issue of the *American Journal of International Law*. Drago's article was titled 'State Loans in their Relation to International Policy'.[63] As he adapted his ideas for a North American audience, Drago built on the logic of his writings on Buenos Aires and Argentina.[64] In his article, Drago argued that there was no tribunal that could settle the matter of debts owed by states to foreign creditors. In contracts between private creditors and a foreign state, reasoned Drago, the government acted as a party subject to the rules of private law, it did not act in 'its character of a sovereign power'.[65]

Drago's view of the state emerged directly from Alberdi's constitutional design for Argentina and Calvo's international law. Indeed, the same prestigious editors and printers that released the first edition of his collection of documents on the Venezuela debt crisis reprinted his intervention on Buenos Aires' debts in a collection titled *Cobro coercitivo de deudas públicas*.[66] According to the editors of the text, his intervention as Attorney General 'could be regarded as a precedent' to his

[58] Drago, *La República Argentina*, p. xi.

[59] Drago, *La República Argentina*, p. 4.

[60] Drago, *La República Argentina*, p. 3.

[61] Drago, *La República Argentina*, pp. 8–9.

[62] Vivot and Paz, *Homenaje*, pp. 21–22.

[63] Luis María Drago, 'State Loans in Their Relation to International Policy', *American Journal of International Law* 1:3 (1907), pp. 692–726.

[64] Note the parallels with Scott on the relationship between sovereignty, the law of nations, and the need for an international court; see Joshua Smeltzer, 'On the Use and Abuse of Francisco de Vitoria: James Brown Scott and Carl Schmitt', *Journal of the History of International Law* 20 (2018), pp. 354–358.

[65] Drago, 'State Loans', pp. 693–694.

[66] Drago, *Cobro*, p. i. Scarfi, *Hidden History*, pp. 1–30. On the Coni printing house see Iván Grondona, *Imprenta Coni. Apuntes para la historia de una imprenta y una dinastía* (Buenos Aires: San Telmo, 1990).

'famous note' to García Mérou since 'the author, fourteen years ago, sustained this doctrine' with regard to 'the internal regime of federal states'.[67]

In his article for the *American Journal of International Law*, Drago explained that in Argentina failures of the state to deliver on contracts were subject to the tribunals that settled matters of private law. When it came to bonds, however, these were 'an exceptional class of obligations'. With regard to this type of contract, the state did act as a sovereign entity: these bonds drawn from public debt were nothing more than 'its currency'. When the government failed to fulfil these contracts, there was 'no tribunal' with a 'jurisdiction' over this class of litigation and it was instead 'created at any moment, spontaneously or through diplomatic intervention'.[68] This principle, argued Drago, was consistent with the ideas set forth in Palmerston's 1848 circular, and was reaffirmed by subsequent British policies.[69] Citing Calvo's ideas, and the international response to his writings, Drago argued that, in the absence of a tribunal that could settle these disputes, they remained the domain of the state which issued public debt.[70]

Drago's argument, as many commentators remarked, left the door open to a state unilaterally declaring default, and this feature led many commentators to reject his proposal.[71] One jurist who cautiously supported Drago's principles was his colleague at The Hague, the Russian humanitarian jurist Fyodor Fyodorovich Martens, who saw the Argentinian's initiative as a means to bolster the new legal institution that he had helped to build, the Permanent Court of Arbitration.[72] This new institution was, in Martens' view, the very tribunal that Drago had been waiting for.[73]

Yet Drago feared there was already an arbiter of American international law. Drago noted that, in light of recent North American diplomacy, '[t]he United States, in order to safeguard the Monroe Doctrine' had assumed 'a sort of supreme magistracy or of superintendence of the South American nations that have fallen behind in the matter of their revenues, making itself the administrator of their finance'. The United States' international police order threatened to erode trust between Latin America and North America: 'This delicate relation would surely contribute to produce estrangement and arouse between the United States and the other nations of America a feeling of envy or jealousy'.[74]

[67] The text was printed with the explicit purpose of influencing the debate on public debts at the diplomatic negotiations at the 1906 Third Pan-American Conference, held in Rio de Janeiro. Drago, *Cobro*, p. 37, n. 1.

[68] Drago, 'State Loans', p. 696.

[69] Drago, 'State Loans', p. 697.

[70] Drago, 'State Loans', p. 703.

[71] Michael Waibel, *Sovereign Defaults before International Courts and Tribunals* (Cambridge: Cambridge University Press, 2011), pp. 35–37.

[72] See Stephen Neff, *Justice among Equals: A History of International Law* (Cambridge: Harvard University Press, 2014), pp. 330–331.

[73] See his measured consideration of Drago's principles in Fyodor Fyodorovich Martens, *Par la justice ver la Paix* (Paris: Charles-Lavauzelle, 1904).

[74] Drago, 'State Loans', p. 722. On Roosevelt and the 'imperialists' see Murphy, *Hemispheric*, p. 142.

In his article, Drago introduced a peculiar term: financial intervention. 'Financial interventions are to-day and have always been a political weapon in the hands of the governments' and the 'right to interfere in the collection of debts' was 'subordinated' to domestic considerations.[75] In line with Calvo's writings, he argued that 'these interventions are always directed against nations that are weak' and 'in no single case has pressure been brought to bear against powerful states'.[76] Drago noted that the Roosevelt Corollary did not give the United States a 'sphere of influence'; instead, it guaranteed the 'commercial independence of the Americas'.[77] But it was not international law that legitimated this commercial independence—as Alberdi had warned, the commercial needs of the strong tilted the scales of power.

The ultimate sin against the Monroe Doctrine, Drago argued, was not default but war over finance. The forceable embargo of a country's assets could lead to war and colonisation: Drago drew the attention of his North American readers to the way in which the United States' failure to assist Juárez's government by temporarily absorbing Mexico's debt to thwart Maximilian's ambitions had led to a French invasion in the Americas.[78] The very threat of conquest, as this example made clear, was incompatible with the principles set out in Monroe's much-vaunted speech: 'violent methods of recovery' of debts 'either represent from the outset, or may ultimately involve, the subordination and conquest which the traditional policy of both Americas forever exclude'.[79] War, he reasoned, could not be used to enforce the repayment of debts for it merely served 'the purpose of a policy of colonisation': it allowed the aggressor to 'gain supremacy or obtain spheres of influence or other advantages pertaining to imperialistic expansion'.[80] Alberdi had pointed to the abolition of capital punishment over bankruptcy and Drago observed that '[t]he law of the Twelve Tables that authorised the creditors to quarter the debtor and to divide his members among themselves cannot obtain for nations within the pale of contemporary civilization'.[81] A common set of global bankruptcy norms would settle financial failure on an international stage.

But the law of the Twelve Tables endured. War over the repayment of public debt was not outlawed. The most consequential impact of Drago's writings was felt at the second Hague Convention of 1907, generally known as the Drago-Porter convention.[82] Thanks to the efforts of the North American jurist Elihu Root, these

[75] Drago, 'State Loans', p. 710.
[76] Drago, 'State Loans', p. 711.
[77] Drago, 'State Loans', p. 715. On the European response to the behaviour of the United States during the Venezuela blockade see Nancy Mitchell, 'The Height of the German Challenge: The Venezuela Blockade, 1902–3', *Diplomatic History* 20:2 (1996), pp. 185–209.
[78] Drago, 'State Loans', pp. 719–720.
[79] Drago, 'State Loans', p. 726.
[80] Drago, 'State Loans', p. 712.
[81] Drago, 'State Loans', p. 705.
[82] And the proliferation of texts on the ethics of foreign debt; see, for example, Jorge Holguín, *Desde cerca: (asuntos colombianos)* (Paris: Ficker, 1908), pp. 307–315.

terms prioritised the use of arbitration and permitted the use of force.[83] Article one of this convention established that contract debts—crucially excluding public debts—did not provide a justification for the use of force. Arbitration, moreover, ought to settle these financial matters.[84] Given the muddled legal nature of many debts that continued to destabilise Latin American economies, this interpretation of intervention was far from useful. Drago voted against this proposal.[85] That same year, during a visit to Buenos Aires, Root was praised by many Argentinians when he endorsed the view that the United States would not use force to demand the repayment of claims from a Latin American government. As he proclaimed this principle, North American armed forces were mobilised in Santo Domingo to enforce the compensation of foreign private claimants.[86] Seven years later, Root would defend the view that the Monroe Doctrine was not a cover for the United States' interventionism a day as US marines reached the Mexican port of Veracruz.[87]

One of the reasons for Root's scepticism of Drago's proposal was his fear that it would turn the world into two 'blocks' made up of creditors and debtors.[88] As a block, debtor countries could unite and leverage their debts against their creditors. US officials ensured that debtor states would instead have to accept arbitration or deal with the consequences of their actions. Whether debts were fair or not—odious or not—would be determined by international courts, and not by national governments. The origins of Root's views on debt dated back to his first diplomatic role when, in the midst of the Spanish–American War, he was asked to establish the legal framework for the governance of Cuba and its relations with the United States. His strategy contributed to the development of the twin logic of humanitarian imperialism and default at the core of the US definition of odious debt.[89] Not only did the Monroe Doctrine, in his view, grant the United States the right to shape its new constitution: it reaffirmed the right of intervention of the United States to ensure the establishment of a republican government in Cuba.[90]

[83] Martha Finnemore, *The Purpose of Intervention: Changing Beliefs about the Use of Force* (Ithaca: Cornell University Press, 2013), p. 37. On Root's approach to Latin America see Scarfi, *Hidden History*, pp. 15–30.

[84] See Rossi, *Whiggish*, p. 60; Wolfgang Benedek, 'Drago-Porter Convention (1907)' in *Max Planck Encyclopedias of International Law* (Oxford: Oxford University Press, 2007) (Online).

[85] Monroe, *Sexton*, p. 236.

[86] Schoultz, *Beneath*, pp. 193–194.

[87] As told by Rossi, *Whiggish*, p. 6.

[88] Vivot and Paz, *Homenaje*, pp. 421–422. Root hoped instead to establish a system based on 'continental consent', see Scarfi, *Hidden History*, p. 3, pp. 15–30.

[89] Scarfi, *Hidden History*, pp. 11–12, p. 50; Anthony Anghie, *Imperialism, Sovereignty and the Making of International Law* (Cambridge: Cambridge University Press, 2012), p. 288. On the Platt Amendment, which turned Cuba into a de facto North American colony see Scarfi, *Hidden History*, pp. 53–54.

[90] Walter LaFeber, 'The Empire of 1898 – and Upheaval', in *The New Cambridge History of American Foreign Relations*. Volume 2 (Cambridge: Cambridge University Press, 2013), pp. 122–147, pp. 143–144. On Monroe and 'imperial anticolonialism' see Sexton, *Monroe*, pp. 5–7, p. 44.

Latin American writers understood that this was another justification for empire. The moral resistance of nations like Mexico and Cuba against this new order would shape American relations for the next century. Mexican officials recovered the ideals of Calvo, Alberdi, and Drago, who had noted that the 'calamity of conquest is masked as a financial intervention', in order to counter the Monroe Doctrine and defend ideas of non-intervention.[91] The American offer of tutelage and an 'arbitrary protectorate', explained Carranza, was a poisoned 'gift' that was imposed on Latin American countries without their consent.[92]

[91] Quoted in Carlos Saavedra Lamas, *Luis María Drago: su obra, proyecciones y trascendencia* (Buenos Aires: Imprenta de la Universidad de Buenos Aires, 1943), p. 13.

[92] Fabia Fernandes Carvalho Veçoso, 'Mexican Post-Revolutionary Foreign Policy and the Spanish Civil War: Legal Struggles over Intervention at the League of Nations', in Kathryn Greenman, Anne Orford, Anna Saunders, and Ntina Tzouvala eds., *Revolutions in International Law: The Legacies of 1917* (Cambridge: Cambridge University Press, 2021), pp. 251–252; Juan Pablo Scarfi, 'Mexican Revolutionary Constituencies and the Latin American Critique of US Intervention', in Greenman, Orford, Saunders, and Tzouvala eds., *Revolutions in International Law*, pp. 229–230.

Conclusion

In the words of Payno, like 'waves at sea that succeeded each other eternally', foreign claims never stopped reaching Latin American shores.[1] The United States ruled the waves and Latin America struggled to stem the tide of intervention. In 1898, the final act of *translatio imperii* saw North America drape its political discourse in the providentialist and progressive principles of the revolution once spearheaded by the Dutch Republic against Spain.[2] *The Atlantic* circulated an article noting that Spaniards still lived 'in the sixteenth century' and a new illustrated edition of Bartolomé de las Casas' *Brevísima Relación de la destrucción de las Indias* was published in New York.[3] This was the fulfilment of a century-long ambition to control Cuba which had once led John Adams to threaten to collaborate with European powers, including Spain, to prevent the island from falling into the hands of a Latin American power.[4]

Following the resolution of the conflict, the perception grew, on both sides of the Atlantic, that a transatlantic cultural *translatio imperii* had taken place. Hispanic American literature had overshadowed the culture of the motherland and a cultural reconciliation was possible.[5] The Spanish government set its sights on a new colonial target: North Africa.[6] But the Spanish–American War of 1898 marked, in the minds of leading Spanish intellectuals, the end of the Spanish

[1] Manuel Payno, *Cuentas, gastos, acreedores y otros asuntos del tiempo de la intervención francesa y del imperio. De 1861 a 1867* (Mexico City: Imprenta de Ignacio Cumplido, 1868), p. 916.

[2] See the quiet splintering of these concepts between North America and the global south in David Armitage, *Civil Wars: A History in Ideas* (New Haven, CT: Yale University Press, 2017), pp. 161–201. For an alternative interpretation of this divide see Claudio Veliz, *The New World of the Gothic Fox: Culture and Economy in English and Spanish America* (Berkeley: University of California Press, 2019).

[3] Henry Charles Lea, 'The Decadence of Spain', *The Atlantic*, July 1989; Tomás Pérez Vejo, *3 Julio de 1898: El significado de una fecha* (Madrid: Taurus, 2020), p. 79.

[4] Sexton, *Monroe*, p. 72.

[5] Rojas, *Las repúblicas de aire. Utopía y desencanto en la revolución de Hispanoamérica* (Madrid: Taurus, 2009), pp. 27–28; Tomás Pérez Vejo, 'La madre por la sangre y la madre intelectual: España y Francia en el imaginario mexicano de mediados del siglo XIX', *Rubrica Contemporánea* 12:23 (2023), pp. 65–83, p. 82. On the broader impact of the war in the formation of Pan-American thought see Dalia Antonia Muller, *Cuban Émigrés and Independence in the Nineteenth-Century Gulf World* (Chapel Hill, NC: University of North Carolina Press, 2018), pp. 210–244; Alejandro Mejías-López, *The Inverted Conquest: The Myth of Modernity and the Transatlantic Onset of Modernism* (Chapel Hill, NC: Vanderbilt University Press, 2009), pp. 85–124. Others rejected the Spanish legacy entirely; for a transversal history of this process see Benedict Anderson, *Under Three Flags: Anarchism and the Anti-colonial Imagination* (London: Verso, 2005).

[6] On the nineteenth-century origins of this imperial ambition see Scott Eastman, *A Missionary Nation: Race, Religion, and Spain's Age of Liberal Imperialism, 1841–1881* (Lincoln: University of Nebraska Press, 2021).

Odious Debt. Edward Jones Corredera, Oxford University Press. © Edward Jones Corredera 2024.
DOI: 10.1093/9780191982200.003.0008

Empire. The foundations of modern Spanish thought were built from the ruins of the war: in the aftermath of the war, the author Emilia Pardo Bazán, in a speech in Paris, coined the term the Black Legend to criticise North American readings of Spain. But Bazán also warned about the rise of its mirror image, a sanitised legend that lionised the colonial violence of Spain's past which would soon be appropriated by General Francisco Franco.[7]

Latin American citizens could not afford to engage in these maudlin lamentations about imperial decline. Cuban officials had to find ways to counter the lack of consideration for their needs among fading and rising empires. The crisis that sparked the initial revolts in Cuba had its origins in Spain's extractive empire—and its perpetual reliance on colonial revenues to mortgage debts. In dire need of funds, mid-nineteenth-century Spain seized the profits generated by trade tariffs in the Philippines and Cuba to finance the administration of the state—and negotiate new loans.[8] This misuse of Cuban rents generated protests and unrest in Havana. In the 1890s, Cuban insurgents destroyed important commercial infrastructure and provoked a serious Spanish military response.[9] Thus began the Cuban War of Independence. Living conditions worsened during the war as a result of the disruptions to agricultural production. This disorder led to a decrease in exports to other nations, including the United States.[10] In the words of a US diplomat, Spanish forces were not efficient enough to quickly quash the rebellion: 'the Spanish Government can only restore peace by producing a graveyard that shall be as large as Cuba herself'.[11] One young British official named Winston Churchill began his journalistic career as a war correspondent in the Caribbean island. Cuba, he warned, was 'between Scylla and Charybdis'. Spain 'overtaxed' its people. The Crown had siphoned off so much of its wealth that its industry had ground to a halt. On the other hand, he reasoned, popular support for the revolution seemed inconsistent and, if successful, the rebels would inherit a 'bankrupt government, torn by race animosities and recurring revolutions'. The United States

[7] Mercedes Tasende, 'Entre la leyenda negra y la leyenda dorada: Emilia Pardo Bazán ante el descubrimiento, la conquista y la colonización española del Nuevo Mundo', *Anales de la literatura española contemporánea* 40:1 (2015), pp. 425–451; 'La conferencia de Doña Emilia Pardo Bazán', *La Época*, 22 May 1899. On the origins, benefits, and drawbacks of the idea of the Black Legend see Edward Jones Corredera, 'When did Spain go to Sleep? An Empire Dead to the World', in Edward Jones Corredera ed., *Supplicant Empires: Searching for the Iberian World in Global History* (Turnhout: Brepols) (Forthcoming).

[8] See Inés Roldán de Montaud, 'Guerra y finanzas en la crisis de fin de siglo: 1895–1900', *Hispania* 57:2 (1997), pp. 611–675, p. 634.

[9] Cuban capital played a significant role in financing the establishment of the first railway in Spain; see Pérez Vejo, *3 Julio de 1898*, pp. 28–29.

[10] John L. Offner, 'McKinley and the Spanish–American War', *Presidential Studies Quarterly* 34:1 (2004), pp. 50–61, pp. 51–52.

[11] Mr. Woodford to Mr. Sherman, 13 September 1897. Papers Relating to the Foreign Relations of the United States, With the Annual Message of the President Transmitted to Congress December 5, 1898. Office of the Historian, Foreign Service Institute. Document 492. (Online).

ought to intervene as a peacemaker: the resolution of a 'speedy peace' was the only way to avoid 'bankruptcy'.[12]

In response to losses incurred by American traders, the United States government intervened in the conflict and framed the liberation of Cuba as a humanitarian intervention.[13] After the defeat of Spain, Cuban officials remained sceptical about the merits of the military presence of the United States on their shores.[14] US periodicals responded to Cuba's desire for independence by castigating its people as ungrateful—they were in need of North American tutelage.[15] Spain, in turn, assumed Cuba's debt as its own and paid a price for its fiscal mismanagement: until 1919, over 35 per cent of the government's yearly budget was spent on liquidating the outstanding payment.[16] Just as citizenship disputes had shaped the diplomatic negotiations of Payno and Alberdi with their Spanish counterparts, the norms of belonging served as a form of penance: Cubans who had fought for Spain and against the revolution were not granted Spanish citizenship. The United States, which received Cuba, Puerto Rico, and the Philippines from Spain, would determine the citizenship status of their peoples.[17] As for those times when 'people ask me what we mean by a stable government in Cuba', Leonard Wood, the US military governor of Cuba, explained, 'I tell them that when money can be borrowed at a reasonable rate of interest and when capital is willing to invest in the Island, a condition of stability will have been reached'.[18]

The North American argument against the assumption of Cuban debts, as scholars have recently shown, turned on the technical, and not moral, argument

[12] Randolph Churchill ed., *Volume 1: Youth, 1874–1896. The Churchill Documents* (Boston: Houghton Mifflin, 2006), pp. 616–621.

[13] On the broader background see Pérez Vejo, *3 Julio de 1898*, pp. 61–102; Lars Schoultz, *Beneath the United States: A History of U.S. Policy Towards Latin America* (Cambridge: Harvard University Press, 2003), pp. 51–57. North American commentators noted the potential geopolitical implications of Spain's large debt. Some believed that since French investors held most of its neighbour's debt, a war might force the participation of France; others argued that its debts prevented it from maintaining an adequate naval force; see Piero Gleijeses, '1898: The Opposition to the Spanish–American War', *Journal of Latin American Studies* 35:4 (2003), pp. 681–719, p. 700, and p. 687.

[14] Louis A. Pérez, Jr., 'Incurring a Debt of Gratitude: 1898 and the Moral Sources of United States Hegemony in Cuba', *The American Historical Review* 104:2 (1999), pp. 356–398, pp. 304–307.

[15] Christopher R. Rossi, *Whiggish International Law: Elihu Root, the Monroe Doctrine, and International Law in the Americas* (Leiden: Brill, 2019), pp. 104–105; Paolo Amorosa, 'Messianic Visions of the United States: International Law, Religion, and the Cuban Intervention, 1898–1917', in Martti Koskenniemi, Mónica García-Salmones Rovira, and Paolo Amorosa eds., *International Law and Religion: Historical and Contemporary Perspectives* (Oxford: Oxford University Press, 2017), pp. 433–454.

[16] Pérez Vejo, *3 Julio de 1898*, p. 31. The government, as scholars have shown, left the door open to renegotiating the matter with the Cuban government; see Inés Roldán de Montaud, 'La deuda pública cubana de la Carta Autonómica al Tratado de París', in Mariano Esteban de Vega, Francisco de Luis Martín, and Antonio Morales Moya eds., *Jirones de hispanidad: España, Cuba, Puerto Rico y Filipinas en la perspectiva de dos cambios de siglo* (Salamanca: University of Salamanca, 2004), pp. 217–246, pp. 244–246.

[17] As noted by Pérez Vejo, *3 Julio de 1898*, pp. 35–36.

[18] Quoted in Sexton, *Monroe*, pp. 217–218.

that Spain had used these loans for its own imperial interests and not for the good of Cuba.[19] It was the perfect foil for an ever-ascending empire that was keen to advocate in favour of the use of foreign private lending as a mechanism that would benefit the recipient state; this was a useful ploy for a nation that would, in the early twentieth century, shift its status from debtor to creditor.[20]

After default

Sack's formulation of odious debt was a strategy of debt repudiation. The Latin American officials under discussion in this book sought to provide instead a set of arguments *against* the prospect of debt repudiation. In their view, when bankruptcy was inevitable, it had to be carried out in a moral way. Fulfilling one's obligations to a community, global or local, remained the way to establish order and peace: creditworthiness, they believed, would lead to more equitable international relations. When this optimism soured, the ire that was once aimed at Spanish tyranny was diverted towards the law of nations and the self-proclaimed foreign arbiters of humanity. It is worth noting that the desacralisation of international law in Latin America emerged before mass secularisation away from the Catholic faith.[21] In the late nineteenth century, it became clear that neither payment nor default would lead to absolution.

In socialism and solidarity, Latin America found new names for redemption. This was the dawn of a new moral economy in the region. In his analysis of conferences which sought to homogenise regional rules of arbitration and establish a Pan-American monetary union, the Cuban poet and revolutionary José Martí, who led and died for the Cuban struggle against Spain, noted that the United States lacked the roots of 'communicative and human liberty' that encouraged a people to 'redeem each other'.[22] The United States, in Martí's view, had supported slavery, seized Mexican lands, and defended non-intervention in the Americas while it actively prevented Latin American states from freeing Cuba from Spain.[23] Martí framed his writings on solidarity, justice, the education of indigenous peoples,

[19] One of the many sharp insights found in the excellent article written by Sarah Ludington, Mitu Gulati, and Alfred L. Brophy, 'Applied Legal History: Demystifying the Doctrine of Odious Debts', *Theoretical Inquiries in Law* 11 (2010), pp. 247–281, pp. 256–257; Mitu Gulati, Sarah Ludington, and Arthur Mark Weisburd, 'A Convenient Untruth: Fact and Fantasy in the Doctrine of Odious Debts (with Response: Reflections on "A Convenient Untruth")', *Virginia Journal of International Law* 48:3. Duke Law School Legal Studies Paper No. 174, p. 629, n. 130.

[20] Scott Nearing and Joseph Freeman, *Dollar Diplomacy: A study in American Imperialism* (New York: Modern Reader Paperbacks, 1969), p. 12.

[21] Eloísa Martín, 'Peter Berger's Theory of Secularization in Latin America: The Two Sacred Canopies', *Journal of the American Academy of Religion* 85:4 (2017), pp. 1137–1146.

[22] The Spanish term 'redención' means both political liberation and salvation. José Martí, 'Nuestra América', *Obras Completas*. Volume 6 (Havana: Editorial de ciencias sociales, 1991), p. 47.

[23] Martí, 'Nuestra América', pp. 47–49.

and the Cuban struggle against Spain through the language of absolution: the war against Spain was a necessary war because man would find 'redemption in the freedom of the *patria*'.[24]

In the twentieth century, a range of Latin American leaders stopped 'seizing the bread from their children's mouths to pay whatever they can to foreign creditors', as Payno once phrased it, and dismissed their obligations towards predatory lenders in order to fulfil the contract with their people.[25] In a binary choice, the prioritisation of the nation's well-being became a rallying cry for the Latin American left. Latin American Marxism granted revolutionary authors a new way to speak about commutative justice, solidarity, and the moral economy. It generated new transvernal and transnational ideological connections through the idea of the proletariat and its international organisations.[26] This totalising discourse replaced earlier terms and debates. In the 1920s, the Peruvian philosopher and admirer of Bolívar, José Carlos Mariátegui, would emerge as the most creative Marxist Latin American thinker of the early twentieth century: as he noted, Latin American states remained 'politically independent and economically colonial' nations: their 'miners' were 'vassals' of European 'capitalists'.[27] Yet emancipation was possible: as Engels had shown, its first stage was 'The Protestant Reformation', which socialists had to implement in Latin America.[28] Recent changes, he continued, such as President Woodrow Wilson's ineffective defence of self-determination, had catalysed the emergence of calls for world revolution.[29] As part of this universalist outlook, Mariátegui analysed Keynes' writings on World War I reparations and the 'allied debt'; whatever parallels there were between the ideas of the British political economist and nineteenth-century Latin American debates were disregarded and replaced by a Marxist framework. In his reading of power relations, Mariátegui noted that the difference that Keynes had drawn between 'political debts' that ought to be consolidated since they had been drawn for the good of a united cause, and 'commercial debts', which were of secondary importance and ought to be paid

[24] José Martí, *Correspondencia con el general Máximo Gómez* (Havana: Editorial de Ciencias Sociales, 1977), p. 28. The scholarship on Martí's thought is extensive. On his life and his views on redemption see Alfred J. López, *José Martí: A Revolutionary Life* (Austin: University of Texas Press, 2014), pp. 153–185.

[25] Payno, *México y sus cuestiones*, p. 41.

[26] For an overview of the topic see Andrés Estefane and Luis Thielemann, 'Latin American Marxism and the Atlantic', *Oxford Research Encyclopedia of Latin American History* (Online). On the translation and dissemination of Marx's writings in Latin America see Horacio Tarcus, *La biblia del proletariado. Traductores y editores de El Capital* (Buenos Aires: Siglo XXI, 2018). On the conceptual challenges behind this reception see José Arico, *Marx y América Latina* (Mexico City: FDCE, 2009).

[27] José Carlos Mariátegui, *Historia de la crisis mundial: conferencias, años 1923 y 1924* (Lima: Amauta, 1971), p. 130. On Mariátegui's philosophy see Mike González, *In the Red Corner: The Marxism of José Carlos Mariátegui* (London: Haymarket, 2019).

[28] José Carlos Mariátegui, *Siete ensayos de interpretación de la realidad peruana*. Prólogo de Aníbal Quijano. Notas, cronología y bibliografía de Elizabeth Garrels (Caracas: Fundación Biblioteca Ayacucho, 2007), p. 148.

[29] José Carlos Mariátegui, *La escena contemporanea* (Lima: Minerva, 1925), p. 49, p. 252.

separately, was irrelevant. Europe would require an extension of the Dawes Plan however its nations distributed these debts. Even the Old World would soon become a debtor to the United States.[30]

A range of private and public North American financial initiatives in Central and Latin America, coupled with military interventions in its political affairs, placed war and debt at the forefront of inter-American relations. As Latin American representatives succeeded in negotiating fairer regional relations through the law of nations, the rise of international financial mechanisms allowed the United States to increase its influence over Latin America and, in particular, Central America. In Salvador Allende's Chile, the jurist Eduardo Novoa Monreal emerged as a moral voice and advocated the nationalisation of the nation's main resource, copper, as a way to avoid foreign debt traps.[31]

But soon the Washington Consensus emerged as a set of proposals for fiscal reform in Latin America.[32] In response, regional trade associations, such as the Latin American Free Trade Association, fostered the rise of stronger forms of regional cooperation, such as Mercosur. Broader debates associated with the Cold War, and failures of the IMF and other North American institutions in the region, intensified tensions over trade with North America. Towards the end of the twentieth century, the IMF contemplated the impossible: its officials held discussions about providing debt relief to Latin American states. Instead, the Brady Bonds delivered debt write-downs.[33] Today, some Latin American states see dollarisation as a way to stabilise the region's economies.[34]

Throughout their history, Latin Americans lent their trust to the Spanish Crown's clemency, the law of nations, and the promise of American unity. The disenchantment with each of these forms of obligation led to a prioritisation of economic visions and material interests. Much of the world in turn continues to see Latin America as El Dorado. When I presented drafts of this book at European universities, audience members would approach me once the discussion had ended to ask about potentially overlooked investment opportunities in Latin America. I would think back to Alberdi's words about the European lack of interest in its people and the fascination with the land and the exports that Latin America could

[30] Mariátegui, *La escena*, pp. 84–96.

[31] See Eduardo Novoa Monreal, *La batalla del cobre. Comentarios y documentos* (Santiago de Chile: Quimantú, 1972); Fabia Fernandes Carvalho and João Roriz, 'Critical Legal Theory Situated: The Work of Eduardo Novoa Monreal as the Legal Adviser of Salvador Allende', in Wanshu Cong and Francisco-José Quintana eds., *Remembering to Reimagine: A Symposium on Salvador Allende, Unfulfilled Promise, and the Future of International Law*. National University of Singapore, CIL Dialogues (Online).

[32] John Williamson, 'A Short History of the Washington Consensus', in Narcís Serra and Joseph E. Stiglitz ed., *The Washington Consensus Reconsidered: Towards a New Global Governance* (Oxford: Oxford University Press, 2008), pp. 14–30.

[33] Edwin M. Truman, 'The Road to the 1980s Write-downs of Sovereign Debt', *Financial History Review* 28:3 (2021), pp. 218–299.

[34] Eric Helleiner, 'Dollarization Diplomacy: US Policy Towards Latin America Coming Full Circle?', *Review of International Political Economy* 10:3 (2003), pp. 406–429.

produce. Latin America may well be the 'forgotten continent'. But while its peoples and their histories are forgotten, its resources are not.[35]

China's influence in Latin America generates a broader question for policy makers and international lawyers: what type of obligations and responsibilities ought to be at the core of global relations?[36] The myth of China's debt traps has now been debunked, and warnings of a Chinese takeover of financial interests in Latin America are growing louder, but they are overblown.[37] There is however no doubt that, in a world ruled by numbers, China offers Latin America leverage. Just as Mexico leveraged the offers of the United States to generate better terms in its commercial and financial exchanges with European states, we may now see Latin American states leverage China's interest in the regions to renegotiate the terms of engagement with the US. It will be the forgotten actor—the people of Latin America—who will have to decide, based on history or expediency, what they owe to the rest of the world. It will be for them to choose whether to follow the neoliberalism of Rivadavia and Courcelle-Seneuil, whether to shoulder new obligations, whether to prioritise the needs of the people, or whether to pursue constitutional reform.[38] This history would suggest that to prioritise the needs of its own would be, after all, to democratise commutative justice and embrace Adams' reformation: to tend to those debts that have been accrued with the consent and for the benefit of the people.

[35] Michael Reid, *Forgotten Continent: A History of the New Latin America* (New Haven: Yale University Press, 2017).

[36] Whether an answer can be agreed across regional interpretations of international law is not clear. On regional systems of international law see Anthea Roberts, *Is International Law International?* (Oxford: Oxford University Press, 2017).

[37] Deborah Brautigam and Meg Rithmire, 'The Chinese "Debt Trap" is a Myth', *The Atlantic*, 6 February 2021. See the excellent "China-Latin America Finance Databases" in Rebecca Ray and Margaret Myers, 'Chinese Loans to Latin America and the Caribbean Database', *Washington and Boston: Inter-American Dialogue and Boston University Global Development Policy Center* (2024) (Online).

[38] Much of the more recent literature on neoliberalism, including the work by Slobodian, has almost entirely overlooked Latin American debates on neoliberalism and nineteenth-century Latin American history. See Quinn Slobodian, *Globalists: The End of Empire and the Birth of Neoliberalism* (Cambridge: Harvard University Press, 2018); Quinn Slobodian and Dieter Plehwe eds., *Market Civilizations: Neoliberals East and South* (Princeton: Princeton University Press, 2022).

Bibliography

Selected periodicals, prints, and manuscripts

Argentina

Biblioteca Nacional Mariano Moreno, Buenos Aires

Drago, Luis María, *El poder marital* (Buenos Aires: El Diario, 1882)
Drago, Martin Luis, *Fallecimiento del doctor Luis María Drago* (Buenos Aires: [s.n.], 1928)
Font, Miguel J. ed., *La mujer: encuesta feminista argentina* (Buenos Aires: Imp. Costa Hnos., 1921)
Saavedra Lamas, Carlos, *Luis María Drago: su obra, proyecciones y trascendencia* (Buenos Aires: Imprenta de la Universidad de Buenos Aires, 1943)

Colombia

Archivo General de la Nación, Bogotá

Hacienda Pública: SR.8,V.9,R.40
Ministerio de Exteriores, DT2, Box 15/508
Ministerio de Exteriores. DT2. Box: 731

Biblioteca Nacional de Colombia

Acevedo Sánchez, María Josefa, *Ensayo sobre los Deberes de los Casados* (Bogotá: Torres Amaya, 1857)
Breve examen del cuaderno publicado en Popayan con el titulo de Opinion de un granadino sobre la division de la deuda colombiana etc. (Bogotá: J. A. Cualla, 1836)
Correo del Orinoco. Numbers 7, 11, 14, 19, 96
Debates de la Cámara del Senado de la República de Colombia del día 4 de febrero del año décimo quinto (Cartagena: Juan Antonio Calvo, 1826)
Gaceta de Cartagena. Number 16
Gaceta de Colombia. Numbers 15, 16, 17, 46, 214, 278, 297, 446, 487
La Miscelánea. Number 24, 26 February 1826
Mosquera, Joaquín, *Opinión de un granadino sobre la división de la deuda colombiana entre los tres Estados de Nueva Granada, Venezuela y Ecuador* (Popayán: Manuel Córdoba, 1836)
Examen de las observaciones del señor senador Joaquín Mozquera sobre el empréstito decretado por la Cámara de Representantes en 28 de abril de 1825 (Bogotá: Impreso por F. M. Stokes, 1826)
Observaciones sobre el empréstito decretado por la Honorable Cámara de Representantes de la República de Colombia, en su decreto de 28 de abril de 1825 (Bogotá: F. M. Stokes, 1825)
Torres, Jerónimo, *Observaciones políticas dirijidas a la gran Convención de Colombia, por el ciudadano que las subscribe* (Bogotá: Imprenta de Nicomedes Lora, 1828)
Opinión del Senador que suscribe sobre la obligación que tiene la República de reconocer los capitales recibidos a censo en este país por el Gobierno antiguo (Bogotá: Imprenta de Salazar, 1826)
Suplemento a la Gaceta de Colombia. Number 246

France

Bibliothèque nationale de France, Paris

Alberdi, Juan Bautista, *España y las repúblicas de la América del Sur* (Paris: J. Kugelmann, 1861)
Martens, Fyodor Fyodorovich, *Par la justice ver la Paix* (Paris: Charles-Lavauzelle, 1904)

Germany

Bayerische Staatsbibliothek Digital Library, Munich

Diario de las actas y discusiones de las cortes: Legislatura de los años de 1820 y 1821. Volumes 1, 5, 6, 10, 11, 13, 17, 18

Mexico

Colegio de México, Mexico City

Constitución Federal de 1824: crónicas. Two volumes (Mexico City: Secretaría de Gobernación, 1974).

Mateos, Juan Antonio, *Historia parlamentaria de los congresos mexicanos de 1821 a 1857.* Volumes 1–2, 4, and Appendix to Volume 2 (Mexico City: J. V. Villada, 1882)

Payno, Manuel, *La reforma social en España y México: apuntes históricos* (Mexico City: Pámpano Servicios Editoriales, 2013)

Tratado de la propiedad: ensayo de un estudio del derecho romano y del derecho público y constitucional en lo relativo a la propiedad (Mexico City: I. Cumplido, 1869)

United Kingdom

Bodleian Library, Oxford University, Oxford

Diario de sesiones de la Junta de Representantes de la Provincia de Buenos Aires (1 May–23 December 1822) (Buenos Aires: Imprenta de la Independencia, 1823)

Spain, its Government and Policy, its Loans and Resources Considered, with Reference to the Claims of its Foreign Creditors (London: Ridgway, Piccadilly, 1839)

British Library, London

Cipriano de Mosquera, Tomás ed., *Memorias sobre la vida del Libertador Simon Bolívar* (New York: S. W. Benedict, 1853)

El Emigrado observador. Numbers 2, 3

Esteva, José Ignacio, *A los españoles ociosos en Londres. Un mexicano ocupado contestando al número 20 de su periódico* (Mexico City: Rivera, 1826)

Ocios de Españoles Emigrados. Numbers 7, 20, 28

The speech of Viscount Palmerston, in reply to the motion of Lord George Bentinck, M.P., for an address to Her Majesty, in favour of the Spanish Bondholders, tried and compared with the fundamental law of this country, as laid down by Blackstone and Locke, and with the principles and rules of Grotius and Vattel (London: Royal Exchange, 1848)

Institute of Latin American Studies, London

Reverente Súplica al ex-rey Carlos Cuarto pidiéndole a su hijo adoptivo el infante don Francisco de Paula para coronarle en las provincias del Rio de la Plata. Por los vasallos del mismo d. Manuel Velgrano y Bernardino Rivadavia (Buenos Aires: Librería Argentina, 1825)

Spain

Biblioteca Nacional de España, Madrid

Exposición presentada á las Cortes por los diputados de ultramar en la sesión de 25 de junio de 1821: sobre el estado actual de las provincias de que son representantes, y medios convenientes para su definitiva pacificación, con una noticia de los trámites que la precedieron y motivaron (Madrid: García y Campot, 1821)

Manifiesto que hace a la nación española el teniente general don Pablo Morillo (Madrid: Imprenta de la Calle de Greda, 1821)

'Reflexiones sobre las deudas del Rey; si estas son del Rei [sic] o del Reino', in *Papeles referentes a las deudas de la Real Hacienda en tiempos de Fernando VI y de Carlos III* (c. 1756–1768). MSS/13814. pp. 1–157

Tornel y Mendívil, José María, *Breve reseña histórica de los acontecimientos mas notables de la nación mexicana: desde el año de 1821 hasta nuestros dias* (Mexico City: Cumplido, 1852)

Biblioteca de la Agencia Española de Cooperación Internacional para el Desarrollo (AECID), Madrid

Riva-Agüero, José de la, *Manifestación histórica y política de la revolución de la América y mas especialmente de la parte que corresponde al Perú, y Rio de la Plata* (Buenos Aires: Expositos, 1818)

Printed and Secondary Sources

Acevedo, Josefa, *A Treatise on Domestic Economy, For the Use of Mothers and Housewives.* Translated by Catherine Davies and Sarah Sánchez (Nottingham: CCCP, 2007).

Acevedo Sánchez, María Josefa, *Ensayo sobre los Deberes de los Casados* (Bogotá: Torres Amaya, 1857)

Acosta, Alberto, *La deuda eterna: una historia de la deuda externa ecuatoriana* (Quito: Libresa, 1990)

Actas del Congreso de Angostura 1819–1820 (Bogotá: Biblioteca de la Presidencia de la República, 1988)

Adelman, Jeremy ed., *Colonial Legacies: The Problem of Persistence in Latin American History* (New York: Routledge, 1999)

Republic of Capital: Buenos Aires and the Legal Transformation of the Atlantic World (Stanford: Stanford University Press, 1999)

Sovereignty and Revolution in the Iberian Atlantic (Princeton: Princeton University Press, 2006)

'Between Order and Liberty: Juan Bautista Alberdi and the Intellectual Origins of Argentine Constitutionalism', *Latin American Research Review* 42:2 (2007), pp. 86-110

Agüero, Alejandro, '¿Provincias o estados? El concepto de provincia y el primer constitucionalismo provincial rioplatense: Un enfoque ius-histórico', *Revista de Historia Americana y Argentina* 54:1 (2019), pp. 137–175

Aguilar Rivera, José Antonio, 'Memoria del cogido imposible: Cádiz y el experimento constitucional atlántico', in Roberto Breña ed., *Cádiz a debate: Actualidad, contexto y legado* (Mexico City: Colegio de México, 2014), pp. 107-130

Alamán, Lucas, *Esposición que hace la Cámara de diputados del Congreso General el apoderado del Duque de Terranova y Monteleone, Sobre las proposiciones presentadas por los señores diputados Don Matías Quintana y Don Miguel Cañedo, relativas á las propiedades que dicho Duque tiene en esta República* (México: José Fernández, 1828)

Disertaciones sobre la historia de la república Megicana, desde la época de la conquista que los españoles hicieron hasta la independencia. Volume 3 (Mexico City: Lara, 1849)

Historia de Méjico desde los primeros movimientos que prepararon su independencia en el año 1808 hasta la época presente. Volume 5 (Mexico City: Lara, 1852)

El reconocimiento de nuestra independencia por España y la unión de los países hispano-americanos. With an introduction by Antonio de la Peña y Reyes (Mexico City: Publicaciones de la Secretaría de Relaciones Exteriores, 1924)

Alberdi, Juan Bautista, *Elementos del derecho público provincial para la República Argentina* (Valparaíso: Mercurio, 1853)

Sistema económico y rentístico de la confederación argentina según su Constitución de 1853 (Valparaíso: Mercurio, 1854)

Condiciones de la union y consolidacion de la República Argentina (Besancon: José Jacquin, 1862)

Diplomacia de Buenos Aires y los intereses americanos y europeos en el Plata con motivo del reciente tratado entre España y la República Argentina (Buenos Aires: Imprenta Hispanoamericana de Cosson, 1864)

La crisis de 1866, ó, Los efectos de la guerra de los aliados en el órden económico y político de las repúblicas del Plata (Paris: Impr. de Dubuisson, 1866)

El Imperio del Brasil ante la democracia de América. Colección de los últimos escritos dados á luz por Don J. B. Alberdi (Paris: Imprenta A.-E. Rochette, 1869)

Obras completas. Volume 6 (Buenos Aires: La Tribuna Nacional, 1886)

De los abusos y victimas del crédito publico sud-americano (Montevideo: El Siglo, 1876)
'Fragmento preliminar al estudio del derecho', in *Obras completas*. Volume 1 (Buenos Aires: La Tribuna Nacional, 1886), pp. 103-142
'Memoria en que el Ministro de la Confederación Argentina en las cortes de Inglaterra: Francia y España da cuenta a su gobierno de los trabajos de su misión, desde 1855 hasta 1860', *Obras completas*. Volume 6 (Buenos Aires: La Tribuna Nacional, 1886), pp. 5–150
'Escritos Económicos', in Juan Bautista Alberdi, *Escritos póstumos*. Volume 1 (Buenos Aires: Imprenta Europa, Moreno, y Defensa, 1895).
'Estudios sobre la colección de tratados de D. Carlos Calvo', in *Escritos póstumos*. Volume 3 (Buenos Aires: Imprenta Europea, Moreno, y Defensa, 1896), pp. 201–280
'Notas para el juicio crítico del "Derecho internacional" de C. Calvo', in *Escritos póstumos. Política exterior de la república argentina. Bibliografía*. Volume 3: (Buenos Aires: Imprenta Europa, Moreno, y Defensa, 1896), pp. 137-280.
Escritos póstumos. Volumes 1 and 3 (Buenos Aires: Imprenta Europea, 1895–1896)
Diplomacia argentina y americana (Buenos Aires: Librería 'La Facultad', 1920)
Sobre la conveniencia de un congreso general americano (Mexico City: UNAM, 1979)
Bases y puntos de partida para la organización política de la República Argentina. Prólogo de Matías Farías (Buenos Aires: Biblioteca del Congreso de la Nación, 2017)
El crimen de la guerra (Buenos Aires: Cadal, 2020)
Albiez-Wieck, Sarah, 'Indigenous Migrants Negotiating Belonging: *Peticiones de cambio de fuero* in Cajamarca, Peru, 17th–18th centuries', *Colonial Latin American Review* 26:4 (2017), pp. 483–508
Alcántara de Somellera, Pedro, *Principios de Derecho Civil*. Noticia preliminar de Jesús H. Paz (Buenos Aires: Instituto de Historia del Derecho Argentino, 1939)
Alejandro de Jesús, Amaro Valencia, '¿Memoria, olvido y perdón? Vaivenes discursivos en la construcción de la historia oficial sobre la Intervención Francesa y el Segundo Imperio Mexicano', *Estudios de historia moderna y contemporánea de México* 64 (2022), pp. 43–68
Alfaro, Eloy, *Ecuador: Deuda Gordiana* (Panama: Imprenta Ramos, 1891); *Deuda Goridiana* (Quito: Imprenta Nacional, 1896)
El ferrocarril trasandino: cartas del Gral. Don Eloy Alfaro (Quito: Imprenta de 'El Tiempo', 1903)
Al-Hussein, Falah Hassan Abed, 'Los cambios y el mercado del dinero medinense', in Eufemio Lorenzo Sanz eds., *Historia de Medina del Campo y su tierra*. Volume 2 (Valladolid: Caja de Ahorros Provincial de Valladolid, 1986), pp. 67–92
Almarza Villalobos, Ángel Rafael, 'Rousseau, Bolívar y las revoluciones de Venezuela', in Gabriel Entin ed., *Rousseau en Iberoamérica* (Buenos Aires: SB Editores, 2018), pp. 121–136
Alonso Torres, Gemma, 'Las relaciones hispano-británicas durante el reinado de Isabel II', *Espacio, Tiempo y Forma, Serie V* (1995), pp. 85–110
Alvarado Luna, Patricio A., 'Reorganizando las nuevas fronteras republicanas: Perú y Bolivia (1826–1836)', *Revista Ciencia y Cultura* 24:44 (2020), pp. 37–62
Álvarez Cuartero, Izaskun and Julio Sánchez Gómez eds., *Visiones y revisiones de la independencia americana: México, Centroamérica y Haití* (Salamanca: Ediciones Universidad de Salamanca, 2005)
Álvarez Macotela, Samantha, *El peso de nuestro descontento la diplomacia británica en torno al paso interoceánico por el istmo de Tehuantepec 1847–1858* (Mexico City: Instituto Mora, 2003)
Amorosa, Paolo, 'Messianic Visions of the United States: International Law, Religion, and the Cuban Intervention, 1898–1917', in Martti Koskenniemi, Mónica García-Salmones Rovira, and Paolo Amorosa eds., *International Law and Religion: Historical and Contemporary Perspectives* (Oxford: Oxford University Press, 2017), pp. 433–454
Rewriting the History of the Law of Nations: How James Brown Scott Made Francisco de Vitoria the Founder of International Law (Oxford: Oxford University Press, 2019)
Anderson, Benedict, *Under Three Flags: Anarchism and the Anti-colonial Imagination* (London: Verso, 2005)
Anderson, Gary A., *Sin: A History* (New Haven: Yale University Press, 2009)
Andrien, Kenneth J., *Andean Worlds: Indigenous History, Culture, and Consciousness under Spanish Rule, 1532–1825* (Albuquerque, University of New Mexico Press, 2001)

Angelis, Pedro de, *Ensayo historico sobre la vida del Exmo. Sr. D. Juan Manuel de Rosas, Gobernador y Capitan General de la Provincia de Buenos Aires* (Buenos Aires: Imprenta del Estado, 1830)

Anghie, Anthony, *Imperialism, Sovereignty and the Making of International Law* (Cambridge: Cambridge University Press, 2012)

Anna, Timothy, *Spain and the Loss of America* (London: University of Nebraska Press, 1983)

The Mexican Empire of Iturbide (Lincoln: University of Nebraska Press, 1990)

Forging Mexico, 1821-7835 (Lincoln: University of Nebraska Press, 1998)

Annino, Antonio et al. eds., *El momento gaditano: La Constitución en el orbe hispánico (1808–1826)* (Madrid: Congreso de los Diputados, 2011)

Antonia Muller, Dalia, *Cuban Émigrés and Independence in the Nineteenth-Century Gulf World* (Chapel Hill: University of North Carolina Press, 2018)

Anzoátegui, Víctor Tau, *Formación del Estado Federal Argentino, 1829–1852: la intervención del gobierno de Buenos Aires en los asuntos nacionales* (Buenos Aires: Perrot, 1965)

Arango, Carlos Camacho, Margarita Garrido Otoya, and Daniel Gutiérrez Ardila eds., *Paz en la República. Colombia, siglo XIX* (Bogotá: Universidad Externado de Colombia, 2018)

Araujo, Ana Lucia, *Reparations for Slavery and the Slave Trade: A Transnational and Comparative History* (New York: Bloomsbury Academic, 2017)

Ardila, Daniel Gutiérrez, 'Colombia y Haití: historia de un desencuentro (1819–1831)', *Secuencia* 81 (2011), pp. 67–93

El reconocimiento de Colombia: diplomacia y propaganda en la coyuntura de las restauraciones, 1819–1831 (Bogotá: Universidad Externado de Colombia, 2012)

'Un sistema para la América independiente', in Alfredo Ávila, Jordana Dym, and Erika Pani eds., *Las declaraciones de independencia: Los textos fundamentales de las independencias de americanas* (Mexico City: Colegio de México, 2013), pp. 441–478

Ardila, Daniel Gutiérrez and Matthias Lok, 'La experiencia de la Restauración a través del lente ultramarino: estudio comparado de la supervivencia política en los Países Bajos y el Nuevo Reino de Granada (1810–1820)', *Revista Universitaria de Historia Militar* 7:15 (2018), pp. 16–38

Argudín, María Luna, 'La épica de la derrota: *Apuntes para la historia de la guerra entre México y los Estados Unidos*', *Fuentes Humanísticas* 54 (2017), pp. 131–145

Argüelles, Agustín, *Elementos de la ciencia de hacienda* (London: Mackintosh, 1825)

Breve respuesta á la representacion de los Comerciantes de Londres (London: Caldero, 1829)

Discurso preliminar a la Constitución de 1812 (Madrid: Centro de Estudios Constitucionales, 1981)

Aristotle, *Politics*. Edited and translated by H. Rackham (Cambridge: Harvard University Press, 1944)

Armitage, David, 'The Declaration of Independence and International Law', *William & Mary Quarterly* 3:54 (2002), pp. 39–64

The Declaration of Independence: A Global History (Cambridge, MA: Harvard University Press, 2007)

Foundations of Modern International Thought (Cambridge: Cambridge University Press)

Civil Wars: A History in Ideas (New Haven, CT: Yale University Press, 2017)

Arico, José, *Marx y América Latina* (Mexico City: FDCE, 2009)

Armas, Mayela, 'Venezuela's Maduro Seeks to Revive Stalled Debt Talks, Bondholders Unimpressed', *Reuters*, 30 September 2019

Autobiografía del general José Antonio Páez. Volume 1 (New York: Impr. Ponce de León, 1878)

Aveni, Anthony F., 'The Measure, Meaning, and Transformation of Aztec Time and Calendars', in Deborah L. Nichols and Enrique Rodríguez-Alegría eds., *The Oxford Handbook of the Aztecs* (Oxford: Oxford University Press, 2017), pp. 107–116.

Bagú, Sergio, *El plan económico del grupo Rivadaviano (1811–1827). Su sentido y sus contradicciones, sus proyecciones sociales, sus enemigos* (Santa Fe: Universidad Nacional del Litoral, 1966)

Baily, Samuel L., 'Sarmiento and Immigration: Changing Views on the Role of Immigration in the Development of Argentina', in Joseph T. Criscenti ed., Sarmiento *and his Argentina* (London: Lynne Rienner Publishers, 1993), pp. 131–142

Barbeyrac, Jean, *Le droit de la guerre, et de la paix*. Par Hugues Grotius. Nouvelle traduction, par Jean Barbeyrac. Volume 1 (Amsterdam: Pierre de Coup, 1724)

Barcena, Manuel, *Manifiesto al mundo la justicia y la necesidad de la independencia de la Nueva España* (Puebla: Imprenta Liberal de Moreno Hermanos, 1821)

Barragan, Yesenia, *Freedom's Captives: Slavery and Gradual Emancipation on the Colombian Black Pacific* (Cambridge: Cambridge University Press, 2021)

Barrel, Callum, *History and Historiography in Classical Utilitarianism, 1800–1865* (Cambridge: Cambridge University Press, 2021)

Barros Charlín, Raymundo, 'Notas sobre Andrés Bello y América Latina', *Estudios Internacionales* 15:57 (198), pp. 104–124

Bartels, Sarah, *The Devil and the Victorians: Supernatural Evil in Nineteenth-Century English Culture* (London: Routledge, 2021)

Baskes, Jeremy, *Indians, Merchants, and Markets A Reinterpretation of the Repartimiento and Spanish-Indian Economic Relations in Colonial Oaxaca, 1750–1821* (Stanford: Stanford University Press, 2000)

Staying Afloat: Risk and Uncertainty in Spanish Atlantic World Trade, 1760–1820 (Redwood: Stanford University Press, 2013)

Bautista y Lugo, Gibran Irving Israel, *Castigar o perdonar: El gobierno de Felipe IV ante la rebelión de 1624 en México* (Unpublished PhD thesis) (México City: UNAM, 2014)

Bazant, Jan, 'La familia Alamán y los descendientes del Conquistador: 1850–1907', *Historia Mexicana* 26:1 (1976), pp. 48–69

Historia de la deuda exterior de México, 1823–1946 (Mexico City: El Colegio de México, 1968)

'Los bienes de la familia de Hernán Cortés y su venta por Lucas Alamán', *Historia Mexicana* 19:2 (1969), pp. 228–247

Becker Lorca, Arnulf, 'International Law in Latin America or Latin American International Law? Rise, Fall, and Retrieval of a Tradition of Legal Thinking and Political Imagination', *Harvard International Law Journal* 47:1 (2006), pp. 283–305

Mestizo International Law: A Global Intellectual History 1842–1933 (Cambridge: Cambridge University Press, 2015)

Bedjaoui, Mohammed, *Ninth Report on Succession of States in respect of matters other than treaties*. United Nations Doc. A/CN.4/301. Volume 2. Part 1 (New York: Yearbook of the International Law Commission, 1977)

Bell, Duncan, 'What is Liberalism?', *Political Theory* 42:6 (2014), pp. 682–715

'Escape Velocity: Ancient History and the Empire of Time', in *Reordering the World: Essays on Liberalism and Empire* (Princeton: Princeton University Press, 2016), pp. 119–147

Bello, Andrés, *Principios de derecho internacional* (Valparaíso: Imprenta de la Capital, 1864)

Principios de derecho internacional (Paris: Librería de Garnier hermanos, 1864)

Obras completas de don Andrés Bello. Volume 10 (Santiago de Chile: Ramírez, 1886)

'Investigaciones sobre la influencia de la Conquista y del sistema colonial de los españoles en Chile', in *Obras completas de Andrés Bello*. Volume 23: *Temas de historia y geografía* (Caracas: Ministerio de Educación, 1957), pp. 153–173

Benedek, Wolfgang, 'Drago-Porter Convention (1907)', in *Max Planck Encyclopedias of International Law* (Oxford: Oxford University Press, 2007)

Benton, Lauren and Kathyrn Walker, 'Law for the Empire: The Common Law in Colonial America and the Problem of Legal Diversity', *Chicago-Kent Law Review* 89 (2014), pp. 937–956

Bentham, Jeremy, *Theory of Legislation*. Translated from the French of Etienne Dumont (London: Trübner & Co, 1864)

Bew, John, '"From an Umpire to a Competitor": Castlereagh, Canning and the Issue of International Intervention in the Wake of the Napoleonic Wars', in Brendan Simms and D.J.B. Trim eds., *Humanitarian Intervention: A History* (Cambridge: Cambridge University Press, 2011), pp. 117–138

Berglund, Susan, 'Mercantile Credit and Financing in Venezuela, 1830–1870', *Journal of Latin American Studies* 17:2 (1985), pp. 371–396

Berruezo León, María Teresa, *La lucha de Hispanoamérica por su independencia en Inglaterra 1800–1830* (Madrid: Ediciones de Cultura Hispánica, 1989)

Bhuta, Nehal, 'The State Theory of Grotius', *Current Legal Problems* 73:1 (2020), pp. 127–176
Blanchard, Peter, *Under the Flags of Freedom: Slave Soldiers and the Wars of Independence in Spanish South America* (Pittsburgh: University of Pittsburgh, 2008)
Blanning, Tim, *The Pursuit of Glory: Europe 1648–1815* (London: Penguin, 2008)
Blaufarb, Rafe, *The Great Demarcation: The French Revolution and the Invention of Modern Property* (Oxford: Oxford University Press, 2006)
Blom, Hans, 'Grotius and Socianism', in Martin Mulsow and Jan Rohls eds., *Socinianism and Arminianism. Antitrinitarians, Calvinists, and Cultural Exchange in Seventeenth-Century Europe* (Leiden: Brill, 2005)
Blumberg, Arnold, 'The Diplomacy of the Mexican Empire, 1863–1867', *Transactions of the American Philosophical Society* 61:8 (1971), pp. 1–152
Bolívar, Simón, *Mensaje del Libertador Presidente de la República de Colombia a la Gran Convención, en el año de 1828* (Bogotá: Impreso por J. A. Cualla, 1826)
Carta de Jamaica (Madrid: Verbum, 2020)
Bolton, Patrick and David Skeel, 'Odious Debts or Odious Regimes?', *Law and Contemporary Problems* 70:4 (2007), pp. 83–107
Borrego Vega, Ana Luz, 'José Mejía Lequerica y José Joaquín de Olmedo, voces americanas en las Cortes de Cádiz', pp. 207–216
Botana, Natalio, *El orden conservador: La política argentina entre 1880 y 1916* (Buenos Aires: Sudamericana, 1977)
La tradición republicana: Alberdi, Sarmiento y las ideas políticas de su tiempo (Buenos Aires: Sudamericana, 1984)
Repúblicas y monarquías. La encrucijada de la independencia (Buenos Aires: Edhasa, 2016)
Bowring, John ed., *The Works of Jeremy Bentham*. Volume 1 (Edinburgh: William Tait, 1843)
Brading, David, *Los orígenes del nacionalismo mexicano*. Translated by Soledad Loaeza Grave (México: Secretaría de Educación Pública, 1973)
Classical Republicanism and Creole Patriotism: Simón Bolívar (1783–1830) and the Spanish American Revolution (Cambridge: Centre for Latin American Studies, 1983)
The First America: The Spanish Monarchy, Creole Patriots, and the Liberal State, 1492–1867 (Cambridge: Cambridge University Press, 1991)
'Francisco Bulnes y la verdad acerca de México en el siglo XIX'. Translated by Lucrecia Orensanz. *Historia Mexicana*, 45:3 (1996), pp. 621–651
Mito y profecía en la historia de México. Translated by Tomás Segura (Mexico City: FDCE, 2004)
Braudel, Fernand, *La Méditerranée et le monde méditerranéen à l'époque de Philippe II*. Two volumes (Paris: Colin, 1949)
Brautigam, Deborah and Meg Rithmire, 'The Chinese "Debt Trap" is a Myth', *The Atlantic*, 6 February 2021.
Breña, Roberto, 'Pensamiento político e ideología en la emancipación americana. Fray Servando Mier y la independencia absoluta de Nueva España', in Francisco Colom González ed., *Relatos de nación. La construcción de identidades nacionales en el mundo hispánico*. Volume 1 (Frankfurt: Vervuert, 2005), pp. 73–102
'En torno al liberalismo hispánico aspectos del republicanismo, del federalismo y del liberalismo de los pueblos en la Independencia de México', in Izaskun Álvarez Cuartero and Julio Sánchez Gómez eds., *Visiones y revisiones de la independencia americana: México, Centroamérica y Haití* (Salamanca: Ediciones Universidad de Salamanca, 2005), pp. 179–204.
El primer liberalismo español y los procesos de emancipación de América 1808–1824. Una revisión historiográfica del liberalismo hispánico (México: El Colegio de México, 2006)
'Diferendos y coincidencias en torno a la obra de François-Xavier Guerra (una réplica a Medófilo Medina Pineda', *Anuario Colombiano de Historia Social y de la Cultura* 38:1 (2011), pp. 281–300
Brett, Annabel, *Liberty, Right and Nature Individual Rights in Later Scholastic Thought* (Cambridge: Cambridge University Press, 1997), pp. 20–24
'Natural Right and Civil Community: The Civil Philosophy of Hugo Grotius', *The Historical Journal* 45:1 (2002), pp. 31–51

Briceño Ruiz, José, 'Los congresos hispanoamericanos en el siglo XIX: identidad, amenazas externas e intereses en la construcción del regionalismo', *Ciclos en la historia, la economía y la sociedad* 26:45 (2015), pp. 88–117

Broggio, Paolo, 'Grace', in Harald Ernst Braun, Erik De Bom, and Paolo Astorri eds., *A Companion to the Spanish Scholastics* (Leiden: Brill, 2022)

Brown, Matthew, 'The Global History of Latin America', *Journal of Global History* 10 (2015), pp. 365–386

Brown, Matthew ed., *Informal Empire in Latin America: Culture, Commerce and Capital* (London: Wiley, 2008)

Brown, Peter, *Augustine of Hippo: A Biography* (Berkeley: University of California Press, 1967)

The World of Late Antiquity: From Marcus Aurelius to Muhammad (London: Thames & Hudson, 1971)

The Ransom of the Soul: Afterlife and Wealth in Early Western Christianity (Cambridge: Harvard University Press, 2015)

Buchenau, Jürgen, 'The Life Cycle of a Trade Diaspora: The German "Colony" in Mexico City, 1821–Present', *Jahrbuch für Geschichte Lateinamerikas* 39 (2002), pp. 275–297

Buchheit, Lee C. and G. Mitu Gulati, 'Odious Debts and Nation-Building: When the Incubus Departs', *Maine Law Review* 60:2 (2008), pp. 478–485

Bucuré, Miriam, 'Militancia y compromiso de Juana Manuela Gorriti', *Quaderns de Filologia. Estudis literaris* 27 (2012), pp. 13–25

Burge, Daniel J., *A Failed Vision of Empire: The Collapse of Manifest Destiny, 1845–1872* (Lincoln: University of Nebraska Press, 2022)

Burgin, Miron, *Aspectos económicos del federalismo argentino* (Buenos Aires: Hachette, 1960)

Burkhart, Louise M., 'The Aztecs and the Catholic Church', in Deborah L. Nichols, and Enrique Rodríguez-Alegría eds., *The Oxford Handbook of the Aztecs* (Oxford: Oxford University Press, 2017), pp. 675–688

Burner, Lisa, 'Tales of Incan Gold in an Era of Guano: Juana Manuela Gorriti's Precious Metal Melodramas', *Hispanic Review* 86:3 (2018), pp. 353–376

Burns, Kathryn, 'Nuns, Kurakas, and Credit: The Spiritual Economy of Seventeenth-Century Cuzco', *Colonial Latin American Review* 6:2 (1997), pp. 185–203

Into the Archive: Writing and Power in Colonial Peru (Durham: Duke University Press, 2010)

Burrow, John, 'Images of Time: From Carlylean Vulcanism to Sedimentary Gradualism', in Stefan Collini, Richard Whatmore, and Brian Young eds., *History, Religion, and Culture British Intellectual History 1750–1950* (Cambridge: Cambridge University Press, 2000), pp. 198–223

Burton Russell, Jeffrey, *Mephistopheles: The Devil in the Modern World* (Ithaca, NY: Cornell University Press, 1990)

Bushnell, David ed., 'The Development of the Press in Great Colombia', *The Hispanic American Historical Review* 30:4 (1950), pp. 432–452

The Santander Regime in Gran Colombia (Newark: University of Delaware Press, 1954)

'The Last Dictatorship: Betrayal or Consummation?', *Hispanic American Historical Review* 63:1 (1983), pp. 65–105

The Making of Modern Colombia: A Nation in Spite of Itself (Berkeley: University of California Press, 1993)

El Libertador: Writings of Simón Bolívar. Translated by Frederick H. Fornoff (Oxford: Oxford University Press, 2013)

Bustamante, Carlos María de, *El nuevo Bernal Díaz del Castillo: ó sea, Historia de la invasión de los Anglo-Americanos en México*. Volumes 1–2 (Mexico City: Vicente García Torres, 1847)

Cadwallader, F. J. J., *In Pursuit of the merchant debtor and bankrupt: 1066–1732*. Two volumes. Volume 1 (Unpublished PhD Thesis) (University of London, 1965)

Caillet-Bois, Ricardo R., 'La Convención Preliminar de Paz celebrada con España en 1823 y las Misiones de Alzaga y Las Heras', *Revista de Historia de América* 6 (1939), pp. 5–46

Calderón Reyes, Clímaco, *Elementos de Hacienda* (Bogotá: La Luz, 1911)

Calvo, Carlos, *Derecho internacional teórico y práctico de Europa y América* (Paris: Durand et Pedone-Lauriel, 1868)

Una página de derecho internacional: o La América del Sur ante la ciencia del derecho de gentes moderno (Paris: Durand, 1864)

Canal Feijóo, Bernardo, *Alberdi y la proyección sistemática del espíritu de Mayo* (Buenos Aires: Losada, 1961)

Candioti, Magdalena and Melina Yangilevich, 'La justicia en la construcción del orden estatal', in Marcela Ternavasio ed., *Historia de la Provincia de Buenos Aires*. Volume 3: De la organización provincial a la federalización de Buenos Aires (1821–1880) (Buenos Aires: UNIPE, 2013), pp. 179–204

Cantú, Roberto, 'La guerra entre México y los Estados Unidos en la novela *El fistol del diablo*, de Manuel Payno', *Literatura Mexicana* 24:1 (2013), pp. 23–43

Cañeque, Alejandro, *The King's Living Image: The Culture and Politics of Viceregal Power in Colonial Mexico* (New York: Routledge, 2004)

Cañizares-Esguerra, Jorge, 'How the "Reformation" Invented Separate Catholic and Protestant Atlantics', *Archive for Reformation History* 108:1 (2017), pp. 245–254

How to Write the History of the New World: Histories, Epistemologies, and Identities in the Eighteenth-Century Atlantic World (Stanford: Stanford University Press, 2001)

Carande, Ramón, *Carlos V y sus banqueros*. Volumes 1 and 2 (Barcelona: Crítica, 1987)

Cárdenas, Elisa, *Roma: el descubrimiento de América* (Mexico City: El Colegio de México, 2018).

Cardinali, Juan Carlos, *Semblanzas y conjeturas en la historia argentina* (Buenos Aires: Biblos, 2004)

Carilla, Emilio, 'El primer biógrafo de Alberdi (José María Torres Caicedo), *Boletín del Instituto Caro y Cuervo* 53:1 (1988), pp. 1–11

Carlos Morales, Carlos Javier de, *Felipe II. El imperio en bancarrota la Hacienda Real de Castilla y los negocios financieros del Rey Prudente* (Madrid: Dilema, 2009)

Carmagnani, Marcello, 'De la economía política a la economía pública: José Canga Argüelles', *Iberian Journal of the History of Economic Thought* 2 (2016), pp. 221–238

Carrithers, David W. and Philip Stewart, 'Statecraft', in *Montesquieu: Discourses, Dissertations, and Dialogues on Politics, Science, and Religion* (Cambridge: Cambridge University Press, 2020)

Carroll, Stuart, *Enmity and Violence in Early Modern Europe* (Cambridge: Cambridge University Press, 2023)

Casals Bergés, Quinti, 'Proceso electoral y prosopografía de los diputados de las Cortes Extraordinarias de Cádiz (1810–1813), *Historia Constitucional* 13 (2012), pp. 194–231

Casasús, Joaquín Demetrio, *Historia de la deuda contraída en Londres* (Mexico City: Imprenta del Gobierno federal, 1885)

Castilla Urbano, Francisco, 'La Escuela de Salamanca y los derechos humanos: una difícil conciliación', *Araucaria* 25:54 (2023), pp. 534–566

Castillo, Lina del, *La invención republicana del legado colonial*. Ciencia, historia y geografía de la vanguardia política colombiana en el siglo XIX (Bogotá: Universidad de los Andes, 2018)

Centeno, Miguel Ángel, *Sangre y Deuda: Ciudades, Estado y construcción de nación en América* Latina (Bogotá: Universidad Nacional de Colombia, 2014)

Chancellor, Edward, *The Price of Time: The Real Story of Interest* (London: Grove Press, 2022)

Chapman-Quevedo, William Alfredo, 'La red sociofamiliar Mosquera y sus relaciones de poder en Popayán, 1832–1836', *Memoria y Sociedad* 14:29 (2010), pp. 37–54

Charles Lea, Henry, 'The Decadence of Spain', *The Atlantic*, July 1989

Charnovitz, Steve, 'The Field of International Economic Law', *Journal of International Economic Law* 17:3 (2014), pp. 607–626

Chevalier, Michel, *Lettres sur l'Amérique du Nord*. Volume 2 (Paris: Charles Gosselin, 1836)

Chiaramonte, José, 'El mito de los orígenes en la historiografía latinoamericana', *Cuadernos del Instituto Ravignani* 2 (1991), pp. 5–40

'El federalismo argentino en la primera mitad del siglo XIX', in Marcello Carmagnani ed., *Federalismos Latinoamericanos: México/Brasil/Argentina* (Mexico City: Fondo de Cultura Económica, 1993), pp. 81–132

Ciudades, provincias, Estados: Orígenes de la Nación Argentina (1800–1846): (Buenos Aires: Ariel Historia, 1997)

'Fundamentos iusnaturalistas de los movimientos de Independencia', *Boletín del Instituto de Historia Argentina y Americana Dr. Emilio Ravignani* 22 (2000), pp. 33–71
Nación y Estado en Iberoamérica. El lenguaje político en tiempos de la independencia (Buenos Aires: Editorial Sudamericana, 2004)
'La Antigua constitución luego de las independencias, 1808–1852', *Desarrollo económico* 50 (2010), pp. 331–361
Chiaramonti, Gabriella, 'El primer constitucionalismo peruano: de Cádiz al primer congreso constituyente', in Antonio Annino and Marcela Ternavasio eds., *El laboratório constitucional iberoamericano: 1807/1808–1830* (Madrid: Iberoamericana, 2012), pp. 135–156
Chipman, Donald E., *Moctezuma's Children: Aztec Royalty under Spanish Rule, 1520–1700* (Austin: University of Texas Press, 2005)
Churchill, Randolph, ed., *Volume 1: Youth, 1874–1896. The Churchill Documents* (Boston: Houghton Mifflin, 2006)
Chust, Manuel and Ivana Frasquet, 'La génesis de las Independencias. La complejidad de un proceso histórico de dimensiones universales', in Manuel Chust and Ivana Frasquet eds., *La patria no se hizo sola: las revoluciones de las independencias iberoamericanas* (Madrid: Silex, 2012), pp. 17–66
Chust, Manuel and José A. Serrano eds., 'La Constitución de 1812: una revolución constitutional bihemisférica', in Antonio Annino y Marcela Ternavasio eds., *El Laboratório constitucional iberoamericano: 1807/1808–1830* (Madrid: Iberoamericana, 2012), pp. 93–114
'El Rey para el pueblo, la constitución para la nación', in Víctor Mínguez and Manuel Chust eds., *El imperio sublevado: monarquía y naciones en España e Hispanoamérica* (Madrid: CSIC, 2014), pp. 225–254
¡Abajo la tiranía! América y España en Revolución 1776–1835 (Barcelona: Silex, 2018)
Clark, A. Kim, *The Redemptive Work: Railway and Nation in Ecuador, 1895–1930* (Lanham: Rowman & Littlefield, 1998)
Clark, Christopher, *Revolutionary Spring: Fighting for a New World* (London: Penguin, 2023)
Claustre, Julie, *Dans les geôles du roi. L'emprisonnement pour dette à Paris à la fin du Moyen Âge* (Paris: Éditions de la Sorbonne, 2007)
Clavel, Damian, 'What's in a Fraud? The Many Worlds of Gregor MacGregor, 1817–1824', *Enterprise & Society* 22:4 (2021), pp. 997–1036
Clavero, Bartolomé, *Mayorazgo: Propiedad feudal en Castilla 1369–1836* (Madrid: Siglo XXI, 1989)
Antidora. Antropología católica de la economía moderna (Milán: Giuffrè Editore, 1991)
Razón de estado, razón de individuo, razón de historia (Madrid: Centro de Constitucionales, 1991)
'Cádiz entre indígenas: Lecturas y lecciones sobre la Constitución y su cultura en tierra de los mayas', *Anuario de Historia del Derecho Español* 65 (1995), pp. 931–992
'"Libraos de Ultramaria!" El fruto podrido de Cádiz', *Revista de Estudios Políticos* 97 (1997), pp. 109–116
'Antropología del sujeto de derechos en Cádiz', *Revista española de la función consultiva* 19 (2013), pp. 99–128
Cohen, Jay, 'The History of Imprisonment for Debt and Its Relation to the Development of Discharge in Bankruptcy', *The Journal of Legal History* 3:2 (1982), pp. 153–171
Colección legislativa de España: continuación de la colección de decretos. Volume 127 (Madrid: Imprenta del Minsiterio de Gracia y Justicia, 1882)
Coleman, Peter J., *Debtors and Creditors in America: Insolvency, Imprisonment for Debt, and Bankruptcy, 1607–1900* (Madison: The State Historical Society of Wisconsin, 1974)
Colley, Linda, *Britons: Forging the Nation 1707–1837* (New Haven: Yale University Press, 2005)
Collin, Richard H., *Theodore Roosevelt's Caribbean. The Panama Canal, the Monroe Doctrine, and the Latin American Context* (Baton Rouge: Louisiana State University Press, 1990)
Colmenares, Germán, *Las Convenciones contra la Cultura* (Bogotá: Tercer Mundo, 1987)
Comín Comín, Francisco, *Las crisis de la deuda soberana en España (1500–2015)* (Madrid: Catarata, 2016)

Conde, José Ignacio y Díaz-Rubín and Javier Sanchiz Ruiz, *Historia genealógica de los títulos y dignidades nobiliarias en Nueva España y México Volumen II. Casa de Austria (siglos XVI–XVII)* (Mexico City: UNAM, 2012)

Conklin, James, 'The Theory of Sovereign Debt and Spain under Philip II', *Journal of Political Economy* 106:3 (1998), pp. 483–513

Constant, Benjamin, *The Liberty of Ancients Compared with that of Moderns* (1819) (Indianapolis: Liberty Fund, 2010)

Conte Corti, Egon, *Maximiliano y Carlota* (Mexico City: FDCE, 1997)

Cooke, John William, *Acción parlamentaria.* Compilation by Eduardo Luis Duhalde (Buenos Aires: Colihue, 2007)

Cooper, Frederick, 'Decolonizations, Colonizations, and More Decolonizations: The End of Empire in Time and Space', *Journal of World History* 33:3 (2022), pp. 491–526

Córdoba Ramírez, Diana Irina, *Los derroteros del liberalismo. Las ideas políticas moderadas de Manuel Payno* (Published PhD Thesis) (Mexico City: UNAM, 2004)

Cortázar, Roberto and Luis Augusto Cuervo, *Congreso de 1825. Senado. Actas* (Bogotá: Imprenta Nacional, 1902)

Cosío Villegas, Daniel, 'La Doctrina Juárez', *Historia Mexicana* 11:4 (1962), pp. 527–545

Covarrubias, José María, *Memorias para servir a la reforma y aumento de la hacienda publica del Imperio Mexicano, presentadas al Soberano Congreso* (Mexico City: Benavente, 1822)

Craven, Matthew, *The Decolonization of International Law: State Succession and the Law of Treaties* (Oxford: Oxford University Press, 2007)

Crawford, James, *The International Law Commission's Article on State Responsibility* (Cambridge: Cambridge University Press, 2002)

The Creation of States in International Law (Oxford: Oxford University Press, 2007)

'Napoleon 1814–1815: A Small Issue of Status', in Inge Van Hulle and Randall C. H. Lesaffer eds., *International Law in the Long Nineteenth Century (1776–1914)* (Leiden: Brill, 2019), pp. 3–19

Crespo, Horacio, 'La tentación monárquica de Alberdi', *Historia Mexicana* 65:2 (2015), pp. 599–628

Cross, Harry E., 'South American Bullion Production and Export, 1550–1750', in J. F. Richards ed., *Precious Metals in the Later Medieval and Early Modern Worlds* (Durham: North Carolina University Press, 1983), pp. 397–424

Cruz Kronfly, Fernando, ed., *Adictos a mí. Cartas a Tomás Cipriano de Mosquera* (1826–1830) (Bogotá: Universidad Nacional de Colombia, 2022)

Cubitt, Geoffrey, 'Revolution, Reaction, Restoration: The Meanings and Uses of Seventeenth-Century English History in the Political Thinking of Benjamin Constant, c.1797–1830', *European Review of History: Revue européenne d'histoire* 14:1 (2007), pp. 21–47

Cuervo, Ángel, y Rufino José Cuervo, *Vida de Rufino Cuervo y noticias de su época. Two volumes* (Paris: Roger and Chernoviz, 1892).

Cuestión Mackintosh (Bogotá: Imprenta de Neo Granadina, 1852).

Cummings, James W., *Towards Modern Public Finance: The American War with Mexico, 1846–1848* (London: Pickering & Chatto, 2009)

Cunningham, Hugh, *The Reputation of Philanthropy since 1750* (Manchester: Manchester University Press, 2020)

d'Altroy, Terence N., 'Inca Political Organization, Economic Institutions, and Infrastructure', in Sonia Alconini and Alan Covey eds., *The Oxford Handbook of the Incas* (Oxford: Oxford University Press, 2018), pp. 205–226

Davis, Teresa, 'The Ricardian State: Carlos Calvo and Latin America's Ambivalent Origin Story for the Age of Decolonization', *Journal of the History of International Law* 23:1 (2020), pp. 32–51

Davies, Catherine, 'La familia republicana: Josefa Acevedo politiza lo doméstico', in Sara Beatriz Guardia ed., *Escritoras del Siglo XIX en América Latina* (Lima, Centro de Estudios la Mujer en la Historia de América Latina, 2012), pp. 153–163

Deardorff, Max, *A Tale of Two Granadas: Custom, Community, and Citizenship in the Spanish Empire, 1568–1668* (Cambridge: Cambridge University Press, 2023)

Deas, Malcolm, 'The Fiscal Problems of Nineteenth-Century Colombia', *Journal of Latin American Studies* 14:2 (1982), pp. 287–328

'Weapons of the Weak?' Colombia and Foreign Powers in the Nineteenth Century', in Matthew Brown ed., *Informal Empire in Latin America: Culture, Commerce and Capital* (London: Wiley, 2008), pp. 173–186

Decock, Wim, 'The Catholic Spirit of Capitalism?', in Wim Decock, Jordan J. Ballor, Michael Germann, and Laurent Waelkens eds., *Law and Religion: The Legal Teachings of the Protestant and Catholic Reformations* (Göttingen: Vandenhoeck & Ruprecht, 2014), pp. 22–44

'Spanish Scholastics on Money and Credit', in David Fox and Wolfgang Ernst eds., *Money in the Western Legal Tradition Middle Ages to Bretton Woods* (Oxford: Oxford University Press, 2016), pp. 267–283

DeJean, Joan, 'Les Capitalistes: The First Capitalists and the Debt Created by Haitian Slavery', *Capitalism: A Journal of History and Economics* 4:1 (2023), pp. 44–72.

Delgado Ribas, Josep, 'La desintegración del imperio español: un caso de descolonización frustrada (1797–1837)', *Illes i Imperis* 8 (2006), pp. 5–44

Delpar, Helen, *Red Against Blue: The Liberal Party in Colombian Politics, 1863–1899* (Tuscaloosa: University of Alabama Press, 1981)

Demetrio Casasús, Joaquín, *Historia de la deuda contraída en Londres con un apéndice sobre el estado actual de la hacienda publica por el Lic.* Joaquín D. Casasus (Mexico City: Imprenta del Gobierno Federal, 1885)

Diario de los debates de la cámara de diputados. Duodécima legislatura constitucional de la Unión (Mexico City: Horcasitas, 1884)

Diaz, Pedro Pablo, José Luis Ramos, and Domingo Navas Spinola eds., *Varios discursos del ciudadano Francisco Antonio Zea* (Caracas: Spinola, 1825)

'Discurso pronunciado por Simón Bolívar ante el Congreso de Venezuela en Angostura, 15 de febrero de 1819'. *Correo del Orinoco*. Number 19, Saturday 20 February 1819. Reprinted in *Coherencia* 16 (2019), pp. 397–424

Ditchfield, Simon, 'Catholic Reformation and Renewal', in Peter Marshall ed., *The Oxford Illustrated History of the Reformation* (Oxford: Oxford University Press, 2015), pp. 152–185

Dodd, Nigel, *The Social Life of Money* (Princeton: Princeton University Press, 2014)

Dover, Paul, *The Information Revolution in Early Modern Europe* (Cambridge: Cambridge University Press, 2021),

Ducey, Michael T., 'Gobierno, legitimidad y movilización: aspectos de la vida electoral en tiempos insurgentes', *Historia Mexicana* 68:4 (2019), pp. 1593–1638

Dunthorne, Hugh, *Britain and the Dutch Revolt, 1560–1700* (Cambridge: Cambridge University Press, 2013)

Drago, Luis María, *La República Argentina y el caso de Venezuela: Documentos, juicios y comentarios relacionados con la nota pasada al ministro argentino en Washington* (Buenos Aires: Coni Hermanos, 1903)

Cobro coercitivo de deudas (Buenos Aires: Hermanos Coni, 1906)

'Argentine Republic: Ministry of Foreign Relations and Worship', *American Journal of International Law* 1:1 (1907), pp. 1–6

'State Loans in Their Relation to International Policy', *American Journal of International Law* 1:3 (1907), pp. 692–726

'Discurso del ex Diputado Nacional Dr. Luis María Drago', in Miguel J. Font ed., *La mujer: encuesta feminista argentina* (Buenos Aires: Imp. Costa Hnos., 1921), pp. 189–194

Drelichman, Mauricio and Hans-Joachim Voth, 'The Sustainable Debts of Philip II: A Reconstruction of Castile's Fiscal Position, 1566–1596', *The Journal of Economic History* 70:4 (2010), pp. 813–842

Lending to the Borrower from Hell: Debt, Taxes, and Default in the Age of Philip II (Princeton: Princeton University Press, 2014)

Dubet, Anne, 'José Patiño y el crédito de Felipe V ¿Un proyecto global?', *Obradoiro de Historia Moderna* 29 (2020), pp. 17–50

Dueñas, Alcira, *Indians and Mestizos in 'the Lettered City': Reshaping Justice, Social Hierarchy, and Political Culture in Colonial Peru* (Boulder: University of Colorado, 2010) Dufour, Alfred. 'Les "Magni hispani" dans l'oeuvre de Grotius', in Frank Grunert and Kurt Seelmann eds., *Die Ordnung der Praxis. Neue Studies zur Spanischen Spätscholastik* (Tübingen: Niemeyer 2001), pp. 351–380

Duncan, Robert H., 'Political Legitimation and Maximilian's Second Empire in Mexico, 1864–1867', *Mexican Studies/Estudios Mexicanos* 12:1 (1996), pp. 27–66

'Maximilian and the Construction of the Liberal State, 1863–1866', in Jaime E. Rodríguez ed., *The Divine Charter: Constitutionalism and Liberalism in Nineteenth-Century Mexico* (Lanham: Rowland & Littlefield Publishers, 2005), pp. 133–166

Durand Flórez, Guillermo, *El Perú en las Cortes de Cádiz.* Volume 1 (Lima: Comisión Nacional del Sesquicentenario de la Independencia del Perú, 1974)

Earle, Rebecca, *Spain and the Independence of Colombia 1810–1825* (Exeter: University of Exeter Press, 2000)

Eastman, Jorge Mario, *Obras selectas: Manuel Murillo Toro* (Bogotá: Cámara de Representantes, 1979)

Eastman, Scott, *Preaching Spanish Nationalism across the Hispanic Atlantic, 1759–1823* (Baton Rouge: Louisiana State University Press, 2012)

A Missionary Nation: Race, Religion, and Spain's Age of Liberal Imperialism, 1841–1881 (Lincoln: University of Nebraska Press, 2021)

Echeverri, Marcela, *Indian and Slave Royalists in the Age of Revolution: Reform, Revolution, and Royalism in the Northern Andes, 1780–1825* (Cambridge: Cambridge University Press, 2016)

Edelstein, Dan, 'From Constitutional to Permanent Revolution: 1649 and 1793', in Keith Michael Baker and Dan Edelstein eds., *Scripting Revolution: A Historical Approach to the Comparative Study of Revolutions* (Redwood City: Stanford University Press, 2015), pp. 118–130

Edling, Max M., 'Peace Pact and Nation: An International Interpretation of the Constitution of the United States', *Past & Present* 240 (2018), pp. 267–303

'"So Immense a Power in the Affairs of War": Alexander Hamilton and the Restoration of Public Credit', *The William and Mary Quarterly* 64:2 (2007), pp. 287–326

Edwards, Sebastian, *The Chile Project: The Story of the Chicago Boys and the Downfall of Neoliberalism* (Princeton: Princeton University Press, 2023)

Eich, Stefan, *The Currency of Politics: The Political Theory of Money from Aristotle to Keynes* (Princeton: Princeton University Press, 2022)

Eire, Carlos, *Reformations: The Early Modern World, 1450–1650* (New Haven: Yale University Press, 2016)

Elena, Eduardo, 'Spinsters, Gamblers, and Friedrich Engels: The Social Worlds of Money and Expansionism in Argentina, 1860s–1900s', *Hispanic American Historical Review* 102:1 (2022), pp. 61–94

Elliott, John, *National and Comparative History: An Inaugural Lecture Delivered Before the University of Oxford on 10 May 1991* (Oxford: Clarendon Press, 1991)

Empires of the Atlantic World: Britain and Spain in America 1492–1830 (New Haven: Yale University Press, 2006)

Eloy Alfaro, Colón, *Eloy Alfaro y el Derecho público de América* (Bogotá: Imprenta de J. V. Barón, 1935)

Ely, James, *The Guardian of Every Other Right: A Constitutional History of Property Rights* (Oxford: Oxford University Press, 2007)

Escosura, Leandro de la, 'The Economic Consequences of Independence in Latin America', in Victor Bulmer-Thomas, John Coatsworth, and Roberto Cortés Conde eds., *The Cambridge Economic History of Latin America* (Cambridge: Cambridge University Press, 2005), pp. 461–504

Escudero, Alfredo Luis, 'The New Age of Andeans: Chronological Age, Indigenous Labor, and the Making of Spanish Colonial Rule', *Hispanic American Historical Review* 103:1 (2023), pp. 1–30

Estefane, Andrés and Luis Thielemann, 'Latin American Marxism and the Atlantic', *Oxford Research Encyclopedia of Latin American History* (Online).

Estep, Raymond, *Lorenzo de Zavala: profeta del liberalismo mexicano*. Translated by Carlos A. Echánove Trujillo. Prologue by Carlos A. Castañeda (Mexico City: Porrúa, 1952)

'Lorenzo de Zavala and the Texas Revolution', *The Southwestern Historical Quarterly* 57:3 (1954), pp. 322–335

Exposición presentada a las Cortes por los diputados de ultramar en la sesión de 25 de junio de 1821: sobre el estado actual de las provincias de que son representantes, y medios convenientes para su definitiva pacificación, con una noticia de los trámites que la precedieron y motivaron (Madrid: García y Campoy, 1821)Fargher, Lane F., Richard E. Blanton, and Verenice Heredia Espinoza, 'Aztec State-Making, Politics, and Empires: The Triple Alliance', in Deborah L. Nichols, and Enrique Rodríguez-Alegría eds., *The Oxford Handbook of the Aztecs* (Oxford: Oxford University Press, 2017), pp. 143–160

Febres-Lores, Fernán Altuve. *La monarquía sin corona: Obras de José María de Pando (1787–1840)* (Lima: Fondo Editorial del Congreso del Perú, 2015)

Feijóo, Bernardo Canal, *Alberdi y la proyección sistemática del espíritu de mayo* (Buenos Aires: Losada, 1961)

Feilchenfeld, Ernst H., *Public Debts and State Succession* (New York: Macmillan, 1931)

Feinerman, James V., 'Odious Debt, Old and New: The Legal Intellectual History of an Idea', *Law and Contemporary Problems* 70:4 (2007), pp. 193–220

Ferdinand VII, *El Rey a los habitantes de ultramar* (Madrid, n.s.)

Fernandes Carvalho Veçoso, Fabia, 'Resisting Intervention through Sovereign Debt: A Redescription of the Drago Doctrine', *TWAIL Review* 1 (2020), pp. 74–92

'Mexican Post-Revolutionary Foreign Policy and the Spanish Civil War: Legal Struggles over Intervention at the League of Nations', in Kathryn Greenman, Anne Orford, Anna Saunders, and Ntina Tzouvala eds., *Revolutions in International Law: The Legacies of 1917* (Cambridge: Cambridge University Press, 2021), pp. 242–268

Fernandes Carvalho, Fabia and João Roriz, 'Critical Legal Theory Situated: The Work of Eduardo Novoa Monreal as the Legal Adviser of Salvador Allende', in Wanshu Cong and Francisco-José Quintana eds., *Remembering to Reimagine: A Symposium on Salvador Allende, Unfulfilled Promise, and the Future of International Law*. National University of Singapore, CIL Dialogues (Online)

Fernández Albaladejo, Pablo, *La crisis de la monarquía* (Barcelona: Crítica, 2009)

Fernández Delgado, Miguel Ángel ed., *Los Sentimientos de la Nación de José María Morelos. Antología documental.* Prólogo de Patricia Galeana. (Mexico City: INEH, 2013)

Fernández Sarasola, Ignacio, *La Constitución de Cádiz: Orígen, contenido y proyección internacional* (Madrid: CEPC, 2011)

'La proyección de los derechos individuales', in Encarna García Monerris and Carmen García Monerris eds., *Guerra, Revolución, Constitución (1808 y 2008)* (Valencia: Universidad de Valencia, 2012), pp. 239–268

Fernández Sebastián, Javier, *Diccionario político y social del mundo iberoamericano. La era de las revoluciones, 1750–1850* (Madrid: CEPC, 2009)

'A Distorting Mirror: The Sixteenth Century in the Historical Imagination of the First Hispanic Liberals', *History of European Ideas* 41:2 (2015), pp. 166–175

'Levantando los planos del porvenir. Sobre el advenimiento del futuro en el mundo hispánico', in Fabio Wasserman ed., *Historia, revolución y temporalidad. Experiencias de tiempo en los mundos iberoamericanos (siglos XVIII y XIX)* (Buenos Aires: Prometeo, 2020), pp. 81–108

Historia conceptual en el Atlántico ibérico: Lenguajes, tiempos, revoluciones (Madrid: FCEE, 2021)

Fernández Sotelo, Rafael Diego, 'Influencias y evolución del pensamiento político de fray Servando Teresa de Mier', *Historia Mexicana* 48:1 (1998), pp. 3–35

Fernández, Susan J., *Encumbered Cuba: Capital Markets and Revolt, 1878–1895* (Gainesville: University Press of Florida, 2002)

Fernández-Salvador, Carmen, 'Uses of Tridentine Artistic Theory in Spanish America: Imaging the Christian Painter in Colonial Hagiography', *Hispanic Research Journal* 21:5 (2020), pp. 495–510

Ferns, Henry Stanley, *Britain and Argentina in the Nineteenth Century* (Oxford: Clarendon Press, 1960)

'The Baring Crisis Revisited', *Journal of Latin American Studies*, 24:2 (1992), pp. 241–273

Ferré, Pedro, *Cuestiones Nacionales: Contestación al 'Lucero', ò, Los falsos y peligrosos principios en descubierto: con la refutación a los autores escondidos bajo el titulo de 'Cosmopolita' y 'Porteño'* (Imprenta del Estado, 1832/1833)

Memoria del brigadier general Pedro Ferre. Octubre 1821 a diciembre 1842 (Buenos Aires: Coni, 1921)

Ferrer, Ada, *Freedom's Mirror Cuba and Haiti in the Age of Revolution* (Cambridge: Cambridge University Press, 2014)

Ferry, Stephen, *Violentology: A Manual of the Colombian Conflict* (New York: Umbrage, 2012).

Finn, Margot, *The Character of Credit. Personal Debt in English Culture, 1740–1914* (Cambridge: Cambridge University Press, 2003)

Finnemore, Martha, *The Purpose of Intervention: Changing Beliefs about the Use of Force* (Ithaca: Cornell University Press, 2013)

Fischer, Sibylle, 'Bolívar in Haiti: Republicanism in the Revolutionary Atlantic', in Carla Calarge et al eds., *Haiti and the Americas* (Jackson: University Press of Mississippi, 2013), pp. 25–53

Flandreau, Marc, 'Pari Passu Lost and Found: The Origins of Sovereign Bankruptcy 1798–1873', *Institute for New Economic Thinking Working Paper Series* 186 (2022), pp. 1–67

Flandreau, Marc and Juan H. Flores, 'Bonds and Brands: Foundations of Sovereign Debt Markets, 1820–1830', *The Journal of Economic History* 69:3 (2009), pp. 646–684

Fleming, Sean, *Leviathan on a Leash: A Theory of State Responsibility* (Princeton: Princeton University Press, 2020)

Flores y Caamaño, Alfredo, *Don José Mejía Lequerica en las Cortes de Cádiz de 1810 a 1813: (o sea el principal defensor de los intereses de la América española en la más grande asamblea de la península)* (Barcelona: Casa Editorial Maucci, 1913)

Flores Zendejas, Jorge, 'The Entanglements of Domestic Polities: Public Debt and European Interventions in Latin America', in Nicolas Barreyre and Nicolas Delalande eds., *A World of Public Debts* (London: Palgrave, 2020), pp. 111–235

Florescano, Enrique, *Memory, Myth, and Time in Mexico. From the Aztecs to Independence* (Austin: University of Texas Press, 1994)

Flórez Estrada, Álvaro, *Examen imparcial de las disensiones de la America con la España: de los medios de su reciproco interés y de la utilidad de los aliados de la España* (Londres: Juigné, 1811)

Floria, Carlos Alberto and Cesar A. García Belsunce, *Historia de los Argentinos.* Volume 1 (Buenos Aires: Larousse, 1992)

Flynn, Dennis O. and Arturo Giráldez, 'Cycles of Silver: Global Economic Unity through the Mid-Eighteenth Century', *Journal of World History* 13:2 (2002), pp. 391–427

Fontán, Carmen, 'Las "Bases" y su influencia en la constitución de 1853', in Carmen Fontán ed., *Juan Bautista Alberdi. Apología y Crítica de su pensamiento* (San Miguel de Tucuman, Argentina: Constitución para Todos, 2011), pp. 259–283

Forrester, Katrina, 'Reparations, History and the Origins of Global Justice', in Duncan Bell ed., *Empire, Race and Global Justice* (Cambridge: Cambridge University Press, 2019), pp. 22–51

Fowler, Will, *Mexico in the Age of Proposals, 1821–1853* (London: Greenwood Press, 1998)

'La historia de la relación entre México y el Reino Unido en el siglo XIX y la polémica sobre el imperio informal británico', in Will Fowler and Marcela Terrazas y Basante eds., *Diplomacia, negocios y política. Ensayos sobre la relación entre México y el Reino Unido en el siglo XIX* (Mexico City: UNAM, 2018), pp. 15–44

Fradera, Josep, 'Reescribir las reglas del juego colonial: discurso, representación, y lobbying', in Scarlett O'Phelan Godoy and Georges Lomné eds., *Voces americanas en las Cortes de Cádiz: 1810–1814* (Lima: Institut Français d'Études Ándines, 2014), pp. 141–156

Frederiksen, M. W., 'Caesar, Cicero and the Problem of Debt', *The Journal of Roman Studies* 56 (1966), pp. 128–141

Frias, Uladislao, *Trabajos legislativos de las primeras Asambleas arjentinas desde la junta de 1811 hasta la disolución del Congreso en 1827: Enero á abril de 1826*. Volume 3 (Buenos Aires: Compañía sud-americana de billetes de banco, 1889)

Friede, Juan, *Los Welser en la conquista de Venezuela* (Caracas: Edime, 1961)

Fritschy, W., 'A "Financial Revolution" Reconsidered: Public Finance in Holland during the Dutch Revolt, 1568–1648', *Economic History Review* 56:1 (2003), pp. 57–89

Fuller, Catherine ed., *The Collected Works of Jeremy Bentham: The Correspondence of Jeremy Bentham*. Volumes 11 and 12 (Oxford: Oxford University Press, 2000)

Furet, François, 'De l'histoire-récit à l'histoire-problème', *Diogène* 89 (1975), pp. 113–130

L'Atelier de l'histoire (Paris: Flammarion, 1982)

Galeana, Patricia, *Las relaciones iglesia-estado durante el Segundo Imperio* (Mexico City: UNAM, 1991).

La disputa por la soberanía (1821–1876) (Mexico City: El Colegio de México, 2010)

Galeano, Eduardo, *Las venas abiertas de América Latina* (Mexico City: Siglo XXI, 1971)

Gallagher, John and Ronald Robinson, 'The Imperialism of Free Trade', *The Economic History Review* 6:1 (1953), pp. 1–15.

Gallo, Klaus, 'Reformismo tardo-ilustrado y utilitario. La "feliz experiencia" y su dimensión europea. 1776–1824', *Trabajos y Comunicaciones* 54 (2021) (Online)

Gandía, Enrique, *Las ideas políticas de la independencia americana* (Buenos Aires: Compañía General Fabril, 1961)

Las ideas políticas de la independencia americana (Buenos Aires: Depalma, 1968)

Rivadavia y su tiempo (Buenos Aires: Claridad, 1990)

Época de Rosas. Part 1 (Buenos Aires: Editorial Claridad, 1994)

García Guerra, Elena María, *Moneda y arbitrios. Consideraciones del siglo XVII* (Madrid: Consejo Superior de Investigaciones Científicas, 2003)

García Mora, Manuel, 'The Calvo Clause in Latin American Constitutions and International Law', *Marquette Law Review* 33:4 (1950), pp. 205–219

Garriga Acosta, Carlos Antonio, 'Cabeza moderna, cuerpo gótico. La Constitución de Cádiz y el orden jurídico', *Anuario de historia del derecho español* 81 (2011), pp. 99–162

'¿Qué era la Constitución de Cádiz?', in Roberto Breña ed., *Cádiz a debate: Actualidad, contexto y legado* (Mexico City: Colegio de México, 2014), pp. 153–174

Gauchet, Thomas and Christine Haynes, 'Restoring Credit in Post-Napoleonic France: Settling French War Claims', *War in History* 27:3 (2020), pp. 433–455

Geddert, Jeremy Seth, 'Too Subtle to Satisfy Many: Was Grotius's Teleology of Punishment Predestined to Fail?', *Grotiana* 38 (2017), pp. 46–69

Gelabert, Juan E., *La bolsa del Rey. Rey, reino y fisco en Castilla (1598–1648)* (Barcelona: Crítica, 1997)

Gelderen, Martin van, *The Political Thought of the Dutch Revolt 1555–1590* (Cambridge: Cambridge University Press, 2002)

Gellman, Irwin, *Good Neighbor Diplomacy: United States Policies in Latin America, 1933–1945* (Baltimore: Johns Hopkins University Press, 2019)

Ghotme, Rafat, *De la debilidad al acomodamiento: la diplomacia de la Nueva Granada frente a Gran Bretaña y Estados Unidos, 1832–1857* (Published PhD Thesis) (Barcelona: Universidad Autónoma de Barcelona, 2016)

Gibbs, Donald L., 'The Economic Activities of Nuns, Friars, and Their Conventos in Mid-Colonial Cuzco', *The Americas* 45:3 (1989), pp. 343–362

Giron, Nicole, 'Manuel Payno, el ir y venir por la Secretaría de Hacienda', in Leonor Ludlow ed., *Los secretarios de Hacienda y sus proyectos (1821–1933)*. Volume 1 (Mexico City: UNAM, 2002), pp. 351–397

Gleijeses, Piero, '1898: The Opposition to the Spanish-American War', *Journal of Latin American Studies* 35:4 (2003), pp. 681–719

Gobat, Miche, 'The Invention of Latin America: A Transnational History of Anti-Imperialism, Democracy, and Race', *The American Historical Review* 118:5 (2013), pp. 1345–1375

Empire by Invitation: William Walker and Manifest Destiny in Central America (Cambridge: Harvard University Press, 2018)

Goldmann, Matthias. 'Putting Your Faith in Good Faith: A Principled Strategy for Smoother Debt Workouts', in Juan Pablo Bohoslavsky and Matthias Goldmann eds., Special Edition on Sovereign Debt, *Yale Journal of International Law* 41:2 (2016), pp. 117–140

Golub, Stephen S. and William Darity, 'The Political Economy of the Latin American Debt Crisis', *Latin American Research Review* 26:1 (1991), pp. 175–215

González Bernaldo, Pilar, 'Estanislao Zeballos and the Argentine Doctrine of Human Private Law: A Micro-Social Approach to the History of Private International Law', *Jus Gentium. Journal of International Legal History* 2:5 (2021), pp. 529–564

González Calderón, Juan Antonio, *Derecho constitucional argentino, historia, teoría y jurisprudencia de la Constitución*. Volume 1 (Buenos Aires: Lajouane, 1923)

González Palencia, Ángel, 'El Conde de Moctezuma, Corregidor de Madrid' [Part 1], *Revista de la Biblioteca, Archivo y Museo* 57 (1948), pp. 373–422

'El Conde de Moctezuma, Corregidor de Madrid' [Part 2], *Revista de la Biblioteca, Archivo y Museo* 58 (1949), pp. 141–208

Gorriti, Juan Ignacio de, *Reflecciones sobre las causas morales de las convulsiones interiores en los nuevos estados americanos y examen de los medios eficaces para reprimirlas: Precedidas de un compendio de la vida pública del autor* (Valparaíso: Imprenta del Mercurio, 1836)

Graaf, Beatrice de, *Fighting Terror after Napoleon: How Europe Became Secure after 1815* (Cambridge: Cambridge University Press, 2020)

Graaf, Beatrice de, Ido de Haan, and Brian Vick ed., *Securing Europe after Napoleon: 1815 and the New European Security Culture* (Cambridge: Cambridge University Press, 2019)

Grafe, Regina, 'An Empire of Debts? Spain and Its Colonial Realm', in Nicolas Barreyre and Nicolas Delalande eds., *A World of Public Debts* (London: Palgrave, 2020), pp. 5–35

Granados García, Aimer, 'Congresos e intelectuales en los inicios de un proyecto y de una conciencia continental latinoamericana, 1826–1860', in Aimer Granados García and Carlos Marichal eds., *Construcción de las identidades latinoamericanas: ensayos de historia intelectual (Siglos XIX y XX)* (México: Colegio de México, 2004), pp. 39–69

Greenfield, Jerome, 'The Mexican Expedition of 1862–1867 and the end of the French Second Empire', *Historical Journal* 63:3 (2020), pp. 660–685.

Greenman, Kathryn, 'The Mexican Revolution: Alien Protection and International Economic Order', in Kathryn Greenman, Anne Orford, Anna Saunders, and Ntina Tzouvala eds., *Revolutions in International Law: The Legacies of 1917* (Cambridge: Cambridge University Press, 2021), pp. 339–364

State Responsibility and Rebels: The History and Legacy of Protecting Investment Against Revolution (Cambridge: Cambridge University Press, 2021)

Grice Hutchinson, Marjorie, *The School of Salamánca: Readings in Monetary Theory 1544–1605* (Oxford: Clarendon Press, 1952)

Griffith Dawson, Frank, 'The Influence of Andrés Bello on Latin-American Perceptions of Non-Intervention and State Responsibility', *British Yearbook of International Law* 57:1 (1986), pp. 253–315

The First Latin American Debt Crisis, The City of London and the 1822–25 Loan Bubble (New Haven: Yale University Press, 1990)

Grondona, Iván, *Imprenta Coni. Apuntes para la historia de una imprenta y una dinastía* (Buenos Aires: San Telmo, 1990)

Grotius, Hugo, 'Hugo Grotius on the Agglomerate Polity of Philip II', *History of European Ideas* 46:3 (2020), pp. 276–291

Annals of the War in the Low Countries. Editing, Translation, and Introduction by Jan Waszink (Leuven: Leuven University Press, 2023)

Grunberg, Bernard, 'Hernán Cortés: un hombre de su tiempo', in María del Carmen Martínez Martínez and Alicia Mayer eds., *Miradas sobre Hernán Cortés* (Frankfurt: Vervuert Verlagsgesellschaft, 2016), pp. 49–66

Guardino, Peter, *The Dead March: A History of the Mexican-American War* (Cambridge: Harvard University Press, 2018)

Guerra, François-Xavier, 'El Olvidado Siglo XIX', in Valentín Vázquez de Prada Vallejo and Ignacio Olábarri Gortázar eds., *Balance de historiografía sobre Iberoamérica: 1945–1988: actas de las IV Conversaciones Internacionales de Historia* (Pamplona: Universidad de Navarra, 1988), pp. 593–631

Modernidad e independencias: ensayos sobre las revoluciones hispánicas (México: FCE, 2010)

Guerra Iñiguez, Daniel, 'Palabras preliminares', in Alfredo N. Vivot and Alberto A. Conil Paz, *Homenaje al doctor Luis M. Drago* (Caracas: Oficina Central de Información, 1976), pp. 9–33

Guerrero, Carolina, *Liberalismo y Republicanismo en Bolívar* (Caracas: Universidad Central Venezuela, 2005)

Guerrero Balfagón, Enrique, 'El reconocimiento de la independencia de Bolivia por España', *Revista de estudios políticos* 135–136 (1964), pp. 181–234

Guillamondegui, Julio César, 'La quiebra en el derecho indiano rioplatense', *Historia* 8:1 (1969), pp. 123–139

Gulati, Mitu, Lee Buchheit, and Robert B. Thompson, 'The Dilemma of Odious Debts', *Duke Law Journal* 56 (2007), pp. 1201–1262

Gulati, Mitu, Sarah Ludington, and Arthur Mark Weisburd, 'A Convenient Untruth: Fact and Fantasy in the Doctrine of Odious Debts (with Response: Reflections on "A Convenient Untruth")', *Virginia Journal of International Law* 48:3. Duke Law School Legal Studies Paper No. 174, pp. 1–47

Gurmendi Dunkelberg, Alonso, 'A Legal History of Consent and Intervention in Civil Wars in Latin America', *Journal on the Use of Force and International Law* 7:1 (2020), pp. 102–121

Gutiérrez, Juan María, 'Fisonomía del saber español; cual deba ser entre nosotros', in *Discursos pronunciados el día de la apertura del salon literario* (Buenos Aires: Imprenta de la Independencia, 1837), pp. 43– 61

Haimovich, Gregory, 'Linguistic Consequences of Evangelization in Colonial Peru: Analyzing the Quechua Corpus of the Doctrina Christiana y Catecismo', *Journal of Language Contact* 10:2 (2017), pp. 193–218

Hale, Charles, *El liberalismo mexicano en la época de Mora*. Translated by Serio Fernández Bravo and Francisco González Aramburu (Mexico City: Siglo XXI, 2012)

Hall, Catherine, Nicholas Draper, and Keith McClelland eds., *Emancipation and the Remaking of the British Imperial World* (Manchester: Manchester University Press, 2014)

Halperín-Donghi, Tulio, *Politics, Economics and Society in Argentina in the Revolutionary Period*. Translated by Richard Southern (Cambridge: Cambridge University Press, 1975)

Guerra y finanzas en los orígenes del Estado argentino (1791 –1850) (Buenos Aires: Belgrano, 1982)

Hamnett, Brian R., *Juárez. El benemérito de las Américas* (Madrid: Biblioteca Nueva, 2006)

'Juárez: La verdadera significación de una presidencia controvertida', in Josefina Zoraida Vázquez ed., *Juárez: historia y mito* (Mexico City: El Colegio de México, 2010), pp. 17–32

La política española en una época revolucionaria (1790–1820) (México: Fondo de Cultura Económica, 2011)

The End of Iberian Rule on the American Continent, 1770–1830 (Cambridge: Cambridge University Press, 2017)

Hann, John H., 'The Role of the Mexican Deputies in the Proposal and Enactment of Measures of Economic Reform Applicable to Mexico', in Nettie Lee Benson, *Mexico and the Spanish Cortes, 1810–1822: Eight Essays* (Austin: University of Texas Press, 1966), pp. 153–184

Harris, Steven M., 'The Global Construction of International Law in the Nineteenth Century: The Case of Arbitration', *Journal of World History* 27:2 (2016), pp. 303–325

Heimbeck, Lea, 'Discovering Legal Silence: Global Legal History and the Liquidation of State Bankruptcies (1854–1907)', in Thomas Duve ed., *Entanglements in Legal History: Conceptual Approaches* (Frankfurt: Max Planck Institute for European Legal History, Frankfurt am Main, 2014), pp. 461–487

Helg, Aline, *Liberty and Equality in Caribbean Colombia, 1770–1835* (Chapel Hill: University of North Carolina Press, 2005)

Helleiner, Eric, 'Dollarization Diplomacy: US Policy Towards Latin America Coming Full Circle?', *Review of International Political Economy* 10:3 (2003), pp. 406–429.
Henderson, Paul, 'Cocoa, Finance and the State in Ecuador, 1895–1925', *Bulletin of Latin American Research* 16:2 (1997) pp. 169–186
Hendrickson, Embert J., 'Roosevelt's Second Venezuelan Controversy', *Hispanic American Historical Review* 50:3 (1970), pp. 482–498
Henry, Jabez, *Outline of a Plan of an International Bankrupt Code for the Different Commercial States of Europe* (London, n.d).
Hepbur, Jarrod, *Domestic Law in International Investment Arbitration* (Oxford: Oxford University Press, 2017)
Hernández del Ángel, Félix, 'Producción periodística de Juan Bautista Morales en la primera mitad del siglo xix (1822–1856)' *Oficio. Revista de historia e interdisciplina* (2022), pp. 51–68
Hernández Carballido, Elvira, 'Un recorrido por las publicaciones de mujeres en el siglo XIX', in Patricia Galeana ed., *Historia de las mujeres en México* (Mexico City: INEHRM, 2015), pp. 157–180
Herrejón Peredo, Carlos, 'El endeudamiento de Hidalgo', *Relaciones. Estudios de historia y sociedad*, 34:133 (2013), pp. 199–223
Herrera León, Fabian, 'Lucas Alamán, estadista y artífice de las misiones por un "Pacto de Familia"', *Revista Mexicana De Política Exterior* 97 (2022), pp. 167–190
Herrera Arroyave, Diana Paola, 'Sobre la Querella Benthamista en Colombia', *Telos* 15:2 (2009), pp. 9–29
Hershey, Amos S., 'The Calvo and Drago Doctrines', *American Journal of International Law* 1:1 (1907), pp. 26–45
Herzog, Tamar, *Is Spain Exceptional? Reflections on Thirty Years of Research and Writing', in Edward Jones Corredera* ed., Supplicant Empires: Searching for the Iberian World in Global History (Turnhout: Brepols) (Forthcoming)
Defining Nations: Immigrants and Citizens in Early Modern Spain and Spanish America (New Haven: Yale University Press, 2003)
Hespanha, Antonio M., *La gracia del derecho: Economía de la cultura en la Edad Moderna.* Edited by Bartolomé Clavero and translated by Ana Cañellas Haurie (Madrid: Centro de Estudios Constitucionales, 1993)
Hilton, Boyd, *The Age of Atonement: The Influence of Evangelicalism on Social and Economic Thought, 1795–1865* (Oxford: Oxford University Press, 1988)
A Mad, Bad, & Dangerous People? England 1783–1846 (Oxford: Oxford University Press, 2006)
Hinrichsen, Simon, *When Nations Can't Default* (Cambridge: Cambridge University Press, 2023)
Historia parlamentaria mexicana: sesiones secretas, 1821–1824. Volumes 1 and 2 (Mexico City: Instituto de Investigaciones Legislativas, 1984)
Historia parlamentaria mexicana. Crónicas: I (mayo–octubre, 1823); Crónicas: II (febrero–marzo, octubre–diciembre, 1824) (Mexico City: Instituto de Investigaciones Legislativas, 1983)
Hodge, John E., 'Carlos Pellegrini and the Financial Crisis of 1890', *Hispanic American Historical Review* 50:3 (1970), pp. 499–523
Hoeflich, M. H., 'Through a Glass Darkly: Reflections upon the History of the International Law of Public Debt in Connection with State Succession Symposium: Default by Foreign Government Debtors', *University of Illinois Law Review* 1 (1982), pp. 39–70
Hogan, Michael, 'Juárez, Maximilian, and the French Occupation of Mexico', in William Beezley ed., *The Oxford Handbook of Mexican History* (Online)
Holguín, Jorge, *Desde cerca: (asuntos colombianos)* (Paris: Ficker, 1908)
Hont, Istvan and Michael Ignatieff eds., *Wealth and Virtue: The Shaping of Political Economy in the Scottish Enlightenment* (Cambridge: Cambridge University Press, 2012)
Horacio López, Luis, *A los colombianos. Proclamas y discursos 1812–1840* (Bogotá: Biblioteca de la Presidencia de la República, 1988)
Huber Abendroth, Hans, 'La deuda pública externa y sus renegociaciones entre 1875 y el arreglo ad referéndum de 1948', in Álvaro Aguirre Badani, Carlos Villegas Quiroga, Hans Huber

Abendroth, Hugo Delgadillo Barea, and Mario Napoleón Pacheco eds., *La deuda externa de Bolivia: 125 años de renegociaciones y ¿cuántos más?* (La Paz: CEDLA, 2001), pp. 25–194

Hudson, Saul, 'Venezuela to Quit IMF, World Bank', *Reuters*, 1 May 2007

Hurtado, Jimena, 'La economía política en los estudios superiores en la segunda mitad del siglo XIX en Colombia: Ezequiel Rojas, sus influencias y programas', in Andrés Álvarez and Juan Santiago Correa eds., *Ideas y políticas económicas en Colombia durante el primer siglo republicano* (Bogotá: Universidad de los Andes, Colombia, 2016), pp. 35–68

Ibarra Bellón, Araceli, *El comercio y el poder en México, 1821–1864: la lucha por las fuentes financieras entre el Estado central y las regiones* (Mexico City: Fondo de Cultura Económica, 1998)

Innes, Joanna, *Inferior Politics: Social Problems and Social Policies in Eighteenth-Century Britain* (Oxford: Oxford University Press, 2009)

Ingenieros, José, *La evolución de las ideas argentinas*. Volume 1 (Buenos Aires: La Revolución, Talleres Gráficos Argentinos, 1918),

Iñurritegui Rodríguez, José María, 'Traducción y geografías del interés en la temprana Ilustración hispana', *Studia historica. Historia moderna* 43:2 (2021), pp. 283–304

Iriarte, Luis, 'Alberdi por Alberdi: Luces y sombras de su pensamiento y accionar político', in Carmen Fontán ed., *Juan Bautista Alberdi. Apología y Crítica de su pensamiento* (San Miguel de Tucuman, Argentina: Constitución para Todos, 2011), pp. 389–456

'Crisis del año XX', in Carmen Fontán ed., *Juan Bautista Alberdi. Apología y Crítica de su pensamiento* (San Miguel de Tucuman, Argentina: Constitución para Todos, 2011), pp. 193–212

"Del centralismo al confederacionismo', in Carmen Fontán ed., *Juan Bautista Alberdi. Apología y Crítica de su pensamiento* (San Miguel de Tucuman, Argentina: Constitución para Todos, 2011), pp. 213–240

Iribarne, Rodolfo Antonio, 'La cuestión capital en 1826', *Universidad de Buenos Aires. Facultad de Derecho. Departamento de Publicaciones* (1970), pp. 185–221

Isabella, Maurizio, *Southern Europe in the Age of Revolutions* (Princeton: Princeton University Press, 2023)

Ittersum, Martine van, *Profit and Principle Hugo Grotius, Natural Rights Theories and the Rise of Dutch Power in the East Indies, 1595–1615* (Leiden: Brill, 2006)

Iurlaro, Francesca, *The Invention of Custom: Natural Law and the Law of Nations, ca. 1550–1750* (Oxford: Oxford University Press, 2021)

Ixchel Atilano, Tania, 'The 1871 Mexican Criminal Code as the Missing Piece in the History of Criminalizing Violations of the Laws of War', *International Review of the Red Cross* 104 (2022), pp. 1650–1683

Jackson, Trevor, *Impunity and Capitalism: The Afterlives of European Financial Crises, 1690–1830* (Cambridge: Cambridge University Press, 2022)

Jaffe, Catherine M. and Elisa Martín-Valdepeñas Yagüe eds., *Society Women and Enlightened Charity in Spain: The Junta de Damas de Honor y Mérito, 1787–1823* (Baton Rouge: Louisiana State University Press, 2022)

Jaksic, Ivan, *Andrés Bello: Scholarship and Nation-Building in Nineteenth-Century Latin America* (Cambridge: Cambridge University Press, 2006)

James Hudson, Peter, *Bankers and Empire: How Wall Street Colonized the Caribbean* (Chicago: Chicago University Press, 2017)

Janssen, Geert H, *The Dutch Revolt and Catholic Exile in Reformation Europe* (Cambridge: Cambridge University Press, 2014)

Jiménez Ángel, Andrés, 'Ciencia, lengua e hispanidad en la construcción de la cultura nacional en Colombia, 1867–1880', *Iberoamericana* 13:50 (2013), pp. 85–99

Johnson, Samuel, *A Dictionary of the English Language. 1755, 1773.* Edited by Beth Rapp Young, Jack Lynch, William Dorner, Amy Larner Giroux, Carmen Faye Mathes, and Abigail Moreshead. 2021 (Online)

Jonas, Raymond, *Habsburgs on the Rio Grande: The Rise and Fall of the Second Mexican Empire* (Cambridge, MA: Harvard University Press, 2024)

Jones, Charles, 'Constituting Argentina, 1810–1860', in Stephen G. H. Roberts and Adam Sharman eds., *1812 Echoes: The Cádiz Constitution in Hispanic History* (Newcastle: Cambridge Scholars, 2013), pp. 264–281

Jones Corredera, Edward, 'Labouring Horizons: Passions and Interests in Jovellanos' *Ley Agraria*', *Dieciocho* 38:2 (2015), pp. 267–290

'"Amazing Rapidity": Time, Public Credit, and David Hume's *Political Discourses*', *Contributions to the History of Concepts* 14:1 (2019), pp. 17–41

'Investing in the Enlightenment: The Financial Revolution and the Global Origins of the Enlightenment in the Spanish Empire', *Storia della Storiografia* 77:1 (2020), pp. 89–111

The Diplomatic Enlightenment: Spain, Europe, and the Age of Speculation (Leiden: Brill, 2021)

'Why International Lawyers Measure Time with a Telescope: Grotian Moments & Richard Falk's Histories of the Future', *Grotiana* 42:2 (2021), pp. 212–228

'How Undiplomatic Memoirs Shaped Enlightenment Reform: Melchor Rafael Macanaz's Memorias and Contexts of Change in Bourbon Spain', in Adriana Luna-Fabritius, Ere Nokkala, Marten Seppel, and Keith Tribe eds., *Political Reason and the Language of Change Reform and Improvement in Early Modern Europe* (London: Routledge, 2023), pp. 198–217

'Free Trade & the Ghost Story of the Bourbon Alliance: Spain, Free Ports, and the Mediterranean Sea, c. 1648–1765', in Giulia Delogu, Koen Stapelbroek, and Antonio Trampus eds., *Free Trade and Free Ports in the Mediterranean* (London: Routledge, 2024), pp. 198-213

'The End of Composite Monarchies: Hugo Grotius' *De iure belli ac pacis* & Mid-Seventeenth-Century Iberian Diplomacy', *English Historical Review* (Forthcoming)

When did Spain go to Sleep? An Empire Dead to the World', in Edward Jones Corredera ed., *Supplicant Empires: Searching for the Iberian World in Global History* (Turnhout: Brepols) (Forthcoming)

'The Laws of Debt: The Paraguayan War (1864–1870) and the Drago Doctrine', in Raphaël Cahen, León Castellanos- Jankiewicz, and Hendrik Simon eds., *The Monroe Doctrine: History, Interpretations, Legacy* (Under review).

Jones Corredera, Edward, ed.,*Supplicant Empires: Searching for the Iberian World in Global History* (Turnhout: Brepols) (Forthcoming)

Julien, Catherine, *Reading Inca History* (Iowa City: University of Iowa Press, 2000)

Julieta Casas, Laura, 'Alberdi y el derecho internacional. La actualidad de su pensamiento', in Carmen Fontán ed., *Juan Bautista Alberdi. Apología y Crítica de su pensamiento* (San Miguel de Tucuman, Argentina: Constitución para Todos, 2011)

Kagan, Richard L., 'Prescott's Paradigm: American Historical Scholarship and the Decline of Spain', *The American Historical Review* 101:2 (1996), pp. 423–446

Kaiser, Axel, 'The Chicago Boys and the Revival of Classical Liberal Economics in Chile', *The Independent Review* 26:3 (2021-2022), pp. 1–22

Kalmanovitz, Salomón, *La idea federal en Colombia durante el siglo XIX* (Bogotá: Banco de la República, Mimeo, 2003)

'Constituciones y crecimiento económico en la Colombia del siglo XIX', *Revista De Historia Economica—Journal of Iberian and Latin American Economic History* 26:2 (2008), pp. 205–241

Kennedy, David, 'International Law and the Nineteenth Century: History of an Illusion', *Nordic Journal of International Law* 65 (1996), pp. 385–420

Kennedy, David and Martti Koskenniemi, *Of Law and the World: Critical Conversations on Power, History, and Political Economy* (Cambridge: Harvard University Press, 2023)

King, Jeff, *The Doctrine of Odious Debt in International Law A Restatement* (Cambridge: Cambridge University Press, 2016)

Klein, Herbert S., 'The Great Shift: the Rise of Mexico and the Decline of Peru in the Spanish American Colonial Empire, 1680–1809', *Revista De Historia Economica—Journal of Iberian and Latin American Economic History* 13:1 (1995), pp. 35–61

Klein, Herbert and Ben Vinson III, *Historia mínima de la esclavitud en América Latina y en el Caribe* (Mexico City: Colegio de México, 2013)

Klein, Matthew and Michael Pettis, *Trade Wars Are Class Wars: How Rising Inequality Distorts the Global Economy and Threatens International Peace* (New Haven: Yale University Press, 2020)

Knight, Alan, 'Debt Bondage in Latin America', in Léonie Archer ed., *Slavery: And Other Forms of Unfree Labour* (New York: Routledge, 2013), pp. 102–117

Bandits and Liberals, Rebels and Saints: Latin America since Independence (Lincoln: University of Nebraska, 2022)

Knott, Sarah, 'Sensibility and the American War for Independence', *American Historical Review* 109:1 (2004), pp. 19–40

Koenigsberger, Helmut, *The Government of Sicily under Philip II of Spain* (London: Staples Press, 1951)

Kolakowski, Leszek, *God Owes Us Nothing: A Brief Remark on Pascal's Religion and on the Spirit of Jansenism* (Chicago: University of Chicago Press, 1995)

Kolla, Edward James, *Sovereignty, International Law, and the French Revolution* (Cambridge: Cambridge University Press, 2017)

Koskenniemi, Martti, *The Gentle Civilizer of Nations: The Rise and Fall of International Law 1870–1960* (Cambridge: Cambridge University Press, 2001)

'Colonization of the "Indies". The Origin of International Law?', in Yolanda Gamarra Chopo ed., *La idea de América en el pensamiento ius internacionalista del siglo XXI: Estudios a propósito de la conmemoración de los bicentenarios de las independencias de las repúblicas latinoamericanas* (Zaragoza: Institución Fernando el Católico, 2010), pp. 43–63, pp. 56–60

To the Uttermost Parts of the Earth: Legal Imagination and International Power 1300–1870 (Cambridge: Cambridge University Press, 2021)

Krauze, Enrique, *Mexico: Biography of Power. A History of Modern Mexico, 1810–1996*. Translated by Hanz Heifetz (New York: Harper Collins, 1997)

LaFeber, Walter, *The New Cambridge History of American Foreign Relations*. Volume 2 (Cambridge: Cambridge University Press, 2013)

Lafit, Facundo, 'El reformismo ilustrado español y napolitano en la Representación de los hacendados de Mariano Moreno', *Anuario del Centro de Estudios Históricos 'Prof. Carlos S. A. Segreti' Córdoba* 21 (2021), pp. 32–53

Landavazo, Marco Antonio, 'Para una historia social de la violencia insurgente: el odio al Gachupín', *Historia Mexicana* 59:1 (2009), pp. 195–225

Lane, Kris, *Potosi: The Silver City That Changed the World* (Berkeley: University of California Press, 2019)

Laplante, Lisa J., 'Outlawing Amnesty: The Return of Criminal Justice in Transitional Justice Schemes', *Virginia Journal of International Law* 49:4 (2019), pp. 915–984

la Parra López, Emilio, *Fernando VII: un rey deseado y detestado* (Barcelona: Tusquets, 2018)

'El Rey ante sus súbditos. Presencia de Fernando VII en el espacio público', *Revista de Historia Constitucional* 20 (2019), pp. 5–23

Lawrence, Mark, 'Constitutional Catechism and the Crowd', *La Révolution française* (Online)

Lecuna, Vicente, *Relaciones diplomáticas de Bolívar con Chile y Buenos Aires: copiadas de los originales existentes en las secciones del Archivo del libertador denominadas de O'Leary y Juan de Francisco Martín*. Volume 1 (Caracas: Imprenta Nacional, 1954)

Leriche, Rosario Janet, 'La política de Entre Ríos en el marco de la crisis directorial y el tratado del Pilar', *Claves* 7:13 (2021), pp. 189–212

Lesaffer, Randall 'Peace Treaties from Lodi to Westphalia', in Randall Lesaffer ed., *Peace Treaties and International Law in European History: From the Late Middle Ages to World War One* (Cambridge: Cambridge University Press, 2004), pp. 9–44

Levaggi, Abelardo, 'El derecho romano en la formación de los abogados argentinos del ochocientos', *Revista de Estudios Histórico-Jurídicos* 10 (1985), pp. 16–33

Levene, Ricardo, 'Notas para la Historia de las Ideas Sociales y Jurídicas Argentinas', *Revista Mexicana de Sociología* 6:3 (1994), pp. 331–346

Liehr, Reinhard, 'Endeudamiento estatal y crédito privado la consolidación de vales reales en hispanoamérica', *Anuario de Estudios Americanos* 41 (1984), pp. 553–578

'La deuda exterior de la Gran Colombia frente a Gran Bretaña, 1820–1860', in Reinhard Liehr ed., *América Latina en la época de Simón Bolívar. La formación de las economías nacionales y los intereses económicos europeos 1800–1850* (Berlin: Colloquium-Verlag, 1989), pp. 465–488

Lienau, Odette. 'Who is the 'Sovereign' in Sovereign Debt?: Reinterpreting a Rule-of-Law Framework from the Early Twentieth Century', *Yale Journal of International Law* 33:1 (2008), pp. 63–111

Rethinking Sovereign Debt: Politics, Reputation, and Legitimacy in Modern Finance (Cambridge: Harvard University Press, 2014)

Loayza, Francisco A., *Juan Santos: el invencible: manuscritos del año de 1742 al año de 1755* (Lima: Editorial Domingo Miranda, 1942)

López, Alfred J., *José Martí: A Revolutionary Life* (Austin: University of Texas Press, 2014)

López, Edwin and Salomón Kalmanovitz, 'La idea federal en el nacimiento de la República colombiana 1810–1828', in Andrés Álvarez and Juan Santiago Correa eds., *Ideas y políticas económicas en Colombia durante el primer siglo republicano* (Bogotá: Universidad de los Andes, Colombia, 2016)

López-Bejarano, Pilar, 'La Justicia de una deuda: el fuero eclesiástico y la deuda pública neogranadina en el período revolucionario', *Illes i imperis* 15 (2013), pp. 29–53

Un Estado a crédito. Deudas y configuración estatal de la Nueva Granada en la primera mitad del siglo XIX (Bogotá: Editorial de la Pontificia Universidad Javeriana, 2015)

López Castellano, Fernando, 'Las Cortes de Cádiz y la implantación del buen orden económico (1810–1814)', *Historia Constitucional* 13 (2012), pp. 233–256

López Domínguez, Luis Horacio, *Obra educativa: la querella benthamista, 1748–1832* (Bogotá: Fundación para la Conmemoración del Bicentenario del Natalicio y el Sesquicentenario de la Muerte del General Francisco de Paula Santander, 1993)

Lovera de-Sola, Roberto, 'Bello crítico en Londres', in *Bello y Londres: Segundo Congreso del Bicentenario*. Volume 2 (Caracas: La Casa de Bello, 1980), pp. 7–33

Lovett, A. W., *Philip II and Mateo Vázquez de Leca: the Government of Spain (1572–1592)* (Geneva: Droz, 1977)

'The Castilian Bankruptcy of 1575', *The Historical Journal* 23:4 (1980), pp. 899–911

Ludington, Sarah, Mitu Gulati, and Alfred L. Brophy, 'A Convenient Untruth: Fact and Fantasy in the Doctrine of Odious Debts', *Virginia Journal of International Law* 48:3 (2008), pp. 595–639

'Applied Legal History: Demystifying the Doctrine of Odious Debts', *Theoretical Inquiries in Law* 11 (2010), pp. 247–281

Ludlow, Leonor ed., 'El Banco Nacional Mexicano y el Banco Mercantil Mexicano: radiografía social de sus primeros accionistas, 1881–1882', *Historia Mexicana* 39:4 (1990), pp. 979–1027

Francisco Bulnes: La deuda inglesa. Colección de artículos publicados en el siglo XIX; estudio sobre la debatida cuestión de la depreciación de la plata (Mexico City: UNAM, 2008), pp. 125–152

Ludlow, Leonor and Carlos Marichal eds., *Banca y poder en México* (1800–1925) (Mexico City: Grijalbo, 1985)

Lupi, Marta, '*Ius Mercatorum* and Statutes of Florence during the 14th and 15th Centuries: The Case of Bankruptcy', *GLOSSAE. European Journal of Legal History* 16 (2019), pp. 204–227

Lynch, John, *Argentine Dictator: Juan Manuel de Rosas 1829–1852* (Oxford: Clarendon Press, 1981)

Simón Bolívar: A Life (New Haven: Yale University Press, 2006)

New Worlds: A Religious History of Latin America (New Haven: Yale University Press, 2012)

Maass, Matthias, 'Catalyst for the Roosevelt Corollary: Arbitrating the 1902–1903 Venezuela Crisis and Its Impact on the Development of the Roosevelt Corollary to the Monroe Doctrine', *Diplomacy & Statecraft* 20:3 (2009), pp. 383–402

Mac-Clure, Oscar, 'El economista Courcelle-Seneuil en el período fundacional de la economía como disciplina en Chile', *Universum (Talca)* 26:1 (2011), pp. 93–108

Macias, Flavia and María Paula Parolo, 'Guerra de independencia y reordenamiento social. La militarización en el norte argentino (primera mitad del siglo XIX)', *Boletín de la Biblioteca del Congreso Nacional* 134:12 (2020), pp. 89–111

Maitland, F. W., *State, Trust and Corporation*. Edited by David Runciman and Magnus Ryan (Cambridge: Cambridge University Press, 2003)

Malamud, Carlos Daniel ed., *Ruptura y reconciliación España y el reconocimiento de las independencias latinoamericanas* (Madrid: Fundación Mapfre, 2012)

Malaspina, Alejandro, 'Axiomas políticos sobre América', in Manuel Lucena Giraldo and Juan Pimentel eds., *Los 'Axiomas políticos sobre la América' de Alejandro Malaspina* (Aranjuez: Sociedad Estatal Quinto Centenario, 1991)

Mälkso, Lauri, 'F.F. Martens and His Time: When Russia Was an Integral Part of the European Tradition of International Law', *European Journal of International Law* 25:3 (2014), pp. 811–829

Mallard, Grégoire, *Gift Exchange: The Transnational History of a Political Idea* (Cambridge: Cambridge University Press, 2019)

Manian, Ilasai and V. Rajesh, *The Russian Revolution and India* (London: Routledge, 2020)

Mangan, Jane E., *Transatlantic Obligations: Creating the Bonds of Family in Conquest-era Peru and Spain* (Oxford: Oxford University Press, 2016)

Mann, Bruce H., *Republic of Debtors: Bankruptcy in the Age of American Independence* (Cambridge: Harvard University Press, 2009)

Marcos Martín, Alberto, 'Medina del Campo en la Época Moderna: del florecimiento a la decadencia. Estructura ocupacional y estructura de la demanda en los siglos XVI, XVII y XVIII: un intento de estimación de la riqueza y su distribución por categorías sociales', in Eufemio Lorenzo ed., *Historia de Medina del Campo y su tierra*. Volume 1 (Medina del Campo: Ayuntamiento de Medina del Campo, 1986), pp. 523–634

Marichal, Carlos, *A Century of Debt Crises in Latin America, from Independence to the Great Depression, 1820–1930* (Princeton: Princeton University Press, 1989)

'Foreign Loans, Banks and Capital Markets in Mexico, 1880–1910', in Reinhard Liehr ed., *La deuda pública en América Latina en perspectiva histórica* (Frankfurt: Iberoamericana, 1995), pp. 337–374.

Bankruptcy of Empire: Mexican Silver and the Wars Between Spain, Britain and France, 1760–1810 (Cambridge: Cambridge University Press, 2009)

Historia mínima de la deuda externa de Latinoamérica (Mexico City: El Colegio de México, 2014)

'El Nacimiento de los estudios internacionales: Comentarios a las obras de José María Caicedo y Carlos Calvo a mediados del siglo XIX', *Foro Internacional* 221 (2015), pp. 707–736

Mariluz Urquijo, José M., 'Manuel Jose Garcia: un eco de Benjamin Constant en el Plata', *Journal of Inter-American Studies* 9:3 (1967), pp. 429–440

Markham Lester, V., *Victorian Insolvency: Bankruptcy, Imprisonment for Debt, and Company Winding-Up in Nineteenth-Century England* (New York: Oxford University Press, 1995)

Martí, José, *Correspondencia con el general Máximo Gómez* (Havana: Editorial de Ciencias Sociales, 1977)

Nuestra América. Prologue by Carlos Battilana y Rodrigo Caresani (Buenos Aires: Biblioteca del Congreso de la Nación, 2019)

Martín, Eloísa, 'Peter Berger's Theory of Secularization in Latin America: The Two Sacred Canopies', *Journal of the American Academy of Religion* 85:4 (2017), pp. 1137–1146

Martin, Jamie, *The Meddlers: Sovereignty, Empire, and the Birth of Global Economic Governance* (Cambridge: Harvard University Press, 2022)

Martínez, Iván Pastoriza, 'Nacionalidad y soberanía. El debate entre Alberdi y Albistur sobre el estatus de los hijos de españoles en la construcción de la extranjería en el Río de la Plata (c. 1852–1869)', *Revista de historia del derecho* 62 (2021), pp. 51–81

Martínez Garnica, Armando, *Historia de la primera República de Colombia, 1819–1831. 'Decid Colombia sea, y Colombia será'* (Bogotá: Editorial Universidad del Rosario, 2018)

Martínez López-Cano, María del Pilar, 'La Iglesia y el crédito en Nueva España: entre viejos presupuestos y nuevos retos de investigación' in María de Pilar Martínez López-Cano ed., *La Iglesia en Nueva España. Problemas y perspectivas de investigación* (Mexico City: UNAM, 2010), pp. 303–352

Martykánová, Darina and Juan Luis Simal, 'Ferdinand and the Sultan: The Metaphor of the Turk and the Crisis of the Spanish Monarchy in the Early Nineteenth Century', *Contributions to the History of Concepts* 10:1 (2015), pp. 1–26

Masiello, Francine, *Between Civilization and Barbarism: Women, Nation, and Literary Culture in Modern Argentina* (Lincoln: University of Nebraska Press, 1992)

'Lost in Translation: Eduarda Mansilla de García on Politics, Gender, and War', in Doris Meyer ed., *Reinterpreting the Spanish American Essay: Women writers of the 19th and 20th Centuries* (Austin: University of Texas Press, 1995), pp. 68–80

Mayer, Jorge, *Alberdi y su tiempo* (Buenos Aires: Editorial Universitaria de Buenos Aires, 1963)

Mayo, Carlos and Jaime Peire, 'Iglesia y crédito colonial: La política crediticia de los conventos de Buenos Aires (1767–1810)' *Revista de Historia de América* 112 (1991), pp. 147–157

Mazower, Mark, *The Greek Revolution: 1821 and the Making of Modern Europe* (London: Penguin, 2021)

McClure, Julia, 'Editors' Forum: Empires of Charity', *New Global Studies* 2:12 (2018)

'Poverty and Empire', in Julia McClure and David Hitchcock eds., *The Routledge History of Poverty, c. 1450–1800* (Abingdon: Routledge, 2020), pp. 39–59

'Conquest by Contract: Property Rights and the Commercial Logic of Imperialism in the Isthmus of Tehuantepec (Southern Mexico)', *Bulletin of Latin American Research*, 41:4 (2022), pp. 557–572

McGraw, Jason, *The Work of Recognition Caribbean Colombia and the Postemancipation Struggle for Citizenship* (Chapel Hill: University of North Carolina Press, 2014)

McKennan, Theodora Louise, *Santander and the Vogue of Benthamism in Colombia and Nueva Granada* (Unpublished PhD thesis) (Chicago: Loyola University, 1970)

Mejía Macía Mejía, Sergio Andrés, *La revolución en letras: La historia de la Revolución en Colombia de José Manuel Restrepo (1781–1863)* (Bogotá: Universidad de Los Andes, 2007)

El pasado como refugio y esperanza: La historia eclesiástica y civil de Nueva Granada de José Manuel Groot (Bogotá: Universidad de los Andes, 2010).

Mejías-Lopez, Alejandro, *The Inverted Conquest: The Myth of Modernity and the Transatlantic Onset of Modernism* (Chapel Hill, NC: Vanderbilt University Press, 2009)

Melo Flórez, Jairo Antonio, 'Clemencia y obediencia. El vínculo amoroso entre el rey y los vasallos del Nuevo Reino de Granada entre 1780 y 1800', *Historia Crítica* 78 (2020), pp. 25–43

Mercado, Juan Carlos, 'Pedro de Angelis y la historia intelectual argentina de la primera mitad del siglo XIX', *Hesperia. Anuario de filología hispánica* 16:2 (2013), pp. 59–72

Mevorach, Irit, *The Future of Cross-Border Insolvency: Overcoming Biases and Closing Gaps* (Oxford: Oxford University Press, 2018)

Mier, Servando Teresa de, *Carta de despedida a los mexicanos: 1821.* Prólogo, notas y cronología de Edmundo O'Gorman (Caracas: Biblioteca Ayacucho, 1978)

Historia de la revolución de Nueva España (Mexico City: CEMC, 1990)

Memorias (Mexico City: Secretaría de Cultura, 2016)

Miller, Nicola, *In the Shadow of the State: Intellectuals and the Quest for National Identity in Twentieth-Century Spanish America* (London: Verso, 1999)

Millington, Thomas, *Debt Politics After Independence: The Funding Conflict in Bolivia* (Gainesville, FA: University Press of Florida, 1992)

Miranda, Francisco de, 'Proclamación a los pueblos del continente colombiano', *Cuadernos de Cultura Latinoamericana* 23 (1978), pp. 5–20

Mirra, Dante, 'La perdurabilidad de la Constitución en las "Bases" de Alberdi', in Carmen Fontán ed., *Juan Bautista Alberdi. Apología y Crítica de su pensamiento* (San Miguel de Tucuman, Argentina: Constitución para Todos, 2011), pp. 323–339

Mitchell, Nancy, 'The Height of the German Challenge: The Venezuela Blockade, 1902–3', *Diplomatic History* 20:2 (1996), pp. 185–210

Mitchener, Kris James and Marc D. Weidenmier, 'The Baring Crisis and the Great Latin American Meltdown of the 1890s', *The Journal of Economic History* 68:2 (2008), pp. 462–500

Mitre, Bartolomé, *Facundo o civilización y barbarie en las pampas argentinas* (Santiago: Imprenta del Progreso, 1845).

Arengas de Bartolomé Mitre. Volume 1. Edited by Alfonso Lamarque (Buenos Aires: Pablo E. Coni, 1875)

Historia de San Martín y de la emancipación Sud-Americana. Volume 4 (Paris: Bouret, 1890)

Molina, Alonso de, *Vocabulario en lengua castellana y mexicana y mexicana y castellana* (Mexico City: Casa de Espinosa, 1571)

Montesquieu, Charles de, *The Spirit of the Laws*. Edited by Anne M. Cohler, Basia Carolyn Miller, and Harold Samuel Stone (Cambridge: Cambridge University Press, 1989)

Moorman, Mary C., *Indulgences: Luther, Catholicism, and the Imputation of Merit* (Steubenville, OH: Emmaus Academic, 2017)

Mora, José Luis María, *México y sus revoluciones*. Three volumes. Volume 1 (Paris: Librería Rosa, 1836)

Morales Cama, Grover Paúl, and Joan Manuel Morales Cama, 'El magistrado Manuel Lorenzo de Vidaurre y el nacimiento de la República', *Revista del Archivo General de la Nación* 31:1 (2016), pp. 123–189

Morales y Ucalde, José, *Manifestación del estado de la hacienda de la república del Perú en fin de abril de 1827* (Lima: J.M. Concha, 1827)

Moreno, Mariano, *Representación de los Hacendados* (1809). Reprinted (Madrid: Biblioteca Virtual Universal, 2003)

Moreno Acevedo, Elda de Jesús, 'Génesis del sistema fiscal mexicano 1821–1824', *Documentos de Trabajo (IELAT)* 40 (2012), pp. 53–69

Morgan, Iwan, 'French Policy in Spanish America: 1830–48', *Journal of Latin American Studies* 10:2 (1978), pp. 309–328

Moyn, Samuel, 'International Law and the Politics of History. By Anne Orford. Cambridge, UK: Cambridge University Press, 2021. Pp. Xii, 382. Index', *American Journal of International Law* 116:4 (2022), pp. 895–900

Mr. Woodford to Mr. Sherman, 13 September 1897. Papers Relating to the Foreign Relations of the United States, With the Annual Message of the President Transmitted to Congress December 5, 1898. Office of the Historian, Foreign Service Institute. Document 492 (Online)

Muldrew, Craig, *The Economy of Obligation: The Culture of Credit and Social Relations in Early Modern England* (London: Palgrave Macmillan, 1998)

Munro, George E., 'Paying for Poland's Partitions', *Journal of Baltic Studies* 20:4 (1989), pp. 327–336

Muñoz Sempere, Daniel, 'Cultural Identity and Political Dissidence: The Periodicals of the Spanish Liberal Exile in London (1810–1841), in Constance Bantman and Ana Cláudia Suriani da Silva eds., *The Foreign Political Press in Nineteenth-Century London: Politics from a Distance* (London: Bloomsbury Publishing, 2017), pp. 33–50

Murphy, Antoin E., *John Law: Economic Theorist and Policy-maker* (Oxford: Oxford University Press, 1997)

Murphy, Gretchen, *Hemispheric Imaginings: The Monroe Doctrine and Narratives of U.S. Empire* (Durham: Duke University Press, 2005)

Musa, Shavana, *Victim Reparation under the Ius Post Bellum: An Historical and Normative Perspective* (Cambridge: Cambridge University Press, 2019)

Nakhimovsky, Isaac, *The Holy Alliance: Liberalism and the Politics of Federation* (Princeton: Princeton University Press, 2024)

Nearing, Scott and Joseph Freeman, *Dollar Diplomacy: A Study in American Imperialism* (New York: Modern Reader Paperbacks, 1969)

Neff, Stephen, *Justice among Equals: A History of International Law* (Cambridge: Harvard University Press, 2014)

Nellen, Henk, *Hugo Grotius: A Lifelong Struggle for Peace in Church and State, 1583–1645* (Leiden: Brill, 2015)

Nichols Barker, Nancy, *The French Experience in Mexico, 1821–1861: A History of Constant Misunderstanding* (Chapel Hill: UNC Press Books, 2018)

Novales, Alberto, *El Trienio Liberal* (Zaragoza: Prensas de la Universidad de Zaragoza, 2020)

Novoa Monreal, Eduardo, *La batalla del cobre. Comentarios y documentos* (Santiago de Chile: Quimantú, 1972)

Nowack, Kerstin, 'Measuring the Passage of Time in Inca and Early Spanish Peru', *Indiana* 30 (2013), pp. 77–98

Núñez, Ignacio, *Noticias históricas, políticas, y estadísticas de las Provincias Unidas del Río de La Plata: con un apéndice sobre la usurpación de Montevideo por los gobiernos portugués y brasilero*

O'Banion, Patrick J., 'Only the King Can Do It: Adaptation and Flexibility in Crusade Ideology in Sixteenth-Century Spain', *Church History* 81:3 (2012), pp. 552–574

Obras completas de don Andrés Bello. Volume 10 (Santiago de Chile: Ramírez, 1886)

Obras completas de Andrés Bello. Volume 23: *Temas de historia y geografía* (Caracas: Ministerio de Educación, 1957)

Obras sueltas de José María Luis Mora, ciudadano mexicano (Mexico City: Editorial Porrúa, 1963)

Obregón, Liliana, 'The Forgotten 19th Century: A New History of a "Latin American" International Law', *Annuaire de La Haye de Droit International* 13 (2000), pp. 27–32

'Between Civilisation and Barbarism: Creole Interventions in International Law' *Third World Quarterly* 27:5 (2006), pp. 815–832

'Completing Civilization: Creole Consciousness and International Law in Nineteenth-Century Latin America', in Anne Orford ed., *International Law and Its Others* (Cambridge: Cambridge University Press, 2006), pp. 247–264

'Construyendo la Región Americana: Andrés Bello y el Derecho Internacional', *Universidad de Los Andes. Revista de Derecho Público* 24 (2010), pp. 1–22

'Carlos Calvo y la profesionalización del derecho internacional', *Revista Latinoamericana de Derecho Internacional* 3 (2015), pp. 1–23

'Empire, Racial Capitalism and International Law: The Case of Manumitted Haiti and the Recognition Debt', Leiden Journal of International Law 31:3 (2018), pp. 597–615

Offner, John L., 'McKinley and the Spanish-American War', *Presidential Studies Quarterly* 34:1 (2004), pp. 50–61

O'Gorman, Edmundo, *La supervivencia política novo-hispana: Reflexiones sobre el monarquismo mexicano* (Mexico City: Fundación cultural de Condumex, 1969)

Ojeda Revah, Mario, *México y la guerra civil española* (Madrid: Turner, 2005)

O'Keefe, Kieran J., 'The Dutch Revolt and Historical Memory in the American Revolution', *The International History Review* 43:3 (2021), pp. 567–578

Olmos Gaona, Alejandro, *La deuda odiosa: el valor de una doctrina jurídica como instrumento de solución política* (Buenos Aires: Ediciones Continente, 2005)

Olveda, Jaime, 'El repudio a la Constitución de Cádiz', in Roberto Breña ed., *Cádiz a debate: Actualidad, contexto y legado* (Mexico City: Colegio de México, 2014), pp. 321-338

Onuf, Peter S., *Statehood and Union: A History of the Northwest Ordinance* (Notre Dame, IN: University of Notre Dame Press, 2019)

Oosterlinck, Kim, *Hope Springs Eternal: French Bondholders and the Repudiation of Russian Sovereign Debt* (Oxford: Oxford University Press, 2016)

'The Historical Context of Sovereign Debt', in Ilias Bantekas, and Cephas Lumina eds., *Sovereign Debt and Human Rights* (Oxford: Oxford University Press, 2018), pp. 13–27

Oosterlinck, Kim, Ugo Panizza, Mark Weidemaier, and Mitu Gulati, 'The Odious Haitian Independence Debt', *Journal of Global Development* 13:2 (2022), pp. 339–378

Ordenanzas de la Ilustre Universidad y Casa de Contratación de la M.N. y M.L. villa de Bilbao: insertos sus reales privilegios (Bilbao: en la oficina de la viuda de Antonio de Zafra y Rueda, 1738)

Orgaz, Raúl A., *Alberdi y el Historicismo* (Córdoba: Rossi, 1937)

Ortega, Francisco, 'Tiempo precario y tiempo eterno: República y moral en la primera mitad del siglo XIX neogranadino', in Fabio Wasserman ed., *Tiempos Críticos: Historia, revolución y temporalidad en el mundo iberoamericano* (siglos XVIII y XIX) (Buenos Aires: Prometeo, 2010), pp. 197–222

Ortemberg, Pablo Marcos, 'El tedeum en el ritual político: usos y sentidos de un dispositivo de pactos en la América española y en la revolución de Mayo', *Anuario del Instituto de Historia Argentina* 10:12 (2010), pp. 199–226

Ortiz de Zevallos, Carlos, *Misiones Peruanas 1820–1826*. Volume 1 (Lima: Comisión Nacional del Sesquicentenario de la independencia del Perú, 1975)

Osorio, Alejandra B., *Inventing Lima: Baroque Modernity in Peru's South Sea Metropolis* (London: Springer, 2008)

O'Sullivan, John Louis, *The Democratic Review*. Volume 14 (New York: Henry Langley, 1844)

Overhoff, Jürgen, 'Benjamin Franklin, Student of the Holy Roman Empire: His Summer Journey to Germany in 1766 and His Interest in the Empire's Federal Constitution', *German Studies Review* 34:2 (2011), pp. 277–286

Owensby, Brian P., *New World of Gain: Europeans, Guaraní, and the Global Origins of Modern Economy* (Redwood: Stanford University Press, 2021)

Padín, Juan Francisco, 'Los albores del derecho internacional en la Universidad de Buenos Aires: la enseñanza de la materia según Antonio Sáenz', *Academia: Revista sobre enseñanza del derecho de Buenos Aires* 27 (2016), pp. 79–99

Pagden, Anthony, *Spanish Imperialism and the Political Imagination: Studies in European and Spanish-American Social and Political Theory 1513–1830* (New Haven: Yale University Press, 1990)

Lords of all the World: Ideologies of Empire in Spain, Britain, and France c. 1500–1800 (New Haven: Yale University Press, 1995)

'Conquest and the Just War The "School of Salamanca" and the "Affair of the Indies"', in Sankar Muthu ed., *Empire and Modern Political Thought* (Cambridge: Cambridge University Press, 2012), pp. 30–60

'Empire, Nation, and Republic in the Transformation of the Modern Hispanic World', in Francisco Colom González and Ángel Rivero eds., *The Traditions of Liberty in the Atlantic World: Origins, Ideas and Practices* (Leiden, The Netherlands: Brill, 2016), pp. 40–60

Pagden, Anthony ed., *Hernán Cortés. Letters from Mexico*. Translated and edited by Anthony Pagden. With an introduction by John Elliott (New Haven: Yale University Press, 1986)

Palti, Elias, *La invención de una legitimidad. Razón y retórica en el pensamiento mexicano del siglo XIX (Un estudio sobre las formas del discurso político)* (Buenos Aires: FCE, 2006)

El tiempo de la política. Lenguaje e historia en el siglo XIX (Buenos Aires: Siglo XXI, 2007)

'La nación argentina entre el ser y el acontecimiento. La controvertida plasmación de una visión genealógica del pasado nacional', in Guillermo Palacios ed., *La nación y su historia, independencias, relato historiográfico y debates sobre la nación* (Mexico City: Colegio de México, 2009), pp. 17–38.

Pani, Erika, '¿"Verdaderas Figuras de Cooper" o 'Pobres Inditos Infelices'? La Política Indigenista de Maximiliano', *Historia Mexicana* 47:3 (1998), pp. 571–604

Para mexicanizar el segundo imperio: el imaginario político de los imperialistas (Mexico City: El Colegio de México, 2001)

'De coyotes y gallinas: Hispanidad, identidad nacional y comunidad política durante la expulsión de españoles', *Revista de Indias* 63:228 (2003), pp. 355–374

'"Ciudadana y Muy Ciudadana"? Women and the State in Independent Mexico, 1810–30', *Gender & History* 18:1 (2006), pp. 5–19

Pan-Montojo, Juan and Juan Luis Simal, 'Exil, finances internationales et construction de l'État: les libéraux et « josephins » espagnols (1813–1851)', *Revue d'histoire du XIXe siècle* 53 (2016), pp. 59–77

Paquette, Gabriel, 'State-Civil Society Cooperation and Conflict in the Spanish Empire: The Intellectual and Political Activities of the Ultramarine Consulados and Economic Societies, c. 1780–1810', *Journal of Latin American Studies* 39:2 (2007), pp. 263–298

Pareja, Francisco Alfaro, 'Capacidades para la paz en las negociaciones para el reconocimiento de la Independencia de Venezuela por parte de España (1833 y 1846)', *Revista de Paz y Conflictos* 7 (2014), pp. 175–194

Parker, Geoffrey, *Imprudent King: A New Life of Philip II* (New Haven: Yale University Press, 2014)

Parry, Jonathan, *The Politics of Patriotism: English Liberalism, National Identity and Europe, 1830–1886* (Cambridge: Cambridge University Press, 2006)

Pas, Hernán, 'Prensa periódica y cultura popular en el Río de la Plata durante el siglo XIX', *Perífrasis. Revista de Literatura, Teoría y Crítica* 9:18 (2018), pp. 11–29

Pasquale, Mariano de, 'Entre la experimentación política y la circulación de saberes: la gestión de Bernardino Rivadavia en Buenos Aires, 1821–1827', *Secuencia* 87 (2013), pp. 51–65

Paul, Tawny, *The Poverty of Disaster: Debt and Insecurity in Eighteenth-Century Britain* (Cambridge: Cambridge University Press, 2019)

Payno, Manuel, *La Convención Española* (Mexico City: Ignacio Cumplido, 1857)

México y el Sr. embajador Don Joaquín Francisco Pacheco (Mexico City: J. Abadiano, 1862)

Carta que sobre los asuntos de México dirige al Sr. General Forey comandante en gefe de las tropas francesas (Mexico City: Imprenta de Vicente García Torres, 1862)

México y sus cuestiones financieras con la Inglaterra, la España y la Francia (Mexico City: Cumplido, 1862)

Vida, aventuras, escritos y viajes del doctor don Servando Teresa de Mier, precedidos de un ensayo histórico por Manuel Payno (Mexico City: Imprenta de Juan Abadiano, 1865)

Cuentas, gastos, acreedores y otros asuntos del tiempo de la intervención francesa y del imperio. De 1861 a 1867 (Mexico City: Imprenta de Ignacio Cumplido, 1868)

El Fistol del Diablo. Novelas de costumbres mexicanas. Texto establecido y estudio preliminar de Antonio Castro Leal (Mexico City: Porrua, 1981)

Los bandidos del Río Frío (Mexico City: Fundación Carlos Slim, n.s.)

Payno, Manuel and José Joaquín Pesado, *Cuestión de Tehuantepec* (Mexico City: Ignacio Cumplido, 1852)

Paz, Juan José and Miño Cepeda, *Eloy Alfaro: Políticas económicas* (Quito: Ministerio de Coordinación de la Política Económica, 2012)

Penry, Elizabeth Henry, *The People Are King: The Making of an Indigenous Andean Politics* (New York: Oxford University Press, 2019)

Pérez Calvo, Eduardo Ricardo, *Vida y trabajos de Carlos Calvo* (Buenos Aires: Dunken, 1996)

Pérez, Jr., Louis A., 'Incurring a Debt of Gratitude: 1898 and the Moral Sources of United States Hegemony in Cuba', *The American Historical Review* 104:2 (1999), pp. 356–398

Pérez Siller, Javier, 'Razones, pasiones y violencia en México. El reconocimiento de la deuda inglesa en 1884', *Nuevo Mundo Mundos Nuevos* (Online)

Pérez Vejo, Tomás, 'España en el imaginario mexicano: el choque del exilio', in Agustín Sánchez Andrés and Silvia Figueroa Zamudio eds., *De Madrid a México. El exilio español y su impacto sobre el pensamiento, la ciencia y el sistema educativo mexicano* (Morelia: Universidad Michoacana de San Nicolás de Hidalgo, 2001), pp. 23–93

'Imaginarios historicistas españoles y mexicanos. Una aproximación iconográfica', in Agustin Sánchez Andrés and Raul Figueroa Esquer eds., *México y España en el siglo XIX. Diplomacia, relaciones triangulares e imaginarios nacionales* (Morelia, UMSNH, 2003), pp. 207–266

España en el debate público mexicano, 1836–1867: aportaciones para una historia de la nación (Mexico City: El Colegio de México, 2008)

'Hispanófobos vs. Hispanófilos. La historia como arma de lucha política en México, 1821–1867', in Agustín Sánchez Andrés and Juan Carlos Pereira Castañares eds., *España y México. Doscientos años de relaciones, 1810–2010* (Morelia: UMSNH, 2010), pp. 125–166

'El imperio que quiso ser una nación', in Roberto Breña ed., *Cádiz a debate: Actualidad, contexto y legado* (Mexico City: Colegio de México, 2014), pp. 63–84

3 de Julio de 1898: El significado de una fecha (Madrid: Taurus, 2020)

'La madre por la sangre y la madre intelectual: España y Francia en el imaginario mexicano de mediados del siglo XIX', *Rubrica Contemporánea* 12:23 (2023), pp. 65–83

Pérez Vejo, Tomás and José María Portillo, 'La Monarquía hispánica en las revoluciones atlánticas: nuevos enfoques', *Araucaria. Revista Iberoamericana de Filosofía, Política, Humanidades y Relaciones Internacionales* 49 (2022), pp. 429–450

Pérez Valdivia, Javier César Puerta Villagaray and Daniel Morán, '"Dos soles no pueden brillar bajo el mismo cielo", La entrevista de Guayaquil entre José de San Martín y Simón Bolívar (1822)', *Desde el Sur* 13(3) (2021) (Online)

Petit, Carlos, *Un Código civil perfecto y bien calculado. El proyecto de 1821 en la historia de la codificación* (Madrid: Editorial Dykinson, 2019)

Peyrou, Florencia, 'The Role of Spain and the Spanish in the Creation of Europe's Transnational Democratic Political Culture, 1840–70', *Social History* 40:4 (2015), pp. 497–517

Phillimore, Robert, *Commentaries Upon International Law.* Volume 1 (Philadelphia: T. & J. Johnson, Law Booksellers, 1854)

Pi-Suñer Llorens, Antonia, *El General Prim y la 'Cuestión de Mexico'* (Published PhD Thesis) (Mexico City: Universidad Nacional Autónoma de México, 1991)

'Manuel Payno y el problema de la deuda española (1848–1862)', *Historia mexicana* 44:1 (1994), pp. 37–72

La deuda española en México. Diplomacia y política en torno a un problema financiero, 1821–1890 (Mexico City: UNAM, 2006)

'Mito y relación en la relación entre Juárez y Prim', in Josefina Zoraida Vázquez, *Juárez: historia y mito* (Mexico City: El Colegio de México, 2010), pp. 89-112

Pistor, Katharina, *Code of Capital: How the Law Creates Wealth and Inequality* (Princeton: Princeton University Press, 2019)

Platt, D. C. M., 'Foreign Finance in Argentina for the First Half-Century of Independence', *Journal of Latin American Studies* 15:1 (1983), pp. 23–47

Plaza Alfonso, Eduardo, 'Las fuentes del derecho internacional de Bello de su periodo londinense; la experiencia y los estudios', in *Bello y Londres: Segundo Congreso del Bicentenario.* Volume 2 (Caracas: La Casa de Bello, 1980), pp. 263–282

Pocock, J. G. A., *The Machiavellian Moment: Florentine Political Thought and the Atlantic Republican Tradition* (Princeton: Princeton University Press, 1975)

Pollmann, Judith, *Catholic Identity and the Revolt of the Netherlands, 1520–1635* (Oxford: Oxford University Press, 2011)

Pola, Angel, ed., *Obras completas de Melchor Ocampo.* Volume 1 (Mexico City: F. Vázquez, 1900)

Portillo, José María, 'La libertad entre evangelio y constitución Notas para el concepto de libertad política en la cultura española de 1812', in José María Portillo and José María Iñurritegui eds., *Constitución en España. Orígenes y destinos* (Madrid: CEPC, 1998), pp. 139–178

Revolución de nación. Orígenes de la cultura constitucional en España, 1780–1812 (Madrid: Centro de Estudios Políticos y Constitucionales, 2000)

'De la Monarquía Católica a la Nación de los Católicos', *Historia y política* 17 (2007), pp. 17–35

Crisis Atlántica: Autonomía e independencia en la crisis de la monarquía hispana (Madrid: Marcial Pons, 2016)

'Rousseau Travestido? Los liberales tomistas en las Cortes de Cádiz', in Gabriel Entin ed., *Rousseau en Iberoamérica. Lecturas e interpretaciones entre Monarquía y Revolución* (Buenos Aires: SB Editores, 2018)

Una historia atlántica de los orígenes de la nación y el Estado (Madrid: Alianza, 2022)

Posada-Carbó, Eduardo, 'Newspapers, Politics, and Elections in Colombia, 1830–1930', *The Historical Journal* 53:4 (2010), pp. 939–962

Posada-Carbó, Eduardo, Joanna Innes, and Mark Philp eds., *The Army of Flanders and the Spanish Road 1567–1659: The Logistics of Spanish Victory and Defeat in the Low Countries' Wars* (Cambridge: Cambridge University Press, 2004)

Re-imagining Democracy in Latin America and the Caribbean, 1780–1870 (New York: Oxford University Press, 2023)

Premo, Bianca, 'Meticulous Imprecision: Calculating Age in Colonial Spanish American Law', *The American Historical Review* 125:2 (2020), pp. 396–406

Press, Steven, *Rogue Empires: Contracts and Conmen in Europe's Scramble for Africa* (Cambridge: Harvard University Press, 2017)

Priest, Claire, *Credit Nation: Property Laws and Institutions in Early America* (Princeton: Princeton University Press, 2021)

Prieto Muñoz, José Gustavo, 'Mixed Claims Commissions in Latin America during the 19th and 20th Centuries: The Development of International Law in between Caudillos and Revolutions', in Raphael Schäfer and Anne Peters eds., *Politics and the Histories of International Law: The Quest for Knowledge and Justice* (Leiden: Brill, 2021), pp. 250–269

Provost, René, *Rebel Courts: The Administration of Justice by Armed Insurgents* (Oxford: Oxford University Press, 2021)

Pruneda, Pedro, *Historia de la guerra de Méjico desde 1861 a 1867* (Madrid: Rojas, 1867)

Queralt, Didac, *Pawned States: State Building in the Era of International Finance* (Princeton: Princeton University Press, 2022)

Quiroz, Alfonso W., *La deuda defraudada: consolidación de 1850 y dominio económico en el Perú* (Lima: Nuevo Mundo, 1987)

Deudas olvidadas: Instrumentos de crédito en la economía colonial peruana 1750–1820 (San Miguel: Pontificia Universidad Católica del Perú, 1993)

Rabe, Stephen G., 'Theodore Roosevelt, the Panama Canal, and the Roosevelt Corollary to the Monroe Doctrine', *IdeAs. Idées d'Amériques* 22 (2023) (Online)

Racine, Karen, 'Matters of Life and Death: Biographies at the Beginning of Independent Mexico, 1820s', in William Beezley ed., *The Oxford Handbook of Mexican History* (Oxford: Oxford University Press, 2020) (Online)

Ramírez, Ignacio, *Obras de Ignacio Ramírez*. Volume 1 (Mexico City: Secretaría de Fomento, 1889)

Ramírez Cabañas, Joaquín, *El empréstito de México a Colombia: recopilación de documentos con una introducción y notas* (México: Publicaciones de la Secretaría de relaciones exteriores, 1930)

Ramírez Rodríguez, Rodolfo, 'Manuel Payno y su polémica participación en las concesiones del Ferrocarril Mexicano', *Relaciones. Estudios de historia y sociedad* 40:158 (2019), pp. 198–231

Rasilla del Moral, Ignacio, 'Francisco de Vitoria's Unexpected Transformations and Reinterpretations for International Law', *International Community Law Review* 15:3 (2013), pp. 287–318

Ratz, Konrad, *Tras las huellas de un desconocido: nuevos datos y aspectos de Maximiliano de Habsburgo*. Prólogo de Patricia Galeana de Valadés (Mexico City: Siglo XXI, 2008).

Ravignani, Emilio ed., *Correspondencias generales de la provincia de Buenos Aires relativas a relaciones exteriores (1820–1824)*. Volume 14 (Buenos Aires: Peuser, 1921)

Ray, Rebecca and Margaret Myers, 'Chinese Loans to Latin America and the Caribbean Database', *Washington and Boston: Inter-American Dialogue and Boston University Global Development Policy Center* (2024) (Online)

Read, Charles, *Calming the Storms: The Carry Trade, the Banking School and British Financial Crises Since 1825* (Cham: Springer, 2023)

Real Academia Española ed., *Diccionario de Autoridades*. Volume 1 (Madrid: Real Academia Española, 1726)

Diccionario de Autoridades. Volume 3 (Madrid: Viuda de Francisco del Hierro, 1732)

Reguera, Marcos, *El imperio de la democracia en América. John O'Sullivan y la formación del concepto de Destino Manifiesto* (Mexico City: Fondo de Cultura Económica) (Forthcoming)

Reid, Michael, *Forgotten Continent: A History of the New Latin America* (New Haven: Yale University Press, 2017)

Reinhart, Carmen and Kenneth Rogoff, *This Time Is Different: Eight Centuries of Financial Folly* (Princeton: Princeton University Press, 2009)

Renan, Ernest, 'What is a Nation?' in Ernest Renan and Matteo Giglioli, *What Is a Nation? And Other Political Writings* (New York: Columbia University Press, 2018), pp. 247–263

Renan, Ernest and Matteo Giglioli, *What Is a Nation? And Other Political Writings* (New York: Columbia University Press, 2018)

Restall, Matthew, *When Montezuma Met Cortés: The True Story of the Meeting that Changed History* (New York: Harper Collins, 2018)

Restrepo, José Manuel, *Historia de la Revolución de la República de Colombia* (Paris: Lib. Americana, 1827)

Historia de la revolución de la República de Colombia en la América Meridional. Volume 4 (Besançon: José Jacquin, 1858)

Restrepo Piedrahita, Carlos, *Actas del Congreso de Cúcuta: 1821* (Bogotá: Fundación Francisco de Paula Santander, 1990)

Revollo Rueda, Marcela, *Epistolario de Joaquín Mosquera (1845–1874)* (Chía: Universidad de la Sabana, 2018)

Reyes Heroles, Jesús, *El liberalismo mexicano*. Volume 3: *Integración de las ideas* (Mexico City: Fondo de Cultura Económica, 1974)

Rieu-Millan, Marie-Laure, *Los diputados americanos en las Cortes de Cádiz (Igualdad o independencia)* (Madrid: CSIC, 1990)

'Presencia Americana en Cádiz y en las Cortes. Encuentros y desencuentros', in Scarlett O'Phelan Godoy y Georges Lomné eds., *Voces americanas en las Cortes de Cádiz: 1810–1814* (Lima: Institut Français d'Études Andines, 2014), pp. 21–38

Riguzzi, Paolo, 'Mexico and the Monroe Doctrines, 1863–1920: From Appropriation to Rejection', Diplomatic History 47:5 (2023), pp. 785–792.

Rinke, Stefan, *Conquistadors and Aztecs: A History of the Fall of Tenochtitlan* (Oxford: Oxford University Press, 2023)

Ripley, Charles, 'The Central American Court of Justice (1907–1918): Rethinking the World's First Court', *Diálogos: Revista Electrónica de Historia* 19:1 (2018), pp. 47–68

Rivera Indarte, José, *Rosas y sus opositores* (Montevideo: Imprenta del Nacional, 1843)

Rivera Serna, Raúl, 'Aspectos de la economía durante la Confederación Perú-Bolivia (1836–1839)', *Anuario de Estudios Americanos* 26 (1969), pp. 611–639

Roberts, Anthea, *Is International Law International?* (Oxford: Oxford University Press, 2017)

Robertson, William Spence, 'The Recognition of the Spanish Colonies by the Motherland', *The Hispanic American Historical Review* 1:1 (1918), pp. 70–91

'The Recognition of the Hispanic American Nations by the United States', *Hispanic American Historical Review* 1:3 (1918), pp. 239–269

'The Tripartite Treaty of London', *The Hispanic American Historical Review* 20:2 (1940), pp. 167–189

'French Intervention in Mexico in 1838', *Hispanic American Historical Review* 24:2 (1944), pp. 222–252

Rocafuerte, Vicente, *Bosquejo ligerisimo de la revolucion de Mégico: desde el grito de Iguala hasta la proclamacion imperial de Iturbide* (Philadelphia: Teracrouef & Naroajeb, 1822)

Ensayo politico: El sistema colombiano, popular, electivo, y representativo, es el que mas conviene á la America independiente (New York: A. Paul, 1823)

Rodas Chaves, Germán, *Eloy Alfaro y Cuba en el siglo XIX* (Havana: Fondo Editorial Casa de las Américas, 2013)

Rodríguez, Linda Alexander, *The Search for Public Policy: Regional Politics and Government Finances in Ecuador, 1830–1940* (Berkeley: University of California Press, 1985)

Rodríguez Arrieta, Marisol, 'Incidencia del derecho natural y de gentes y el derecho de propiedad en el proceso de manumisión de la provincia de Maracaibo (1810–1835), *Historia Caribe* 5:14 (2009), pp. 35–58

Rodríguez Gutiérrez, Francisco Javier, *El Doctor José Miguel Ramos de Arizpe, de súbdito a ciudadano. Documentos, 1808–1822* (Saltillo: Congreso del Estado de Coahuila, 2008)

Rodríguez O., Jaime E., *The Emergence of Spanish America: Vicente Rocafuerte and Spanish Americanism, 1808–1832* (Berkeley: University of California Press, 1975)

'La Constitución de 1824 y la formación del Estado mexicano', *Historia* 'La transición de colonia a nación: Nueva España, 1820–1821', *Historia Mexicana* 43:2 (1993), pp. 265–322
Mexicana 40:3 (1991), pp. 507–535

The Divine Charter: Constitutionalism and Liberalism in Nineteenth-Century Mexico (Lanham: Rowman and Littlefield, 2005)

'We Are Now the True Spaniards': Sovereignty, Revolution, Independence, and the Emergence of the Federal Republic of Mexico, 1808–1824 (Stanford: Stanford University Press, 2012)

Rodríguez Salgado, María José, *Un imperio en transición: Carlos V, Felipe II y su mundo, 1551–1559* (Barcelona: Crítica, 1992)

Rodulfo Corté, Santos, 'La creación de Bolivia y la Santa Alianza', *Boletín de la Academia Nacional de la Historia* 84 (2001), pp. 109–124

Rojas, Ezequiel, *Teoría del crédito público i privado con su aplicación al de los Estados Unidos de Colombia* (Funza: Imprenta del Estado, 1863)

Filosofía moral (Bogotá: Imprenta de la Nación, 1868)

'Una Defensa' (1872), in Camilo González, Carlos Arturo López, Rusbel Martínez, María Cristina Conforti Rojas, and Marcela Forero Rey eds., *Textos filosóficos de Ezequiel Rojas: compilación y presentaciones* (Bogotá: Portal Pontificia Universidad Javeriana, 2017), pp. 294–346

Rojas, Rafael, *La escritura de la independencia: el surgimiento de la opinión pública en México* (Mexico City: Taurus/CIDE, 2003)

Las repúblicas de aire. Utopía y desencanto en la revolución de Hispanoamérica (Madrid: Taurus, 2009)

Rojas, Rafael, Antonio Annino, and Francisco A. Eissa-Barroso, *La independencia: los libros de la patria* (México: CIDE, 2008)

Rojas de Ferro, Cristina, 'The "Will to Civilization" and Its Encounter with Laissez-Faire', *Review of International Political Economy* 2:1 (1995), pp. 150–183

Roldán de Montaud, Inés, 'Guerra y finanzas en la crisis de fin de siglo: 1895–1900', *Hispania* 57:2 (1997), pp. 611–675

'La deuda pública cubana de la Carta Autonómica al Tratado de París', in Mariano Esteban de Vega, Francisco de Luis Martín, and Antonio Morales Moya eds., *Jirones de hispanidad: España, Cuba, Puerto Rico y Filipinas en la perspectiva de dos cambios de siglo* (Salamanca: University of Salamanca, 2004), pp. 217–246

Romagnoli, Alejandro, 'El proyecto historiográfico de Martín García Mérou: Sus lecturas de Alberdi, Echeverría y Sarmiento', *Prismas* 27 (2023), pp. 89–108

Roper, Lyndal, *Luther: Renegade and Prophet* (London: Vintage, 2017)

Rosa, Alfonso, *Fidel Castro y la deuda externa* (Havana: Editora Política, 1989)

Rosales, Antulio, 'Going Underground: The Political Economy of the "Left Turn" in South America', *Third World Quarterly* 34:8 (2013), pp. 1443–1457

Roshchin, Evgeny, 'The Hague Conferences and "International Community": A Politics of Conceptual Innovation', *Review of International Studies* 43:1 (2017), pp. 177–198

Rosen, Frederick, *Bentham, Byron, and Greece: Constitutionalism, Nationalism, and Early Liberal Political Thought* (Oxford: Oxford University Press, 1992),

Rosenthal, Joshua M., 'Conditional Clemency after the Golpe de Melo of 1854: Constitutionalism and Tradition in Early Republican Colombia', *Historia Crítica* 63 (2017), pp. 75–96

'The Indultados of Tescua: Criminal Rebellion and Judicial Reckoning during the War of the Supremes', *Anuario Colombiano de Historia Social y de la Cultura* 39:2 (2012), pp. 131–156

Rossi, Christopher R., *Whiggish International Law: Elihu Root, the Monroe Doctrine, and International Law in the Americas* (Leiden: Brill, 2019)

Ruan, Felipe E., 'The Probanza and Shaping a Contesting Mestizo Record in Early Colonial Peru', *Bulletin of Spanish Studies* 94:5 (2017), pp. 843–869

Ruíz Moreno, Isidoro, *Relaciones hispano-argentinas: de la guerra a los tratados* (Buenos Aires: R.J. Pellegrini, 1981)

Rule, John C., and Ben S. Trotter, *A World of Paper: Louis XIV, Colbert de Torcy, and the Rise of the Information State* (Montreal: McGill-Queen's Press, 2014)

Ryan, Maeve, *Humanitarian Governance and the British Antislavery World System* (New Haven: Yale University Press, 2022)

Sabato, Hilda, *Republics of the New World: The Revolutionary Political Experiment in Nineteenth-Century Latin America* (Princeton: Princeton University Press, 2018)

Sack, Alexander Nahum, *Les effets des transformations des états sur leurs dettes publiques et autres obligations financières. Traité juridique et financier, etc.* (Paris: Sirey, 1927)

Sáenz, Antonio, *Instituciones Elementales sobre el derecho natural de gentes.* Noticia preliminar de Ricardo Levene (Buenos Aires: Instituto de Historia del Derecho Argentino, 1939)

Safford, Frank, *Historia de Colombia: País fragmentado, sociedad dividida*. Translated by Marco Palacios and Ángela García (Bogotá: Ediciones Uniandes, 2011)

Sainlaude, Stève, *France and the American Civil War: A Diplomatic History* (Oxford: Oxford University Press, 2019)

Salazar Cáceres, Carlos Gabriel, *Ezequiel Rojas: vida y pensamiento* (Boyacá: Academia Boyacense de Historia, 2006)

Salcedo-Bastardo, José Luis, 'Bello y los "Symposiums" de Grafton Street', in John Lynch ed., *Andrés Bello: the London Years* (Richmond: Richmond Publication Company, 1982), pp. 57–64

Salvatore, Ricardo D., *Wandering Paysanos. State Order and Subaltern Experience in Buenos Aires During the Rosas Era* (Durham: Duke University Press, 2003)

Salvucci, Richard J., *Textiles and Capitalism in Mexico: An Economic History of the Obrajes, 1539–1840* (Princeton: Princeton University Press, 1988)

Politics, Markets, and Mexico's 'London Debt,' 1823–1887 (New York: Cambridge University Press, 2009)

Sánchez Agesta, Luis, 'Introducción', in Agustín de Argüelles, *Discurso preliminar a la Constitución de 1812* (Madrid: Centro de Estudios Políticos y Constitucionales, 1987)

Sánchez Andrés, Agustín, 'La diplomacia hispano-mexicana: de la intervención tripartita a la caída del imperio', in Clara E. Lida and Andrés Lira eds., *España y el imperio de Maximiliano: finanzas, diplomacia, cultura e inmigración* (Mexico City: El Colegio de México, 1999), pp. 105–178

'México', in Carlos Daniel Malamud ed., *Ruptura y reconciliación España y el reconocimiento de las independencias latinoamericanas* (Madrid: Fundación Mapfre, 2012), pp. 37–52

'Las dificultades del reinicio. Las relaciones entre España y Ecuador durante la minoridad de Isabel II, 1834–1843', in Agustín Sánchez Andrés and Marco Antonio Landavazo eds., *Conflicto y reconciliación. España y las naciones hispanoamericanas en el siglo XIX* (Madrid: Marcial Pons, 2021), pp. 275–308

Sánchez Andrés, Agustín and Fabrián Herrera León, *Contra todo y contra todos: la diplomacia mexicana y la cuestión española en la Sociedad de Naciones, 1936–1939* (Las Palmas: Ediciones Idea, 2011)

Sánchez Andrés, Agustín and Juan Carlos Pereira Castañares eds., *España y México. Doscientos años de relaciones, 1810–2010* (Morelia: UMSNH, 2010)

Sánchez Andrés, Agustín and Marco Antonio Landavazo eds., *Conflicto y reconciliación*. España y las naciones hispanoamericanas en el siglo XIX (Madrid: Marcial Pons, 2021)

Sánchez Andrés, Agustín and Silvia Figueroa Zamudio eds., *De Madrid a México. El exilio español y su impacto sobre el pensamiento, la ciencia y el sistema educativo mexicano* (Morelia: Universidad Michoacana de San Nicolás de Hidalgo, 2001)

Sanchiz Ruiz, Javier and Juan Gómez Gallardo Latapí, 'Las falsas paternidades del Padre de la Patria', *Estudios de historia moderna y contemporánea de México* 44 (2012), pp. 49–93

Sanjurjo, Jesús, *In the Blood of Our Brothers Abolitionism and the End of the Slave Trade in Spain's Atlantic Empire, 1800–1870* (Tuscaloosa: University of Alabama Press, 2021)

Sanz Ayán, Carmen, *Los banqueros y la crisis de la monarquía hispánica de 1640* (Madrid: Marcial Pons, 2013)

Sarmiento, Domingo, *La condición del extranjero en América* (Buenos Aires: La Facultad, 1928)

Scalabrini Ortiz, Raúl, *Política británica en el Río de la Plata* (Barcelona: Editorial del Sol, 2001)

Scarfi, Juan Pablo, 'La emergencia de un imaginario latinoamericanista y antiestadounidense del orden hemisférico: de la Unión Panamericana a la Unión Latinoamericana (1880–1913)', *Revista Complutense de Historia de América* 39 (2013), pp. 81–104

El imperio de la ley. James Brown Scott y la construcción de un orden jurídico interamericano (Buenos Aires: FCE, 2014)

'Globalizing the Latin American Legal Field: Continental and Regional Approaches to the International Legal Order in Latin America', *Revista Brasileira de Política Internacional* 61:2 (2015), pp. 1–12

'Excepcionalismo estadounidense y hegemonía legal hemisférica: La Corte Suprema de Justicia de Estados Unidos como modelo imperial de justicia internacional para Centroamérica y América Latina y su influjo en el Sistema Interamericano', *Revista Latinoamericana de Derecho Internacional* 4 (2016), pp. 1–22

'In the Name of the Americas: the Pan-American Redefinition of the Monroe Doctrine and the Emerging Language of American International Law in the Western Hemisphere, 1898–1933', *Diplomatic History* 40:2 (2016), pp. 189–218

The Hidden History of International Law in the Americas: Empire and Legal Networks (Oxford: Oxford University Press, 2017)

Denaturalizing the Monroe Doctrine: The Rise of Latin American Legal Anti-Imperialism in the Face of the Modern US and Hemispheric Redefinition of the Monroe Doctrine', *Leiden Journal of International Law* 33:3 (2020), pp. 541–555

'Mexican Revolutionary Constituencies and the Latin American Critique of US Intervention', in Kathryn Greenman, Anne Orford, Anna Saunders, and Ntina Tzouvala eds., *Revolutions in International Law: The Legacies of 1917* (Cambridge: Cambridge University Press, 2021), pp. 218–241

Schell, Deise Cristina, 'El archivero de Rosas: Pedro de Angelis y la producción del Archivo Americano', *Estudios de Teoría Literaria. Revista digital: artes, letras y humanidades* 9:20 (2020), pp. 369–380

Schipani, Sandro ed., *Dalmacio Vélez Sarsfield e il diritto latinoamericano* (Padova: CEDAM, 1991)

Schmieder, Ulrike, 'Spain and Spanish America in the System of the Holy Alliance: The Importance of Interconnected Historical Events on the Congresses of the Holy Alliance', *Review (Fernand Braudel Center)* 38 (2015), pp. 147–169

Schlez, Mariano Martin, *The Woodbine Parish Report on the Revolutions in South America (1822): The Foreign Office and Early British Intelligence on Latin America* (Liverpool: Liverpool University Press, 2022)

Schmitt, Roberto, 'Finanzas públicas, Puerto y recursos financieros', *Historia de la Provincia de Buenos Aires.* Volume 3: De la organización provincial a la federalización de Buenos Aires (1821–1880) (Buenos Aires: UNIPE, 2013), pp. 205–224

Schofield, Philip, *Utility and Democracy: The Political Thought of Jeremy Bentham* (Oxford: Oxford University Press, 2006)

Schofield, Philip and Jonathan Harris eds., *'Legislator of the World': Writings on Codification, Law, and Education* (Oxford: Oxford University Press, 1998)

Schoultz, Lars, *Beneath the United States: A History of U.S. Policy Towards Latin America* (Cambridge: Harvard University Press, 2003)

Schwartz, Daniel, 'Juan Bautista Alberdi and the Mutation of French Doctrinaire Liberalism in Argentina', *History of Political Thought* 30:1 (2009), pp. 140–165

Schwartz, Stuart, *Blood and Boundaries: The Limits of Religious and Racial Exclusion in Early Modern Latin America* (Waltham: Brandeis University Press, 2020)

All Can Be Saved: Religious Tolerance and Salvation in the Iberian Atlantic World (New Haven: Yale University Press, 2008)

Scott, James Brown, *The Hague Peace Conferences of 1899 and 1907.* Volume 1 (Baltimore: Johns Hopkins Press, 1909)

Sovereign States and Suits before Arbitral Tribunals and Courts of Justice (New York: New York City, 1925)

'Asociación Francisco de Vitoria', *The American Journal of International Law* 22:1 (1928), pp. 136–139

'The Good Neighbor Policy', *American Journal of International Law* 30:2 (1936), pp. 287–290

Semo, Enrique, *La conquista, catástrofe de los pueblos originarios* (Mexico City: Siglo XXI, 2019)

Sexton, Jay, *Debtor Diplomacy Finance and American Foreign Relations in the Civil War Era 1837–1873* (Oxford: Oxford University Press, 2014)

'The Monroe Doctrine in an Age of Global History', *Diplomatic History* 47:5 (2023), pp. 845–870

Jay Sexton, *The Monroe Doctrine: Empire and Nation in Nineteenth Century America* (New York: Hill and Wang, 2011),

Shakespeare, William, *Julius Caesar.* Edited by Arthur Raleigh Humphreys (Oxford: Oxford University Press, 1998)

Sharman, Adam, *Deconstructing the Enlightenment in Spanish America: Margins of Modernity* (London: Routledge, 2020)

Shawcross, Edward, 'When Montevideo Was French: European Civilization and French Imperial Ambitions in the River Plate, 1838–1852', *European History Quarterly* 45:4 (2015), pp. 638–661

France, Mexico and Informal Empire in Latin America, 1820–1867: Equilibrium in the New World (London: Springer, 2018)

Shea, Donald, *The Calvo Clause: A Problem of Inter-American and International Law and Diplomacy* (Minneapolis: University of Minnesota Press, 1955)

Shumway, Nicolas, *The Invention of Argentina* (Berkeley: University of California Press, 1991)

Simal, Juan, *Emigrados. España y el exilio internacional, 1814–1834* (Madrid: CEPC, 2012)

'National Credit and the International Financial Market: The Spanish Debt and its Foreign Bondholders, 1820–1834', *Journal of Iberian and Latin American Studies* 25:3 (2019), pp. 381–402

'José Canga Argüelles (1771–1842), la deuda pública española y el compromiso creíble: política y economía en tiempos de revolución y exilio', in Darina Martykánova and Juan Pan Montojo eds., *Misioneros del capitalismo: Aventureros, hombres de negocio y expertos transnacionales en el siglo XIX* (Granada: Comares, 2023), pp. 3–26

Simon, Joshua, *The Ideology of Creole Revolution: Imperialism and Independence in American and Latin American Political Thought* (Cambridge: Cambridge University Press, 2017)

Sims, Harold, *The Expulsion of Mexico's Spaniards, 1821–1836* (Pittsburgh: University of Pittsburgh Press, 1990)

Singh, Devin, *Divine Currency: The Theological Power of Money in the West* (Stanford: Stanford University Press, 2018)

Skeel Jr., David A., *Debt's Dominion: A History of Bankruptcy Law in America* (Princeton: Princeton University Press, 2003)

Skinner, Quentin, 'Meaning and Understanding in the History of Ideas', *History & Theory* 8:1 (1969), pp. 3–53

'The sovereign state: a genealogy', in Hent Kalmo and Quentin Skinner eds., *Sovereignty in Fragments: The Past, Present, and Future of a Contested Concept* (Cambridge: Cambridge University Press, 2010), pp. 26-46

Slack, Paul, *From Reformation to Improvement: Public Welfare in Early Modern England* (Oxford: Oxford University Press, 1998).

Slobodian, Quinn, *Globalists: The End of Empire and the Birth of Neoliberalism* (Cambridge: Harvard University Press, 2018)

Slobodian, Quinn and Dieter Plehwe eds., *Market Civilizations: Neoliberals East and South* (Princeton: Princeton University Press, 2022)

Sluga, Glenda, 'Economic Insecurity, 'Securities' and a European Security Culture after the Napoleonic Wars', in Beatrice de Graaf, Ido de Haan, and Brian Vick ed., *Securing Europe after Napoleon: 1815 and the New European Security Culture* (Cambridge: Cambridge University Press, 2019), pp. 288–305

Smeltzer, Joshua, 'On the Use and Abuse of Francisco de Vitoria: James Brown Scott and Carl Schmitt', *Journal of the History of International Law* 20 (2018), pp. 345–372

Soberanes Fernández, José Luis, 'La abolición de la esclavitud en México', *Ars Iuris* 50 (2015), pp. 247–259

Soen, Violet, 'Challenges to Clemency: Seneca, Lipsius and the Dutch Revolt', in Astrid Steiner-Weber, Alejandro Coroleu, Domenico Defilippis, Roger Green, Fidel Rädle, Valery Rees, Dirk Sacré, Marjorie Woods, and Christine Wulf eds., *Acta Conventus Neo-Latini Upsaliensis. Proceedings of the Fourteenth International Congress of Neo-Latin Studies* (Uppsala 2009. Volume 2 (Leiden/Boston, 2012), pp. 1039–1048

'The Clementia Lipsiana: Political Analysis, Autobiography and Panegyric', in Erik de Bom et al., *(Un)masking the Realities of Power Justus Lipsius and the Dynamics of Political Writing in Early Modern Europe* (Leiden: Brill, 2011), pp. 207–231

Soledad Barbón, Maria, *Colonial Loyalties: Celebrating the Spanish Monarchy in Eighteenth-Century Lima* (Notre Dame, IN: University of Notre Dame Press, 2019)

Soll, Jacob, *Free Market: The History of an Idea* (New York: Basic Books, 2022)
Somos, Mark, 'Virtue', in Randall Lesaffer and Janne E. Nijman eds., *The Cambridge Companion to Hugo Grotius* (Cambridge: Cambridge University Press, 2021), pp. 91–117
Somos, Mark and Joshua Smeltzer, 'Vitoria, Suárez, and Grotius: James Brown Scott's Enduring Revival', *Grotiana* 41:1 (2020), pp. 137–162
Sonenscher, Michael, *Before the Deluge; Public Debt, Inequality, and the Intellectual Origins of the French Revolution* (Princeton: Princeton University Press, 2007)
Capitalism: The Story behind the Word (Princeton: Princeton University Press, 2022)
Souto, Nora, 'El debate en torno a la "capitalización" de Buenos Aires de 1826 y la cuestión de la soberanía', *IX Jornadas Interescuelas/Departamentos de Historia, Córdoba: Universidad Nacional de Córdoba* (2003), pp. 1–12
Sparks, Tom, *Self-Determination in the International Legal System Whose Claim, to What Right?* (London: Hart, 2023)
Stapelbroek, Koen, 'Vattel and the Seven Years' War', in Peter Schröder ed., *Concepts and Contexts of Vattel's Political and Legal Thought* (Cambridge: Cambridge University Press, 2021), pp. 101–120
Stedman Jones, Gareth, *An End to Poverty: A Historical Debate* (New York: Columbia University Press, 2008)
Stein, Stanley and Barbara Stein, *The Colonial Heritage of Latin America* (New York: Oxford University Press, 1970)
Silver, Trade, and War: Spain and America in the Making of Early Modern Europe (Baltimore: Johns Hopkins University Press, 2000)
Stensland, Monica, *Habsburg Communication in the Dutch Revolt* (Amsterdam: Amsterdam University Press, 2012)
Stevenson, John, 'The "Moral Economy" of the English Crowd: Myth and Reality', in Anthony J. Fletcher and John Stevenson eds., *Order and Disorder in Early Modern England* (Cambridge: Cambridge University Press, 1985), pp. 218–238Stoetzer, O. Carlos, *The Scholastic Roots of the Spanish American Revolution* (New York: Fordham University Press, 1979)
Straumann, Benjamin, *Roman Law in the State of Nature: The Classical Foundations of Hugo Grotius' Natural Law* (Cambridge: Cambridge University Press, 2015)
Suanzes-Carpegna, Joaquín Varela, *La monarquía doceañista (1810–1837). Avatares, encomios y denuestos de una extraña* forma de gobierno (Madrid: Marcial Pons, 2013)
Sugawara, Masae ed., *La deuda pública de España y la economía novohispana, 1804–1809* (Mexico City: INAH, 1976)
Stiglitz, Joseph, 'Odious Rulers, Odious Debts', The Atlantic, November 2003
Szuchman, Mark D., 'From Imperial Hinterland to Growth Pole: Revolution, Change, and Restoration in the Río de la Plata, in Mark D. Szuchman and Jonathan Charles Brown, *Revolution and Restoration: The Rearrangement of Power in Argentina, 1776–1860* (Lincoln: University of Nebraska Press, 1994), pp. 1–26
Tah Ayala, Einer David, 'El principio de no intervención en América Latina: el corolario Roosevelt y la Doctrina Drago', *Intersticios sociales* 21 (2021), pp. 173–195
Tarcus, Horacio, *La biblia del proletariado. Traductores y editores de El Capital* (Buenos Aires: Siglo XXI, 2018).
Tasende, Mercedes, 'Entre la leyenda negra y la leyenda dorada: Emilia Pardo Bazán ante el descubrimiento, la conquista y la colonización española del Nuevo Mundo', *Anales de la literatura española contemporánea* 40:1 (2015), pp. 425–451
Tenenbaum, Barbara A., 'Money, and Mischief the British in Mexico, 1821-1862', *The Americas* 35:3 (1979), pp. 317-339
México en la época de los agiotistas, 1821–1857 (Mexico City: Fondo de Cultura Económica, 1985)
'Banqueros sin bancos: el papel de los agiotistas en México', in Leonor Ludlow and Carlos Marichal eds., *Banca y poder en México (1800–1925)* (Mexico City: Grijalbo, 1985), pp. 75–98
The Politics of Penury: Debts and Taxes in Mexico, 1821–1856 (Alburquerque: University of New Mexico Press, 1986)

'Taxation and Tyranny; Public Finance during the Iturbide Regime, 1821–1823', in Jaime E. Rodríguez, *The Independence of México and the Creation of the New Nation* (Los Angeles: University of California Press, 1989), pp. 201–213

'Mexico's Money Market and the Internal Debt, 1821–1855', in Reinhard Liehr ed., *La deuda pública en América Latina en perspectiva histórica* (Frankfurt: Iberoamericana, 1995), pp. 254–292

'Manuel Payno, Financial Reform, and Foreign Intervention in Mexico, 1855–1880', in Vicente Peloso and Barbara A. Tenenbaum eds., *Liberals, Politics, and Power: State Formation in Nineteenth-Century Latin America* (Athens: University of Georgia Press, 1996), pp. 212–234

'The Early Republic and Santa Anna', in William Beezley ed., *The Oxford Handbook of Mexican History* (Oxford: Oxford University Press, 2021) (Online)

Tenenbaum, Barbara A. and Sergio Negrete, 'Manuel Payno y los bandidos del erario mexicano, 1848–1873', *Historia Mexicana* 44:1 (1994), pp. 73–106

Teran, Emilio María, *Informe al jefe supremo general Eloy Alfaro sobre la deuda anglo-ecuatoriana extendido* (Quito: Imprenta Nacional, 1899)

Ternavasio, Marcela, 'Las reformas rivadavianas en Buenos Aires y en el Congreso General Constituyente (1820–1827)', in Noemí Goldman ed., *Nueva historia de Argentina. Revolución, república, confederación (1806–1852)*. Volume 3 (Buenos Aires: Editorial Sudamericana, 2001), pp. 159–198

'Construir poder y dividir poderes. Buenos Aires durante la "feliz experiencia" rivadaviana', *Boletín del Instituto de Historia Argentina y Americana "Dr. Emilio Ravignani"* 26 (2004), pp. 7–43

'La revolución y sus silencios', in Marco Palacios ed., *Las independencias hispanoamericanas. Interpretaciones 200 años después* (Bogotá: Norma, 2009), pp. 157–181

Historia de la Argentina. 1806–1852 (Buenos Aires: Siglo XXI, 2009)

Historia de la Provincia de Buenos Aires. Volume 3: De la organización provincial a la federalización de Buenos Aires (1821–1880) (Buenos Aires: UNIPE, 2013)

La revolución del voto: Política y elecciones en Buenos Aires, 1810–1852 (Buenos Aires: Siglo XXI, 2016)

Los juegos de la política. Las independencias hispanoamericanas frente a la contrarrevolución (Buenos Aires: Siglo XXI, 2021)

Thompson, E. P., 'The Moral Economy of the English Crowd in the Eighteenth Century', *Past & Present* 50 (1971), pp. 76–136

Thornton, Christy, *Revolution in Development Mexico and the Governance of the Global Economy* (Berkeley, University of California Press, 2021)

Todd, David, 'A French Imperial Meridian, 1814–1870', *Past & Present* 210:1 (2011), pp. 155–186

A Velvet Empire: French Informal Imperialism in the Nineteenth Century (Princeton: Princeton University Press, 2021)

Todd, David and Alexia Yates, 'Public Debt and Democratic Statecraft in Nineteenth-Century France', in Nicolas Barreyre and Nicolas Delalande eds., *A World of Public Debts* (London: Palgrave, 2020), pp. 79–106.

Tomás y Valiente, Francisco, 'La prisión por deudas en los Derechos castellano y aragonés', *Anuario de Historia del Derecho Español* 30 (1960), pp. 249–490

Topik, Steven C., 'When Mexico Had the Blues: A Transatlantic Tale of Bonds, Bankers, and Nationalists, 1862–1910', *The American Historical Review* 105:3 (2000), pp. 714–738

Torre Villar, Ernesto de la, 'La política americana durante la Intervención Francesa en México. Notas para su estudio', *Revista de Historia de América* 63–64 (1967), pp. 13–67

Torres, Camilo, 'Memorial de Agravios' (1809), *Boletín de la Sociedad Geográfica de Colombia* 66 (1960), pp. 1–23

Torres, Victor Manuel, 'El pensamiento político de Ignacio Ramírez', *Historia Mexicana* 12:2 (1962), pp. 190–228

Torres Caicedo, José María, *Unión latino-americana, pensamiento de Bolívar para formar una liga americana: su origen y sus desarrollos y estudio sobre la gran cuestión que tanto interesa a los estados débiles, a saber : un gobierno legítimo es responsable por los daños y perjuicios ocasionados a los extranjeros por las facciones?* (Paris: Rosa y Bouret, 1865)

Townsend, Camilla, *Annals of Native America: How the Nahuas of Colonial Mexico Kept Their History Alive* (Oxford: Oxford University Press, 2017)

Fifth Sun: A New History of the Aztecs (Oxford: Oxford University Press, 2019)

Treiman, Israel, 'Escaping the Creditor in the Middle Ages', *Law Quarterly Review* 43 (1927), pp. 230–231

'Acts of Bankruptcy: A Medieval Concept in Modern Bankruptcy Law' *Harvard Law Review* 52:2 (1938), pp. 189–215

Trejo, Evelia, 'Lorenzo de Zavala en el uso de la palabra', *Estudios de historia moderna y contemporánea de México* 20 (2000), pp. 41–66

Tribe, Keith, 'Reform: Elements for a Conceptual History', in Adriana Luna-Fabritius, Ere Nokkala, Marten Seppel, and Keith Tribe eds., *Political Reason and the Language of Change Reform and Improvement in Early Modern Europe* (London: Routledge, 2022), pp. 23–43

Truman, Edwin M., 'The Road to the 1980s Write-downs of Sovereign Debt', *Financial History Review* 28:3 (2021), pp. 218–299

Tunino, John, 'The Americas in the Rise of Capitalism', in John Tutino ed., *New Countries: Capitalism, Revolutions, and Nations in the Americas, 1750–1870* (Durham, NC: Duke University Press, 2017), pp. 25–70

'Capitalism, Christianity, and Slavery: Jesuits and New Spain, 1572–1767', *Journal of Jesuit Studies* 8 (2011), pp. 11–36

Turlington, Edgar, *Mexico and Her Foreign Creditors* (New York: Columbia University Press, 1930)

Tzouvala, Ntina, *Capitalism as Civilisation: A History of International Law* (Cambridge: Cambridge University Press, 2020)

Uribe-Uran, Victor M., *Honorable Lives: Lawyers, Family, and Politics in Colombia, 1780–1850* (Pittsburgh: Pittsburgh University Press, 2000)

Usunáriz, Jesús M., 'El padre ante el parto en la España de los siglos XVI y XVII', *Hipogrifo. Revista de literatura y cultura del Siglo de Oro* 6:1 (2018), pp. 1–20

Varela Suanzes-Carpegna, Joaquín, *La teoría del Estado en las Cortes de Cádiz* (Madrid: Centro de Estudios Políticos y Constitucionales, 2012)

Vattel, Emer de, *Le droit des gens ou principes de la loi naturelle, appliqués â la conduite et aux affaires des nations et des souverains.* Volume 1 (Neuchâtel: Société Typographique, 1773)

The Law of Nations, Or, Principles of the Law of Nature, Applied to the Conduct and Affairs of Nations and Sovereigns, with Three Early Essays on the Origin and Nature of Natural Law and on Luxury. Edited and with an Introduction by Béla Kapossy and Richard Whatmore (Indiannapolis: Liberty Fund, 2008)

Vause, Erika, *In the Red and in the Black: Debt, Dishonor, and the Law in France between the Revolutions* (Charlottesville: University of Virginia Press, 2018)

Vélez Rendón, Juan Carlos, 'Las luchas narrativas de una nación escindida. La historiografía colombiana del siglo XIX', in Guillermo Palacios ed., *La nación y su historia, independencias, relato historiográfico y debates sobre la nación* (Mexico City: Colegio de México, 2009), pp. 39–80

Veliz, Claudio, *The New World of the Gothic Fox: Culture and Economy in English and Spanish America* (Berkeley: University of California Press, 2019)

Vicuña Guengerich, Sara, 'Inca Women under Spanish Rule: Probanzas and informaciones of the colonial Andean elite', in Mónica Díaz and Rocío Quispe-Agnoli eds., *Women's Negotiations and Textual Agency in Latin America, 1500–1799* (London: Routledge, 2016), pp. 118–141

Viejo Yharrassarry, Julián, *Amor proprio y sociedad comercial en el siglo XVIII hispano* (Bilbao: Universidad del País Vasco, 2018)

Vilches, Elvira, *New World Gold: Cultural Anxiety and Monetary Disorder in Early Modern Spain* (Chicago: University of Chicago Press, 2010)

Villegas Revueltas, Silvestre, *Deuda y diplomacia. La relación México-Gran Bretaña, 1824–1884* (Mexico City: UNAM, 2005)

Viola, Lora Anne, *The Closure of the International System: How Institutions Create Political Equalities and Hierarchies* (Cambridge: Cambridge University Press, 2020)
Vivot, Alfredo N. and Alberto A. Conil Paz, *Homenaje al doctor* Luis M. *Drago* (Caracas: Oficina Central de Información, 1976)
Vizcarra, Catalina, 'Guano, compromisos creíbles y el pago de la deuda externa peruana del siglo XIX', *Economía* 34 (2011), pp. 9–39
Voekel, Pamela, *For God and Liberty Catholicism and Revolution in the Atlantic World, 1790–1861* (Oxford: Oxford University Press, 2022)
Voigt, Lisa, *Spectacular Wealth: The Festival of Colonial South American Mining Towns* (Austin: University of Texas Press, 2016)
Vries, Jan, *The Industrious Revolution: Consumer Behavior and the Household Economy, 1650 to the Present* (Cambridge: Cambridge University Press, 2008)
Waibel, Michael, *Sovereign Defaults before International Courts and Tribunals* (Cambridge: Cambridge University Press, 2011)
Waisman, Sergio, *Dreams and Realities: Selected Fiction of Juana Manuela Gorriti* (New York: Oxford University Press, 2003)
Waldron, Jeremy, 'Two Conceptions of Self-Determination', in Samantha Besson and José Luis Martí eds., *The Philosophy of International Law* (Oxford: Oxford University Press 2010), pp. 397–413
Walker, David, *Kinship, Business, and Politics: The Martínez del Río Family in Mexico, 1823–1867* (Austin, Texas: University of Texas Press, 1987)
Walker Howe, Daniel, *What Hath God Wrought: The Transformation of America, 1815–1848* (Oxford: Oxford University Press, 2007)
Wasserman, Fabio, 'El concepto de nación y las transformaciones del orden político en Iberoamérica, 1750–1850', *Jahrbuch für Geschichte Lateinamerikas* 45 (2008), pp. 197–220
'La historia como concepto y como práctica: conocimiento histórico en el Río de la Plata (1780–1840)', *História da Historiografia: International Journal of Theory and History of Historiography* 3:4 (2010), pp. 15–36
'Presentación', in Fabio Wasserman ed., *Tiempos Críticos: Historia, revolución y temporalidad en el mundo iberoamericano (siglos XVIII y XIX)* (Buenos Aires: Prometeo, 2010), pp. 11–32
'De la revolución al historicismo romántico: experiencias de tiempo y política en el Río de la Plata (1780–1850)' in Fabio Wasserman ed., *Tiempos Críticos: Historia, revolución y temporalidad en el mundo iberoamericano* (siglos XVIII y XIX) (Buenos Aires: Prometeo, 2010), pp. 169–196
Tiempos Críticos: Historia, revolución y temporalidad en el mundo iberoamericano (siglos XVIII y XIX) (Buenos Aires: Prometeo, 2010)
El mundo en movimiento: el concepto de Revolución en Iberoamérica y el Atlántico norte (siglos XVII–XX) (Buenos Aires: Miño y Dávila Editores, 2019)
Wasserman, Martín, *Las obligaciones fundamentales. Crédito y consolidación económica durante el surgimiento de Buenos Aires* (Buenos Aires: Prometeo, 2017)
Weinberg, Félix, *Florencio Varela y 'El Comercio del Plata'* (Bahía Blanca: Instituto de Humanidades Universidad Nacional del Sur, 1970)
Weller, Leonardo, 'Government versus Bankers: Sovereign Debt Negotiations in Porfirian Mexico, 1888–1910', *The Journal of Economic History* 75:4 (2015), pp. 1030–1057
Wennerlind, Carl, *Casualties of Credit: The English Financial Revolution, 1620–1720* (Cambridge: Harvard University Press, 2011).
Whatley Pierson, William, 'Alberdi's Views on the Monroe Doctrine', *Hispanic American Historical Review* 3:3 (1920), pp. 362–374
Whatmore, Richard, *The End of Enlightenment:* Empire, Commerce, Crisis (London: Allen Lane, 2023)
Whitehead, Laurence, 'Latin America as a Mausoleum of Modernities', in Luis Roniger and Carlos Waisman eds., *Globality and Multiple Modernities. Comparative North American and Latin American Perspectives* (Brighton: Sussex Academic Press, 2002), pp. 29–65

Williamson, John, 'A Short History of the Washington Consensus', in Narcís Serra and Joseph E. Stiglitz eds., *The Washington Consensus Reconsidered: Towards a New Global Governance* (Oxford: Oxford University Press, 2008), pp. 14–30

Wobeser, Gisela von, *Dominación colonial. La consolidación de Vales Reales en Nueva España, 1804–1812* (Mexico City: UNAM, 2003)

'La consolidación de vales reales como factor determinante de la lucha de independencia en México, 1804–1808', *Historia Mexicana* 56:2 (2006), pp. 373–425

Woll, Allen, *A Functional Past: The Uses of History in Nineteenth-Century Chile* (Baton Rouge: Louisiana State University Press, 1982)

Wright, Winthrop, *British-Owned Railways in Argentina: Their Effect on the Growth of Economic Nationalism, 1854–1948* (Austin: University of Texas Press, 1974)

Young, Eric van, *The Other Rebellion: Popular Violence, Ideology, and the Mexican Struggle for Independence* (Stanford: Stanford University Press, 2001)

A Life Together: Lucas Alamán and Mexico, 1792–1853 (New Haven: Yale University Press, 2021)

'Between Bustamante and Burke: Lucas Alamán's Historical Project', *Korpus* 21:1 (2021), pp. 395–418

Zavala, Lorenzo, *Ensayo histórico de las revoluciones de Mégico: desde 1808 hasta 1830* (Paris: Dupont and Laguionie, 1831)

Zea, Francisco, 'Mediación entre España y América', in Diaz, Pedro Pablo, José Luis Ramos, and Domingo Navas Spinola eds., *Varios discursos del ciudadano Francisco Antonio Zea* (Caracas: Spinola, 1825), pp. 1–80

Zeltsman, Corinna, *Ink under the Fingernails: Printing Politics in Nineteenth-Century Mexico* (Berkeley: University of California Press, 2021)

Zendejas, Juan Flores, 'Crying on Lombard Street: Fixing Sovereign Defaults in the 1890s', *European Review of History: Revue européenne d'histoire* 19:6 (2012), pp. 979–997

'Explaining Latin America's Persistent Defaults: an Analysis of the Debtor–Creditor Relations in London, 1822–1914', *Financial History Review* 27:3 (2020), pp. 319–339

Zendejas, Juan Flores and Felipe Ford Cole, 'Sovereignty and Debt in Nineteenth-Century Latin America', in Pierre Penet, and Juan Flores Zendejas eds., *Sovereign Debt Diplomacies: Rethinking Sovereign Debt from Colonial Empires to Hegemony* (Oxford: Oxford University Press, 2021), pp. 49–72

Zertuche Muñoz, Fernando, Felipe Remolina Roqueñí, Victor Manuel Ruiz Naudal, and Juan Mateos eds., *Historia parlamentaria de los congresos mexicanos, 1824–1828* (Mexico City: Cámara de Diputados, Instituto de Investigaciones Legislativas, Asuntos Editoriales: Miguel Ángel Porrúa, 1997)

Zoraida Vázquez, Josefina, *Manuel Crecencio Rejón* (Mexico City: Senado de la República, 1987)

'El federalismo mexicano, 1823–1847', in Marcello Carmagnani ed., *Federalismos Latinoamericanos: México/Brasil/Argentina* (Mexico City: Fondo de Cultura Económica, 1993), pp. 15–50

Juárez: historia y mito (Mexico City: El Colegio de México, 2010)

Index

For the benefit of digital users, indexed terms that span two pages (e.g., 52–53) may, on occasion, appear on only one of those pages.